D0215473

Capital Budgeting
under
Uncertainty

Raj Aggarwal
John Carroll University, Cleveland, Ohio

PRENTICE HALL Englewood Cliffs, New Jersey 07632

Library of Congress Cataloging-in-Publication Data

Capital budgeting under uncertainty : new and advanced perspectives
  a book / edited by Raj Aggarwal.
      p.   cm.
    "April 1991."
    Includes bibliographical references.
    ISBN 0-13-117250-6 (case)
    1. Capital budget.   2. Capital investments.   I. Aggarwal, Raj.
  HG4028.C4C352 1993
  658.15`4--dc20
                                                                92-7467
                                                                   CIP

Acquisition Editor: *Leah Jewell*
Production Editor: *Edith Pullman*
Copy Editor: *Carol J. Dean*
Cover Design: *Ben Santora*
Prepress Buyer: *Trudy Pisciotti*
Manufacturing Buyer: *Patrice Fraccio*

 © 1993 by Prentice-Hall, Inc.
a Simon & Schuster Company
Englewood Cliffs, New Jersey 07632

All rights reserved. No part of this book may be
reproduced, in any form or by any means,
without permission in writing from the publisher.

Printed in the United States of America

10 9 8 7 6 5 4 3 2 1

ISBN 0-13-117250-6

Prentice-Hall International (UK) Limited, *London*
Prentice-Hall of Australia Pty. Limited, *Sydney*
Prentice-Hall Canada Inc., *Toronto*
Prentice-Hall Hispanoamericana, S.A., *Mexico*
Prentice-Hall of India Private Limited, *New Delhi*
Prentice-Hall of Japan, Inc., *Tokyo*
Simon & Schuster Asia Pte. Ltd., *Singapore*
Editora Prentice-Hall do Brasil, Ltda., *Rio de Janeiro*

for Karen and Sonia

Contents

PART I CAPITAL BUDGETING CONCEPTS

PART II ASSESSING RISKY CASH FLOWS

PART III ASSESSING CASH FLOWS IN A COMPETITIVE ENVIRONMENT

PART IV EVALUATING GROWTH OPTIONS IN INVESTMENTS

PART V STRATEGIC APPLICATIONS OF CAPITAL BUDGETING

PREFACE

This book presents new perspectives on the process of capital budgeting in a business. Capital budgeting decisions involve investments in assets that provide benefits over more than one period. The perspectives presented here cover both theoretical and practical issues related to the process of capital budgeting in a business—issues not generally covered in this range and detail in most other books on this topic. This book presents advanced topics in the theory and practice of capital budgeting.

This book is suitable for adoption in advanced undergraduate and graduate courses in corporate finance, managerial finance, capital budgeting, strategic planning, and other areas of business. It is also designed to be useful to business managers who are responsible for capital budgeting either as analysts or decision makers. Thus the book is also suitable for use in selected executive development programs and for purchase by managers and corporate libraries. It includes contributions from outside the United States and takes a global approach to the analysis of capital budgeting; therefore it is suitable for worldwide use.

The number of books published each year seems to rise exponentially. The number of new books on business subjects, including those that cover various aspects of finance, also seems to follow this general trend. What, if anything, sets this book apart? First, it covers a very important topic. The topic of capital budgeting deals with the analysis and selection of capital expenditure decisions. Capital expenditure decisions are an important and critical managerial responsibility in most businesses. Such decisions certainly influence and many times determine the survival and long-term growth of a business. Capital budgeting decisions are also a major mechanism for implementing business strategy. Poor capital budgeting procedures have been blamed for the competitive decline of businesses and of the United States. Thus it is clear that capital budgeting decisions are very important.

However, there is a second more important reason for this book. The process of capital budgeting is treated inadequately in most books that cover this topic. Each book treats only a part of the topic, and no book with as comprehensive a treatment of this topic as has been undertaken here is currently available. Books and courses on managerial and corporate finance generally do an excellent job describing and explaining the capital budgeting process after project benefits and costs have been converted to a set of estimated future cash flows. Books and courses on industrial economics describe the role of industrial structure on the profitability of companies and their capital investments but rarely deal with the procedures necessary for analysis of capital expenditure decisions in a business. Books and courses on strategic planning describe the process of developing a sustainable competitive advantage to ensure the long-run survival, profitability, and growth of a firm but also do not deal with the issues and procedures related to capital budgeting in a business. With regard to capital budgeting, books on decision theory may focus on decision making and procedures for assessing uncertainty and risk but generally do not cover the process of converting project descriptions into a series of estimates of future cash flows or the process of estimating the uncertainty and risk associated with those future cash flows. Capital budgeting involves understanding and using techniques from all these areas, and most treatments of the topic do a poor job of integrating the various areas in the analysis of capital budgeting. This book is a modest attempt to present the theory and practice of capital budgeting from these different perspectives.

This book fills an important gap in the literature on capital budgeting. While there are some books that focus on capital budgeting and others that are collections of advanced topics in finance, currently there is no book in print that is a collection of chapters on advanced topics focused on capital budgeting issues. This book on advanced topics on the theory and practice of capital budgeting is designed to fill this gap. Each of the chapters selected for this volume has been revised based on comments from a peer blind refereeing process and represents a new contribution to current thinking in this area.

Many more chapters were submitted for this book than could be accepted for publication. Unfortunately, many good papers could not be included, but I am grateful to all those who submitted their work for consideration. As the editor, I am also grateful to the reviewers for their assistance in suggesting revisions and selecting the articles that appear here. David Schirm and Siva Ramakrishnan also provided useful comments on Chapter 2. I am also thankful for the support provided by John Carroll University and the Edward J. and Louise E. Mellen Foundation. The continuing encouragement for my professional activities provided by Dean Frank Navratil has been invaluable, as has been the intellectual environment and feedback provided by my colleagues at John Carroll University, Harvard University, and at the International University of Japan. The dedicated assistance provided by my secretary, Anita Fratantonio, and by my student assistants, Robert Moussaid, John Stenger, and

Mary Wood, has also greatly facilitated the completion of this volume. They deserve and have my thanks and appreciation.

Raj Aggarwal
Chesterland, Ohio

REVIEW BOARD

THOMAS C. CHIANG, Professor of Finance, Drexel University, Philadelphia, PA

EDWARD J. FARRAGHER, Professor of Finance, Oakland University, Rochester, MI

LAWRENCE J. GITMAN, Professor of Finance, San Diego State University, San Diego, CA

EDWARD GRUCA, Assistant Professor of Finance, Case Western Reserve University, Cleveland, OH

THOMAS J. HINDELANG, Professor of Finance, Drexel University, Philadelphia, PA

JAMES E. HODDER, Professor of Finance, University of Wisconsin, Madison, WI

LAURENT JACQUE, Associate Professor of Business, University of Minnesota, Minneapolis, MN

PETER KOVEOS, Professor of Finance, Syracuse University, Syracuse, NY

CHENG-FEW LEE, Professor of Finance, Rutgers University at New Brunswick, New Brunswick, NJ

EDWARD M. MILLER, Professor of Finance, University of New Orleans, New Orleans, LA

R. CHARLES MOYER, Professor of Finance, Wake-Forest University, Winston-Salem, NC

PETER RITCHKEN, Associate Professor of Finance, Case Western Reserve University, Cleveland OH

JACKY C. SO, Associate Professor of Finance, Southern Illinois University at Edwardsville, Edwardsville, IL

LUC A. SOENEN, Professor of Finance, Cal Poly State University, San Luis Obispo, CA

GEORGE TSETSEKOS, Associate Professor of Finance, Drexel University, Philadelphia, PA

MICHAEL C. WALKER, Professor of Finance, University of Cincinnati, Cincinnati, OH

JOHN WINGENDER, Associate Professor of Finance, Oklahoma State University, Stillwater, OK

CONTRIBUTORS

RAJ AGGARWAL, Mellen Professor of Finance, John Carroll University, Cleveland, Ohio

TAMIR AGMON, Managing Director, Clali & Associates Financial Management, Tel Aviv, Israel

JAMES S. ANG, Cullom Professor of Finance, Florida State University, Tallahasse, Florida

MOSHE BEN HORIN, Professor of Business Administration, The Hebrew University, Jerusalem, Israel; Professor of Business Administration, Northeastern University, Boston, Massachusetts

LEROY D. BROOKS, Professor of Finance, University of South Carolina, Columbia, South Carolina

STEPHEN P. DUKAS, Associate Professor of Finance, Kansas State University, Manhattan, Kansas

PAUL FALLONE, Professor of Mathematics, University of Connecticut, Storrs, Connecticut

M. ANDREW FIELDS, Associate Professor of Finance, University of Delaware, Newark, Delaware

CARMELO GIACCOTTO, Department of Finance, School of Business Administration, University of Connecticut, Storrs, Connecticut

FERNANDO GOMEZ-BEZARES, Professor of Finance, Deusto University, Bilbao, Spain

CHARLES W. HALEY, Professor of Finance, University of Washington, Seattle, Washington

ROBERT E. JENSEN, Jones Distinguished Professor of Business, Trinity University, San Antonio, Texas

EERO KASANEN, Associate Professor of Finance, Helsinki School of Economics, SF-00100 Helsinki, Finland

W. CARL KESTER, Professor of Business Administration, Harvard Business School, Boston, Massachusetts

YONG H. KIM, Professor of Business Administration, University of Cincinnati, Cincinnati, Ohio

MOON H. LEE, Department of Finance and Management Science, University of Saskatchewan, Saskatoon, Canada

LATHA SHANKER, Associate Professor of Finance, Concordia University, Montreal, Canada

BARRY N. STEDMAN, Associate Professor of Architecture, University of Cincinnati, Cincinnati, Ohio

LENOS TRIGEORGIS, Assistant Professor of Finance, Boston University, Boston, Massachusetts

1

Introduction
and Chapter Reviews

RAJ AGGARWAL

Capital budgeting under uncertainty is an important topic. Many contend that the focus on discounted cash flow techniques in evaluating new capital investments is inappropriate, as it has contributed to our loss of international competitiveness. Others have contended that such criticisms are incorrect and that capital budgeting techniques are not inappropriate but are often misapplied.[1] In any event, the evaluation of new investments is an important part of the process whereby firms create value, and thus it can have significant implications for the competitive position of a firm or a country.

Capital budgeting is usually an exercise in estimating the net value of future cash flows and other benefits as compared to the initial investment required. The one thing certain about the future is its uncertainty. Thus all capital budgeting is really under uncertainty, and it can be argued that the title of this book is a tautology. Nevertheless, traditional capital budgeting procedures often ignore or postpone consideration of the uncertainty inherent in estimates of future benefits.

Uncertainty in capital budgeting can have many sources. First, even for well-defined, tangible, and fairly certain benefits, there are a number of sources of estimation and measurement error. For fairly stable environments, capital budgeting procedures are being improved with better statistical forecasting tools that reduce estimation errors. An additional source of measurement and estimation errors can be cost accounting systems that often involve approximations of overhead allocation. Further, because of the unique nature of each application, new capital equipment may not work exactly as estimated, resulting in unexpected variations in labor, material, inventory, or other costs.[2]

Second, all positive net present value (NPV) projects depend explicitly or implicitly on natural or artificially created market imperfections. It is often difficult to forecast the stability of market imperfections over time, especially since they are likely to depend on competitor reactions. There may be a number of discontinuities in the effects of competitor actions, particularly for strategic capital investments subject to positive feedbacks, where an initial competitive advantage can lead to an additional advantage. Such discontinuities make it difficult to estimate future benefits from an investment.[3]

Third, traditional capital budgeting procedures have generally ignored the valuation of options created by an investment. Such options are valuable whether or not they are exercised and should be included in assessing the benefits of such an investment. The valuation of real options associated with an investment is often difficult and depends on estimates of the uncertainties being reduced by the options. A set of options commonly given inadequate attention in traditional capital budgeting procedures involves the continuing management of an investment after the initial accept/reject decision. As an example, management has the option to delay the investment. Another option available to management in each time period is the option to continue or to temporarily or permanently shut down the project. In addition, management generally also has options to make changes in operating procedures to enhance the value of the project as new information becomes available.[4]

Fourth, as the burgeoning research on risk assessment indicates, there is considerable imprecision and systematic bias in the estimation and valuation of risky alternatives. For example, probability estimates are subject to bias because of phenomena such as anchoring, framing, and regret. Fifth, in addition to uncertainties in the estimation of future benefits and cost, uncertainties in inflation and interest rates, capital market imperfections, and changing tax rates make the estimation of an appropriate discount rate also difficult and subject to error.[5]

Sixth, agency costs and information asymmetry can also influence the efficiency of the capital budgeting process. The capital investment process can be segmented into three phases: identifying the set of investment alternatives, selecting the right investment, and implementing and managing the investment. The capital budgeting process has to work well in each of these phases for investments to be value-enhancing. Mistakes and inefficiencies in any one of these phases can offset even outstanding skills and efficiency in the other phases. However, agency costs due to differences in the goals, objectives, and utility functions among owners, managers at different levels, creditors, and other stakeholders introduce inefficiencies in each stage of the capital budgeting process, and the selection and management of new investments may not be economically optimal.[6]

As this brief discussion indicates, capital budgeting is subject to a number of uncertainties, and procedures for estimating and overcoming such uncertainties can be very useful. The collection of articles put together for this book attempts to address this need, and a brief review of each of the remaining chapters follows.

The next three articles, Chapters 2 through 4, form the first main part of this book. They focus on capital budgeting concepts useful in a multiperiod setting. They show the need to extend traditional capital budgeting analysis and propose some procedures that may be used to augment traditional approaches to make them more realistic.

Chapter 2, "A Brief Overview of Capital Budgeting Under Uncertainty," by Raj Aggarwal, introduces the topic by providing an explanation of the basics and a brief overview. By taking a broad overview of the topic this chapter provides a conceptual framework for placing each of the subsequent chapters in context. In addition, it provides an initial guide to the literature of capital budgeting and it also fills in the gaps that are inevitably left in any collection of specialized topics.

Chapter 3, "A Modern Theory of Finance Analysis of Differences Between Accounting and Economic Rates of Return," by Robert E. Jensen, shows how computation of both the accounting and economic rates of return can be improved by correcting and adjusting for variations in assumed reinvestment rates and utility of returns due to variations in the state of the economy. This chapter also provides some practical procedures that can be used to make these adjustments.

Chapter 4, "Corporate Capital Budgeting: Contributions of Finance Theory and an Extension Under Multiperiod Uncertainty," by Charles Haley, extends the single-period valuation model to develop a multiperiod value-additive model. This chapter also provides a framework for classifying capital projects and for estimating their risk characteristics.

The next three articles, Chapter 5 through 7, form the second part of this collection. They focus on some technical areas and techniques that are usually considered too specialized or theoretical to be included in most textbooks but which are actually very practical. These chapters present techniques for assessing risky cash flows which in many cases are represented more realistically by nonnormal return distributions.

Chapter 5, "Penalized Net Present Value: Net Present Value Penalization with Normal and Beta Distributions," by Fernando Gómez-Bezares, provides some practical recommendations for making capital budgeting decisions when full probability distributions are not or cannot be known economically. It also develops procedures for use when project returns can be better approximated by the beta distribution.

Chapter 6, "An Application of the Lognormal Distribution to Risk Analysis," by Moon Kim, shows how a three-level forecast of an input variable may be fitted to a log-normal distribution. This chapter also explains the use of lognormal probability distributions in a Hertz-type simulation or risk analysis for assessing capital projects.

Chapter 7, "Managerial Risk Preferences and Investment Decisions Under Uncertainty: A Gamma Preference Framework," by Barry Stedman and Yong Kim, shows how the gamma function may be used to overcome the need to know managerial utility preferences in making capital budgeting decisions when markets are less than perfect and the usual separation of investment and financing decisions breaks down.

The next three articles, Chapters 8 through 10, form the third part of this book. They focus on capital budgeting procedures useful in multiperiod and competitive environments. They show the procedures that may be used to augment traditional approaches to make them more realistic.

Chapter 8, "An Application of the Box-Jenkins Methodology to Capital Budgeting," by Paul Fallone and Carmelo Giaccotto, presents analytical solutions to the problem of selecting a project with stationary and nonstationary serially correlated cash flows. It models the impact of serial dependency in cash flows on the expected NPV of the investment. While there are many reasons for serial dependence in project cash flows, as indicated earlier, one reason may be the positive feedback effects of a competitive advantage.

Chapter 9, "Capital Budgeting and the Learning Curve Phenomenon," by Andrew Fields, provides a procedure for assessing the effect of the learning curve on operating costs and thus on the amount and timing of cash flows from an investment. The procedures modeled include the impact of changes in the learning rate and other variables on project risk and NPV.

Chapter 10, "Some Implications of Competition for Capital Investment," by James Ang and Stephen Dukas, develops a capital budgeting model that incorporates both competitive intensity and asymmetric information. It shows that both competitive intensity and the duration of an investment are important decision variables and that capital budgeting procedures that ignore changes in competitive intensity may seriously overstate the net present value and the internal rate of return (IRR) of such investments.

The next three chapters, Chapters 11 to 13, form the fourth part of this collection. They focus on some areas neglected to varying degrees in many textbooks but which are drawing increasing interest in the profession. These articles use the fresh perspectives provided by contingent claims analysis to expand the definition of value used in traditional capital budgeting procedures to include intangibles such as flexibility and other options. These chapters provide insights that help reconcile the often divergent approaches taken by traditional capital budgeting and strategic planning procedures.

Chapter 11, "Turning Growth Options Into Real Assets," by Carl Kester, applies the contingent claims perspective to show how the practical strategic problems of timing a capital investment and of sequencing a project investment within a larger capital program can be reconciled with the traditional objective of maximizing shareholder wealth. This chapter provides an important bridge between traditional capital budgeting and strategic planning.

Chapter 12, "Flexibility, Synergy, and Control in Strategic Investment Planning," by Eero Kasanen and Lenos Trigeorgis, contends that in view of the options available (at least to shut down or to continue a project) during the life of most capital investments, capital budgeting is more than just an accept/reject decision and should be part of the firm's ongoing planning and control mechanisms. The authors show that the active management of an investment can add value beyond what can be assessed when the investment is first proposed or approved.

Chapter 13, "Capital Budgeting and the Utilization of Full Information: Performance Evaluation and the Exercise of Real Options," by Tamir Agmon, presents additional insights into how managing a capital investment by revising the original operating strategy can or cannot add value. He points out that it is important, however, to design a performance evaluation mechanism that is consistent with the information set used in the initial decision.

The next four articles, Chapters 14 through 16, form the fifth and last part of this book. They focus on practical issues and provide examples of applications of capital budgeting techniques.

Chapter 14, "Capital Budgeting for Replacements With Unequal Remaining Life," by LeRoy Brooks, reviews the literature in this area and attempts to integrate into manageable formulas the various issues that impact the replacement problem. These formulas include modifications that account for variations in the time horizon and the amount of information available.

Chapter 15, "The Make-or-Buy Decision in Capital Budgeting," by Moshe Ben-Horim and Latha Shanker, applies the capital budgeting process to assess the make-or-buy decision. The authors show that the decision to make is favored by the use of debt financing and by anticipated inflation.

Chapter 16, "Justifying Strategic Investments: The Case of Flexible Manufacturing Technology," by Raj Aggarwal, is an application of the adjusted net present value approach in assessing the mix of tangible, intangible, and strategic benefits and options created by investments in flexible new manufacturing equipment. The proposed model is designed to provide a framework that can be augmented to reflect the strategic characteristics of any investment.

As this brief overview indicates, the chapters in this book present a wide range of issues and significant contributions that extend our understanding of the capital budgeting process. The procedures and models presented here should also contribute toward making the practice of capital budgeting less prone to error and more useful in enhancing a firm's competitive position and value. As this collection of articles also indicates, there is room for additional research in this area. The authors of these chapters and I invite reader comments and suggestions.

NOTES

1. For details of these contentions see, for example, Hayes and Garvin (1982), Hodder (1986), Landau (1988), and Meyers (1987).
2. See, for example, Johnson and Kaplan (1987) and Kaplan (1984).
3. Competitive effects, including destabilizing positive feedback of an initial competitive advantage associated with new investments, have been modeled by, for example, Arthur (1990), Bailey and Friedlaender (1982), Dixit (1989), Mills (1988), and Roberts (1987).
4. The literature exploring the role of real options in valuing new investment proposals is expanding rapidly and includes Aggarwal and Soenen (1989), Baldwin (1982), Brennan and Schwartz (1985), Carlson (1989), Kester (1984), Majd and Pyndick (1987), Mason and Merton (1985), McDonald and Siegle (1985, 1986), Sick (1989), Siegle et al. (1987), and Trigeorgis and Mason (1987).
5. See, for example, Arrow (1982), Machina (1987, 1989), and MacCrimmon and Wehrung (1986).
6. Agency and information asymmetry issues in capital budgeting have been explored in many books and papers, including Aggarwal (1978), Heckerman (1975), Jensen and Meckling (1976), and Myers and Majluf (1987).

REFERENCES

AGGARWAL, RAJ (1978). "Corporate Use of Sophisticated Capital Budgeting Procedures: A Strategic Perspective," *Interfaces* 10 (No. 2, April), pp. 31–34.

AGGARWAL, RAJ, and LUC A. SOENEN (1989). "Project Exit Value as a Measure of Flexibility and Risk Exposure," *Engineering Economist* 35 (No. 1, Fall), pp. 39–54.

ARTHUR, W. BRIAN (1990). "Positive Feedbacks in the Economy," *Scientific American* 261 (No. 2, February), pp. 92–99.

ARROW, KENNETH J. (1982). "Risk Perception in Psychology and Economics," *Economic Inquiry* 20 (No. 1, January), pp. 1–9.

BAILEY, E. E., and A. F. FRIEDLAENDER (1982). "Market Structure and Multi-product Industries," *Journal of Economic Literature* 20 (No. 2, June), pp. 1024–1048.

BALDWIN, CARLISS Y. (1982). "Optimal Sequential Investment When Capital Is Not Readily Reversible," *Journal of Finance* 37 (No. 3, June), pp. 763–782.

BRENNEN, MICHAEL J., and EDUARDO S. SCHWARTZ (1985). "Evaluating Natural Resource Investments," *Journal of Business* 58 (No. 1, April), pp. 135–157.

CARLSSON, BO (1989). "Flexibility and the Theory of the Firm," *International Journal of Industrial Organization* 7 (No. 2, June), pp. 179–203.

COOPER, IAN, and JULIAN R. FRANKS (1983). "The Interaction of Financing and Investment Decisions When the Firm Has Unused Tax Credits," *Journal of Finance* 38 (No. 2, May), pp. 571–583.

DIXIT, AVINASH (1989). "Entry and Exit Decisions Under Uncertainty," *Journal of Political Economy* 97 (No. 3, May), pp. 620–638.

HAYES, ROBERT H., and DAVID A. GARVIN (1982). "Managing as If Tomorrow Mattered," *Harvard Business Review* (No. 3, May–June), pp. 71–79.

HECKERMAN, DONALD G. (1975). "Motivating Managers To Make Investment Decisions," *Journal of Financial Economics* 2 (No. 2, June), pp. 273–292.

HODDER, JAMES E. (1986). "Evaluation of Manufacturing Investments: A Comparison of U.S. and Japanese Practices," *Financial Management* 15 (No. 1, Spring), pp. 17–24.

JENSEN, MICHAEL C., and WILLIAM H. MECKLING (1976). "Theory of the Firm: Managerial Behavior, Agency Costs, and Ownership Structure," *Journal of Financial Economics* 3 (No. 3, October), pp. 305–360.

JOHNSON, H. THOMAS, and ROBERT S. KAPLAN (1987). *Relevance Lost: The Rise and Fall of Management Accounting* (Boston: Harvard Business School Press).

KAPLAN, ROBERT S. (1984). "Yesterday's Accounting Undermines Production," *Harvard Business Review* 62 (No. 4, July–August), pp. 95–101.

KESTER, W. CARL (1984). "Today's Options for Tomorrow's Growth," *Harvard Business Review* 62 (No. 2, March–April), pp. 67–75.

LANDAU, RALPH (1988). "U.S. Economic Growth," *Scientific American* 258 (No. 6, June), pp. 44–52.

MACCRIMMON, KENNETH R., and DONALD A. WEHRUNG (1986). *Taking Risks* (New York: Free Press).

MACHINA, MARK J. (1987). "Choice Under Uncertainty: Problems Solved and Unsolved," *Economic Perspectives* 1 (No. 1, January–February), pp. 121–154.

MACHINA, MARK J. (1989). "Dynamic Consistency and Non-Expected Utility Models of Choice Under Uncertainty," *Journal of Economic Literature* 27 (No. 4, December), pp. 1622–1688.

MAJD, SAMAN, and ROBERT S. PYNDICK (1987). "Time to Build, Option Value, and Investment Decisions," *Journal of Financial Economics* 18 (No. 1, March), pp. 7–27.

MASON, SCOTT P., and ROBERT C. MERTON (1985). "The Role of Contingent Claims Analysis in Finance," in Edward Altman and Marti Subrahmanian (eds.), *Recent Advances in Corporate Finance* (Homewood, Ill.: Richard D. Irwin), pp. 149–158.

McDonald, Robert L., and Daniel R. Siegle (1985). "Investments and the Value of the Firm When There Is an Option To Shut Down," *International Economic Review* 26 (No. 2, June), pp. 331–349.

McDonald, Robert L., and Daniel R. Siegle (1986). "The Value of Waiting to Invest," *Quarterly Journal of Economics* 101 (No. 4, November), pp. 707–727.

Mills, David E. (1988). "Pre-Emptive Investment Timing," *Rand Journal of Economics* 19 (No. 1, Spring), pp. 114–122.

Myers, Stewart C. (1987). "Finance Theory and Financial Strategy," *Midland Corporate Finance Journal* 5 (No. 1, Spring), pp. 6–13.

Myers, Stewart C., and Nicholas S. Majluf (1984). "Corporate Financing and Investment Decisions When Firms Have Information Investors Do Not Have," *Journal of Financial Economics* 13 (No. 2, June), pp. 187–221.

Roberts, John (1987). "Battles for Market Share: Incomplete Information, Aggressive Strategic Planning and Competitive Dynamics," in Truman F. Bewley (ed.), *Advances in Economic Theory* (New York: Cambridge University Press), pp. 157–195.

Sick, Gordon (1989). *Capital Budgeting With Real Options*, Monograph Series in Finance and Economics, No. 1989-3 (New York: New York University), pp. 1–78.

Siegle, Daniel R., James L. Smith, and James L. Paddock (1987). "Valuing Offshore Oil Properties with Options Pricing Models," *Midland Corporate Finance Journal* 5 (No 1, Spring), pp. 22–30.

Stulz, Rene (1982). "Options on the Minimum or Maximum of Two Risky Assets," *Journal of Financial Economics* 10 (No. 2, July), pp. 161–185.

Trigeorgis, Lenos, and Scott P. Mason (1987). "Valuing Managerial Flexibility," *Midland Corporate Finance Journal* 5 (No. 1, Spring), pp. 14–21.

2

A Brief Overview
of Capital Budgeting
Under Uncertainty

RAJ AGGARWAL

ABSTRACT

This chapter is a brief review and summary of the literature related to capital budgeting under uncertainty. As this literature is quite voluminous, this review is not comprehensive. This review and summary is deliberately nontechnical, and it highlights only the major strands and issues in the literature related to capital budgeting under uncertainty. The goal of this brief review and summary is to provide an introduction to the literature on capital budgeting under uncertainty. This review also clarifies some common conundrums and misunderstandings associated with capital budgeting, including the alleged inconsistency between business strategy and capital budgeting. Finally, it is hoped that this review will encourage further thought and, perhaps, attempts to clarify the many issues related to capital budgeting that still remain murky.

I. INTRODUCTION

The process of capital budgeting generally covers all long-term capital expenditures, including investments in machines, buildings, pollution control equipment, advertising campaigns, options to buy or lease real estate, and other expenditures that have benefits extending beyond one time period. Thus it covers a wide range of business activity and, as capital budgeting is the process of allocating capital for long-term investments, it is a central and critical aspect of implementing business strategy. Capital budgeting is also an important process that certainly influences and perhaps even determines the long-run survival, growth, and value of a business. Mistakes and inefficiencies in capital budgeting can indeed mean business failure and bankruptcy for a firm. Inefficiencies in the process of capital budgeting have also been blamed for the competitive decline of the United States (Hays and Garvin, 1982).

Management of the capital budgeting process in a business is generally a significant and important responsibility of top management. According to the chief executive officer of Emerson Electric, "The job of management is to identify and successfully implement business investment opportunities" (Knight, 1992). However, most proposals for long-term investment are generally initiated by the part of the business that is also likely to implement such a proposal or is likely to be most affected by or benefit from it. Thus the organizational structure and reward systems in a business are likely to influence the generation of capital budgeting proposals. Once a capital project is proposed, it is likely to move up through the corporate hierarchy until it is approved or rejected. For large and critical projects, this decision may be made only at the highest levels in a business organization. The ability of the project to add to the value of the business and the consistency of the proposed project with the overall strategy of the business are two of the more important dimensions along which such proposals are likely to be evaluated.

These processes of generating and evaluating capital budgeting proposals become more complex as the size of the business grows. The separation of owners and managers introduces many aspects of agency problems into the process. In addition, such separation, and the complexity and size of many capital budgeting proposals, mean that communications between managers and suppliers of capital and other monitors of the project are likely to be influenced by issues explored in the literature on financial signaling. In a decentralized multidivisional business environment, the capital budgeting process also involves procedures for evaluating, motivating, and rewarding project managers, as well as procedures used to allocate capital among competing divisions that may often face different industrial and national environments. Finally, businesses generally want to improve their capital budgeting process, and thus may undertake to varying degrees what is generally known as a postaudit of projects that have been or are being implemented.

As projects grow larger and more complex, their initial evaluation also becomes more complex. This is especially true for capital budgeting projects involving long time horizons, new business areas or unproven technology, uncertain competitive reactions, and other factors that are difficult to assess and evaluate. Capital investment projects undertaken in a perfectly competitive market environment cannot create value, as any benefits in excess of related costs are competed away. Capital budgeting projects can create value only if they take advantage of market imperfections. Thus the evaluation of capital expenditure proposals involves assessment of the related market imperfections.

As this brief discussion indicates, the process of capital budgeting involves assessments along some very difficult and challenging dimensions, especially as capital budgeting involves the estimation and valuation of future benefits. First, as discussed above, the process must identify and then prepare a plan to exploit market imperfections that are preferably not known or exploitable by other businesses. Second, the level and riskiness of future cash flows associated with the proposed project must be estimated. Third, the value of trade-offs across time periods must be assessed, that is, the incremental value of earlier benefits must be assessed. Finally, the utility implications of uncertain or risky future benefits must be assessed before a capital expenditure decision can be made. All these assessments are analytically challenging, and it has been widely suggested that capital budgeting is still more of an art than a science even though much progress has been made in reducing the subjectivity in assessing uncertainty, risk, utilities, and time value trade-offs.

The first few sections of this chapter review the traditional domain of capital budgeting—topics likely to be covered in many books on financial management and on capital budgeting. The last few sections deal with some issues related to capital budgeting that have not been discussed widely in such books. However, these issues may help clarify some conundrums such as the alleged inconsistencies between capital budgeting and business strategy.

II. MEASURES OF PROJECT VALUE UNDER CERTAINTY

The first step in the valuation of a project is to convert its benefits into estimates of incremental cash flows for each of the future time periods in the life of the project. In this section, it is temporarily assumed that these cash flows are known with certainty—an unrealistic assumption to be certain, but nevertheless one that is useful for expository purposes. Once the benefits of a capital budgeting project have been converted into cash flows for each time period, its attractiveness can be estimated either in absolute or relative terms. The measure of attractiveness must then be compared to a minimum acceptable value or a hurdle rate in order to reach an approval decision for the project.

Conversion of the project description into projected after-tax cash flow estimates can be quite challenging. For example, projects may involve the use of existing facilities that may be shared with other projects. In such cases, costs associated with the facilities must be estimated and allocated to the project if there are specific alternative uses. The cash flow impacts of improvements in product quality, manufacturing flexibility, and customer service may be difficult to estimate. Similarly, the estimation and allocation of overhead expenses to project cash flows can also present many challenges (Kaplan, 1984). Further, estimates of future benefits generally become more uncertain as the time horizon lengthens. In many cases, therefore, it may be useful to limit the number of time periods for which explicit estimates of cash flows are made. In such cases, the terminal value of a project must be estimated at the end of the time horizon—a time horizon based on the ability to estimate future cash flows rather than on the economic life of the project. Project cash flow estimates may also be unduly influenced by managers so that they meet stated corporate hurdle rates and other acceptance criteria (Aggarwal, 1980).

Many businesses use measures of project attractiveness based on the effects of the project on the reported accounting income of a business. An example of such a measure is the accounting rate of return (ARR), a rate obtained by dividing the project's incremental profits averaged over its life by its average investment (often the average of the beginning and the ending investments). While this procedure ignores project cash flows and their temporal distribution (thereby assuming a zero rate of discount), it allows project worth to be assessed in accounting terminology that may already be familiar to many managers and to many of their outside monitors.

Another measure of project attractiveness even more widely used in business is the payback period—defined simply as the time it takes to recover the initial investment. Again, it is an easy measure to compute and understand. However, it not only ignores the time value of money but also ignores cash flows after the payback period, a potentially more serious shortcoming. Because of this last characteristic, the payback period is best suited for assessing and comparing projects with conventional patterns of cash flows where project cash flows decline similarly over time and project lives are comparable. Use of the payback period to assess capital budgeting emphasizes projects with large cash flows in the early years—a characteristic that is useful is assessing projects where uncertainty and risk increase rapidly with time. Such a procedure can also be critically useful for businesses facing bankruptcy or other challenges to their survival. However, its use can also limit the long-run growth of a business. One reason for the persistence of the payback and the ARR methods for assessing capital expenditure decisions may be the continuing use of managerial compensation schemes tied to short-term accounting earnings (Statman, 1982).

These two procedures for assessing capital expenditure proposals do not account for the time value of money. However, investment funds come from savings and, as savings are a form of postponed consumption, savers lend only to receive increases in their purchasing power. This expected increase in purchasing power associated with lending means that money has time value (Fisher, 1930). Further, money generally has many alternative uses, and the rate of return on its best alternative use is considered its opportunity cost. Thus funds invested in a capital project have time value that must be reflected in evaluating future cash flows. This cost of capital, generally expressed in terms of a percentage per year, can be broken down into three components: the real riskless cost of money or the increase in purchasing power for a riskless loan, an additional amount to compensate for expected inflation, and, finally, a premium to compensate for the risk involved in the loan or investment because of possible default and/or the lack of liquidity at maturity.

As these variables are likely to change depending on the time period covered by a loan, the resulting nominal rate of interest depends on the term or maturity of the investment. There are many theories of the term structure, that is, how nominal interest rates vary with maturity. Theoretically, the term structures should be known for each future time period in order to evaluate the exact present value of a future set of cash flows. In fact, the valuation of many securities and investments with fixed and known future cash flows can generally be improved with better forecasts of the term structure and the appropriate discount rate applicable to future cash flows. In capital budgeting practice, however, the much lower degree of accuracy associated with the estimates of projected cash flows that characterize investments in real assets overwhelms the need for such accuracy in estimates of the term structure.

Since most businesses face alternative investment opportunities for their capital and many of these investment alternatives (especially those associated with fixed-income securities) have well-defined rates of return, they may prefer to assess capital budgeting projects also in terms of their internal rate of return (IRR). The IRR is defined as the rate of return on the project investment reflected in its set of future cash inflows. It is often calculated by finding the discount rate that equates the present value of all cash inflows to the present value of all project cash outflows (investments). This calculated value of the project IRR is compared to a hurdle rate, for example, the rate on return of alternative investments with the same maturity and risk. A project is an attractive project if the IRR equals or preferably exceeds this hurdle rate.

However, use of the IRR as a measure of project attractiveness in capital budgeting may have some limitations. First, the IRR assumes that all project cash inflows are reinvested in other projects at a rate of return that equals the IRR. This may be an unrealistic assumption, especially for outstanding projects that have unusually high or low IRRs. Second, it may be difficult or impossible to calculate a single, unambiguous IRR for a project when its future cash flows change sign more than once, that is, become negative after being positive, or vice versa, more than once. It can be shown that the number of mathematically correct IRRs for a series of cash flows equals the number of times the cash flows change sign. The economic interpretation of these multiple rates of return is almost always challenging and sometimes impossible.

Many businesses are interested in capital budgeting projects that add to the value of the firm. The net present value (NPV) of a project is the amount by which the proposed capital budgeting project will add to the present worth of the business. The NPV is obtained by calculating the present value of project cash inflows less the present value of project cash outflows. While this measure of project attractiveness is widely favored in business, it has limitations. First, calculation of the NPV requires an estimate of the appropriate discount rate—a discount rate that reflects the risk, maturity, and other characteristics of the project. In some cases, different discount rates may have to be estimated for different time periods or for different components of the cash flows. The development of such estimates may present formidable challenges, especially as market measures of firm beta are likely to differ from the appropriate asset betas, in part because of the influence of growth opportunities on observed betas (Myers and Turnbull, 1977). Thus the assessment and calculation of appropriate project discount rates can be subjective and controversial in many cases, and challenging in most cases. Second, calculation of the NPV assumes that project cash inflows are reinvested in other projects at a rate of return that equals the discount rate used to calculate the NPV—an assumption that may not be too unrealistic. In order to make this reinvestment assumption explicit, some businesses may calculate the net future value of a proposed capital expenditure. On balance, the NPV is recommended in most finance textbooks as the best overall measure of project attractiveness.

In this simplified analysis, these measures of project attractiveness assume that project lives are similar. If that is not the case, then each project is replicated until all projects being compared have similar lives. Similarly, it is assumed that cash flows for each project are independent of cash flows for other projects. If there are interdependencies among certain projects, such projects must be grouped together before being compared to other groups of projects. The measures of project attractiveness discussed above also assume that the projects being evaluated are small relative to the overall size of the company and that these projects will not change the overall riskiness or the optimal capital structure of the business. As discussed later, the simple NPV rule cannot be applied in many cases, especially if the project involves the valuation of option-like contingent claims or when a project changes the optimal capital structure of a firm (Black, 1988).

Variations in project size are treated differently by each of these measures of project attractiveness. Measures like the NPV tend to emphasize the adoption of larger projects, as such projects tend to have higher NPVs. In order to overcome this bias, some businesses use a related size-free measure, the profitability index, calculated by dividing the present value of cash inflows by the present value of cash outflows or the project investment. Rate-of-return measures like the ARR, the IRR, and the profitability index, and the payback method, treat projects of all sizes equally. However, the use of such size-free measures of project attractiveness that do not favor larger projects might lead to the acceptance of many small projects. Such a situation may strain the managerial or other resources available to a business that are necessary for the project (in other words, it may induce nonlinearities into the resource costs reflected in project cash flows). In such cases, businesses may have to use multiperiod mathematical programming models for assessing capital budgeting projects (Thompson, 1976). The mathematical programming approach to the analysis and selection of capital budgeting projects is also recommended for firms facing capital rationing, that is, firms with limited funds and an inability to undertake all positive-NPV projects (Weingartner, 1977).

The analysis of capital budgeting projects discussed above has assumed that future cash flows are known with certainty. This is clearly an unrealistic assumption. The one thing certain about the future is that it is uncertain. Since all capital budgeting involves assessment of future benefits, all capital budgeting involves assessment of risky future cash flows. The discussion in the next section is more realistic, as it covers capital budgeting analysis for risky projects.

III. TRADITIONAL APPROACHES TO PROJECT RISK ANALYSIS

The first step in traditional risk analysis of capital expenditure proposals is usually to classify the proposed projects into different categories, for example, projects involving new businesses (higher risk) versus expansion projects in existing businesses (lower risk), projects involving new technology versus those using existing and well-known technologies, and projects in environments with high levels of competition or of political, foreign exchange, or inflation risks versus projects without such risks. Naturally, such high-risk projects, large projects, and projects that are strategically or otherwise important normally undergo much more extensive risk analysis than do other projects. Risk analysis of proposed capital expenditure projects should account for the variability and stability of market imperfections giving rise to the value-adding nature of the proposed capital investment. More generally, risk analysis should account for the variability and uncertainty in variables that influence and determine a project's profitability.

The analysis of capital budgeting projects must distinguish among conditions of ignorance, uncertainty, and risk. It is generally assumed that if all project outcomes cannot even be enumerated reasonably, the situation must be dealt with using an analysis useful under conditions of ignorance. If project outcomes can be enumerated but probabilities cannot be assigned to the outcomes, it is considered a situation under uncertainty. If, however, probabilities can be assigned to the various outcomes, the situation is suitable for risk analysis.

The analysis of projects under ignorance or uncertainty generally uses techniques from game theory and is generally specific to the nature of the industry and business involved. The first step in capital budgeting analysis under uncertainty is generally to develop a payoff matrix relating the level of project benefits for each project for each of the enumerated future outcomes. The next step is to apply a decision rule to select the best choice among the alternative projects. A number of decision rules have been developed for such cases. For example, one rule, the Laplace rule, recommends that all outcomes be implicitly assigned equal probabilities and that the project with the highest average outcome be selected. The maximin rule suggests selecting the alternative that provides the best results under the worst possible outcome conditions. In contrast, the maximax rule is a more optimistic approach, and it suggests selecting the alternative that provides the best results under the best possible outcome conditions. Other decision rules reflect weighted averages of the pessimistic and the optimistic approaches (Thuesen and Fabrycky, 1989). A more detailed analysis of capital budgeting under uncertainty is likely to reflect insights and procedures based on game theory applied to specific industry and competitive situations (Dixit and Nalebuff, 1991; Rasmusen, 1989).

Nevertheless, it seems that in general there is an advantage in developing probability estimates for the various project outcomes, as analysis of projects under risk is more developed than under uncertainty. Many measures of risk in a projected cash flow have been developed and are used in capital budgeting analysis. The most common measure is the variance of the expected cash flows. Because investors may be concerned only with negative consequences, risk may be measured by the semivariance, as it reflects only negative variation from the mean (Porter, Bey, and Lewis, 1975). Modern finance theory has argued that in efficient capital markets, the covariance of the expected cash flows with the general market index is a better measure of risk. Investor utility has also been shown to depend on the higher moments, such as skewness and kurtosis, of the distribution of expected cash flows, with a positive utility for the odd moments and a negative utility for the even moments (Scott and Horvath, 1980). A comprehensive measure of risk ideally reflects the shape of the complete distribution of expected cash flows, including its higher moments. In such cases, risk may be measured and assessed using stochastic dominance techniques that rely on the shape of the cumulative probability distribution (Jean and Helms, 1986). Fortunately, however, only the first two moments, the mean and the variance, are needed to describe the most common distribution, the normal distribution.

One of the easiest approaches to risk analysis is to first identify the variables likely to vary from their estimates and the likely range of these variations. As a second step, the NPV or another measure of project attractiveness is recalculated for various reasonable values of the input variables to assess how sensitive the measure of project attractiveness is to changes in these variables. Such a sensitivity analysis provides a range of values rather than a point estimate of the project's attractiveness. In cases involving investments in manufacturing, such a sensitivity analysis may be guided by a model, such as cost-volume-profit (CVP) analysis, that relates fixed and variable costs.

In other cases, risk assessment may be assisted by a decision tree analysis of the business situation surrounding the proposed capital budgeting project. The decision tree can be a convenient procedure for summarizing and assessing the major events, alternatives, and outcomes associated with a projected investment. For larger and more important projects, project sensitivity analysis can be, and is, generalized into simulation analysis. In simulation analysis, the probability distribution of the input variables is used to determine the frequency with which values are calculated for the selected measure of project attractiveness. These calculations result in an output in the form of a probability distribution of the selected measure of project attractiveness.

Finally, these approaches to risk analysis and assessment must be related to the procedures used to estimate the effect of project risk on the value of a project. Generally, one of two mutually exclusive approaches is used: certainty-equivalent cash flows (CECFs) or risk-adjusted discount rates (RADRs). With the CECF approach, estimated future risky cash flows are adjusted downward to their certainty-equivalent values, and the resulting certain cash flows are then discounted at the risk-free rate (Sick, 1986). Naturally, the certainty-equivalent factor used to obtain certain cash flows from risky ones should be lower for higher levels of risk. Estimating the exact values for these certainty equivalents can be challenging, and many procedures for making these estimates have been developed (Levy and Sarnat, 1990). With the RADR approach, risky cash flows are discounted at a risk-adjusted discount rate that is higher for riskier cash flows. Unlike the adjustment for risk in the CECF approach, which can be specified for each time period, the use of a single RADR implies an exponential compounding of the adjustment for risk over time. In addition, risk in estimating the RADR can cause projects to be over-valued (Butler and Schachter, 1989).

The previous sections have reviewed the various issues associated with procedures used to assess capital budgeting proposals under conditions of certainty, ignorance, uncertainty, and risk. The next section illustrates the application of capital budgeting analysis to a few selected special situations such as capital budgeting under inflation and for multi-divisional and multinational companies. It also illustrates use of the adjusted net present value rule in capital budgeting.

IV. SELECTED APPLICATIONS OF CAPITAL EXPENDITURE ANALYSIS

A. Capital Budgeting and Inflation

Inflation influences not only a project's future cash flows but also the opportunity cost of funds used as the discount rate (Brenner and Venzia, 1983). However, these opposing influences on the present values of project cash flows do not generally cancel out, especially since tax shields related to depreciation are fixed in nominal terms at the beginning of the project (Ang, 1987). Further, different rates of inflation may influence market dynamics and related cash flows differently, with perhaps unequal influences on costs and revenues (Ezzell and Kelly, 1984). Very high rates of inflation may also lead to government price controls and other types of economic and political instability. Finally, only expected rates of inflation are generally reflected in nominal interest rates in efficient markets. The effects of even expected inflation on the attractiveness of a proposed capital expenditure should account for the specific and different effects of such inflation on the various component cash flows and on the opportunity costs of funds (Rappaport and Taggart, 1982). For example, tax asymmetries normally lead to a bias against high-risk projects (Heaton 1987). Unexpected inflation and its effects on proposed capital expenditures must be estimated separately from the effects of expected inflation. While the procedures for analyzing and managing expected rates of inflation can be easily included in traditional capital budgeting procedures with mostly minor modifications, the risks posed by unexpected inflation must be analyzed and managed with procedures related to options and their pricing (Baldwin and Ruback, 1986).

B. Capital Budgeting in Multidivisional Companies

Capital budgeting in multidivisional companies faces some additional challenges not faced by other companies. For example, division managers must be motivated to have goals consistent with those of the firm. The degree of independence enjoyed by the divisions may determine the capital budgeting process in a multidivisional company. In many such cases, the capital budgeting process may involve two stages. In a multidivisional firm, capital may first be allocated among the divisions based on strategic considerations, and then individual capital projects may be assessed and approved at a divisional level (Scapens and Sale, 1981). In such cases it has been suggested that appropriate corporate systems for divisional capital budgeting be based on a set of internal transfer prices for the capital supplied by the headquarters that reflect the overall strategic goals of the business (Obel and Vanderweide, 1979). As an alternative, it has been suggested that the use of divisional capital budgets may also be effective in a decentralized firm (Taggart, 1987). In the case of a centralized capital budgeting process, risks, returns, and attractiveness of projects in many different businesses must be compared in order to make capital expenditure decisions. The discount rate or the minimum-hurdle rate should vary from division to division, as it reflects the business risks of a given division.

With the availability of market and other data on publicly traded companies in the same business as a given division (pure plays), observed market betas can be adjusted for financial leverage and differences in growth options to calculate the asset beta for such a division. This asset beta can then be used along with the division's estimated or imputed leverage, cost of debt, and other data in the cost-of-capital calculation for the division (Fuller and Kerr, 1981). However, these procedures for determining divisional hurdle rates may have many limitations in practice (Thode, 1986). In the absence of pure play alternatives that are publicly traded, the estimation of such divisional hurdle rates may present formidable challenges and may ultimately be subjective.

C. Capital Budgeting in Multinational Companies

Like a domestic company, a multinational company (MNC) must develop estimates of the investment needed and the net cash flow generated by a proposed foreign capital investment. It must also assess the riskiness of these cash flows. Finally, it must summarize the cash flow and risk analysis information in a measure of desirability for the project such as the net present value. The company can then compare the proposed investment with other possibilities and make a go or no-go decision. Although this basic outline of the steps necessary in evaluating a specific long-term foreign investment is not much different from that followed in evaluating a domestic capital investment, the cross-border nature of the foreign investment may require consideration of a number of additional factors such as the effect of currency and political risks on the project's value (Folks and Aggarwal, 1988). Foreign exchange risk arises out of the fact that the value of a foreign currency is subject to change, and political risk results from regulatory changes in the ability to move cash flows across borders effectively and efficiently.

One of the issues that arises in an MNC has to do with the perspective adopted in assessing a capital budgeting proposal. Should the proposed capital investment be evaluated from the viewpoint of the local firm or from the viewpoint of the parent company, especially since the latter may have supplied only part or none of the initial investment for the project? The objective of maximizing shareholder wealth in the case of a wholly owned or majority-owned foreign affiliate indicates that the parent company perspective should be used. When using the parent company perspective, the project should be evaluated in terms of the parent's currency, with the parent company's net initial investment and its net receipt of cash flows from the project discounted at a rate appropriate for the risks of the project cash flows and based on the inflation rate of the parent's currency.

However, cash flows to the parent company depend not just on the performance of the project but also on what proportion of the local cash flows is remitted to the parent. For example, because of tax considerations it may not be optimal to remit all project cash flows to the parent, especially since in many cases some or all of these cash flows must be sent back to be reinvested in the foreign affiliate. In addition, since the value added to a foreign affiliate by a project is normally reflected in the value of the parent company, it may be better, even for shareholders' wealth maximization, to evaluate a foreign capital proposal from the perspective of its local affiliate. In such cases, the total investment for the project is compared to its cash flows discounted at a rate that reflects the local inflation rate and the riskiness of the project. In practice, most MNCs use at least the local perspective to evaluate a foreign project, and some MNCs supplement the local perspective with a present value analysis from the parent's perspective. In such cases, the foreign affiliate perspective is the primary basis for a go or no-go decision, while the parent perspective is used to ensure that the structure of the project investment and the remittance of the cash flows to the parent are consistent with corporate objectives.

As indicated above, when taking the local currency perspective, the discount rate should reflect a realistic assessment of the expected local inflation rate. This may be especially difficult given that capital markets in many foreign countries are often not free or efficient and interest rates do not reflect market expectations. Project cash flows should also reflect the advantages of using any subsidized financing that may have been used to finance the project.

When using the parent currency perspective, the discount rate should reflect the expected inflation rate in the parent currency, and foreign currency cash flows should be converted to parent currency cash flows using projected exchange rates. These projections often are based on the assumption that purchasing power parity will hold during the life of the project. In such cases, it may be possible to take initial-year cash flows and assume that increases in local inflation will be offset exactly by declines in the exchange rate related to purchasing power parity. However, if significant deviations from purchasing power parity are expected, such a simplifying assumption is inappropriate. In addition, high inflation rates may be accompanied by government price controls and a company may face a lag between allowed price increases and inflation, or it may be accompanied by other economic and even political instability. In such cases, simply assuming that purchasing power parity will hold may be insufficient, and additional analysis to reflect these factors should be undertaken.

An additional factor that adds to the complexity of international capital budgeting is diversity in the international tax laws faced by an MNC. Should project cash flows be valued after all taxes, that is, after taxes paid at the foreign affiliate and at the parent company levels? The answer normally seems to be yes. However, the timing and actual possibility of having to pay parent country income taxes depend on remittance policies and the use of other tax-reducing mechanisms, such as tax havens and transfer prices. Thus the procedures and tax rates used to calculate after-tax cash flows for a foreign capital expenditure depend on the situation in a specific company.

Ideally, in an MNC, capital should be allocated to projects globally wherever it can earn the highest rate of return for the owners. In practice, this objective is hard to achieve, especially because it is difficult to compare risks internationally on an objective and quantitative basis. Projects from different countries differ not only with regard to their business or commercial risks but also with regard to the degree of political risk they face. In addition, it is not easy to assess the systematic portion of the total risk of a foreign capital project and thus to develop the appropriate risk-adjusted discount rate that should be used to assess the project. Although a foreign project may seem to have higher overall risks than a domestic project, it also may offer greater opportunities for risk diversification.

As in the case of domestic operations, normal capital budgeting procedures are often inadequate in valuing projects in which a significant objective is to position the firm for possible future expansion, that is, to generate a viable option for expansion that may or may not be exercised at some point in the future. Similarly, it is important that the MNC relate the funding of capital projects to its strategic plans for foreign operations.

D. The Adjusted Net Present Value Method

The adjusted net present value (ANPV) method can be used to value a proposed capital expenditure when the investment and financing decisions cannot be separated. This section illustrates its application for a proposed capital expenditure for an MNC. The ANPV approach is particularly suitable for such projects since traditional approaches to capital budgeting, such as the calculation of net present value using the corporate cost of capital, are often inadequate in a multinational setting. For example, the traditional NPV approach assumes that financing and investment decisions can be separated and that the corporate capital structure represents the mix of financing appropriate for the project being considered. Thus the traditional NPV calculation is particularly likely to be inappropriate in the case of capital projects in a multinational setting, especially in view of significant international variations in capital structure norms and the widespread use of subsidized project-specific financing, loan guarantees, and insurance against political risks. In addition, political and currency risks may be unsystematic in nature for a capital budgeting proposal in a multinational firm, and, further, project systematic risk may not reflect the systematic risk of the parent company. Thus the adjusted net present value approach has been widely suggested as being more appropriate for the capital budgeting process in a multinational corporation.

The ANPV approach differs from the traditional NPV approach in a number of ways. It uses an all-equity discount rate that reflects local inflation and interest rates and the systematic part of the business risk of a particular project. In addition, it uses the value-additivity approach, and the ANPV calculation adds to the present value of the operating cash flows the present value of after-tax amounts of any subsidies inherent in project-specific financing, as well as the present value of debt-related tax shields reflecting the capital structure appropriate for the particular project being evaluated. Consequently, the ANPV approach encourages the decision maker to adjust project cash flows for specific project-related subsidies, and, in addition, project risks are accounted for by adjusting cash flows rather than by making adjustments to the discount rate. Thus the ANPV approach allows calculation of the project NPV to easily reflect the specific risks, capital structure, financing, and other conditions associated with a project in a given country.

As an example, consider the following formulation for the adjusted net present value of a project being considered by a foreign affiliate of an MNC (Folks and Aggarwal, 1988):

$$\text{ANPV} = -I_0 + \sum_1^n \frac{CF_i}{(1 + k_e)^i} + \sum_1^n \frac{T_i}{(1 + k_d)^i}$$

$$+ \sum_1^n \frac{S_i}{(1 + k_d)^i} + \sum_1^n \frac{O_i}{(1 + k_e)^i} + \frac{TV_n}{(1 + k_e)^n}$$

where I_0 = initial investment

k_e = all-equity cost or discount rate reflecting the riskiness and diversification benefits of the project

k_d = cost of debt

n = number of periods in the investment horizon

CF_i = after-tax net cash inflows for period i

T_i = tax shield on debt service payments for period i reflecting the capital structure of the affiliate undertaking the project

S_i = after-tax value of special financial or other subsidies associated with the project for the period i

O_i = estimated value in period i of any options, such as the ability to enter a new business created by the project

TV_n = estimated terminal value in period n at the end of the investment horizon, which also can be the estimated present value of compensation received for an expected government takeover.

The first term covers the initial investment. The second term reflects the present value of the net after-tax cash inflows the project is expected to generate. These cash inflows are discounted at the all-equity cost that reflects the business risk associated with the project. The third term reflects the present value of the tax savings associated with use of debt in the capital structure. By explicitly accounting for the tax shields, it is possible to account for the unique capital structure being used by the affiliate undertaking the project. The fourth term reflects the present value of any financial or other subsidies often received by international projects from home, host, or other governments. The fifth term reflects the value of any options, such as the ability to enter a new business, whether exercised or not, generated by the project. These values may be zero or very small, at least for the first few years, and may often be difficult to estimate. Nevertheless, the ANPV approach at least provides an opportunity to value these options.

The last term reflects the estimated terminal value at the end of the investment horizon. Although there are many ways to estimate the terminal value, one approach commonly used is to set it equal to the present value of all future cash flows, that is, equal to $CF/(k - g)$, where CF is the annual cash flow after the investment horizon, k is the discount rate, and g is the expected growth rate for these cash flows. Another approach that may be used for projects in politically unstable environments is to allow the terminal value to reflect the expected present value of a possible future amount received as compensation for government takeover of the project. Other aspects of political risk also may be modeled as additional terms in the ANPV formulation.

As this example illustrates, the ANPV method allows for explicit valuation of each cost and benefit associated with a project. The illustration used here included the use of a financial structure specified for the project being evaluated, subsidized financing sources and other investment subsidies unique to the project, and the political risks of expropriation associated with the project. Additional aspects of the project, such as blockages of funds by host governments, may also be modeled as additional terms in the ANPV formulation.

Prior sections have provided a brief review and illustrative applications of capital budgeting analysis. However, the attractiveness of a capital budgeting proposal depends, sometimes critically, on the reactions of competitors and the economic environment of the business. Thus market conditions and industry structure can be expected to greatly influence the riskiness of proposed capital expenditures. The next section addresses some of these issues. Other sections cover other aspects of capital budgeting not dealt with adequately in ordinary and textbook discussions of capital budgeting.

IV. THE ECONOMICS OF CAPITAL BUDGETING

A. Industrial Economics and Capital Budgeting

Capital investment projects undertaken in a perfectly competitive market environment cannot create value, as any benefits in excess of related costs are competed away. Capital budgeting projects can create value only if they take advantage of market imperfections. Thus the evaluation of capital expenditure proposals involves assessment of the related market imperfections. The ability of a firm to identify and exploit such market imperfections depends on the nature and structure of the project's industry.

Variations in business profitability have been shown to depend on a firm's market share in an industry and on the nature and structure of the industry, including its capital intensity and growth rate. The concentration of firms in an industry and the significance of entry and exit barriers are also likely to influence the profitability of capital expenditure proposals in the industry. While entry barriers are likely to increase the attractiveness of such investments, exit barriers may have an opposite effect. As a first approximation, it is contended that for an entry decision, product prices must exceed variable costs and the interest cost on the fixed costs of entry; and similarly for exit decisions—product prices must go below the variable cost less the interest cost on the fixed costs of exit. However, in the presence of sunk costs it has been shown that such decisions are no longer symmetric and there is hysteresis; that is, it is not optimal to reverse a decision when prices move back (Dixit, 1989).

The nature of industry structure is likely to influence some types of investments more than others. For example, investments in other firms in the form of mergers and acquisitions, or in the form of foreign direct investments, are likely to be heavily influenced by expectations of antitrust actions by other firms in the industry or by other government regulations. Similarly, decisions regarding foreign direct investments are also likely to be influenced by industry structure and other aspects of industrial structure in the host country. Capital expenditures in research and development, advertising, and other means for achieving and maintaining product differentiation are also likely to be greatly influenced by industry structure. Using the example of the corn wet-milling industry, industry growth rates and competitor reactions have been shown to influence capacity expansion decisions and the evolution of industry concentration (Porter and Spence, 1982).

The influence of industry structure on capital budgeting also includes the effects of economies of scale and scope, learning or experience curves, and other forms of increasing returns. Such influences which frequently take the form of positive feedback loops can greatly affect firm market shares, industry structures, and the profitability of related capital investments. These dynamic effects can interact with historical accidents, selecting an equilibrium and locking an industry or a firm into an outcome that is not necessarily the best or easily predictable (Arthur, 1989). A common example used to illustrate these positive feedback effects is the evolution of the VCR market where the VHS system came to dominate the technically superior Beta system (Anderson, Arrow, and Pines, 1988). Learning curve and scale effects have also been shown to influence many aspects of corporate strategy, including investment, pricing, and production decisions (Majd and Pindyck, 1989; Lieberman, 1987). For effective entry deterrence in such cases, a firm may have to invest in projects having negative NPVs when they are first reviewed.

The ability of a business to develop capital expenditure projects that result in positive NPVs may depend on patents, on other unique technological or managerial skills, or on the ownership of unique natural resource(s). More generally, it arises from a firm's managerial resources, reputation, market position, and scale, all of which may have been developed over time to act as barriers to entry or exit. Much literature on strategic analysis has been devoted to the development of such sustainable strategic advantages. These competitive advantages provide firms valuable options to grow through the undertaking of positive-NPV investments. The decision to invest is thus similar to the decision to exercise a call option (McDonald and Siegel, 1986). The application of contingent claims analysis (CCA) and options pricing models (OPMs) to capital budgeting decisions are reviewed next.

B. Valuing Options Embedded in Capital Expenditure Projects

Many capital budgeting projects are considered strategic in nature, and such projects have embedded options that provide flexibility in responding to changes in the business, regulatory, or competitive environment. Further, there is often some flexibility in the start date of a project, projects may have varying degrees of reversibility, and capital budgeting projects may differ with regard to the flexibility with which they can be ended or abandoned (Pindyck, 1991). As an example, urban land is best valued using an options pricing approach that recognizes that the value of land should reflect not only its value based on its best immediate use but also its value if building is delayed for one or more years (Titman, 1985). Similarly, machinery that has multiple uses in addition to its use in the specific project being considered is likely to be more valuable and present a lower risk of loss if the project fails (Aggarwal and Soenen, 1989). In many cases, the extent of project flexibility in a series of projects may influence their optimal sequence (Kester, 1984). These competitive, timing, and other aspects of flexibility in capital budgeting projects must be articulated, assessed, and valued.

There are many reasons why a project may be irreversible and why flexibility may be especially valuable (Sick, 1989). For example, the expenditure may result in capital that is firm- or industry-specific, such as marketing and advertising expenditures which are particularly firm-specific. In addition, there may be a number of implementation or other costs that reduce the alternative use or liquidation value of project expenditures to less than their original value. The well-known "lemons problem" (Ackerlof, 1970), severance pay, reclamation costs, and other government regulations may also contribute to these forms of irreversibility. As an example, the sunk costs associated with opening and closing a mine combined with the variability of the price of the output means that mining decisions exhibit some hysteresis and options pricing models can be used to guide such decisions (Brennan and Schwartz, 1985).

There are numerous other examples of the application of CCA and OPMs in the analysis of capital expenditures (Bjerksund and Ekem, 1990). For example, when sequential irreversible investment opportunities arrive at random and the firm has limited investment funds, the simple NPV rule leads to overinvestment (Baldwin, 1982). For projects that can be delayed, the decision to invest depends not only on the discount rate but also on its uncertainty, with the uncertainty in discount rates delaying the investment (Ingersoll and Ross, 1992). For projects that take time to build, that is, where there is a maximum rate at which the initial investment can be completed, uncertainty magnifies the effects of irreversibility because the minimum expected value of a project required for it to proceed increases the longer it takes to build (Majd and Pindyck, 1987). In contrast, for cases where initial investment can provide information that reduces uncertainty in the future value of a project, it may be appropriate to undertake investments that initially have a negative NPV (Roberts and Weitzman, 1981). For similar reasons, it is contended that traditional capital budgeting procedures may deter investment in innovation (Baldwin, 1991).

In general, as this brief discussion indicates, it is clear that option pricing analysis can be useful in assessing the value of active and continuing management of a capital project where a project may be delayed, accelerated, or changed in response to new developments (Kensinger, 1987). In such cases, managerial flexibility must be valued (Trigeorgis and Mason, 1987). For example, investments in flexible production technology must be valued using option pricing models (Triantis and Hodder, 1990). However, since an option can be exercised only once, a firm loses the value of the option to make the investment later, once a decision has been made to make an investment (Demers, 1991). Consequently, it has been recommended "that in many cases capital projects should be undertaken only when their present value is at least double their direct costs" (Pindyck, 1988, p. 969). In any case, there is little question that the valuation of project flexibility has become a major new source of attention in the capital budgeting literature in recent years.

This brief analysis of the industrial economics and contingent claims associated with capital expenditure proposals illustrates some reasons why there seem to be inconsistencies between business strategy and conventional capital budgeting. Conventional capital budgeting generally seems to ignore many of the issues discussed in this section. The next section on organizational issues covers other issues that are also ignored or dealt with inadequately in many conventional textbook discussions of capital budgeting.

V. ORGANIZATIONAL ISSUES IN CAPITAL BUDGETING

A. Agency Costs and Asymmetric Information

An agency relationship is established when one party (the principal) engages another party (the agent) to perform services for the former. However, principals and agents may not operate with the same information set and may not have the same utility functions. Thus rational utility maximization by managers may not be consistent with owner wealth maximization. Nevertheless, in most large businesses and in many small businesses, managerial functions are largely performed by professional nonowner managers. Consequently, managerial compensation schemes have to be designed and implemented to align managerial and owner goals. In such cases, owners must monitor managers for compliance with these compensation contracts and, at equilibrium, optimal monitoring expenditures still leave some residual agency costs that are not eliminated (Fama, 1980).

It should be noted that the principal-agent problem occurs in many areas of operation in a business firm. This is especially true because a business firm is considered a nexus of numerous formal and informal contracts between many stakeholders, for example, owners, bondholders, managers, employees, suppliers, customers, and the communities where the firm operates (Aggarwal and Chandra, 1990). Transaction costs theories have analyzed various forms of decentralized organizational structures as to their business effectiveness and their ability to reduce these residual agency costs (Williamson, 1981). It has been shown that the organizational form used by a business influences its investment decisions (Fama and Jensen, 1985).

Agency considerations indicate that managers may exhibit higher risk aversion than may be optimal for the owners because it is not possible for managers to diversify their investment in human capital which may be largely firm-specific (Thakor, 1990). In such cases, firm capital investment is likely to reflect this higher-than-optimal risk aversion (Holmstrom and Weiss, 1985). In order to protect their reputations and preserve their human capital, managers may also engage in herd behavior, making investment decisions that are nonoptimal for the business and ignoring contrary private information (Scharfstein and Stein, 1990). Managers also may differ greatly in terms of their propensity to take risks depending on their socioeconomic background (MacCrimmon and Wehrung, 1990). In designing contracts for motivating managers, it is important to account for the costs faced by owners in obtaining the superior information about a project possessed by the manager (Heckerman, 1975). In addition to principal-agent problems, capital budgeting procedures must also account for the costs of collecting and processing the information needed to make capital budgeting decisions (Kaplan, 1984). It has been noted that because of these information costs, managers may be able to appropriate excess or residual corporate slack (Antle and Eppen, 1985). Managers are also likely to entrench themselves and favor implicit contracts and investments having a higher value under their management (Shleifer and Vishny, 1989). It has been suggested that appropriate financing policies be used to limit managerial discretion in such cases (Stulz, 1990).

Agency cost analysis has also been used to analyze conflicts between bondholders and stockholders. It has been shown that equity holders face incentives to undertake risky investments that transfer wealth from bondholders to themselves (Jensen and Meckling, 1976). It is also now well known that equity holders in a leveraged firm may forgo positive NPV investments if a sufficient fraction of the project value accrues to debt holders (Myers, 1977). Thus conflicts between stock- and bondholders that are unmitigated by other mechanisms are likely to lead to underinvestment and investment in risky projects.

While these agency- and information asymmetry-related costs reduce the efficiency of the capital budgeting process in a business, this process may also be influenced by imperfections in the capital budgeting environment. The next section addresses these issues and reviews their impact.

VI. IMPERFECTIONS IN THE ENVIRONMENT OF CAPITAL BUDGETING

A. Imperfections in Capital Markets

It has been noted that temporal fluctuations in aggregate investment levels in the U.S. economy have been four to five times the fluctuations in output during the postwar period. These variations in U.S. investment/output ratios are also much larger than those observed in other industrial countries (Greenwald and Stiglitz, 1988). Some economists have contended that these cycles in investment/output ratios are associated with capital market imperfections that, for example, make internally generated capital cheaper and preferable to externally generated capital (Fazzari, Hubbard, and Petersen, 1988). In the presence of excess and free cash flows, it has been contended that managers are likely to overinvest rather than return the excess cash flows to the investors (Jensen, 1986). This effect has been confirmed empirically for oil exploration and paper industries where investment levels have been related to the level of free cash flows (Griffin, 1988; Strong and Meyer, 1990). In contrast, firms that face declines in internally generated cash flows reduce the level of their capital investments; that is, managers of such firms operate in environments characterized to varying degrees by capital rationing.

There are a number of reasons why a firm may operate under conditions of capital rationing. Managers may avoid raising external capital to avoid the associated intense monitoring by outside suppliers of capital. Such external scrutiny may reduce the benefits that can be expropriated by managers. In addition, external financing is generally more expensive than internal financing. One reason for the higher cost of external financing related to the observed differences between the lending and borrowing rates resulting from the cost of financial intermediation, is the additional cost of flotation involved in a new public issue of securities. To the extent that a firm can use less costly external financing, such as bank loans or debt issues or private placements of its new securities, it can reduce this differential cost advantage of internal financing. In addition, in the United States and in most other countries, external equity financing faces tax disadvantages compared to debt financing (Auerbach, 1983). Finally, because of information asymmetries, external suppliers of financing have less information about business investments than do managers, causing suppliers of external financing to demand a premium (Greenwald, Stiglitz, and Weiss, 1984). In such cases, a firm is unlikely to issue new securities and to underinvest compared to what may be optimal (Myers and Majluf, 1984).

B. Political Costs of Reported Earnings

Some projects may be adopted or rejected on the basis of their influence on reported earnings regardless of their ability to add to the value of the business. This may be so even though accounting data often do not reflect economic reality. For example, the time value of money is unevenly or rarely used in the various accounting standards applicable for U.S. companies (Aggarwal and Gibson, 1989). However, it has been documented that accounting choices do have economic consequences (Holthausen and Leftwich, 1983).

There can be a number of reasons for the influence of accounting data on capital budgeting decisions even though such influences seem to imply deviations from economic rationality. First, as discussed above, managerial compensation may reflect reported earnings. Second, loan covenants and other contractual arrangements with outside stakeholders may depend on reported earnings and other accounting data. Third, noncontractual but implicit agreements between the firm and its various stakeholders may be influenced by reported accounting data. For example, higher reported earnings may lead to demands for higher wages and salaries, lower prices for output and higher prices for inputs, and a higher probability of governmental regulation (Aggarwal, 1991). It seems clear that decision making under uncertainty is heavily influenced in a number of ways by the availability of accounting and other information at different stages of the decision process (Hirshleifer and Riley, 1979).

C. Interaction of Capital Budgeting With Business Financing

Most capital budgeting analysis assumes the validity of the separation principle, which states that a firm's financing and investment decisions should be separate; that is, a firm's financing decisions should be made to minimize its cost of capital, while its investment decisions should independently maximize firm value. However, in many cases, because of capital market imperfections (as discussed above) the conditions for the separation principle may be violated (Rotemberg and Scharfstein, 1990). For example, borrowing and lending rates may differ, tax schedules may be nonlinear and interact with proposed investments, leasing a capital asset may involve embedded financing subsidies, and financial distress costs may depend on accounting data rather than economic values. In such cases, capital budgeting decisions may be influenced by and influence the firm's financing decisions; that is, the investment and financing decisions may have to be considered jointly. The ANPV methodology described earlier is much more suitable than the normal NPV calculation in such cases and for assessing the attractiveness of a capital expenditure project that results in a change in the firm's optimal financing mix. As an example, it has been shown that the flexibility and capital intensity of the production technology used by a firm have been shown to influence its risk and cost of capital (Booth, 1991). The technology used by a firm can also influence agency costs of debt and its optimal debt ratio (Kim and Maksimovic, 1990). A firm's assets in place and its investment options may influence its equity market risk (Chung and Charoenwong, 1991).

D. Deviations From the Expected Utility Rule for Risky Decisions

Organizations and individuals face a number of challenges in assessing probabilistic events and their consequences accurately (Arrow, 1982). Decision science research has articulated and documented a number of systematic deviations from "rational behavior" in assessing uncertain outcomes (Fishburn, 1989). For example, it has been documented that risk aversion is asymmetric; that is, people tend to pay more to avoid a risk than for the equal possibility of a gain. A closely related phenomenon is the high value attached to the fear of regret, especially when associated with an investment that has a poor reputation (Thaler, 1991). While it is commonly believed that decision makers maximize their expected utility, it has been documented that utility functions that are concave at low levels of wealth and convex at high levels of wealth are more consistent with observed behavior (Friedman and Savage, 1948).

In addition to the changing curvature of the utility function with regard to expected value and wealth, decision analysis is further complicated by violations of linearity in probability (Machina, 1987). For example, it has been documented that indifference curves related to expected values are not parallel but "fan out" in what is known as the Allais paradox (Allais and Hagen, 1979). The Allais paradox is actually considered to be part of a wider phenomenon known as the common consequence effect where Samuelson's independence axiom is violated. As an example of such a case, winning a top prize in a lottery has been shown to provide more utility than winning a bottom prize of the same value in a different lottery (Bell, 1985).

Decision makers have also been documented to display the preference reversal phenomenon: Choices regarding winning or losing a gamble are based primarily on the probability of winning or losing, while buying and selling prices are determined primarily by the dollar amounts involved (Grether and Plott, 1979). It has been documented that investors are influenced by prior losses and gains when making decisions concerning risky investments (Thaler and Johnson, 1990). These conceptual contentions of the effects of sunk costs and prior losses and gains have been empirically documented for investment decisions in the U.S. nuclear power industry (De Bondt and Makhija, 1988).

Similarly, framing also influences decisions. In framing, unrelated contextual data or a reference point unduly affects the outcome of a risky choice (Tversky and Kahneman, 1986). Judgments regarding probabilistic events are also influenced by phenomena such as availability (easy recallability), representativeness (similarities based on superficial characteristics), and anchoring (relatedness to an initial number). Thus framing a decision may provide an "anchor" and elicit responses related to availability and representativeness and may have a great deal of influence on its outcome (MacCrimmon and Wehrung, 1986). For example, it has been documented that while new information leads to adjustments in the prior anchor in the right direction, such adjustments are generally too small. In addition, investors and managers have been found to be particularly poor judges of the expected value of remote possibilities such as winning a major lottery (Tversky and Kahneman, 1981). For example, the abandonment decision has been shown to be governed by aspects related to prospect theory as discussed above (Statman and Caldwell, 1987).

These difficulties in assessing risky outcomes and deviations from the expected utility rule have a number of influences on the capital budgeting process. Because of these and other limitations of expected utility models, a number of alternative models of decision making under uncertainty are being investigated (Machina, 1989). Similarly, decisions involving assessments over long horizons with limited information may be improved with the use of special algorithms developed for this purpose (Geanakopolis and Gray, 1991).

E. Practical Aspects of Imperfections in Capital Budgeting

It is widely contended that strategic allocation of capital in a business is different from its allocation based on financial criteria (Gale and Branch, 1987). In fact, it is often suggested that strategic considerations should overrule financial considerations in setting hurdle rates and in allocating capital (Donaldson, 1972; Ellsworth, 1983). It seems that a major reason for these alleged differences between strategic and financial bases in assessing capital expenditure decisions has been the lack of comprehensiveness in traditional finance-based capital budgeting analysis.

As the comments above indicate, traditional discussions of capital budgeting procedures leave out many significant aspects of the process. For example, it seems that a large part of the differences between financial and strategic allocations of capital may be traced to the recognition and treatment of growth options in the capital allocation process. However, as discussed above, traditional finance-based capital budgeting analysis typically has also ignored explicit consideration of competitive reactions and associated industrial economics, the options embedded in capital expenditure proposals, and the problems induced by market imperfections and deviations from expected utility decision rules.

Market failures and externalities in the markets for goods and services, often acerbated by ill-defined property rights and "free rider" problems, have also been considered to be responsible for the failure of traditional capital budgeting procedures in most cases of capital investment for social goals (Quinn and Winginton, 1981). Such market failures mean that many of the resources used and the benefits generated by a project are unlikely to be priced appropriately by market mechanisms (Cowen, 1988).

While the discussion above makes clear that our models of the capital budgeting process fail to capture many of its significant aspects, it seems that corporate practice in this area may not suffer from as many limitations. A number of studies have examined and found an increasing adoption of sophisticated capital budgeting techniques by businesses (Bierman, 1988; Aggarwal, 1980). Interestingly, no clear relationship between the use of sophisticated capital budgeting techniques and corporate performance has been documented (Haka, Gordon, and Pinches, 1985). Fortunately, companies seem to use techniques that, on average, are viewed favorably by equity markets, as the announcement of capital expenditure decisions by industrial firms has been found to be associated with positive abnormal equity market returns (McConnell and Muscarella, 1985). It seems that corporate managers make appropriate intuitive adjustments in practice to ensure that, on average, capital expenditure proposals add to rather than reduce firm value.

VI. CONCLUSIONS

This chapter has been a brief review and summary of the literature related to capital budgeting under uncertainty. As this literature is quite voluminous, this review has not been comprehensive but has been deliberately nontechnical. It has highlighted only the major themes and issues in the literature related to capital budgeting under uncertainty. The goals of this brief review and summary have been to provide an introduction to the literature on capital budgeting under uncertainty and to shed some light on the alleged inconsistencies between business strategy and capital budgeting.

Imperfections in capital markets, agency costs, difficulties in valuing embedded options, the importance and political costs of accounting data, and deviations from rational decision making related to the psychological aspects of assessing uncertain and risky outcomes, all contribute to making the practice of capital budgeting closer to an art and farther from a science than is desirable. Fortunately, this brief review also provides directions for further investigation designed to reduce the art and increase the science in our understanding of capital budgeting. Thus it is hoped that this review will also encourage further thought and, perhaps, attempts to clarify the many issues related to capital budgeting that still remain unclear.

REFERENCES

ACKERLOF, GEORGE A. (1970). "The Market for Lemons: Quality Uncertainty and the Market Mechanism," *Quarterly Journal of Economics* 84 (No. 3, August), pp. 488–500.

AGGARWAL, RAJ (1980). "Corporate Use of Sophisticated Capital Budgeting Techniques," *Interfaces* 10 (No. 2, April), pp. 31–34.

AGGARWAL, RAJ (1991). "Management of Accounting Exposure to Currency Changes: Role and Evidence of Agency Costs," *Managerial Finance* 17 (No. 4), pp. 10–22.

AGGARWAL, RAJ, and GYAN CHANDRA (1990). "Stakeholder Management: Opportunities and Challenges," *Business* 40 (No. 4, October–November–December), pp. 48–51.

AGGARWAL, RAJ, and CHARLES H. GIBSON (1989). *Discounting in Financial Accounting and Reporting* (Morristown, N.J.: Financial Executives Research Foundation).

AGGARWAL, RAJ, and LUC SOENEN (1989). "Project Exit Value as a Measure of Flexibility and Risk Exposure," *Engineering Economist* 35 (No. 1, Fall), pp. 39–54.

ALLAIS, MAURICE, and OLE HAGEN, eds. (1979). *Expected Utility Hypothesis and the Allais Paradox* (Dordrecht, The Netherlands: D. Reidel).

ANDERSON, PHILIP W., KENNETH J. ARROW, and DAVID PINES, eds. (1988). *The Economy as an Evolving Complex System* (Reading, Mass.: Addison-Wesley).

ANG, JAMES (1987). "Tax Asymmetries and the Optimal Investment Decision of the Firm," *Engineering Economist* 32 (No. 2, Winter), pp. 135–161.

ANTLE, RICK, and GARY EPPEN (1985). "Capital Rationing and Organizational Slack in Capital Budgeting," *Management Science* 31 (No. 2, February), pp. 163–174.

ARROW, KENNETH, J. (1982). "Risk Perception in Psychology and Economics," *Economic Inquiry* 20 (No. 1, January), pp. 1–9.

ARTHUR, W. BRIAN (1989). "Competing Technologies, Increasing Returns, and Lock-in by Historical Events," *The Economic Journal* 99 (No. 1, March), pp. 116–131.

AUERBACH, ALAN J. (1983). "Taxation, Corporate Finance, and the Cost of Capital," *Journal of Economic Literature* 21 (No. 3, September), pp. 448–500.

BALDWIN, CARLISS Y. (1982). "Optimal Sequential Investment When Capital Is Not Readily Reversible," *Journal of Finance* 37 (No. 3, June), pp. 763–782.

BALDWIN, CARLISS Y. (1991). "How Capital Budgeting Deters Innovation—And What to Do About It," *Research Technology Management* 34 (No. 6, November–December), pp. 39–45.

BALDWIN, CARLISS Y., and RICHARD S. RUBACK (1986). "Inflation, Uncertainty, and Investment," *Journal of Finance* 41 (No. 3, July), pp. 657–669.

BELL, DAVID E. (1985). "Disappointment in Decision Making Under Uncertainty" *Operations Research*, 33 (No. 1, January–February), pp. 1–27.

BIERMAN, HAROLD (1988). *Implementing Capital Budgeting Techniques* (Cambridge, Mass: Ballinger).

BJERKSUND, PETTER, and STEINER EKERN (1990). "Managing Investment Opportunities Under Price Uncertainty: From "Last Chance" to "Wait and See" Strategies, *Financial Management* 19 (No. 3, Autumn), pp. 65–83.

BLACK, FISCHER (1988). "A Simple Discounting Rule," *Financial Management* 17 (No. 2, Summer), pp. 7–11.

BOOTH, LAURENCE (1991). "The Influence of Productive Technology on Risk and Cost of Capital," *Journal of Financial and Quantitative Analysis* 26 (No. 1, March), pp. 109–127.

BRENNAN, MICHAEL J., and EDUARDO S. SCHWARTZ (1985). "Evaluating Natural Resource Investments," *Journal of Business* 58 (No. 2, April), pp. 135–157.

BRENNER, MENACHEM, and IZTHAK VENZIA (1983). "The Effects of Inflation and Taxes on Growth Investments and Replacement Policies," *Journal of Finance* 38 (No. 5, December), pp. 1519–1527.

BUTLER, J. S., and BARRY SCHACHTER (1989). "The Investment Decision: Estimation Risk and Risk Adjusted Discount Rates," *Financial Management* 18 (No. 4, Winter), pp. 13–22.

CHUNG, KEE H., and CHARLIE CHAROENWONG (1991). "Investment Options, Assets in Place, and the Risk of Stocks," *Financial Management* 20 (No. 3, Autumn), pp. 21–33.

COWEN, TYLER, ed. (1988). *The Theory of Market Failure* (Fairfax, Va.: George Mason University Press and the Cato Institute).

DE BONDT, WERNER F. M., and ANIL K. MAKHIJA (1988). "Throwing Good Money After Bad?: Nuclear Power Plant Investment Decisions and the Relevance of Sunk Costs," *Journal of Economic Behavior and Organization* 10 (No. 2, September), pp. 173–199.

DEMERS, MICHEL (1991). "Investment Under Uncertainty, Irreversibility and the Arrival of Information Over Time," *Review of Economic Studies* 58 (No. 2, April), pp. 333–350.

DIXIT, AVINASH (1989). "Entry and Exit Decisions Under Uncertainty," *Journal of Political Economy* 97 (No. 3, May), pp. 620–638.

DIXIT, AVINASH, and BARRY NALEBUFF (1991). *Strategic Thinking* (New York: Free Press).

DONALDSON, GORDON (1972). "Strategic Hurdle Rates for Capital Investments," *Harvard Business Review* 50 (No. 2, March–April), pp. 50–58.

ELLSWORTH, RICHARD R. (1983). "Subordinate Financial Policy to Corporate Strategy," *Harvard Business Review* 61 (No. 6, November–December), pp. 170–182.

EZZELL, JOHN R., and WILLIAM A. KELLY (1984). "An APV Analysis of Capital Budgeting Under Inflation," *Financial Management* 13 (No. 3, Autumn), pp. 657–669.

FAMA, EUGENE F. (1980). "Agency Problems and the Theory of the Firm," *Journal of Political Economy* 88 (No. 2, April), pp. 288–307.

FAMA, EUGENE F., and MICHAEL C. JENSEN (1985). "Organizational Forms and Investment Decisions," *Journal of Financial Economics* 14 (No. 1, March), pp. 101–119.

FAZZARI, STEVEN, R. GLEN HUBBARD, and BRUCE PETERSEN (1988). "Financing Constraints and Corporate Investment," *Brookings Papers on Economic Activity* (No. 1, Spring), pp. 141–206.

FISHBURN, PETER C. (1989). "Foundations of Decision Analysis," *Management Science* 35 (No. 4, April), pp. 387–405.

FISHER, IRVING (1930). *The Theory of Interest* (New York: Macmillan).

FOLKS, WILLIAM R., and RAJ AGGARWAL (1988). *International Dimensions of Financial Management* (Boston: PWS-Kent Publishing).

FRIEDMAN, MILTON, and LEONARD SAVAGE (1948). "The Utility Analysis of Choices Involving Risk," *Journal of Political Economy* 56 (No. 4, August), pp. 279–304.

FULLER, RUSSELL J., and HALBERT S. KERR (1981). "Estimating the Divisional Cost of Capital: An Analysis of the Pure Play Technique," *Journal of Finance* 36 (No. 5, December), pp. 997–1009.

GALE, BRADLEY T., and BEN BRANCH (1987). "Allocating Capital More Effectively," *Sloan Management Review* 29 (No. 1, Fall), pp. 21–31.

GEANAKOPOLIS, JOHN, and LARRY GRAY (1991). "When Seeing Further Is Not Seeing Better," *SFI Bulletin* 6 (No. 2), pp. 4–9.

GREENWALD, BRUCE, and JOSEPH STIGLITZ (1988). "Examining Alternative Macroeconomic Theories," *Brookings Papers on Economic Activity* (No. 1, Spring), pp. 202–220.

GREENWALD, BRUCE, JOSEPH STIGLITZ, and ANDREW WEISS (1984). "Information Imperfections in the Capital Market and Macroeconomic Fluctuations," *American Economic Review* 74 (No. 2, May), pp. 194–199.

GRETHER, DAVID M., and CHARLES R. PLOTT (1979). "Economic Theory of Choice and the Preference Reversal Phenomenon," *American Economic Review* 69 (No. 4, September), pp. 623–638.

GRIFFIN, JAMES M. (1988). "A Test of the Free Cash Flow Hypothesis: Results from the Petroleum Industry," *Review of Economic Statistics* 70 (No. 1, February), pp. 76–82.

HAKA, SUSAN F., LAWRENCE A. GORDON, and GEORGE E. PINCHES (1985). "Sophisticated Capital Budgeting Selection Techniques and Firm Performance," *Accounting Review* 60 (No. 4, October), pp. 651–669.

HAYS, ROBERT H., and DAVID A. GARVIN (1982). "Managing as If Tomorrow Mattered," *Harvard Business Review* 50 (No. 3, May–June), pp. 70–79.

HEATON, HAL (1987). "On the Bias of the Corporate Tax Against High Risk Projects," *Journal of Financial and Quantitative Analysis* 22 (No. 3, September), pp. 365–371.

HECKERMAN, DONALD G. (1975). "Motivating Managers to Make Investment Decisions," *Journal of Financial Economics* 2 (No. 3, September), pp. 273–292.

HIRSHLEIFER, JACK, and JOHN G. RILEY (1979). "The Analytics of Uncertainty and Information—An Expository Survey," *Journal of Economic Literature* 42 (No. 4, December), pp. 1375–1421.

HOLMSTROM, BENGT, and LAURENCE WEISS (1985). "Managerial Incentives, Investment, and Aggregate Implications: Scale Effects," *Review of Economic Studies* 52 (No. 3, July), pp. 403–425.

HOLTHAUSEN, ROBERT W., and ROBERT W. LEFTWICH (1983). "The Economic

Consequences of Accounting Choice," *Journal of Accounting and Economics* 5 (No. 2, August), pp. 77–117.

INGERSOLL, JONATHAN E., and STEPHEN A. ROSS (1992). "Waiting to Invest: Investment and Uncertainty," *Journal of Business* 65 (No. 1, January), pp. 1–29.

JEAN, WILLIAM H., and BILLY P. HELMS (1986). "Stochastic Dominance as a Decision Model," *Quarterly Journal of Business and Economics* 25 (No. 1, Winter), pp. 65–101.

JENSEN, MICHAEL C. (1986). "Agency Costs of Free Cash Flow, Corporate Finance, and Takeovers," *American Economic Review* 76 (No. 2, May), pp. 323–329.

JENSEN, MICHAEL C., and WILLIAM MECKLING (1976). "Theory of the Firm, Managerial Behavior, Agency Costs, and Ownership Structure," *Journal of Financial Economics* 3 (No. 4, October), pp. 305–360.

KAPLAN, ROBERT (1984). "The Evolution of Management Accounting," *Accounting Review* 59 (No. 3, July), pp. 390–418.

KENSINGER, JOHN W. (1987). "Adding the Value of Active Management Into the Capital Budgeting Equation," *Midland Corporate Finance Journal* 5 (No. 1, Spring), pp. 31–42.

KESTER, W. CARL (1984). "Growth Options and Investment: Reducing the Guesswork in Strategic Capital Budgeting," *Harvard Business Review* 52 (No. 2, March–April), pp. 153–160.

KIM, MOSHE, and VOJISLAV MAKSIMOVIC (1990). "Technology, Debt and the Exploitation of Growth Options," *Journal of Banking and Finance* 14 (No. 6, December), pp. 1113–1131.

KNIGHT, CHARLES F. (1992). "Emerson Electric: Consistent Profits, Consistently," *Harvard Business Review* 70 (No. 1, January–February), pp. 57–69.

LEVY, HAIM, and MARSHALL SARNAT (1990). *Capital Investment and Financing Decisions*, 4th ed. (Englewood Cliffs, N.J.: Prentice-Hall).

LIEBERMAN, MARVIN B. (1987). "The Learning Curve, Diffusion, and Competitive Strategy," *Strategic Management Journal* 8 (No. 5, September–October), pp. 441–452.

MACCRIMMON, KENNETH R., and DONALD A. WEHRUNG (1986). *Taking Risks: The Management of Uncertainty* (New York: Free Press).

MACCRIMMON, KENNETH R., and DONALD A. WEHRUNG (1990). "Characteristics of Risk Taking Executives, "*Management Science* 36 (No. 4, April), pp. 422–435.

MACHINA, MARK J. (1987). "Choices Under Uncertainty: Problems Solved and Unsolved," *Journal of Economic Perspectives* 1 (No. 1, Summer), pp. 121–154.

MACHINA, MARK J. (1989). "Dynamic Consistency and Non-Expected Utility Models of Choice Under Uncertainty," *Journal of Economic Literature* 27 (No. 4, December), pp. 1622–1668.

MAJD, SAMAN, and ROBERT S. PINDYCK (1987). "Time to Build, Option Value, and Investment Decisions," *Journal of Financial Economics* 18 (No. 1, March), pp. 7–27.

MAJD, SAMAN, and ROBERT S. PINDYCK (1989). "The Learning Curve and Optimal

Production Under Uncertainty," *Rand Journal of Economics* 20 (No. 3, Autumn), pp. 331–343.

McCONNELL, JOHN J., and CHRIS J. MUSCARELLA (1985). "Corporate Capital Expenditure Decisions and the Market Value of the Firm," *Journal of Financial Economics* 14 (No. 3, September), pp. 399–422.

McDONALD, ROBERT, and DANIEL R. SIEGEL (1986). "The Value of Waiting to Invest," *Quarterly Journal of Economics* 101 (No. 4, November), pp. 707–727.

MYERS, STEWART C., and NICHOLAS S. MAJLUF (1984). "Corporate Financing Decisions When Firms Have Investment Information That Investors Do Not," *Journal of Financial Economics* 13 (No. 2, June), pp. 187–220.

MYERS, STEWART C., and STUART M. TURNBULL (1977). "Capital Budgeting and the Capital Asset Pricing Model: Good News and Bad News," *Journal of Finance* 32 (No. 2, June), pp. 321–333.

OBEL, BORGE, and JAMES VANDERWEIDE (1979). "On the Decentralized Capital Budgeting Problem Under Uncertainty," *Management Science* 25 (No. 9, September), pp. 873–883.

PINDYCK, ROBERT S. (1988). "Irreversible Investment, Capacity Choice, and the Value of the Firm," *American Economic Review* 78 (No. 5, December), pp. 969–985.

PINDYCK, ROBERT S. (1991). "Irreversibility, Uncertainty, and Investment," *Journal of Economic Literature* 29 (No. 3, September), pp. 1110–1148.

PORTER, MICHAEL E., and A. MICHAEL SPENCE (1982). "The Capacity Expansion Process in a Growing Oligopoly: The Case of Corn Wet Milling," in John J. McCall, ed., *The Economics of Information and Uncertainty* (Chicago: University of Chicago Press), pp. 259–309.

PORTER, R. BURR, ROGER P. BEY, and DAVID C. LEWIS (1975). "The Development of a Mean-Semivariance Approach to Capital Budgeting," *Journal of Financial and Quantitative Analysis* 10 (No. 4, November), pp. 639–649.

QUINN, G. DAVID, and JOHN C. WINGINTON (1981). *Analyzing Capital Expenditures: Private and Public Perspectives* (Homewood, Ill.: Richard D. Irwin).

RAPPAPORT, ALFRED, and ROBERT TAGGART (1982). "Evaluation of Capital Expenditure Proposals Under Inflation," *Financial Management* 11 (No. 1, Spring), pp. 5–13.

RASMUSEN, ERIC (1989). *Games and Information* (Oxford: UK: Basil Blackwell).

ROBERTS, KEVIN, and MARTIN L. WEITZMAN (1981). "Funding Criteria for Research, Development, and Exploration Projects," *Econometrica* 49 (No. 5, September), pp. 1261–1288.

ROTEMBERG, JULIO J. and DAVID S. SCHARFSTEIN (1990). "Shareholder-Value Maximization and Product Market Competition" *Review of Financial Studies* 3 (No. 3), pp. 367–391.

SCAPENS, R. W., and J. TIMOTHY SALE (1981). "Performance Measurement and Formal Capital Expenditure Controls in Divisionalized Companies," *Journal of Business Finance and Accounting* 8 (No. 3, Autumn), pp. 389–420.

SCHARFSTEIN, DAVID S., and JEREMY C. STEIN (1990). "Herd Behavior and Investment," *American Economic Review* 80 (No. 3, June), pp. 465–479.

SCOTT, ROBERT C., and PHILIP A. HORVATH (1980). "On the Direction of Preference for Moments of Higher Order Than the Variance," *Journal of Finance* 35 (No. 4, September), pp. 915–919.

SHLEIFER, ANDREI, and ROBERT W. VISHNY (1989). "Management Entrenchment: The Case of Manager-Specific Investments," *Journal of Financial Economics* 25 (No. 1, November), pp. 123–139.

SICK, GORDON A. (1986). "Certainty Equivalent Approach to Capital Budgeting," *Financial Management* 15 (No. 4, Winter), pp. 23–32.

SICK, GORDON A. (1989). *Capital Budgeting With Real Options* (New York: Solomon Brothers Center, New York University).

STATMAN, MEIR (1982). "The Persistence of the Payback Method: A Principal-Agent Perspective," *Engineering Economist* 27 (No. 2, Winter), pp. 95–100.

STATMAN, MEIR, and DAVID CALDWELL (1987). "Applying Behavioral Finance to Capital Budgeting: Project Terminations," *Financial Management* 16 (No. 4, Winter), pp. 7–15.

STRONG, JOHN S., and JOHN R. MEYER (1990). "Sustaining Investment, Discretionary Investment, and Valuation: A Residual Funds Study of the Paper Industry," in R. Glenn Hubbard, ed., *Asymmetric Information, Corporate Finance and Investment* (Chicago: University of Chicago Press), pp. 127–148.

STULZ, RENE M. (1990). "Managerial Discretion and Optimal Financing Policies," *Journal of Financial Economics* 26 (No. 1, July), pp. 3–27.

TAGGART, ROBERT A. (1987). "Allocating Capital Among a Firm's Divisions: Hurdle Rates vs. Budgets," *Journal of Financial Research* 10 (No. 3, Fall), pp. 177–189.

THAKOR, ANJAN (1990). "Investment Myopia" and the Internal Organization of Capital Allocation Decisions" *Journal of Law, Economics and Organization* 6 (No. 1, Spring), pp. 129–154.

THALER, RICHARD H. (1991). *The Winner's Curse: Paradoxes and Anomalies of Economic Life* (New York: Free Press).

THALER, RICHARD H., and ERIC J. JOHNSON (1990). "Gambling With the House Money and Trying to Break Even: The Effects of Prior Outcomes on Risky Choice," *Management Science* 36 (No. 6, June), pp. 643–660.

THODE, STEPHEN F. (1986). "The Trouble With Divisional Hurdle Rates," *Business Horizons* 29 (No. 1, January–February), pp. 62–66.

THOMPSON, HOWARD E. (1976). "Mathematical Programming, the Capital Asset Pricing Model, and Capital Budgeting of Interrelated Projects," *Journal of Finance* 31 (No. 1, March), pp. 125–131.

THUESEN, GEORGE J., and W. J. FABRYCKY (1989). *Engineering Economy* (Englewood Cliffs, N.J.: Prentice-Hall).

TITMAN, SHERIDAN (1985). "Urban Land Prices Under Uncertainty," *American Economic Review* 75 (No. 3, June), pp. 505–514.

TRIANTIS, ALEXANDER J. and JAMES E. HODDER, (1990), "Valuing Flexibility as a Complex Option" *Journal of Finance* 45 (No. 2, June), pp. 549–565.

TRIGEORGIS, LENOS, and SCOTT P. MASON (1987). "Valuing Mangerial Flexibility," *Midland Corporate Finance Journal* 5 (No. 1, Spring), pp. 14–21.

TVERSKY, AMOS, and DANIEL KAHNEMAN (1981). "The Framing of Decisions and the Psychology of Choice," *Science* 211, (No. 4481), pp. 453–458.

TVERSKY, AMOS, and DANIEL KAHNEMAN (1986). "Rational Choice and the Framing of Decisions," *Journal of Business* 59 (No. 4, Part 2, October), pp. 251–278.

WEINGARTNER, H. MARTIN (1977). "Capital Rationing: *n* Authors in Search of a Plot," *Journal of Finance* 32 (No. 5, December), pp. 1403–1431.

WILLIAMSON, OLIVER (1981). "The Modern Corporation: Origins, Evolution, and Attributes," *Journal of Economic Literature* 19 (No. 4, December), pp. 1537–1568.

3

A Modern Theory
of Finance Analysis of
Differences Between Accounting and
Economic Rates of Return

ROBERT E. JENSEN

ABSTRACT

Attempts to compare economic (internal) rates versus accounting rates of return persist in both theory and practice. This article was inspired by the attempt by Steele (1986) to compare economic and accounting rates of return for a British firm called Briton Ltd.

The main purposes of this article are to propose that the computation of economic and accounting rates of return can be improved both by adjusting for erroneous cash flow reinvestment assumptions and by allowing for variation in the utility of returns according to the depression or boom state of the economy. This is accomplished so as to be coherent with market (systematic) risk as conceived in what has become popularly known as the "modern theory" of finance.

The market risk adjustments (MRA) proposed in this paper reduce the differences between economic and accounting rates of return; they can be made practical by means of the graphical sensitivity analysis presented. These propositions are applied to the Briton Ltd. data provided by Steele. Although precise parameter estimation is impractical, the article focuses on sensitivity analysis ranges.

I. BACKGROUND

Debates concerning accounting rate of return (ARR) patterns versus internal (economic) rate of return (IRR) patterns have raged for decades. Much of this literature is a reiteration (with refinements) of arguments against ARR rooted in Paton and Stevenson (1918), Canning (1929), and Alexander (1950).[1] Studies by Peasnell (1977, 1981, 1982a) extended the finding by Kay (1976, 1978) that IRR is a weighted average of ARR. Although most of the research has been of a theoretical nature, there have been a number of efforts to estimate economic (IRR) rates of return ex post for ongoing real-world business firms; for example, see Ijiri (1978, 1979, 1980), Salmi (1982), Salamon (1985), and Steele (1986).

To my knowledge, no writer to date has infused the "modern theory" of finance into the ARR-versus-IRR controversy. In particular, the modern theory appears contrary to traditional ARR and IRR calculations in two important respects:

1. The modern theory entails time adjustments by discounting at riskless rates rather than discounting at cash flow streams at a constant IRR or ARR over the entire life of a firm or project.
2. The modern theory adjusts cash flow streams for market (systematic) risk. This, in turn, implicitly recognizes that firms having greater dependency on a boom (or depression) economic state will be valued lower (or higher) in capital markets; for example, see Banz and Miller (1978, p. 656).

I have discovered no literature that explicitly proposes adjusting either IRR or ARR for the modern theory implications of items 1 and 2 above. *The modern theory proposes discounting at riskless rates for valuing both riskless and risky uncertain payoffs into a certainty-equivalent present value.* Riskless rates for risky return discounting are advocated in the modern theory by Rubinstein (1973, 1974, 1976), Geske (1977, 1979), Brennan (1979), Banz and Miller (1978), Cox and Ross (1976), Cox, Ross, and Rubinstein (1979), Gehr (1981), and many others.

The modern theory of finance is rooted in the portfolio theory of Markowitz (1959) and extensions to the capital asset model pricing (CAPM) theory of Sharpe (1963), Lintner (1965a, b), and Mossin (1966). The essential feature of this theory is the distinction between marked (systematic) and individual asset (unsystematic) risk. This newer theory holds that returns should be adjusted *only* for market risk, because unsystematic risk can be eliminated by investment (portfolio) diversification. However, CAPM was conceived as a single-period market risk adjustment (MRA) model and does not hold up with multiperiod discounting (because of nonstationarities of key parameters). The modern theory extensions of market risk adjustment for multiperiod analysis rely more heavily upon arbitrage pricing theory (APT) and the options pricing method (OPM) approaches in time-state-preference theory contexts.

The evolution of modern theory from CAPM to APT and OPM for multiperiod analysis has been largely driven by efforts to make newer theory more practical and of value for real-world problems.[2] To date, however, the modern theory is still plagued by impracticality and parameter estimation difficulties. Restrictive assumptions are replaced by other restrictive assumptions that, to date, have impeded the use of real-world multiperiod ex ante analysis for business decisions.[3]

The impracticality of the modern theory in ex ante analysis, however, need not stand in the way of its practicality in ex post analysis. This is especially relevant if a "reasonable range" can be derived for parameters via a sensitivity analysis. *This chapter will attempt to apply such a sensitivity analysis to ex post analysis of both IRR and ARR for a real-world firm.*

There are also traditional issues (aside from modern theory issues) inherent in ex ante discounting analysis. These are summarized by Aggarwal and Gibson (1989, pp. 4–5) as (1) estimates of future cash flows, (2) estimates of the interest rate, (3) the role of market imperfections, and (4) estimates of materiality. When concentrating on an entire firm (as opposed to individual assets within a firm) and a relatively long time interval, issues 3 and 4 regarding market imperfections and materiality are of less concern. Issues 1 and 2 are overcome in part by focusing this article upon ex post rather than ex ante analysis. There are three key advantages to our ex post performance analysis relative to ex ante analysis:

1. A firm's cash flows (e.g., dividends and stock sales) to and from its owners are known with certainty ex post.
2. Ownership exchange (share trading) values provide clues as to equity values ex post. Marginal trading values, however, are not generally error-free indicators of total value.
3. The states (booms versus depressions) of the market economy are much easier to estimate ex post.

II. PREVIEW OF FINDINGS

This article was inspired, in large measure, by a case study of a real-world British firm (Briton Ltd.) analyzed by Steele (1986). For the period 1969 through 1980, the Briton Ltd. traditional economic rate of return (nominal) was *nearly zero* ($\hat{r} = 0.0027$); British riskless (nominal) rates always exceeded 5.5% and were sometimes in excess of 11%. This reported 0.27% economic rate of return is quite misleading because

1. The regular *annual dividends from Briton Ltd. could have been reinvested risk-free at much higher rates than $\hat{r} = 0.0027$*. The 0.27% economic rate of return derived by Steele, unfortunately, implicitly assumes that all shareholders reinvested each year at a negligible 0.27% rate. Such a minuscule rate is far short of the riskless alternatives available to them from 1969 through 1980.

2. The reported $\hat{r} = 0.0027$ ignores market risk in the sense that dividends and equity values in the modern theory have greater marginal utility in periods of recession than in periods of boom. However, such varying utilities are ignored in the traditional economic (internal) rate of return computations.

This chapter will ultimately derive a market risk-adjusted (MRA) economic rate of return (r) range that is more in line with the capital markets theory in the sense that market risk-adjusted cash flows are assumed to be reinvested at observed risk-neutral rates as proposed in Bierman and Smidt (1980), Cox and Rubinstein (1979), and Gehr (1981). A major drawback is that r cannot be known either ex ante or ex post. The key obstacle is that calculation of r implicitly assumes that the market risk preferences of all investors are known. This clearly is unrealistic.

However, it is not unrealistic to perform a sensitivity analysis in terms of a composite marginal preference ratio ($\tilde{m}$) defined later in this article. It is possible to analyze $\tilde{m}$ over a broad range that is nearly certain to encompass the unknown ex post composite ratio for investors. Across the time span from 1969 through 1980, it is highly unlikely that $\tilde{m}$ is less than 0.80 or greater than 1.20 for reasons to be discussed. Within the range $0.80 \leq \tilde{m} \leq 1.20$ and using observed riskless rates in Great Britain for 1969 through 1980, the MRA economic rate of return of Briton Ltd. lies in the range $0.0123 \leq r \leq 0.0357$. Across an even tighter, but likely, range, $0.90 < \tilde{m} < 1.10$, the MRA economic rate of return is $0.0175 < r < 0.0271$, which varies by less than $0.0271 - 0.0175 = 0.0096$ or less than 1% (with $r = 0.02243$ when $\tilde{m} = 1.00$ depicting market risk neutrality).

The Briton Ltd. varying patterns of r versus a constant $\hat{r} = 0.0027$ are compared in Figure 3.1. It is evident that the $\hat{r} = 0.0027$ economic rate of return is much too low and is very misleading for any realistic market risk conditions during 1969 through 1980. The estimates of this article for Briton Ltd. lie in the $0.0175 < r < 0.0271$ range. It is much more meaningful to use r as a basis of comparison with accounting rates of return than the $\hat{r} = 0.0027$ traditional economic rate of return. The sensitivity analysis depicted in Figure 3.1 shows that market risk is not the major shortcoming of $\hat{r} = 0.0027$ for Briton Ltd. Rather, the major problem lies in the totally misleading assumption (in the $\hat{r} = 0.0027$ computation) that Briton Ltd. dividends are reinvested at 0.27% (far below much higher riskless rates). The Figure 1 computations of r assume reinvestment at riskless rates in Great Britain during the 1969 through 1980 period.

Steele also derives the weighted average accounting rate of return as $\hat{a} = 0.1286$ (or 12.86%) for the 1969 through 1980 period in the life of Briton Ltd. This procedure unrealistically assumes all dividends are

Figure 3.1

Sensitivity of the MRA economic rate of return to $\tilde{m}$ for Briton Ltd.

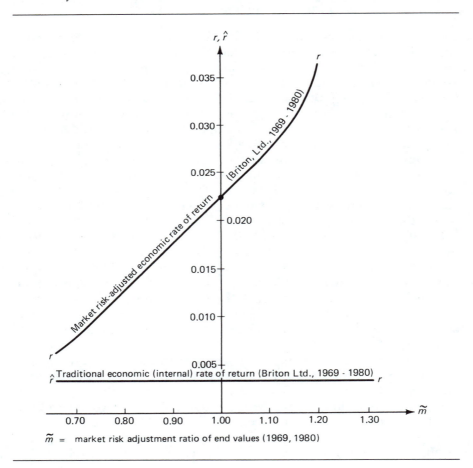

$\tilde{m}$ = market risk adjustment ratio of end values (1969, 1980)

reinvested by investors each year at a 12.86% annual return. It also makes no modern theory allowance for differential utilities of accounting returns in recessions and booms. In this chapter a market risk-adjusted accounting rate of return (a) will be derived. The patterns of traditional ($\hat{a}$) versus MRA (a) accounting rates of return for Briton Ltd. are contrasted in Figure 3.2. Even in a risk-neutral setting (where $\tilde{m} = 1.00$) there is a difference between $\hat{a}$ and a because the computation of MRA accounting return (a) utilizes riskless rates of return rather than the unrealistic constant $\hat{a} = 12.86\%$ from 1969 through 1980.

Steele (1986) computes an $\hat{e} = \hat{r} - \hat{a} = 0.0027 - 0.1286 = -0.1259$ "error term" and concludes (p. 9), "Unhappily, in this instance, the error

Figure 3.2

Sensitivity analysis of MRA accounting rate of return for Briton Ltd.

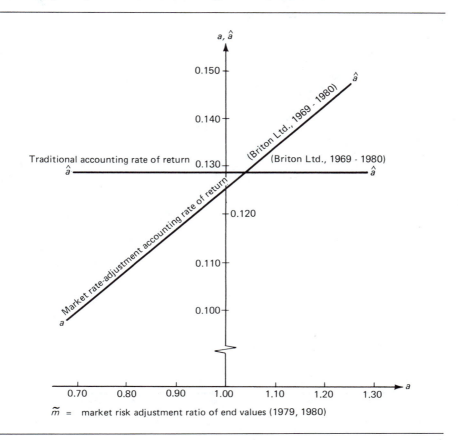

term is empirically significant, and the valuation of the opening and closing assets are important." *What he is implying is that the 1969 (opening) and 1980 (closing) differences between Briton Ltd. market and book values of equity are so different as to give rise to a significant error term (ê = − 0.1259) in economic versus accounting rates of return.*

Our attempts to replace the $\hat{e}$ and e patterns for Briton Ltd. are shown in Figure 3.3. Market risk adjustment does not eliminate the error term but does reduce the error.

Figure 3.3

Sensitivity analysis of traditional $\hat{e} = (\hat{r} - \hat{a})$ versus MRA $e = r - a$.

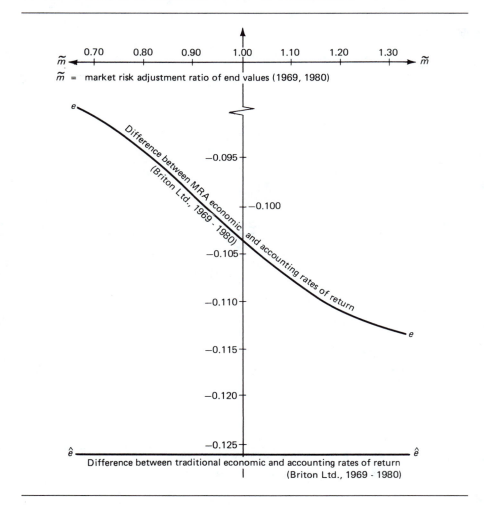

$\tilde{m}$ = market risk adjustment ratio of end values (1969, 1980)

Difference between traditional economic and accounting rates of return
(Briton Ltd., 1969 - 1980)

III. NOTATION SUMMARY

Over any specified interval of time $(y - 1, x)$, for $y < x$ integers, let $\hat{r} = \hat{R}_y^x$ depict the traditional economic (internal) rate of return for year y through year x. Similarly, let $\hat{a} = \hat{A}_y^x$ depict the corresponding average annual accounting rate of return. Additional terms are as follows:

t = interval of time which is usually read "year t." A project or firm being evaluated begins in year 1 and ceases to exist after year n. The subinterval of time $(y - 1, x)$ may be one or more years anywhere in the lifetime $(0, n)$ of the firm for $y \geq$ and $x \leq n$.

p_t = accounting net profit that in theory could be distributed to shareholders at the end of the year t. If P_t is negative (depicting a loss), then shareholders could in theory invest P_t into the firm to cover this loss.

C_t = net cash flow to and from owners (shareholders) in year t. For convenience it is assumed that C_t cash flows occur on the last day of the year. The $P_t - C_t$ difference arises from differences in the timing of accounting revenues and expenses. It also arises because C_t includes equity cash investments and withdrawals (e.g., dividends) that are excluded from the P_t measurement.

B_t = accounting book value of equity at the end of year t as reported in financial statements. Since depreciation and many other expenses and revenues are usually estimated, $\hat{B}_t$ differs from "ideal" B_t book values based upon unknown ideal economic depreciation time allocations as first envisioned by Hotelling (1925)

$\hat{V}_t$ = estimated value of equity at the end of year t as determined by actual market agreement of investors; for example, Steele (1986) assumes $\hat{V}_t$ is the total equity aggregation of a firm's marginal security price trades near the end of the year. In theory, $\hat{V}_t$ depicts the equilibrium market value, at time t, of all future subjectively forecasted cash flows from time $t + 1$ through time n when the firm expires. In reality, investors may have differing, heterogeneous forecasts of how long (n) the firm will survive, future cash flows, future investment opportunities, future states of the economy, future inflation, risks, and so on.

$\hat{r}$ = $\hat{R}_y^x$ = ex post economic (internal) rate of return of a project or firm (from $t = y - 1$ *through* $t = x$) using beginning value $\hat{V}_y$, ending value $\hat{V}_x$, and actual cash flows $C_y, \ldots, C_x$ known ex post. This is also frequently symbolized in the literature as $\hat{r} =$ internal rate of return.

$r = R_y^x =$ MRA economic rate of return that assumes market risk-adjusted cash flows are reinvested at risk-neutral rates of return from $t = y$ through $t = x$.

$r^* =$ riskless rate in terms of the modern theory.[2]

$\hat{a} = \hat{A}_y^x =$ accounting rate of return computed on the basis of reported B_t accounting book values of ownership equity. Rather unfortunately this is also sometimes called the "pseudo" economic (internal) rate of return [e.g., Steele (1986)].

$a = A_y^x =$ accounting rate of return computed on the basis of reported $\hat{B}_t$ accounting book values adjusted for market risk. Market risk-adjusted dividends are assumed to be reinvested by shareholders at risk-neutral rates, which is consistent with the modern theory of finance [e.g., see Rubinstein (1973)].

At $t = x$, the ex post market economic rate of return that equates $\hat{r}$ and $\hat{R}_y^x$ is

$$\hat{V}_{y-1} = \left[\sum_{t=y}^{x-1} C_t (1 + \hat{r})^{-t} \right] + [(C_x + \hat{V}_x)(1 + \hat{r})^{-x})] \tag{1}$$

If $\hat{V}_{y-1}$ and $\hat{V}_x$ equity value estimates are available, a MRA economic rate of return is $r = \hat{R}_y^x$ that equates

$$\hat{V}_{y-1} (1 + r)^x = \frac{1}{m(y, s)} \left[\sum_{t-y}^{x-1} m(t, s)C_t \prod_{i=t+1}^{x} (1 + r_i^*) \right]$$
$$+ (C_x + \hat{V}_x) \, \tilde{m} \tag{2}$$

where $m(y, s)$ and $m(t, s)$ are market risk adjustment factors and $\tilde{m}$ is a ratio to be defined later. Because $m(y, s)$, $m(t, s)$, and $\tilde{m}$ parameters are virtually impossible to derive empirically, sensitivity analysis over a relevant range of their feasible values may lend insights into the upper and lower bounds of r.

Based on a finding by Kay (1978) and extended in Theorem 3 of Peasnell (1982a), the average accounting rate of return ex post is the rate of return $\hat{a} = \hat{A}_y^x$ that equates

$$\hat{B}_{y-1} = \left[\sum_{t-y}^{x-1} C_t(1 + \hat{a})^{-t} \right] + [(C_x + \hat{B}_x)(1 + \hat{a})^{-x}] \tag{3}$$

It is evident that $\hat{r} = \hat{a}$ [making Equations (1) and (3) identical] provided the end values are equal, that is, that $\hat{B}_{y-1} = \hat{V}_{y-1}$ and $\hat{B}_x = \hat{V}_x$. Kay (1978) demonstrated that $\hat{r} = \hat{a}$ over the entire lifetime of a firm or project (where $y = 1$ and $x = n$) and that $\hat{r}$ is also a weighted average of annual accounting rates of return. But in the interim intervals for $y > 1$ and $x < n$, the $\hat{r}$-versus-$\hat{a}$ economic and accounting rates of return are generally unequal [except in the limiting case of economic depreciation rates first discovered by Hotelling (1925) which implicitly assume $\hat{B}_t = \hat{V}_t$ and constant reinvestment rates across the time interval $(y - 1, x)$].

IV. PURPOSES OF THIS CHAPTER

The focus of this chapter is upon the error term $\hat{e} = \hat{E}_y^x$ that equates Equation (1) economic ($\hat{r}$) and Equation (3) accounting ($\hat{a}$) rates of return as follows:

$$\hat{E}_y^x = \hat{R}_y^x = \hat{A}_y^x$$
$$\hat{e} = \hat{r} - \hat{a} \tag{4}$$

The $\hat{e} = \hat{E}_y^x$ value is widely called the error term in earlier literature. Such terminology is unfortunate since the implication is generally that the $\hat{r}$ economic rate of return is some sort of ideal toward which accountants should aspire in deriving the $\hat{a}$ accounting rate of return. Actually, $\hat{r}$ and $\hat{a}$ are derived with different premises and purposes, as discussed in Jensen (1986) in greater detail.

Be that as it may, $\hat{e} = \hat{E}_y^x$ is widely referred to as the error term and will be accordingly referred to as such here. Many writers go so far as to claim that (since $\hat{e}$ is often significant in analytical models, simulation models, and practice) the accounting rate of return is misleading.[1]

Kay (1978), Wright (1978a), and Peasnell (1982) discuss theoretical conditions under which the $\hat{e}$ error term in Equation (4) is negligible. In a case study of a British accounting firm called Briton Ltd. (formerly British Ropes Ltd.) for the years $y = 1969$ through $x = 1980$, Steele (1986) estimates that $\hat{a} = 0.1286$ and $\hat{r} = 0.0028$. My calculations from his tables yield $\hat{r} = 0.002717$ [which differs only slightly from the $\hat{r} = 0.0028$ reported by Steele (p. 9) and incorrectly printed in his Table 3 as $\hat{r} = 0.0003$]. The error term in Equation (4) becomes $\hat{e} = -0.1259$. Steele (1986, p. 9) concludes (emphasis added):

> The estimate of 12.86 percent which was reached earlier, based entirely on accounting book values taken from published financial accounts, should properly be referred to as a pseudo IRR. *Unhappily, in this instance the error term is empirically significant, and the valuation of the opening and closing assets is important.*

The terminology "pseudo IRR" ($\hat{a}$) and "economic IRR" ($\hat{r}$) used by Steele implies that $\hat{a}$ should ideally equal $\hat{r}$. This is highly controversial, but I will not debate the issue in theory here. The focus will be limited to the drawbacks in how $\hat{r}$ and $\hat{a}$ are traditionally calculated.

The major purpose of this chapter is to demonstrate that the economic IRR (i.e., $\hat{r}$) may be full of so much reinvestment and market risk error that it is a very poor criterion on which to judge traditional accounting ($\hat{a}$) rates of return. Improved criteria, market risk-adjusted rate of return (r) in place of $\hat{r}$ and MRA rate of return (a) in place of $\hat{a}$, are proposed here. The MRA, r, and a values cannot be exactly known even ex post, but they can be ranged by sensitivity analysis.

V. PSEUDO REINVESTMENT ERROR

Some intuitively obvious generalization as to when $\hat{r} - r$ corrections will or will not be significant are listed below, where C_x cash flows are net cash payouts of a business firm to its owners or added cash investments by owners:

1. Firms that have low payout ratios (i.e., firms that plow back a high proportion of earnings) tend to have smaller $\hat{r} - r$ corrections than firms with high payout ratios.
2. A firm that has increasing payouts *ceteris paribus* tends to have smaller $\hat{r} - r$ corrections than a firm with decreasing payouts even though for both firms total payout $C_y + \cdots + C_x$ is identical.
3. Firms whose ending equity value $\hat{V}_x$ is large relative to $C_y + \cdots + C_x$ payouts have a much smaller $\hat{r} - r$ correction than when $\hat{V}_x$ is relatively small.
4. Firms that have smaller interim owner-added investments have much smaller $\hat{r} - r$ corrections than when C_t values are relatively large negative numbers.
5. When the time interval for calculating economic rate of return is relatively short (e.g., 2 years) the $\hat{r} - r$ pseudo reinvestment corrections will be very small because there is not sufficient time for cash flow reinvestments to matter. The correction will be larger over much longer periods such as 10 to 20 years.

It is possible that firms may have a relatively small $\hat{r} - r$ pseudo reinvestment correction and, at the same time, $\hat{r} - r$ is still large in relation to a very small $\hat{r}$ traditional economic rate of return. This happens when a firm has not done very well in a period of rather high riskless rates of return. For example, consider the following:

Case A: A firm has a $\hat{r} = \hat{R}_1^t = 0$ traditional rate of return and $r = R_1^t > 0$.

Case B: A firm has $\hat{r} = \hat{R}_1^t < 0$ and $r = R_1^t > 0$.

In case A, it is implicitly assumed in the traditional economic rate of return ($\hat{r}$) that all C_t cash outflows do not earn anything when invested elsewhere by consumers. In case B it is implicitly assumed that such cash outflows are reinvested elsewhere at the same loss rate as experienced by the firm that distributed the dividends. *Both reinvestment assumptions are dubious and are part of the weakness of traditional $\hat{r}$ economic rate of return calculations that "defy logic."* In such instances, the $\hat{r} - r$ pseudo reinvestment correction adjusts to a more reasonable reinvestment assumption. The correction will be large relative to $\hat{r}$ so long as the firm performed considerably worse than riskless government bonds.

A business firm can reinvest earnings each year, that is, sacrifice C_t payouts for the purpose of enhancing $\hat{V}_t$ equity value. The $\hat{r} - r$ reinvestment correction arises only when C_t payout owners can reinvest or consume "outside the firm."

Consider the two sixteenth-century Venetian trading ventures whose cash flows are given in Jensen (1986, pp. 116–119):

Ship A	Ship B
$\hat{V}_0 = 10,000$ ducats	$\hat{V}_0 = 10,000$ ducats
$C_1 = 0$ ducats	$C_1 = 21,000$ ducats
$C_2 = 0$ ducats	$C_2 = -10,000$ ducats
$C_3 = 0$ ducats	$C_3 = 0$ ducats
$C_4 = 0$ ducats	$C_4 = 0$ ducats
$C_5 = 0$ ducats	$C_5 = 0$ ducats
$C_6 = 17,714$ ducats	$C_6 = 1026$ ducats
$\hat{V}_6 = 0$ ducats	$\hat{V}_6 = 0$ ducats
$\hat{r} = 0.1000$	$\hat{r} = 0.4086$

In this instance, ship B had a much higher 40.86% traditional economic rate of return than ship A's 10.00%. For simplicity, suppose there were neither depression nor boom states in Venice over those 5 years and that Venetian risk-free bonds yielded 2% per annum. In such circumstances, the market risk-adjusted economic rates of return are $\hat{r} = 0.1000$ for ship A and $\hat{r} = 0.1588$ for ship B.

In summary, the pseudo reinvestment correction is 0.0000 for ship A and -0.2468 for ship B:

Ex Post Components of $\hat{r}$	Ship A	Ship B
Traditional economic rate of return, $\hat{r}$	0.1000	0.4086
Minus pseudo reinvestment error component, $\hat{r} - r$	−.0000	−0.2498
Reinvestment error adjusted, r	0.1000	0.1588
Minus market risk component (discussed later)	−0.0000	−0.0000
Minus risk-free rate component	−0.0200	−0.0200
Ex post nominal return on nonmarket risk	0.0800	0.1388

The point here is that ship A has an $\hat{r} - r = 0$ reinvestment error correction because it neither returned interim cash dividends nor received additional interim cash investments. In contrast, ship B has a very large $\hat{r} - r = +0.2498$ (24.98%) reinvestment error correction because it returned a large $C_1 = 21,000$ ducat dividend and received a large $C_2 = -10,000$ ducat interim investor cash input. *Reinvestment error correction can arise only if there are interim cash flows between the firm and its owners.* Hence, ship A needs no reinvestment error correction, whereas ship B needs a lot of it. Returns attributable to reinvestment are termed "hypothetical returns" in the Jensen (1986) discussion of these Venetian ventures.

VI. THE REAL WORLD OF ECONOMIC CYCLES AND VARYING RISKLESS RATES

For added realism, suppose $m(t, s)$ market risk modifiers exist that convert a C_t cash flow (when the economy was ex post observed to be in state s) into market risk-adjusted equivalents equal to $m(t, s)C_t$. The $m(t, s)$ modifiers under a CAPM approach are given by the bracketed term in Equation (10) of Bierman and Smidt (1980, p. 326). However, CAPM and other proposed methods (arbitrage pricing theory and options pricing methods) are not yet practical for real-world calculation of market risk modifiers.[3]

Suppose $s < 0$ depicts the intensity of a depression and $s > 0$ depicts the intensity of a boom in the marketwide economy. For the time being assume s lies on the real line and $p(t, s)$ depicts the probability that the economy is in state s at time t. Under a market risk proposition, equal cash flows do not have equal marginal utilities in the following risk conceptualization in Hirshleifer (1965), "'the state preference approach leads to a generalized concept which might be called 'conservative behavior'—of which ordinary risk aversion in the sense of minimizing variability of outcome is only a special case." This proposition is stated concisely by Banz and Miller (1978, p. 656), who publish $S(t, s)$ risk adjustment present value factors (intended for practical application in adjusting a cash flow stream for market risk differentials), "For equal probabilities the current price of a claim to funds in a state in which funds are hard to come by (as in a depression) will be higher than one in an ebullient state where everything is paying off handsomely." Intended business firm use of their tables has not transpired.

Consistent with the market risk proposition, suppose there exist multiplicative $m(t, s)$ market risk preference modifiers (for each $1.00 of cash flow in state s at time t) that monotonically decrease on s as follows under the market risk proposition:

$1 < m(t, s) < \infty$ if $s < 0$ signifies depression states. The current claim value of a depression dollar is higher because "funds are hard to come by."

$m(t, s) = 1$ if $s > 0$ signifies a market risk-neutral state.

$0 < m(t, s) < 1$ if $s < 0$ signifies boom states. The claim value of a boom dollar "will have a lower value per dollar of expected return."

The $m(t, s)$ is also a measure of the intensity of a boom or a depression. For example, $m(t, s) = 0.95$ implies s a mild boom state in which $1.00 cash flow is worth only $0.95 under the market risk proposition. It is mild relative to an $m(t, s) = 0.75$ boom. Conversely, $m(t, s) = 1.05$ implies s is a mild depression in which each $1.00 return is worth $1.05. This is mild relative to an $m(t, s) = 1.25$ depression. The $m(t, s)$ market risk modifiers adjust for market (systematic) risk only in the well-known context of Markowitz (1959), Sharpe (1963), and Lintner (1965). Hence, a $1.00 return is adjusted by the same $m(t, s)$ whether it flows in at time t in state s from ownership of a solid government bond asset or of a temperamental racehorse asset. Individual asset (unsystematic) risk is considered diversifiable in portfolios and is not the type of risk being discussed here. For example, under the capital asset pricing model, the bracketed terms in Equation (10) in Biermann and Smidt (1980, p. 326) constitute $m(t, s)$ estimates that conform to the market risk proposition. A possible means of estimating $m(t, s)$ is discussed in the Appendix. Current data are not available, however, for my proposed estimation approach.

Without loss of generality, the s measure of depression/boom intensity of the ecomomy will be somewhat arbitrarily defined as

$s = 1 - m(t, s)$ for $s < 0$ values of depression states.
$s = -1 + 1/m(t, s)$ for $s > 0$ values of boom states.
$s = 0$ for a market risk-neutral state.

It is important to distinguish a risk-neutral economy [where $m(t, s) = 1$ for all s on the real line] and a risk-neutral *state* in a risk-preferential economy [where $m(t, s) = 1$ *only* when $s = 0$]. The market risk proposition assumes the economy is not risk-neutral.

Assume s is the observed state of the world economy ex post for period t. If $m(t, s)$ were known along with r_i^* riskless rates, exact market risk adjustments would be feasible. Let r depict the MRA economic rate of return that can be calculated so as to equate the left and right sides of the following equation (note that s may depict different economic states in $m(y, s)$ versus $m(x, s)$ versus $m(t, s)$):

$$m(y, s)\hat{V}_{y-1} (1 + r)^x = \left[\sum_{t=y}^{x-1} m(t, s)\, C_t \prod_{i=t+1}^{x} (1 + r_i^*) \right]$$
$$+ m(x, s)\, (C_x + \hat{V}_x) \qquad (5)$$

In a risk-neutral economy, all $m(t, s) = 1$ such that Equation (5) reduces to

$$\hat{V}_{y-1} (1 + r)^x = \left[\sum_{t=y}^{x-1} C_t \prod_{i=t+1}^{x} (1 + r_i^*) \right] + (C_x + \hat{V}_x) \qquad (6)$$

Equation (6) may also be utilized when market risk adjustments are ignored but cash flows are all assumed to be reinvested at riskless rates.

VII. APPLICATION TO THE FIRM BRITON LTD.

Steele (1986) examined year-end (December 31) stock trading prices of a United Kingdom business firm known as Briton Ltd. (formerly British Ropes Ltd.). These prices were used to estimate the $\hat{V}_t$ equity values shown in Table 3.1. Steele also provided the cash flow C_t amounts for the corresponding years (assuming year-end flows). He did not consider risk-free rates or systematic (market) risk. Estimates of risk-free 91-day treasury bills in the United Kingdom are added to Steele's data in Table 3.1. The traditional ($\hat{r}$) economic rates of return computed from Equation (1) are contrasted in Table 3.2 with reinvestment rate-corrected (r) rates computed from Equation (10). The Briton Ltd. rate of return corrections ($\hat{r} - r$) range from -0.0203 in 1979 to 0.0238 in 1971. For the entire 1969 through 1980 span in the life of Briton Ltd., the $\hat{r} - r$ reinvestment rate correction is about 2%:

$$\hat{r} = \hat{R}_{1969}^{1980} = 0.0027$$
$$r = R_{1969}^{1980} = 0.0024$$
$$\hat{r} - r = -0.0197 \approx 2.0\%$$

TABLE 3.1   Briton Ltd. Cash Flows and Equity Values Along With United
Kingdom Risk-Free Rates and Consumer Price Indexes

t	Year	Cash Flow,[a] C_t (thousand £)	Equity Value,[a] V_t (thousand £)	Treasury Bill Rates,[b] r_t^f	Accounting Book Value[a] (£)
0	1968		32335	0.0709	26782
1	1969	1623	26651	0.0764	27435
2	1970	1395	30098	0.0701	30424
3	1971	1715	45424	0.0557	31889
4	1972	1380	42426	0.0554	34075
5	1973	1182	31362	0.0934	37310
6	1974	1352	19069	0.1137	44198
7	1975	−6172	75839	0.1018	61458
8	1976	−1935	66241	0.1112	76325
9	1977	2625	59922	0.0768	82449
10	1978	3617	58266	0.0851	88243
11	1979	2691	31642	0.1298	88901
12	1980	1914	21870	0.1511	90372
		11387			

[a] Cash flows and some of the other data in this table are provided in Steele (1986, p. 5).
[b] United Kingdom 91-day treasury bill rates are tabulated in *International Financial Statistics* (Washington, D.C.: Bureau of Statistics of the International Monetary Fund, 1974–1981).

The above 2.0% pseudo reinvestment correction factor is not large in an absolute sense, but it is large relative to the $\hat{r} = 0.0027 \approx 0.0\%$ traditional economic rate of return for Briton Ltd. over the 12-year span. *In fact, the $\hat{r} = 0.0027$ calculation implicitly assumed that Briton Ltd. shareholders could not earn more than 0.27% elsewhere from the Table 1 dividends they received.* This is highly unlikely, as these shareholders could invest in riskless government treasury bills paying the relatively high rates shown in Table 3.1. *The $\hat{r} - r \approx 2.0\%$ pseudo reinvestment correction factor adjusts the rate of return upward for more realistic reinvestment conditions.* The 2% correction is lower than the riskless rates, but this is due to the impact of the equity value loss from $\hat{V}_{1968} = £ 32,335$ to $\hat{V}_{1980} = £ 21,870$ in the r calculation.

It should be pointed out that in the Table 3.2 calculations of r economic rates of return, it was not possible to adjust r_t^* risk-free rates in the United Kingdom for systematic market risk (that adjusts cash flows and values for varying marginal utilities of returns in depressions versus booms). Such data are not available. Difficulties in this regard are discussed in Notes 2 and 3. Sensitivity analysis will be a focus later to allow the analysis to transpire without specifying exact market risk adjustments.

TABLE 3.2   Briton Ltd. Economic Rates of Return: Traditional $\hat{r}$ Versus r (Using Table 1 Risk-Free Discount Rates)

t	Year	Equation $(1)^a$ $\hat{r} = {}_1\hat{R}_t$	Equation (10) $r = {}_1R_t$	Pseudo Reinvestment Error, $\hat{r} - r$
0	1968			
1	1969	−0.1256	−0.1256	0.0000
2	1970	0.0123	0.0137	−0.0014
3	1971	0.1637	0.1598	0.0238
4	1972	0.1134	0.1012	0.0112
5	1973	0.0398	0.0427	−0.0029
6	1974	−0.0291	−0.0114	−0.0177
7	1975	0.1466	0.1413	0.0053
8	1976	0.1040	0.1027	0.0013
9	1977	0.0843	0.0849	0.0006
10	1978	0.0790	0.0802	0.0012
11	1979	0.0249	0.0452	0.0203
12	1980	0.0027	0.0224	−0.0197

^{a} The $\hat{r} = {}_1\hat{R}_t$ rates are termed "economic internal rate of return" by Steele (1986). My calculations agree for each year except for the 1980 $r = 0.0003$ reported in Steele's Table 3, p. 10. This must be a mistake since Steele reports a 1980 $r = 0.0028$ in the text. My computation of $\hat{r} = 0.0027$ differs only slightly from the $\hat{r} = 0.0028$ derived by Steele for the $\hat{r} = {}_1\hat{R}_{12}$ traditional economic rate across the 12-year time interval from 1969 through 1980.

VIII. SENSITIVITY ANALYSIS OF BRITON LTD. RISK-FREE RATE VARIATION

The 91-day British treasury bill rates r_t^* shown in Table 3.1 were utilized in calculating r economic rates of return for Briton Ltd. in Table 3.2. It might be disputed that these rates are not error-free estimates of the true risk-free rate. However, because C_t cash flows for Briton Ltd. are small relative to $\hat{V}_t$ equity values, we do not anticipate that an error in estimating risk-free rates will have a significant impact on $r = R^{1980}_{1969}$ rates of return. Comparison of a ridiculously low average $r^* = 0.02$ versus an absurdly high average $r^* = 0.14$ is provided in Table 3.3. Even at such extreme outliers, the impacts on r economic rates of return are very small for Briton Ltd. across the years 1969 through 1980. This is primarily due to the fact that dividend payouts are quite low relative to equity values and the decline in equity value from $\hat{V}_{1969} = £\,32,355$ to $\hat{V}_{1980} = £\,21,870$ over the 12-year period.

   In conclusion, the calculations of r returns in Tables 3.2 and 3.3 (adjusted for pseudo reinvestment error) for Briton Ltd. are highly insen-

TABLE 3.3   Briton Ltd. Sensitivity Analysis Relative to Risk-Free Rate Variation

		EQUATION (1)	EQUATION (10)		
			$r^f = 0.02$,	r^f = Table 3.1,	$r^f = 0.14$,
t	Year	$r = {}_1R_t$	$r = {}_1R_t$	$r = {}_1R_t$	$r = {}_1R_t$
0	1968				
1	1969	−0.1256	−0.1256	−0.1256	−0.1256
2	1970	0.0123	0.0125	0.0137	0.0155
3	1971	0.1637	0.1583	0.1598	0.1628
4	1972	0.1134	0.1079	0.1012	0.1150
5	1973	0.0398	0.0381	0.0427	0.0494
6	1974	−0.0291	−0.0269	−0.0114	−0.0039
7	1975	0.1466	0.1360	0.0143	0.1460
8	1976	0.1040	0.0963	0.1027	0.1082
9	1977	0.0843	0.0785	0.0849	0.0901
10	1978	0.0790	0.0737	0.0802	0.0859
11	1979	0.0249	0.0242	0.0356	0.0440
12	1980	0.0027	0.0053	0.0169	0.0279

sitive to wide ranges of error in estimating riskless rates of return in the United Kingdom. This is the case even over a relatively long time span from 1969 through 1980. The results will be more sensitive for firms with higher payout ratios.

IX. SENSITIVITY ANALYSIS OF BRITON LTD. MRA ECONOMIC RATE OF RETURN

One might naively suspect that, whenever r economic rates of return are highly insensitive to estimation errors in risk-free discount rates, the r rates of return will also be insensitive to market risk adjustments of discount rates. *Such is not the case, however, because the differing marginal utilities for $\hat{V}_{y-1}$ and $\hat{V}_x$ end values must also be considered, unlike the Table 3.2 and Table 3.3 computations that implicitly assume that a monetary return in a boom state has the same marginal utility as an identical amount of money in a depression.* Across time $t = y - 1$ through time $t = x$, the relative market risk ratio of end market risk adjustment factors can be defined as

$$\tilde{m} = \frac{m(x, s)}{m(y, s)} \tag{7}$$

For example, suppose year y was a mild recession year for which $s = 0.0400$. In contrast, year x was a mild boom year depicted by $s = 0.0638$. Suppose the corresponding market risk adjustment factors are

$m(y, -0.0400) = 1 - (-0.0400) = 1.04$ and $m(x, 0.0638 = 1/1.0638 \approx 0.94$. The market risk ratio is then

$$\tilde{m} = 1.04/0.94 = 1.1063 \tag{8}$$

Equation (5) can then be rewritten as

$$\hat{V}_{y-1} (1 + r)^x = \frac{1}{m(y, s)} \left[\sum_{t-y}^{x-1} m(t, s) \, C_t \prod_{i=t+1}^{x} (1 + r_i) \right]$$
$$+ (C_x + \hat{V}_x)\tilde{m} \tag{9}$$

In this case r is an ideal or market risk-adjusted rate of return (ignoring inflation) that is corrected for both market risk and pseudo reinvestment error. Unfortunately, it is not practical to measure this ideal in real life. It can, however, be analyzed over a sensitivity range.

In order to facilitate a graphical analysis, some simplifications of Equation (9) are possible provided that:

1. C_t cash flows are relatively small such as in companies like Briton Ltd. with low payout ratios and a large difference between beginning (V_y) and ending (V_x) equity values.
2. The $m(t, s)C_t/m(y, s)$ ratios offset over time such that, when aggregated, the $m(t, s)$ multipliers have a relatively small net effect.
3. The $(C_x + V_x)\tilde{m}$ component is relatively large.

In such instances, Equation (9) can be recast in a simplified form:

$$\hat{V}_{y-1} (1 + r)^x = \left[\sum_{t-y}^{x-1} C_t \prod_{i=t+1}^{x} (1 + r_i^*) \right] + (C_x + \hat{V}_x)\tilde{m} \tag{10}$$

Equation (10) is easier to work with than Equation (9), because it is possible to graph r (MRA economic rate of return) as a function of $\tilde{m}$ (the ratio of end value market risk adjustments that reflect varying marginal utilities in the economy at $t = y - 1$ versus $t = x$ points in time that experience differing states of the economy).

Because $\tilde{m}$ cannot be known for the economy, a sensitivity analysis of r over a wide range of $\tilde{m}$ possibilities is important in evaluating whether market risk significantly affects economic rates of return. For Briton Ltd. the result is rather dramatic if s_x is quite unlike the s_{y-1} state of the economy. A graph of r as a function of $\tilde{m}$ was provided earlier in the sensitivity analysis graph in Figure 3.1. Recall that r is very insensitive to variations in the r^* risk-free rate for reasons discussed earlier. Figure 3.1, in comparison, reveals that r is not as insensitive to variations in the $\tilde{m}$ market risk adjustment ratio. This is largely because the end value $V_x = V_{1980} = \text{£ } 21{,}870$ is large relative to the aggregate Briton Ltd.

C_t cash flows shown in Table 3.1. A much higher payout ratio would have increased the risk-free rate sensitivity relative to MRA sensitivity.

X. SENSITIVITY ANALYSIS OF BRITON LTD. MRA ACCOUNTING RATE OF RETURN

Recall that r is the MRA economic rate of return compared with traditional $\hat{r}$ economic (internal) rate of return in Figure 3.1. In an analogous fashion, let the letter a depict the MRA accounting rate of return to be compared with the traditional ($\hat{a}$) accounting rate of return. Equation (9) may be recast for an MRA accounting rate of return ($a = A_y^x$):

$$\hat{B}_{y-1} (1 + a)^x = \frac{1}{m(y, s)} \left[\sum_{t-y}^{x} m(t, s_t) C_t \prod_{i=t+1}^{x} (1 + r_i^*) \right]$$
$$+ (C_x + \hat{B}_x)\tilde{m} \qquad (11)$$

Also recall that $r = a$ whenever $y - 1 = 0$ and $x = n$ signifying the lifetime of the firm. Similarly $r = a$ for a firm's life span but not necessarily interim subintervals where $x < n$. With the simplifications discussed earlier, the simplified version of Equation (10) relating r to $\tilde{m}$ may be recast to relate a to $\hat{m}$:

$$\hat{B}_{y-1} (1 + a)^x = \left[\sum_{t-y}^{x-1} C_t \prod_{i=t+1}^{x} (1 + r_i^*) \right] + (C_x + \hat{B}_x)\tilde{m} \qquad (12)$$

Equation (12) facilitates graphical sensitivity analysis of the market risk-adjusted accounting rate of return ($\hat{a}$), with $\tilde{m}$ as defined previously in Equation (11). In Figure 3.3, the $\hat{e} = \hat{r} - \hat{a}$ and $e = r - a$ error terms were contrasted on a sensitivity analysis basis with respect to the $\tilde{m}$ market risk adjustment ratio. The MRA (e) error is less than the traditional ($\hat{e}$) error over the relevant range of $\tilde{m}$ for 1969 through 1980. Steele concludes that the $\hat{e} = 0.0027 - 0.1286 = -0.1259$ error term is "empirically significant." In this context, the e error term ranging from -0.0921 (when $\tilde{m} = 0.70$) to -0.1060 (when $\tilde{m} = 1.20$) is also significant. However, it is argued in this article that e is more meaningful than $\hat{e}$ because

1. The traditional $\hat{e}$ computation utilizes differing and inconsistent divided reinvestment rates. The e computation uses empirical riskless rates.
2. The traditional $\hat{e}$ calculation ignores market risk differences in boom and recession states of the economy, whereas the e pattern in Figure 3.3 includes market risk adjustments.

XI. CONCLUSION AND LIMITATIONS

Market risk adjustment is not intended to eliminate the $e = r - a$ differences between economic and accounting rates of return. It may, however, tend to reduce such differences. More importantly, adjusting for market risk leads to theoretical improvements in economic (r) and accounting (a) rates of return by adjusting for inconsistent cash flow reinvestment errors and varying market risk.

The Equation (9) approach for computing r and the Equation (11) approach for computing a require that the $m(t, s_t)$ market risk adjustment factors be known (from whence $\bar{m}$ may also be derived). This is not practical in reality, but if upper and lower bounds can be placed on $m(t, s)$ factors, sensitivity analysis may be utilized to derive ranges of possible values. Using a graphical approach, ranges for r, a, and e were derived in Figures 3.1 through 3.3 for Briton Ltd.

Many of the hurdles of ex ante analysis are overcome by focusing on performance measurement in an ex post analysis such as for the years 1969 through 1980 for Briton Ltd. Many hurdles and limitations, nevertheless, still remain. Some of the major ones are as follows:

1. Difficulty in estimating $\hat{V}_t$ values of the firm. In this chapter I used the Table 1 values derived for Briton Ltd. by Steele (1986). Steele uses share trading prices and multiplies by the number of outstanding shares. This is an exceedingly controversial approach for estimating total equity value. In reality, there are no reliable methods for estimating total equity value unless the entire firm is purchased for cash.

2. Difficulty in measuring riskless rates in alternate states of the economy.

3. Collapsing of yearly market risk factors into a single ratio derivation of $\bar{m}$ in Equation (7). It would be better to use disaggregated $m(t, s)$ parameters as shown in Equation (5). These are difficult to derive ex ante or ex post for states of the economy that might have transpired.

APPENDIX: A THEORETICAL PROPOSAL FOR ESTIMATING $m(t, s)$ MARKET RISK MODIFIERS

The $m(t, s)$ market risk modifiers are not familiar concepts in the literature of economics, finance, or accounting. They are however, implicit in asset valuation approaches proposed by Bierman and Smidt (1980) using CAPM theory and Banz and Miller (1978) using option pricing methods (on grounds that the CAPM is not suited for miltiperiod valuation).

The $m(t, s)$ is a measure of the intensity of a boom or a depression. For example, $m(t, s) = 0.95$ implies s is a mild boom state in which $1.00 cash flow is worth only $0.95 under the market risk proposition. It is mild relative to an $m(t, s) = 0.75$ boom. Conversely, $m(t, s) = 1.05$ implies s is a mild depression in which each $1.00 return is worth $1.05. This is mild relative to an $m(t, s) = 1.25$ depression. The $m(t, s)$ market risk modifiers adjust for market (systematic) risk only in the well-known context of Markowitz (1959), Sharpe (1963), and Lintner (1965). Hence, a $1.00 return is adjusted by the same $m(t, s)$ whether it flows in a time t in state s from ownership of a solid government bond asset or of a temperamental racehorse asset. Individual asset (unsystematic) risk is considered diversifiable in portfolios and is not the type of risk being discussed here. For example, under the capital asset pricing model, the bracketed terms in Equation (10) in Bierman and Smidt (1980, p. 326) constitute $m(t, s)$ estimates that conform to the theory that cash flows (dividends) returned to shareholders in states of depression have greater value than equal returns in boom states.

Banz and Miller (1978, p. 665) conceptualize each state s as an "equally probable" range of return of a market portfolio (emphasis added):

> Our estimates of state prices are presented in Tables 2–4 for three alternative state patterns (3, 5, and 20 states), *each defined to yield approximately equal state probabilities*. Given the data limitations in most capital budgeting applications, the use of more than five states (or perhaps even more than three states) smacks of overkill, but should more states be needed in any problem or should unequal probability intervals be desired, they can be obtained by aggregation from the 20-state tables.

Hence, for an $n = 3$-, 5-, or 20-state table, state probability $P(t, s) = 1/n$. Banz and Miller $S(t, s)$ state price tables also provide forecasts of annualized risk-free rates such that $D(t, s)$ discount factors can be estimated. The underlying market risk factors residually become

$$m(t, s) = \frac{S(t, s)}{P(t, s)\, D(t, s)}$$

$$= \frac{S(t, s)}{(1/n)\, [1/d(t, s)]^t}$$

The six $S(t, s)$ contingency state prices given by Banz and Miller (1978, Table 2) for the $n = 3$ state tables disaggregate as follows:

$m(1, 1) = 3(1.0018)^1\, (0.5398) = 1.6223 > 1$ to depict a relatively severe depression state in the first year.

$m(1, 2) = 3(1.0018)^1 (0.1672) = 0.8752 < 1$ to depict a slight boom considered to be a normal state in the first year.

$m(1, 3) = 3(1.0018)^1 (0.1672) = 0.5025 < 1$ to depict a much more ecstatic boom state in the first year

$m(2, 1) = 3(1.0030)^2 (0.533) = 1.6095 < 1$ to depict a relatively severe depression state in the second year.

$m(2, 2) = 3(1.0030)^2 (0.2915) = 0.8798 < 1$ to depict a slight boom considered to be a normal state in the second year.

$m(2, 3) = 3(1.0030)^2 (0.1693) = 0.5110 < 1$ to depict a much more ecstatic boom state in the second year.

If more up-to-date tables such as those provided by Banz and Miller in 1978 were available, it would be possible to compute $m(t, s)$ market risk modifiers in the manner illustrated above. Unfortunately, no such tables are available. Thus for purposes of this chapter $m(t, s)$ sensitivity analysis was proposed rather than point estimation of $m(t, s)$ market risk modifiers. No tables comparable to the Banz and Miller tables exist for the 1969–1980 capital markets in the United Kingdom. This prompted the use of sensitivity analysis for estimating Briton Ltd. market risk-adjusted economic rate of return.

NOTES

1. Noted antagonists of ARR include Swalm (1958), Carlson (1964), Solomon (1966, 1970), Sarnat and Levy (1969), Stauffer (1971), Gordon (1974), Livingston and Salamon (1971), Wright (1978), Stark (1982), Fisher and McGowan (1983), and Long and Ravenscraft (1984). Counter arguments providing limited support for ARR and/or criticism of IRR as a performance standard are found in Vatter (1966), Beaver and Dukes (1973), Kay (1976, 1978), Gonedes and Dopuch (1979), Beaver (1981), Mepham (1978, 1979), Van Breda (1981, 1984), Freeman, Ohlson and Penman (1982), Beaver and Landsman (1983), Beaver, Griffin and Landsman (1982), Horowitz (1984), Martin (1984), Jensen (1986a), and Edwards, Kay, and Mayer (1987). Following the controversial Fisher and McGowan (1983) paper, Fisher (1984) published a rejoinder in which he laments (p. 509):

   > *Judging from some of the comments I have received, only some of which are published above, you would think that John McGowan and I had defaced a national monument. We have been accused of claiming that all accounting data are useless, of making it difficult for expert economists to testify about monopoly, and even of implying that "most of applied economics is misguided."*

   General analysis of such a complex and multifaceted debate is provided in Jensen (1986a). A useful reprint of key articles appears in Brief

(1986). A historical perspective is provided by Lee (1980). Papers of indirect interest along these same lines include Brief, Merino, and Weiss (1980), Beaver and Demski (1979), Beaver (1981), Blocher and Stickney (1979), and Shriver (1987). Notable references from the vast literature of valuation and economic income include Edwards and Bell (1961), Sterling (1972), Chambers (1966), and Canning (1929). Newer cash recovery rate IRR estimation approaches that are highly controversial in nature have been advocated by Ijiri (1978, 1979, 1980), Salami (1981), Salamon (1982, 1985, 1988), Stark (1987), and Griner and Stark (1988). AICPA (1953), stresses: "Depreciation is a process of allocation, not valuation." One of the strongest cases for the allocation basis of accounting is found in Paton and Littleton (1940).

2. The modern theory of finance evolved from a large body of literature focused on ex ante asset valuation. It's history is briefly sketched by Jensen and Smith (1984) and reviewed in greater depth in Copeland and Weston (1983). Linkage with financial statement analysis is extensively analyzed and reviewed by Gonedes and Dopuch (1988). This newer theory embraces the time-state-preference model (TSPM), the capital asset pricing model, arbitrage pricing theory, the option pricing model, and Modigliani and Miller (MM) models that can all be combined into a coherent modern theory [e.g. see Hsia (1981)]. In TSPM, the economy is viewed as having alternative states at each future point in time. Investor preferences for monetary returns are deemed to vary inversely with the state of the economy; that is, the worse the depression, the higher the economic value of each $1.00 return. The CAPM deems the only relevant investment risk as market (systematic) risk that increases with positive covariance of an asset's returns with the state of the market economy (as reflected in the return of a market portfolio for the CAPM). There are a number of variations on the CAPM (e.g., discrete versus continuous, wealth-oriented versus consumption-oriented, quadratic utility versus bivariate lognormal-based). All variations have some rather troublesome underlying assumptions (random walk price changes, perfect capital markets, parameter stationarity) that inhibit applications of the CAPM, especially for longer-term capital budgeting decisions.

  Approaches for longer-term ex ante valuation have been proposed using APT and OPM theories that both assume (unknown) value of an asset can be estimated from market values of other assets that can be combined into portfolios having cash return equivalencies to the projected returns of the capital budgeting asset in question. Liabilities may also be valued for the levered firm, linking the CAPM, APT, and the OPM with MM theory.

  Many problems remain in ex ante valuation under the modern theory for real-world investment decision; for example, see Devinney and Stewart (1988) for a summary of the most serious problems. Less attention is given in the modern theory to ex post performance evaluation which is often viewed as the domain of financial accounting. Nothing, to my knowledge, appears on the ex post theory.

3. For example, APT is an innovative approach for overcoming the need in the CAPM and the OPM to specify underlying probability distributions and societal risk preferences. The theory [as proposed by Ross (1976, 1978) and

illustrated in Cox, Ross, and Rubinstein (1979)] is very promising for valuing capital budgeting proposals. However, the restrictive distributional assumptions are replaced by an (almost) equally restrictive assumption that managers can forecast *and link* both a capital budgeting project cash flow stream and a comparison asset cash flow stream *without* knowing the states of the economy (and equivalently societal risk preferences) that are likely to impact upon cash flows and comparison asset prices. Computer software linking APT with capital budgeting and the cost of capital estimation is available from the Alcar Group. I thank Karen J. Frederick for sending me information about this from The Alcar Group, Inc., 5215 Old Orchard Road, Suite 600, Skokie, Ill.

REFERENCES

AGGARWAL, RAJ and CHARLES H. GIBSON. (1989). *Discounting in Financial Accounting* (Morristown, NJ: Financial Executives Research Foundation).

AICPA (1953). *Accounting Research Bulletin* 43. (June), chap. 9, sec. C, par. 5.

ALEXANDER, S. S. (1950). "Income Measurement in a Dynamic Economy," *Five Monographs on Business Income* (New York: American Institute of Accountants), pp. 1–95.

ARMSTRONG, P. (1987). "The Rise of Accounting Control in British Capitalist Enterprises," *Accounting, Organizations and Society* 12, pp. 415–436.

ARROW, KENNETH (1964). "The Role of Securities in the Optimal Allocation of Risk Bearing," *Review of Economic Studies* 31, pp. 91–96.

BANZ, R. W., and M. H. MILLER (1978). "Prices for State-Contingent Claims: Some Estimates and Applications," *Journal of Business* 51, pp. 653–672.

BEAVER, W. H. (1981). *Financial Reporting: An Accounting Revolution* (Englewood Cliffs, N.J.: Prentice-Hall).

BEAVER, W. H., and J. S. DEMSKI (1979). "The Nature of Income Measurement," *Accounting Review* 54, pp. 38–46.

BEAVER, W. H., and R. DUKES (1973). "Interperiod Tax Allocation and Delta Depreciation Methods: Some Empirical Results," *Accounting Review* 48, pp. 549–559.

BEAVER, W. H., P. A. GRIFFIN, and W. R. LANDSMAN (1982). "The Incremental Information Content of Replacement Cost Earnings," *Journal of Accounting and Economics* 3, pp. 15–39.

BEAVER, W. H., and W. R. LANDSMAN (1983). *Incremental Information Content of Statement 33 Disclosures* (Stamford, Conn.: Financial Accounting Standards Board).

BECKER, S. W., and BROWNSON, F. O. (1964). "What Price Ambiguity? Or the Role of Ambiguity in Decision Making," *Journal of Political Economy* 73, pp. 62–73.

BIERMAN, JR., H. B., and S. SMIDT (1980). *The Capital Budgeting Decision* (New York: Macmillan). A 1988 seventh edition is also available.

BLOCHER, F., and C. STICKNEY (1979). "Duration and Risk Assessments in Capital Budgeting," *Accounting Review* 54, pp. 180–188.

BREEDEN, D. T., and R. H. LITZENBERGER (1978). "Prices of State-Contingent Claims Implicit in Option Prices," *Journal of Business* 51, pp. 621–641.

BRENNAN, M. J. (1979). "The Pricing of Contingent Claims in Discrete Time Models," *Journal of Finance* 34, pp. 53–68.

BRIEF, R. P., ed. (1986). *Estimating the Economic Rate of Return From Accounting Data* (New York: Garland).

BRIEF, R. P. (1985). "Limitations of Using the Cash Recovery Rate to Estimate the IRR: A Note," *Journal of Business, Finance, and Accounting* 12, pp. 473–475.

BRIEF, R. P., B. MERINO, and J. WEISS (1980). "Cumulative Financial Statements," *Accounting Review* 55, pp. 480–490.

CANNING, J. B. (1929). *The Economics of Accounting* (New York: Ronald Press).

CARLSON, R. S. (1964). "Measuring Period Profitability: Book Yield Versus True Yield." Ph.D. Thesis, Graduate School of Business, Stanford University.

CHAMBERS, R. J. (1966). *Accounting, Evaluation and Economic Behavior* (Englewood Cliffs, N.J.: Prentice Hall).

CONNOLLY, R. A., and M. HIRSCHEY (1988). "Concentration and Profits: A Test of the Accounting Bias Hypothesis," *Journal of Accounting and Public Policy* pp. 313–334.

COPELAND, J. E., and J. F. WESTON (1983). *Financial Theory and Corporate Policy* (Reading, Mass.: Addison-Wesley).

COX, J. C., and S. A. ROSS (1976). "The Valuation of Options for Alternative Stochastic Processes," *Journal of Financial Economics* 3, pp. 145–166.

COX, J. C., S. A. ROSS, and M. E. RUBINSTEIN (1979). "Option Pricing: A Simplified Approach," *Journal of Financial Economics* 7, pp. 229–263.

COX, J. C., and M. E. RUBINSTEIN (1985). *Options Markets* (Englewood Cliffs, N.J.: Prentice-Hall).

D'ARCY, S. P., and N. A. DOHERTY (1988). *The Financial Theory of Pricing Property-Liability Insurance Contracts*, S.S. Huebner Foundation Monograph No. 15 (Homewood, Ill.: Richard D. Irwin).

DEVINNEY, M. D., and D. W. STEWART (1988). "Rethinking the Product Portfolio: A Generalized Investment Model," *Management Science*, 34, pp. 1080–1095.

EDWARDS, E. O., and P. W. BELL (1961). *The Theory and Measurement of Business Income* (Berkeley: University of California Press).

EDWARDS, J., J. KAY, and C. MAYER (1987). *The Economic Analysis of Accounting Profitability* (Oxford: Clarendon Press).

EINHORN, HILLEL J., and ROBIN M. HOGARTH (1985). "Ambiguity and Uncertainty in Probabilities Inference," *Psychological Review* 92, pp. 433–461.

ELLSBERG, DANIEL (1961). "Risk, Ambiguity and the Savage Axioms," *Quarterly Journal of Economics* 75, pp. 643–669.

FAMA, E. F. (1976). *Foundations of Finance* (New York: Basic Books).

FAMA, E. F. (1970). "Efficient Capital Markets: A Review of Theory and Empirical Work," *Journal of Finance* 25 (May), pp. 383–417.

FAMA, E. F., and M. H. MILLER (1972). *The Theory of Finance* (New York: Holt, Rinehart and Winston).

FELDSTEIN, M. S., and L. H. SUMMERS (1977). "Is the Rate of Profit Falling?" *Brookings Papers on Economic Activity* 1, pp. 211–228.

FELLNER, WILLIAM (1961). "Distortion of Subjective Probabilities as a Reaction to Uncertainty," *Quarterly Journal of Economics* 75, pp. 670–692.

FISHER, F. M., (1984). "The Misuse of Accounting Rates of Return: Reply," *American Economic Review* 74, pp. 509–517.

FISHER, F. M., and J. J. McGOWAN (1983). "On the Misuse of Accounting Rates of Return to Monopoly Profits," *American Economic Review* 73, pp. 82–97.

FREEMAN, R. N., J. A. OHLSON, and S. H. PENMAN (1982). "Book Rate of Return and Prediction of Earnings Changes: An Empirical Investigation," *Journal of Accounting Research* 20, pp. 639–653.

GEHR, A. (1981). "Risk-Adjusted Capital Budgeting Using Arbitrage," *Financial Management* 12, pp. 14–19.

GESKE, R. (1977). "The Valuation of Corporate Liabilities as Compound Options," *Journal of Financial and Quantitative Analysis* 12, 541–552.

GESKE, R. (1979). "The Valuation of Compound Options," *Journal of Financial Economics* 6, pp. 63–81.

GONEDES, NICHOLAS J., and NICHOLAS DOPUCH (1988). *Analysis of Financial Statements: Financial Accounting and the Capital Market*, SAR #30 (Sarasota, Fla.: American Accounting Association).

GONEDES, NICHOLAS J., and NICHOLAS DOPUCH (1979). "Economic Analysis and Accounting Techniques: Perspectives and Proposals," *Journal of Accounting Research* 17, pp. 384–410.

GORDON, L. A. (1974). "Accounting Rate of Return vs. Economic Rate of Return," *Journal of Business Finance and Accounting*, 1, pp. 343–356.

GRINER, E. H., and A. W. STARK (1988). "Cash Recovery Rates of Return, and the Estimation of Economic Performance," *Journal of Accounting and Public Policy* 7, pp. 293–312.

HAY, D. A. and D. J. MORRIS (1979). *Industrial Economics: Theory and Evidence* Oxford: Oxford University Press).

HILL, T. P. (1979). *Profits and Rates of Return* (Paris: Organization for Economic Cooperation and Development).

HIRSHLEIFER, J. (1965). "Investment Decision Under Uncertainty: Choice Theoretic Approaches," *Quarterly Journal of Economics* 79, pp. 509–536.

HIRSHLEIFER, J. (1966). "Investment Decision Under Uncertainty: Application of the State Preference Approach," *Quarterly Journal of Economics* 80, pp. 252–277.

HOLLAND, D. M., and S. C. MAYERS (1979). "Trends in Corporate Profitability and Capital Costs," in R. Lindsay (ed.), *The Nation's Capital Needs: Three Studies*, (New York: Committee for Economic Development).

HOROWITZ, IRA (1984). "The Misuse of Accounting Rates of Return: Comment," *American Economic Review* 74, pp. 492–493.

HOTELLING, H. (1925). "A General Mathematical Theory of Depreciation," *Journal of the American Statistical Association* 20 (September), pp. 340–353.

HSIA, C. (1981). "Coherence of the Modern Theories of Finance," *Financial Review* 16, pp. 27–41.

IJIRI, Y. (1978). "Cash Flow Accounting and Its Structure," *Accounting, Auditing, and Finance* 1, pp. 331–348.

IJIRI, Y. (1979). "Convergence of Cash Recovery Rate," in Y. Ijiri and A. B. Whinston (eds.), *Quantitative Planning and Control* (New York: Academic Press), pp. 259–267.

IJIRI Y. (1980). "Recovery Rate and Cash Flow Accounting," *Financial Executive* 48, pp. 54–60.

JACOBSON, R. (1987). "The Validity of ROI as a Measure of Business Performance," *American Economic Review* 77, pp. 470–478.

JENSEN, M. C., and C. W. SMITH, JR. (1984) "The Theory of Corporate Finance: A Historical Overview," in M. C. Jensen and C. W. Smith (eds.), *The Modern Theory of Corporate Finance* (New York: McGraw-Hill), pp. 2–21.

JENSEN, R. E. (1986a). "'The Befuddled Merchant of Venice': More on the 'Misuse' of Accounting Rates of Return Vis-á-Vis Economic Rates of Return," *Advances in Public Interest Accounting* 1, pp. 113–166.

JENSEN, R. E. (1986b). "Discount Rate Risk Adjustments and Diversification Theory: Paradoxical Impacts of Market Risk Adjustments on Optimum Portfolio Decisions in Multiperiod Settings," Working Paper 144, Trinity University, San Antonio, Tex.

JENSEN, R. E. (1986c). "Capital Budgeting Under Risk and Inflation," *Advances in Accounting* 3, pp. 255–279.

JENSEN, R. E., (1987). "A Fairy Tale Prompted by 'The Economics of Real Estate Decisions'," Working Paper 155, Trinity University, San Antonio, Tex.

JENSEN, R. E. (1988a). "Does a Ross Economy Lunch Really Cost as Much as a Hirshleifer Cusine Complete With o_m Dessert?" Working Paper 149, Trinity University, San Antonio, Tex.

JENSEN, R. E. (1988b). "Sensitivity Analysis of the Components of 'Error' in Accounting Versus Economic Rate of Return Measurements: Infusion of the Modern Theory of Finance," Working Paper 156, Trinity University, San Antonio, Tex.

JENSEN, R. E. (1988c). "Some Theoretical Implications of the 'Modern Theory' of Finance and Time State Preference Models for Accounting, Economic, and Monopoly Excess Rates of Return: Part I. Background," Working Paper 170, Trinity University, San Antonio, Tex.

JENSEN, R. E. (1988d). "Some Theoretical Implications of the 'Modern Theory' of Finance and Time State Preference Models for Accounting, Economic, and Monopoly Excess Rates of Return: Part II. Analysis of Monopoly Power," Working Paper 170, Trinity University, San Antonio, Tex.

JENSEN, R. E. (1989). "Recent Advances in the "Modern Theory" of Finance That Make It Possible to Identify Some of the Monopoly Power Ingredients of

Ex Post Accounting Rate of Return," Working Paper No. 173, Trinity University, San Antonio, Tex.

KAPLAN, R. S. (1984). "The Evolution of Management Accounting," *Accounting Review* 59, pp. 390–418.

KAY, J. A. (1976). "Accountants, Too, Could be Happy in a Golden Age: The Accountants' Rate of Profit and the Internal Rate of Return," *Oxford Economic Papers* 28, pp. 447–460.

KAY, J. A. (1978). "Accounting Rate of Profit and Internal Rate of Return: A Reply," *Oxford Economic Papers* 30, pp. 469–470.

LEE, T. A. (1980). *Income and Value Measurement: Theory and Practice* (Baltimore: University Park Press).

LINTNER, J. (1965a). "The Valuation of Risk Assets and the Selection of Risky Investments in Stock Portfolios and Capital Budgets," *Review of Economics and Statistics* 47, pp. 13–37.

LINTNER, J. (1965b). "Security Prices and Maximal Gains From Diversification," *Journal of Finance* 20, pp. 587–616.

LIVINGSTON, J. L., and G. L. SALAMON (1970). "Relationship Between the Accounting and the Internal Rate or Return Measure: A Synthesis and an Analysis," *Journal of Accounting Research* 8, pp. 199-216.

LONG, W. F., and D. J. RAVENSCRAFT (1984). "The Misuse of Accounting Rates of Return: Comment," *American Economic Review* 74, pp. 494–500.

MARKOWITZ, H. (1959). *Portfolio Selection* (New Haven: Yale University Press).

MARTIN, S. (1984). "The Misuse of Accounting Rates of Return: Comment," *American Economic Review* 74, pp. 501–506.

MEPHAM, M. J. (1978). "A Reinstatement of the Accounting Rate of Return," *Accounting and Business Research*, pp. 178–190.

MEPHAM, M. J. (1979). "A Note to 'A Reinstatement of the Accounting Rate of Return'," *Accounting and Business Research* 52, pp. 74–75.

MOSSIN, J. (1966). "Equilibrium in a Capital Asset Market," *Econometrica* 34, pp. 768–783.

NEWMAN, C. M., and I. J. CZECHOWICZ (1983). *International Risk Management* (Morristown, N.J.: Financial Executives Research Foundation).

PARKER, R. H., and G. C. HARCOURT (1969). *Readings in the Concept and Measurement of Income* (Cambridge: Cambridge University Press).

PATON, W. A., and A. S. LITTLETON (1940). *An Introduction to Corporate Accounting Standards* (Sarasota, Fla.: American Accounting Association).

PATON, W. A., and R. A. STEVENSON (1918). *Principles of Accounting* (New York: Macmillan, especially chap. 20.

PEASNELL, K. V. (1977). "The CCA Depreciation Problem—An Analysis and Proposal," *Abacus* 13, pp. 212–219.

PEASNELL, K. V. (1981). "On Capital Budgeting and Income Measurement," *Abacus* 17, pp. 52–67.

PEASNELL, K. V. (1982). "Some Formal Connections Between Economic Values and Yields and Accounting Numbers," *Journal of Business Finance and Accounting* 9, pp. 361–381.

RAPPAPORT, ALFRED (1986). *Creating Shareholder Value* (New York: Free Press).

ROSS, S. A. (1976). "The Arbitrage Theory of Capital Asset Pricing," *Journal of Economic Theory* 3, pp. 343–362.

ROSS, S. A. (1978). "A Simple Approach to the Valuation of Risky Streams," *Journal of Business* 51, 453–475.

RUBINSTEIN, M. E. (1973). "A Mean-Variance Synthesis of Corporate Financial Theory," *Journal of Finance* 28, pp. 167–181.

RUBINSTEIN, M. E. (1974). " An Aggregation Theorem for Securities Markets," *Journal of Financial Economics* 1, pp. 225–244.

RUBINSTEIN, M. E. (1976). "The Valuation of Uncertain Streams and the Pricing of Options," *Bell Journal of Economics* 7, pp. 407–425.

SALAMON, G. L. (1982). "Cash Recovery Rates and Measures of Firm Profitability" *American Economic Review* 72, pp. 292–302.

SALAMON, G. L. (1985). "Accounting Rates of Return," *American Economic Review* 75, pp. 495–504.

SALAMON, G. L. (1988). "On the Validity of Accounting Rate of Return in Cross-sectional Analysis: Theory, Evidence and Implications," *Journal of Accounting and Public Policy* 7, pp. 267–292.

SALMI, T. (1981). "Estimating the Internal Rate of Return from Published Financial Statements," *Journal of Business Finance and Accounting* 9, pp. 68–74.

SARNAT, M., and H. LEVY (1969). "The Relationship of Rules of Thumb to the Internal Rate of Return: A Restatement and Generalization," *Journal of Finance* 24, pp. 479–490.

SHARPE, W. F. (1963). "A Simplified Model for Portfolio Analysis," *Management Science* 9, pp. 277–293.

SHRIVER, K. A. (1987). "An Empirical Examination of the Effects of Alternative Measurement Techniques on Current Cost Data," *Accounting Review* 68, pp. 79–96.

SOLOMON, E. (1966). "Return on Investment: The Relation of Book Yield to True Yield," *Research in Accounting Measurement* (Sarasota, Fla.: American Accounting Association).

SOLOMON, E. (1970). "Alternative Rate of Return Concepts and Their Implications for Utility Regulations," *Bell Journal of Economics* 1, (Spring), pp. 65–81.

SOLOMONS, DAVID (1961). "Economic and Accounting Concepts of Income," *Accounting Review* 36, pp. 374–383.

STARK, A. W. (1982). "Estimating the Internal Rate of Return From Accounting Data," *Oxford Economic Papers* 34, pp. 520–525.

STARK, A. W. (1987) "On the Observability of the Cash Recovery Rate," *Journal of Business, Finance, and Accounting* 14, pp. 99–108.

STAUFFER, T. R. (1971). "The Measurement of Corporate Rates of Return: A Generalized Formulation," *Bell Journal of Economics* 2, pp. 434–469.

STEELE, A. (1986). "A Note on Estimating the Internal Rate of Return from Published Financial Statements," *Journal of Business Finance and Accounting* 13, pp. 1–13.

STERLING, R. L. (1972). "Decision Oriented Financial Accounting," *Accounting and Business Research* 45, pp. 198–208.

SWALM, R. O. (1958). "On Calculating the Rate of Return on Investment," *Journal of Industrial Engineering* 37, pp. 99–103.

VAN BREDA, M. F. (1981). *The Prediction of Corporate Earnings* (Ann Arbor, Mich.: UMI Research Press). Van Breda, M. F. (1984). "The Misuse of Accounting Rates of Return: Comment," *American Economic Review* 74, pp. 507–508.

VATTER, W. J. (1966). "Income Models, Book Yield, and Rate of Return," *Accounting Review* 41, pp. 681–698.

WEI, K. C. J. (1988). "An Asset Pricing Theory Unifying the CAPM and APT," *Journal of Finance* 43, pp. 881–892.

WILLIAMS, N. P. (1981). "Influences on the Profitability of Twenty-two Industrial Sectors," Bank of England Discussion Paper 5.

WRIGHT, F. K. (1978). "Accounting Rate of Profit and Internal Rate of Return," *Oxford Economic Papers* 30, pp. 464–468.

4

Corporate Capital Budgeting: Contributions of Finance Theory and an Extension Under Multiperiod Uncertainty*

CHARLES W. HALEY

ABSTRACT

This chapter is divided into two main parts. In the first part we review briefly the major contributions made by finance theory to corporate capital budgeting in practice. In the second part we look at some models that extend the theory and may ultimately influence practice. We begin with a brief history of theoretical developments relevant to capital budgeting. No attempt is made here to provide a survey of the huge volume of literature, but rather we try to highlight major developments.

I. THE DEVELOPMENT OF CAPITAL BUDGETING THEORY

The primary goal of finance theory, as applied to capital budgeting, has been to provide a means for determining which of the set of investment

*This research was supported by a grant from the Center for Study of Banking and Financial Markets.

options available to a firm will provide the maximum benefit to the firm's stockholders. In its simplest form, the problem can be stated as determining whether the undertaking of a given capital investment that is economically independent of all other possible investments will benefit the stockholders. The theory has identified the measure of benefit to be the market value of the firm's common stock reduced to the problem of identifying how undertaking a capital project will affect stock values. The dominant model has been and continues to be some form of discounted cash flow (DCF) analysis.

Although discounted cash flow techniques of project evaluation were known by industrial engineers early in the twentieth century, the beginning of developments that would change corporate practice occurred in 1951. In this year Dean (1951) and Lutz and Lutz (1951) published books that sparked an extensive examination of capital budgeting methodology by academics during the 1950s. A collection of the major articles of this period can be found in Solomon (1959), and a summary of the concepts that were developed is provided by Solomon (1963). By the mid-1960s the use of the net present value (NPV) and the internal rate of return (IRR) approaches to capital budgeting was being taught in finance and accounting courses throughout the United States at both graduate and undergraduate levels. The discount rate or cutoff rate to be used in this technique was identified as the "firm's cost of capital" with, perhaps, some adjustment for risk. Solomon (1959, p. 76) was pessimistic as to whether any systematic risk adjustment methods would be forthcoming.

The mid-1960s was also a period in which mathematical models of capital market equilibrium under conditions of risk were first developed. These models indicated that systematic risk, usually measured by a security's beta with respect to the market, was the only relevant risk. Many authors took this concept and developed implications for corporate capital budgeting. The primary result was the proposition that diversification per se should be irrelevant. This proposition implies that firms can evaluate projects without considering statistical interactions with other investments of the firm—past, present, or future.

The development of precise analytic procedures of risk adjustment in capital budgeting has been slower. Although there is substantial agreement among theorists as to the value of mean-variance-based models in a single-period setting, their application to the corporate capital budgeting problem is still being debated. The valuation of assets that provide multiperiod streams of uncertain cash flows remains a central problem in financial theory. [Although it was not identified as such by Weston (1981) in his review of finance theory.] It should not be surprising then that the newer models of valuation have not achieved widespread application in practice even after 20 years of development.

A. The Diffusion of Theory into Practice

Over the years many surveys have been made to determine how capital budgeting is actually being done in major U.S. corporations. Istvan (1961) reported (based on personal interviews) that of 48 large firms, only 5 were using "time-adjusted" evaluation techniques in 1960. Surveys carried out during the 1960s and 1970s, such as Vaughn (1968), Klammer (1972), Schall, Sundem, and Geibeek (1978), and Gitman and Forrester (1977) show an increasing usage of discounted cash flow techniques. By the mid-1970s over 85% of the large firms in these surveys reported that they were using some form of DCF. By 1982, according to a survey undertaken by Gitman and Mercurio (1982), the majority of financial executives in Fortune 1000 companies were aware of mean-variance pricing models, although procedures based on these models were used by a minority of firms.[1] Moreover these studies show that firms appear to evaluate projects without regard for diversification considerations, which is consistent with the prescriptions of financial theory.

Thus we can say that financial theory has a significant impact on corporate practice in the past 25 years. The spread of DCF methods from journal articles, through the classroom, to corporate decision making must be considered a major success for academics in the finance field. However, Solomon's pessimism, expressed over 20 years ago, concerning the development of risk adjustment procedures appears to have been justified.[2] At best we have only a rough idea as to how to achieve this despite substantial work in the area.

II. MULTIPERIOD EXTENSIONS OF MEAN-VARIANCE MODELS

The models developed to date seem to suffer from one or more of the following deficiencies:

1. Difficult to apply in practice
2. Not based on standard capital market theory—the capital asset pricing model (CAPM) or arbitrage pricing theory (APT)
3. Based on highly restrictive assumptions regarding the time pattern of risk (risk-adjusted discount rate approaches).

Three articles that are not subject to these particular criticisms are Fama (1977), Myers and Turnbull (1977), and Sick (1986). [See Sick (1989) for a presentation of the basic ideas.] Sick argues that operational capital budgeting models can be built on a single-period capital market model that encompasses both the CAPM and APT. The earlier papers by Fama and by Myers and Turnbull provided a method based on the CAPM. The major differences among the approaches of these authors are their assumptions regarding the nature of revisions in expectations of cash flows over time. Fama and Myers and Turnbull assume that expectations are revised in a proportional manner, whereas Sick assumes that revisions are additive.

We seek to build on the work of these authors by examining alternative specifications of the revision of expectations, including the earlier assumptions as special cases. A general class of capital budgeting models is developed where the specific model to be used depends on the nature of the project to be undertaken. That is, different projects may require different valuation procedures, although each procedure (or model) is a member of the same general class. Each model can also be reduced to the same simple certainty-equivalent and risk-adjusted discount rate valuation equations. However, the assumptions required and the implied magnitudes of the resulting discount rates or certainty-equivalent factors differ according to the model and the characteristics of the project. Being able to identify the determinants of risk for a project and the assumptions regarding the risk are useful, even if a simple, constant discount rate model is used to evaluate projects.

III. THE BASIC MODEL

Assume that the value additivity principle (VAP) holds in the capital markets. Applied to two cash flows $\tilde{Y}_1^1$ and $\tilde{Y}_1^2$ to be received in period 1, the VAP states that the market value of the cash flows received together is equal to the sum of the market values of the cash flows received separately. That is, if V_0^1 and V_0^2 are the time-zero market values of $\tilde{Y}_1^1$ and $\tilde{Y}_1^2$, respectively, and

$$\tilde{Y}_1^T = \tilde{Y}_1^1 + \tilde{Y}_1^2$$

then the market value of $\tilde{X}_1^T$ is V_0^T, where

$$V_0^T = V_0^1 + V_0^2$$

Value additivity is a property of perfect capital markets and is therefore a characteristic of the CAPM, APT, and consumption-based CAPM models. Sick (1986) has shown that when the VAP holds, the market value of any single-period cash flow $\tilde{Y}_1$ can be represented by an equation of the form

$$V_0 = \frac{E_0(\tilde{Y}_1) - q_1 \, \text{cov}_0(\tilde{Y}_1, \tilde{Z}_1)}{1 + z_1} \tag{1}$$

where $E_0(\tilde{Y}_1)$ = expected value of cash flow $\tilde{Y}_1$ with the expectation at time zero

$\text{cov}_0(\tilde{Y}_1, \tilde{Z}_1)$ = covariance of $\tilde{Y}_1$ with random factor $\tilde{Z}$ based on expectations at time zero

q_1 and z_1 = constants that characterize equilibrium in the markets; z_1 is always the equilibrium rate of return for any asset or portfolio of assets for which $\text{cov}_0 (\tilde{Y}_1, \tilde{Z}_1) = 0$

The interpretations of $\tilde{Z}_1$, q_1, and z_1 depend on the particular capital market model used. For example, in a K-factor APT model,

$$q_1 = 1.0$$

$$\tilde{Z}_1 = \sum_{k=1}^{K} \lambda_{k1} \, \tilde{f}_{k1}$$

where $\tilde{f}_{k1}$ = the priced risk factor

λ_{k1} = market prices associated with factor

z_1 = the equilibrium rate of return on the zero-beta portfolio

For ease of exposition and interpretation, we assume that the CAPM is the appropriate model; however, the results can always be restated and interpreted in the more general form of Equation (1). In the CAPM we have

$\tilde{Z}_1 = \tilde{r}_{m1}$, the rate of return in the market portfolio

$z_1 = i_1$,   the riskless rate of interest

$q_1 = \lambda_1$,   the slope of the capital market line.

In addition we assume that the market process underlying $\tilde{r}_m$ is stationary and that the term structure of interest is flat and given for all future periods. Thus we can drop the time subscripts for $\tilde{r}_m$, λ, and i. The market valuation relationship shown by Equation (2) is therefore assumed to hold in each and every future period.

$$V_t = \frac{E_t(\tilde{Y}_{t+1}) - \lambda \, \text{cov}_t(\tilde{Y}_{t+1}, \tilde{r}_m)}{1 + i} \tag{2}$$

In applying single-period models to multiperiod cash flows, the major problem arises in specifying precisely the source and nature of the uncertainty in the cash flows.[3] One potential source of uncertainty is a change in capital market equilibrium conditions. We have ruled this out by assuming λ and i are given. A second source could be nonstationarity in the market process which has also been assumed away. Remaining are uncertainties in what the actual realization of $\tilde{Y}_T$ will be at time T, the fundamental uncertainty in the problem, and uncertainty in how the (subjective) probability distribution of $\tilde{Y}_T$ will change over time (from $t = 0$ to $t = T - 1$). The focus of this chapter is on this process of expectational revision and its implication for capital budgeting.

A. The Revision of Expectations

Consider the problem of specifying today's ($t = 0$) market value of an asset that T periods from now (at $t = T$) will pay the owner a single cash flow of $\tilde{X}_T$. We assume that T is known and therefore not a source of uncertainty.[4] Suppose, for the moment, that no new information about the cash flow will be received between $t = 0$ and $t = T - 1$; therefore there will be no revision of expectations regarding $\tilde{X}_T$. If this is true and Equation (2) holds for each period, then there is no uncertainty in the future value of the asset. The only uncertainty is the realization of $\tilde{X}_T$. The time-zero market value of the asset is

$$V_{0,T} = [E_0(\tilde{X}_T) - \lambda \, \text{cov}_0(\tilde{X}_T, \tilde{r}_m)] \sum_{t=1}^{T} (1 + i)^{-t} \tag{3}$$

In Equation (3) the market certainty equivalent of the cash flow occurring at time T is discounted back to the present at the riskless rate of interest. No additional adjustment of risk is required.

Now consider the problem when new information about $\tilde{X}_T$ may be forthcoming and expectations may be revised. We know that the value of the asset at time $T - 1$ will be

$$V_{T-1,T} = \frac{E_{T-1}(\tilde{X}_T) - \lambda \text{cov}_{T-1}(\tilde{X}_T, \tilde{r}_m)}{1 + i} \tag{4}$$

Note that the expectations are shown as of $T - 1$. The value of the asset at $T - 2$ is more complex. Applying the single-period model,

$$V_{T-2,T} = \frac{E_{T-2}(\tilde{V}_{T-1,T}) - \lambda \, \text{cov}_{T-2}(\tilde{V}_{T-1,T}, \tilde{r}_m)}{(1 + i)} \tag{5}$$

$\tilde{V}_{T-1,T}$ is an uncertain quantity as of $T - 2$ because there may be a revision of expectations regarding $\tilde{X}_T$. From the perspective of $T - 2$, we do not know what $E_{T-1}(\tilde{X}_T)$ and $\text{cov}_{T-1}(\tilde{X}_T, \tilde{r}_m)$ will be. That is, as of $T - 2$,

$$V_{T-1,T} = \frac{\tilde{E}_{T-2}(\tilde{X}_T) - \lambda \, \text{cov}_{T-2}(\tilde{X}_T, \tilde{r}_m)}{(1 + i)} \qquad (6)$$

where the $\sim$ indicates random variables.

To identify the potential areas of uncertainty more precisely it is helpful to break the covariance into separate terms as follows:

$$\text{cov}(\tilde{X}_T, \tilde{r}_m) = \rho_{x,m} \, CV_x \, \sigma_m \, E(\tilde{X}_T) \qquad (7a)$$
$$= C_T \, E(\tilde{X}_T) \qquad (7b)$$

where σ_m = standard deviation of $\tilde{r}_m$

$\rho_{x,m}$ = coefficient of correlation between $\tilde{X}_T$ and $\tilde{r}_m$

CV_x = coefficient of variation of $\tilde{X}_T$ $[\sigma_x/E(\tilde{X}_T)]$

C_T = relative covariance $(\rho_{xm}CV_x\sigma_m)$

From our assumption of the stationarity of $\tilde{r}_m$, σ_m is a constant. $E(\tilde{X}_T)$ is presumably subject to revision and is a separate term in Equation (6). The behavior of the two distribution parameters $\rho_{x,m}$ and CV_x is not clear; however, Fama (1977) argues that they must be taken as known quantities in order for the CAPM to apply. In any case we assume that the distribution parameters are constants, as this assumption substantially simplifies the analysis. Thus C_T, the relative covariance, is a constant. We are therefore left with only the changes in $E(\tilde{X}_T)$ as a source of uncertainty. In this view of the world, the distribution of $\tilde{X}_T$ becomes more diffuse as $E(\tilde{X}_T)$ increases, and more compact as $E(\tilde{X}_T)$ decreases. Note also that we can express the basic market valuation Equation (2) in this notation as

$$V_t = \frac{(1 - \lambda C_t)E(\tilde{Y}_{t-1})}{1 + i}$$

Thus the assumptions that the market risk premium λ (or λ_t) is given and that the relative covariances C_t are given imply that the certainty-equivalent factors $1 - \lambda C_t$ are given for the cash flows in question for all t.

Two assumptions regarding the stochastic behavior of $E(\tilde{X}_T)$ have appeared in the literature. Fama (1977) and Myers and Turnbull (1977) assumed that changes are proportional, that is,

$$\tilde{E}_t(\tilde{X}_T) = E_{t-1}(\tilde{X}_T) \, (1 + \tilde{p}_t) + \tilde{e}_t \qquad (8)$$

where $\tilde{e}_t$ is pure noise and $\tilde{p}_t$ may be correlated with $\tilde{r}_m$ and with $\tilde{p}_{t-1}$. Both $\tilde{p}_t$ and $\tilde{e}_t$ have expected values of zero.

Sick (1986) proposes an alternative additive model.[5]

$$\tilde{E}_t(\tilde{X}_T) = E_{t-1}(\tilde{X}_T) + \tilde{d}_t \qquad (9)$$

where $\tilde{d}_t$ has the same properties as $\tilde{p}_t$ but with a different scale. This additive model produces somewhat different valuation relationships than the proportional model (although both are certainty-equivalent valuation models), and determining which one best describes an actual process of expectational revision is no easy task.

We can make some general comments regarding the implications of the two models. Proportional revision implies some sort of compound growth process is at work. For example, suppose the cash flow under consideration results from the sale of land 5 years from now. One of the factors influencing the price of the land is the rate of inflation, which is normally taken to be growth-type process. Assuming that we are working with nominal cash flows, we suspect that many projects have a growth element arising from inflation.

Additive revisions can arise for many reasons. For example, suppose the cash flow arises from the sale of some commodity at a contractually fixed price. The uncertainty might be due to the actual amount of the commodity that can be produced—coal from a mine, grapes from a vineyard, and so on. In such cases additive revisions of expectations seem more reasonable than proportional.

From these examples we can see that both additive and proportional changes can easily characterize a particular cash flow. When the vineyard is planted, both the future yield and the price of the grapes are uncertain. There can be additive changes in expectations regarding yields, and proportional changes in expectations regarding prices. Thus a more general model is needed with both additive and proportional revision incorporated. We can combine Equations (8) and (9) to obtain

$$\tilde{E}_t(\tilde{X}_T) = E_{t-1}(\tilde{X}_T)\,(1 + \tilde{p}_t) + \tilde{d}_t \tag{10}$$

Our focus will be in this more general form for the revision of expectations. We now need to consider more deeply why expectations might be revised.

B. Sources of Information

Expectations are revised only on the basis of new information. This is a fundamental characteristic of efficient markets that was assumed in the underlying equilibrium relationship, Equation (1). Further, only the systematic relationship between the arrival of new information and the market return $\tilde{r}_m$ affects market values a priori. Ultimately then, only the covariances between $\tilde{p}_t$ and $\tilde{r}_m$ and between $\tilde{d}_t$ and $\tilde{r}_m$ affect value. However, it may be useful to distinguish between two possible sources for new information. One source is information directly impounded in $\tilde{r}_m$. This includes all general economic events. The other source is of importance when we consider capital investments involving multiperiod cash flows. Realization of the cash flow in period t is apt to provide information regarding future cash flows. Since the realization $\tilde{X}_t$ is, in general, correlated with $\tilde{r}_m$, any revisions in expectations of future cash flows $\tilde{X}_T$, $T > t$, must be related to $\mathrm{cov}(\tilde{X}_t, \tilde{r}_m)$. Given the potential for two sources of information, the use of two different types of impact (proportional and additive) seems desirable. Further, although it is not necessary, we will assume for expositional purposes that proportional effects are due to information linked to general economic activity, whereas additive effects are due to information specific to the cash flows of the project but still correlated with the market return $\tilde{r}_m$.[6]

C. Valuation

As shown in the Appendix, the present value of a stream of cash flows $\tilde{X}_t$, $t = 1, n$ can be written as

$$V_0 = \sum_{t=1}^{n} \frac{\left[\overline{X}_t \prod_{\tau=1}^{t-1}(1 - \lambda\, g_{\tau,t}) - \lambda \sum_{t=1}^{t-1} a_{\tau,t} \right](1 - \lambda\, C_t)}{(1 + i)^t} \tag{11}$$

where n = time period for the last possible cash flow

$\overline{X}_t \equiv E_0(\tilde{X}_t)$, the expectation as of time 0 for the cash flow occurring at time t

$g_{\tau,t} \equiv \mathrm{cov}\,(\tilde{p}_{t-\tau,t},\, \tilde{r}_m)$, the "growth" covariance, a nondimensional number representing the covariance of the proportional change in the expectation of the period t cash flows occurring τ periods before the cash flow of time $t - \tau$

$a_{\tau,t} \equiv \mathrm{cov}[\tilde{d}_{t-\tau,t},\, \tilde{r}_m]$, the additive covariance, a dollar-dimensional number representing the covariance of the additive change in the expectation of the period t cash flows occurring τ periods before the cash flow at time $t - \tau$

The remaining terms are as previously defined. We assume that all terms in Equation (11) are known as of time 0.

The obvious problem with any application of Equation (11) to capital budgeting decisions is the substantial data requirement. There are n^2 risk factors that must be estimated along with n expected values of the cash flows. Therefore we shall look at some special cases.

First, assume that the information flow is uniform and symmetric such that $g_{\tau,t} = g_{\tau,t-1}$ and $a_{\tau,t} = a_{\tau,t-1}$ for all t. Here there is pure time structure of expectational risk. The change in expectations for each cash flow at a given time before its realization has the same covariances as all other cash flows. Thus we can drop the double subscripts on the expectational covariances to obtain g_τ and a_τ. The only remaining risk that is unique to a particular cash flow is captured by C_t. We can therefore consider possible time patterns for g_τ and a_τ. In general it seems unlikely that g_τ and a_τ are increasing functions of τ. Information received today is unlikely to have a greater impact on the expectation of a cash flow 10 years from now than it will on the expected value of the cash flow next year. If anything, one would think that g_τ and a_τ are decreasing functions of τ. If we assume g_τ and a_τ to be constants, the result is a conservative valuation formula.

$$V_0 = \sum_{t=1}^{n} \frac{[\overline{X}_t(1 - \lambda\, g)^{t-1} - \lambda\, a(t - 1)]\,(1 - \lambda\, C_t)}{(1 + i)^t} \tag{12}$$

Further, since we have captured a natural increase in the uncertainty of future cash flows through the expectational changes, there is no obvious reason why the C_t-adjusted covariances should have any particular time pattern. Equation (12) is worthwhile when there is unusual uncertainty associated with a particular cash flow, for example, the salvage value of an asset. However for "well-behaved" cash flows, we can assume C_t to be constant as well. We are left with the simplest complete valuation formula for multiperiod revisions of expectations shown as Equation (13).

$$V_0 = (1 - \lambda C) \sum_{t=1}^{n} \frac{\overline{X}_t(1 - \lambda g)^{t-1} - \lambda a(t - 1)}{(1 + i)^t} \tag{13}$$

Equation (13) is complete because it contains all three possible sources of risk: (1) specific cash flow risk as measured by the adjusted covariance of the cash flow itself C, (2) risk due to proportional revisions of expectations as measured by g, and (3) risk due to additive revisions of expectations as measured by a. It is also a conservative formula under the arguments advanced in the development of Equation (12). Indeed Equations (12) and (13) may be too conservative, as we will see in Section IV. As an alternative, consider the case where the revision of expectations occurs for the expected cash flow in period $t + 1$ only. Equation (11) reduces to

$$V_0 = \frac{\overline{X}_1(1 - \lambda C_1)}{1 + i} + \sum_{t=2}^{n} \frac{[\overline{X}_t(1 - \lambda g_{1,t}) - \lambda a_{1,t}]\,(1 - \lambda C_t)}{(1 + i)^t} \tag{14}$$

In contrast to Equation (11), there is only one set of risk adjustments for each period's cash flows. We can describe this case as single-period risk adjustment. We can simplify Equation (14) by assuming C_t, $g_{1,t}$, and $a_{1,t}$ are constants and obtain the parallel to Equation (13).

$$V_0 = \frac{\overline{X}_1(1 - \lambda C)}{1 + i} + (1 - \lambda C) \sum_{t=2}^{n} \frac{\overline{X}_t(1 - \lambda g) - \lambda a}{(1 + i)^t} \tag{15}$$

As a final set of relationships, we provide the formulas for level perpetuities $\overline{X}_t = \overline{X}$ for $t = 1, \infty$. These are used in examples in Section D.

Multiperiod revisions: perpetuity version of Equation (13):

$$V_0 = \frac{\overline{X}(1 - \lambda C)}{i + \lambda g} - \frac{\lambda_a(1 - \lambda C)}{i^2} \tag{16}$$

Single-Period revisions: perpetuity version of Equation (15):

$$V_0 = \frac{(1 - \lambda C)\,[\overline{X}(1 + i - \lambda g) - \lambda a]}{i(1 + i)} \tag{17}$$

D. Numerical Illustrations

The following numerical examples of valuation using Equations (16) and (17) are intended to provide some insight into the nature of the risk adjustments being made and the relative magnitudes of these adjustments. We use the relationship between the linear slope coefficient b (beta) and the covariance between two random variables X and Y as a way to interpret the magnitudes of the covariances C, g, and a. That is,

$$\tilde{y} = c + b\tilde{X} + \tilde{E}$$

$$b = \frac{\mathrm{cov}(\tilde{X}, \tilde{Y})}{\mathrm{var}(\tilde{X})}$$

or

$$\mathrm{cov}(\tilde{X}, \tilde{Y}) = b \, \mathrm{var}\,(\tilde{X}) \tag{18}$$

For example, suppose that $\tilde{X} = \$120$ for all t, $\lambda = 4.0$, $i = 6\%$, and the standard deviation of the rate of return on the market portfolio is 20%. If the cash flows are riskless (C, g, and a are zero), the market value of the asset is \$2000 (\$120/0.06).

Suppose that a 10% point change in the market rate of return in any period is, on average, associated with a 5% change in the cash flow for that period. This implies that b for the relationship between relative cash flows (cash flows divided by their expected value) and the market return is 0.05/0.10 = 0.5. Since the variance of the rate of return on the market portfolio is 0.04 (0.2^2), by assumption, the relative covariance C can be calculated from Equation (18) as

$$C = b \, \mathrm{var}(\tilde{r}_m)$$

$$= 0.5(0.04)$$

$$= 0.02$$

If there is no risk due to revisions of expectations (g and a are zero), the market value of the asset from Equation (16) or (17) is

$$V_0 = \frac{\overline{X}(1 - \lambda C)}{i}$$

$$= \$170[1 - 4(0.02)]/0.06]$$

$$= \$110.4/0.06$$

$$= \$1840$$

In other words, the certainty equivalent of $120 per year is $110.40 per year, given the assumed relative covariance, and the market value of the asset is $1840. The impact on value from this source of risk is $160 ($2000 − $1840), and the market expected rate of return for this asset is

$$\bar{r} = \$120/\$1840$$

$$= 6.52\%$$

Now consider the impacts of revisions and expectations, keeping all other assumptions. Suppose there are no additive revisions (a is zero). For a 10 percentage point change in the market rate of returns in any period, there is on average a 5% revision of expectations regarding *all* cash flows in the future. In other words, if the market rate of return is 10 percentage points higher in 1992 than it was in 1991, the expected value of all cash flows from 1993 on will, on average, increase 5% from what was expected at the beginning of 1992. The value of b is again 0.5, and the value of g is 0.02, the same value as C. Substitution into Equation (16) gives

$$V_0 = \frac{\overline{X}(1 - \lambda C)}{i + \lambda g}$$

$$= \$110.40/(0.06 + 0.08)$$

$$= \$789$$

The reduction in value from this added risk is $1051 ($1840 − $789), and the expected rate of return for the asset is 15.2% ($120/$789).

Now suppose in addition that there is an additive revision of expectations such that for every 10 percentage point change in the market rate of return, there is a $5 change in the expected value of all future cash flows. The implied value for b here is $50 ($5/0.10), and therefore the additive covariance (a) is $2 ($50 × 0.04). Substitution of all values in Equation (16) gives

$$V_0 = \frac{\overline{X}(1 - \lambda C)}{i + \lambda g} - \frac{\lambda a(1 - \lambda C)}{i^2}$$

$$= \$789 - \$2044$$

$$= -\$1255$$

Therefore the additive risk factor reduces the value by $2044, making the value of the overall cash flow negative. The reason for such a large risk adjustment is the assumption of constant revisions of expectations for all future periods. The additive factor is especially sensitive in this respect. Thus the use of conservative assumptions in Equations (12), (13), and (16) appears to be excessively so.

Suppose, instead, the magnitudes of g and a are as assumed above but there is only a single revision of expectations such that Equation (17) applies. In this case,

$$
\begin{aligned}
V_0 &= \frac{(1 - \lambda C)[\overline{X}(1 + i - \lambda g) - \lambda a]}{i(1 + i)} \\
&= \frac{(1 - \lambda C)\overline{X}(1 + i - \lambda g)}{i(1 + i)} - \frac{\lambda a(1 - \lambda C)}{i(1 + i)} \\
&= \frac{\$110.40(1.06 - 0.08)}{0.06(1.06)} - \frac{\$8(0.92)}{0.06(1.06)} \\
&= \$1701 - \$116 \\
&= \$1585
\end{aligned}
$$

Thus the reduction in value from the proportional revision term is only $139 ($1840 − $1701) for the case where $g = 0$. The reduction in value from the additive term is only $116. The differences in risk and values between multiperiod revisions and single-period revisions are huge.

The results of this section indicate that market values are extremely sensitive to the timing of revisions of expectations. At the moment we have little knowledge about this phenomena, yet such knowledge is needed for the objective valuation of risky cash flows.

E. Conclusion and Future Directions

We have developed a general valuation model extending a single-period, value-additive relationship to multiperiods. The resulting Equation (11) is the basis for a general class of valuation relationships of which prior authors' developments are special cases. There are many such special cases that fall under the general model. It is hypothesized that there are different types of projects, each type conforming to a particular special case of Equation (11). Future research is required to identify and clarify projects along these lines. In addition, research into means of estimating the risk characteristics of projects is sorely needed. The present article provides a framework for such research.

APPENDIX

In this Appendix we use our assumption regarding revisions of expectations, Equation (10), plus the single-period valuation model, Equation (2), to develop Equation (11), the value of a cash flow $\tilde{X}_t$ occurring T periods from now (time 0). We begin with the value of the cash flow one period before its receipt, time $T - 1$. From Equation (2),

$$V_{T-1,T} = \frac{E_{T-1}(\tilde{X}_T) - \lambda \, \text{cov}(\tilde{X}_T, \tilde{r}_m)}{1 + i} \tag{A1}$$

As noted in the body of the chapter we assume that λ and i are known with certainty and, for convenience, assume them to be constant so that time subscripting is not necessary. Similarly, we assume $\tilde{r}_m$ to be drawn from a stationary distribution, which is consistent with the assumptions of constant i and λ.[7]

We assume that as of time $T - 1$ all quantities in Equation (A1) are known. However, as of time $T - 2$, $V_{T-1,T}$ is uncertain, and therefore the value of $\tilde{X}_T$ is

$$V_{T-2,T} = \frac{E_{T-2}(\tilde{V}_{T-1,T}) - \lambda \, \text{cov}(\tilde{V}_{T-1,T}, \tilde{r}_m)}{1 + i} \tag{A2}$$

We now need to consider the source of uncertainty in V_{T-1} from the perspective of time $T - 2$. We assume that all uncertainty at $T - 2$ is due to potential revision of the expected value of $\tilde{X}_T$ between $T - 2$ and $T - 1$. That is,

$$\tilde{V}_{T-1,T} = \frac{\tilde{E}_{T-1}(\tilde{X}_T) - \lambda \, C_T \, \tilde{E}_{T-1}(\tilde{X}_T)}{1 + i} \tag{A3}$$

where $C_T = \rho_{X,m}\sigma_m \, CV_X$ as per Equations (7a) and (7b). C_T is the relative covariance of $\tilde{X}_T$ and $\tilde{r}_m$ and is assumed to be a given parameter of the distribution of $\tilde{X}_T$. Therefore,

$$\tilde{V}_{T-1} = \frac{\tilde{E}_{T-1}(\tilde{X}_T)(1 - \lambda \, C_T)}{1 + i} \tag{A4}$$

From our assumed revision relationship expressed in Equation (10), we have

$$\tilde{E}_{T-1}(\tilde{X}_T) = \tilde{E}_{T-2}(\tilde{X}_T)(1 + \tilde{p}_{T-1}) + \tilde{d}_{T-1} \tag{A5}$$

and by substitution of (A5) into (A4),

$$\tilde{V}_{T-1} = \frac{[E_{T-2}(\tilde{X}_T)(1 + \tilde{p}_{T-1}) + \tilde{d}_{T-1}](1 - \lambda \, C_T)}{1 + i} \tag{A6}$$

and

$$E_{T-2}(\tilde{V}_{T-1}) = \frac{E_{T-2}(\tilde{X}_T)(1 - \lambda\, C_T)}{1 + i} \tag{A7}$$

$$\text{cov}(\tilde{V}_{T-1,T}, \tilde{r}_m) = \frac{[E_{T-2}(\tilde{X}_T)\, \text{cov}(\tilde{p}_{T-1}, \tilde{r}_m) + \text{cov}(\tilde{d}_{T-1}, \tilde{r}_m)]\,(1 - \lambda\, C_T)}{1 + i} \tag{A8}$$

Define

$$g_{1,T} \equiv \text{cov}(\tilde{p}_{T-1}, \tilde{r}_m) \tag{A9}$$

$$a_{1,T} \equiv \text{cov}(\tilde{d}_{T-1}, \tilde{r}_m) \tag{A10}$$

Both g_1 and a_1 are assumed to be known constants. The subscripts identify them as being associated with the revisions taking place one period before realization of the cash flow occurring at time T. Thus, in general,

$$g_{\tau,T} \equiv \text{cov}(\tilde{p}_{T-\tau,T}, \tilde{r}_m) \tag{A11}$$

$$a_{\tau,T} \equiv \text{cov}(\tilde{d}_{T-\tau,T}, \tilde{r}_m) \tag{A12}$$

Using Equations (A9) and (A10) to simplify Equation (A8) and substituting the result plus Equation (7a) into Equation (7b), we have

$$V_{T-2,T} = \frac{[E_{T-2}(\tilde{X}_T)(1 - \lambda\, g_{1,T}) - \lambda a_{1,T}](1 - \lambda\, C_T)}{(1 + i)^2} \tag{A13}$$

If we back up one more period to $T - 3$, we can go through a similar procedure to obtain

$$V_{T-3,T} = \frac{[E_{T-3}(\tilde{X}_T)(1 - \lambda g_{1,T})(1 - \lambda g_{2,T}) - \lambda(a_{1,T} + a_{2,T})](1 - \lambda C_T)}{(1 + i)^3} \tag{A14}$$

Thus following this scheme we arrive at

$$V_{0,T} = \frac{\left[E_0(\tilde{X}_T) \prod_{\tau=1}^{T-1} (1 - \lambda g_{\tau,T}) - \lambda \sum_{\tau=1}^{T-1} a_{\tau,T}\right] (1 - \lambda C_T)}{(1 + i)^T} \tag{A15}$$

Equation (A15) expresses the current (time-zero) market value of a single cash flow $\tilde{X}_T$ in terms of the current expectation of the cash flow and a variety of risk factors: $g_{\tau,T}$, $a_{\tau,T}$, and C_T.

Suppose that we have a stream of cash flows $\tilde{X}_t$, $t = 1, n$. By the value additivity principle the total value of the stream V_0 must be the sum of the values of the individual cash flows. Thus

$$V_0 = \sum_{t=1}^{n} V_{0,t} \tag{A16}$$

We know the value of any single cash flow is given by Equation (A15). Since all expectations of future cash flows are as of time 0, we can simply denote $E_0[\tilde{X}_t]$ as $\bar{X}_t$ and obtain V_0 as

$$V_0 = \sum_{t=1}^{n} \frac{\left[\bar{X}_t \prod_{\tau=1}^{t-1} (1 - \lambda g_{\tau,t}) - \lambda \sum_{\tau=1}^{t-1} a_{\tau,t} \right] (1 - \lambda C_t)}{(1 + i)^t} \tag{A17}$$

Equation (A17) is Equation (11), which we set out to derive.

NOTES

1. The survey questions permitted multiple responses by a single person, so that a precise percentage is not known. At least 22% of the respondents said that mean-variance methods of risk assessment were in use. However, the use could have been in estimating the firm's cost of equity rather than in adjusting for risk in specific projects. The survey was not designed to distinguish the nature of usage.

2. In a 1985 survey of CFOs of the Fortune 1000, Kim, Crick, and Kim (1986) report that 14% of respondents made no risk adjustments, 48% made subjective adjustments, and 29% adjusted the discount rate in unspecified ways. Several respondents used more than one approach.

3. In this application, the value of any asset is the value of the total cash flows paid to the holders of securities with claims against those assets (interest dividends, principal payments, and so on). Thus the cash flows are net of taxes, of costs associated with financial distress, and so on. [See Haley and Schall (1978), especially Appendix A.]

4. Uncertainty as to T is not an issue here. For assets involving multiperiod cash flows, the uncertainty in T reduces to uncertainty in how long the cash flows will persist, that is, the life of the asset. However, such assets can always be treated as having potentially infinite lives with the expected value of the cash flows approaching zero beyond their normal life.

5. In an additive model $\tilde{e}_t$ can be combined with $\tilde{d}_t$ without affecting the final results.

6. Textbook writers often describe the diversifiable component of the total risk from an asset (e.g., a firm's stock) as being a specific or unique risk associated with the asset. This description is not accurate since a specific or unique event (such as a strike) can still be statistically correlated with the market despite the absence of a direct causal link.

7. Nonstationarity of $\tilde{r}_m$ is probably inconsistent with the assumptions of constant i and λ. Conversely, time variation of i or λ suggests time variation of the distribution of $\tilde{r}_m$.

REFERENCES

BANZ, ROLF W., and MERTON H. MILLER (1978). "Prices for State-Contingent Claims: Some Estimates and Applications," *Journal of Business* 51, No. 4, pp. 653–672.

BOGUE, M. C., and R. ROLL (1974). "Capital Budgeting of Risky Projects with 'Imperfect' Markets for Physical Capital," *Journal of Finance* 30, pp. 601–613.

BOHREN, OYVIND (1983). "The Validity of Conventional Valuation Models Under Multi-period Uncertainty," *Journal of Business Finance and Accounting* 11, pp. 199–211.

BREEDEN, DOUGLAS T. (1979). "An Intertemporal Asset Pricing Model with Stochastic Consumption and Investment Opportunities," *Journal of Financial Economics* 7, No. 3, pp. 265–296.

BREEDEN, DOUGLAS T., and R. H. LITZENBERGER (1978). "Prices of State-Contingent Claims Implicit in Option Prices," *Journal of Business* 51, No. 4, pp. 621–651.

BRENNAN, MICHAEL J. (1973). "An Approach to the Valuation of Uncertain Income Streams," *Journal of Finance* 29, pp. 661–674.

DEAN, JOEL (1951). *Capital Budgeting* (New York: Columbia University Press, 1951).

FAMA, EUGENE (1970). "Efficient Capital Markets: A Review of Theory and Empirical Work," *Journal of Finance* 25, pp. 383–417.

FAMA, EUGENE (1977). "Risk-Adjusted Discount Rates and Capital Budgeting under Uncertainty," *Journal of Financial Economics* 5, pp. 3–24.

GITMAN, LAWRENCE J., and JOHN R. FORRESTER, JR. (1977). "A Survey of Capital Techniques Used by Major U.S. Firms," *Financial Management* (Fall), pp. 66–71.

GITMAN, LAWRENCE J., and VINCENT A. MERCURIO (1982). "Cost of Capital Techniques Used by Major U.S. Firms: Survey and Analysis of Fortune's 1000," *Financial Management* (Winter), pp. 21–29.

HALEY, CHARLES W., and LAWRENCE D. SCHALL (1978). "Problems With the Concept of the Cost of Capital," *Journal of Financial and Quantitative Analysis* 13, pp. 847–870.

ISTVAN, D. F. (1961). "The Economic Evaluation of Capital Expenditures," *Journal of Business* 34 (January), pp. 45–51.

KIM, SUK H., TREVOR CRICK, and SEUNG H. KIM (1986). "Do Executives Practice What Academics Preach," *Management Accounting* (November), pp. 49–52.

KLAMMER, THOMAS (1972). "Empirical Evidence of the Adoption of Sophisticated Capital Budgeting Techniques," *Journal of Business* 45 (October), pp. 387–397.

LUTZ, FRIEDRICH and VERA LUTZ (1951). *The Theory of Investment of the Firm* (Princeton, N.J.: Princeton University Press, 1951).

MYERS, STEWART C. (1974). "Interactions of Corporate Financing and Investment Decisions—Implications for Capital Budgeting," *Journal of Finance* 29, pp. 1–25.

MYERS, STEWART C., and STUART TURNBULL (1977). "Capital Budgeting and the Capital Asset Pricing Model: Good News and Bad News," *Journal of Finance* 32, pp. 321–333.

ROSS, STEPHEN (1978). "A Simple Approach to the Valuation of Risky Streams," *Journal of Business* 51, pp. 453–475.

SCHALL, LAWRENCE D., GARY L. SUNDEM, and WILLIAM R. GEIJSBECK JR. (1978). "Survey and Analysis of Capital Budgeting Methods," *Journal of Finance* 33, (March), pp. 281–292.

SICK, GORDON A. (1986). "A Certainty Equivalent Approach to Capital Budgeting," *Financial Management* 15 (Winter), pp. 23–32.

SICK, GORDON A. (1989). "Multi-period Risky Project Valuation: A Mean-Covariance Certainty-Equivalent Approach," in C. F. Lee (ed)., *Advances in Financial Planning and Forecasting* 3 (No. 1), pp. 1–36.

SOLOMON, EZRA (1959). *The Management of Corporate Capital* (New York: Free Press, 1959).

SOLOMON, EZRA (1963). *The Theory of Financial Management* (New York: Columbia University Press, 1963).

STAPLETON, R. C., and M. G. SUBRAHMANYAM (1978). "A Multi-Period Equilibrium Asset Pricing Model," *Econometrica* 46, pp. 1077–1096.

VAUGHN, DONALD E. (1968). "Capital Budgeting: Organization and Procedures," *Southern Journal of Business* (April), pp. 105–115.

WESTON, J. FRED (1981). "Developments in Finance Theory," *Financial Management* 10, pp. 5–22.

5

Penalized Present Value: Net Present Value Penalization With Normal and Beta Distributions

Fernando Gómez-Bezares

ABSTRACT

Starting from the Markowitz model but referring to net present values, we put forward the use of "straight lines" instead of the traditional indifference curves, which simplifies the matter greatly. Assuming the net present value interest in investment decisions, a new decision criterion appears: the penalized present value. If the net present value has a normal distribution, the analysis can be simplified even further, extending itself afterward to beta distribution cases, qualifying us to consider situations of asymmetry.

I. INTRODUCTION

Many writers distinguish between risk and uncertainty, the situations in the first case being those where probability distributions are known. In this chapter it is assumed that these distributions exist, but that, as usually happens in practice, we do not reach a full understanding of them. Thus we try to help the reader make decisions about investment selections by taking reliable factors into account. This view forces us to make important simplifications, something that can be criticized from a theoretical viewpoint but which is helpful, as the more accurate alternatives theoretically speaking are very difficult to put into practice—at least according to my experience as a consultant. The methodology described here has already been undertaken by some important companies. I shall try to explain its theoretical basis and the conclusions deriving from it.

Following the Markowitz (1952, 1959) theory on portfolio management, let us assume that there is aversion to risk and that we can make decisions according to the mean μ and the standard deviation σ of the expected returns [for its implications, see Gómez-Bezares (1987, pp. 316–317)]. A map of possible portfolios is brought forward in which every single portfolio is characterized by its values within the binomial (μ, σ); this map can be like the *ABCDEF* map in Figure 5.1. There are also a number of upsloping indifference curves. Each investor, according to his or her indifference curve system, invests in the portfolio that reaches the highest curve possible (such portfolios are placed on the *AB* curve, called the *efficient frontier*).

If we refer to wealth increments instead of rates of return, which are normally used in these kinds of studies, we will get μ and σ for the net present value (NPV) of the different decisions (e.g., Van Horne, 1986, p. 220), so that we can operate in a similar way. According to this model, when investment decisions are to be made, we calculate the mean μ and the standard deviation σ for the NPV of the different options; we place them on a map like the one in Figure 5.1, and we look for

Figure 5.1

Utility analysis of investment alternatives.

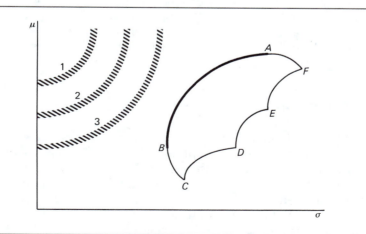

the optimum one according to our indifference curve system. But it is extremely difficult to take this last step. Besides, we must point out the diversifiable and nondiversifiable extent of the risk; we also have to deal with the problem related to the existence of more than one period of time, and so on [for a first approach, see Copeland and Weston (1988)]; but we shall not take these considerations into account. For the sake of clarity, let us concentrate on an individual project for the time being, as if it did not have anything to do with the other ones.

II. LINEAR PENALIZATION

To find a practical solution to this problem, I have been suggesting (e.g., Gómez-Bezares, 1987, 1988, 1989) that decisions be made according to a criterion of the $\mu - t\sigma$ type, which implies that when looking at the Markowitz portfolio map, we use indifference straight lines of the $\mu = Z + t\sigma$ type; on solving for Z, we obtain $Z = \mu - t\sigma$, which is the *criterion for decision.* Thus if we have indifference straight lines like the ones in Figure 5.2, with a t slope, C and D portfolios are equivalent, as both have the same value Z; E is better, as it has a higher value Z; and so on. Therefore, we can make decisions either by following the Z function $(Z = \mu - t\sigma)$ or by using a map of indifference straight lines.

Figure 5.2

Indifference lines for investment decision-making.

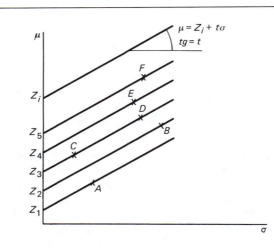

We have been considering Z, the wealth obtained when there is no risk involved (we consider this identical to a null standard deviation); thus Z_3 is equivalent to C and D. Therefore, it is a certainty equivalent, which we call penalized present value (PPV), as it is NPV penalized by risk (PPV $= Z = \mu - t\sigma$). Once the system is assumed, decisions are made by choosing the highest PPV. In order to calculate the NPV before penalization, we must use the risk-free rate as a discount rate, for penalization turns up later on when subtracting t standard deviations.

The use of indifference straight lines is a simplification that can be justified because of its practical advantages and, because as an approximation, the indifference curves can be considered a compound of short, straight lines. This is why the PPV is acceptable when comparing similar projects; it does not seem to be correct to use the same coefficient of penalization (t) for large projects (which determine the future of the company) as for small ones. In fact, the real problem relies on the correlation between the project at stake and other projects (not only those within the company, as the shareholders can diversify as well). Our methodology consists of analyzing the project in an individual way, and t varies according to the correlation between this project and the other ones.

III. BRIEF THEORETICAL CONSIDERATIONS

Going back to the previous analyses, let us introduce some theoretical considerations here (Gómez-Bezares, 1987, pp. 312–314). The NPV has a very important property, its additivity. What we mean by this term is that the NPV of a number of different independent investments can be added in order to obtain the NPV of the total investment. Under certainty conditions, such a property is obvious almost immediately. The situation becomes more complicated when risk is involved. This problem is usually solved by taking only the systematic risk into account. If we adjust the discount rate k for that risk and if we calculate its NPV, we see that the NPV is still additive (so that we can evaluate decisions according to their contribution to the total NPV); but the distinction between systematic and diversifiable risk gives rise to dubious results in practice.

The other possibility is the use of the concept of total investment. According to this theory, we should not analyze investments in isolation but as a whole, including those operating investments and those to be released (all the investments of a particular company). Thus we have a number of different possible investment portfolios, each with its own distribution of the NPV (characterized by two parameters $\mu(NPV)$ and $\sigma(NPV)$, according to our conditions), and we choose the most interesting one. However, this view is not very convincing either, as it presumes that shareholders are absolutely incapable of diversifying, which is false. Nevertheless, this idea appears implicitly in the actions of many managers working for big companies.

This is a very complex problem indeed, to which there is no unified answer in the financial world. One solution can be the use of both approaches jointly (Van Horne 1986, p. 223), qualitatively choosing a compromise between both options. In practice, and depending on the perfectness of the market, the appropriate thing to do fluctuates between one side and the other.

Bearing in mind the PPV, we can operate in a similar way, penalizing according to either systematic or total risk; however, it is difficult to put both systems into practice. We shall try to present a feasible method, although we will have to overlook theoretical perfection. For the time being, let us suppose that the important factor is the risk that new projects cause to the company as a whole; if we consider similar kinds of risk, then what matters is the relative size of such projects (in relation to a particular company). Small ones are diversified by the company itself, as it undertakes a number of similar projects at the same time. Large ones do not have that property and therefore present a risk to the company. Thus the former should not be penalized, while the latter should be (so that t varies according to the size of the investment).

When we approached the study of projects in an individual way, we did not discuss correlation among investments. But the covariance of the new project in relation to the previous ones, and therefore its correlation, can be very different (even if it is much more complicated to calculate). If it is high and positive, then penalization must be high as well; if it is equal to zero, then penalization must be lower; there may even be situations in which strong negative correlations are involved, which result in negative penalization.

It is also possible to rank penalization according to potential shareholder diversification, which is especially useful when referring to big companies whose shareholders usually hold quite diversified portfolios.

By way of a conclusion, the PPV can offer an alternative to the traditional NPV adjustments according to risk. These cases have been thoroughly discussed; for example, the risk-adjusted rate of return valuation formula and the certainty-equivalent valuation formula can be included in the capital asset pricing model (CAPM), the problems related to the existence of multiperiods, the application of arbitrage pricing theory (APT), and so on. [For a good approach to these problems, see Copeland and Weston (1988, chaps. 7 and 12) where some key points are discussed.] But these analyses, which are of great theoretical importance, are very difficult to put into practice.

The PPV may give way to studies similar to those already mentioned, and perhaps that will happen in the future. But the PPV is based on feasibility—thus the reader should excuse a certain lack of theoretical profundity, as we shall concentrate on the different courses of action based on the data that companies usually hold.

Finally, I would like to comment on the danger springing from the fact that financial theory loses contact with reality itself when it offers solutions that are hardly feasible. The PPV avoids this risk by giving priority to feasibility.

IV. PPV AND THE DISTRIBUTION OF NPV

We know from previous comments that NPV linear penalization according to risk results in a Z value:

$$Z = \mu(NPV) - t\sigma(NPV) \tag{1}$$

This can be rewritten as

$$Z = \mu - t\sigma \tag{2}$$

which is called the penalized present value:

$$PPV = \mu - t\sigma \tag{3}$$

If we assume that the NPV has a normal distribution, the value $\mu - t\sigma$ leaves to its left the same probability as t leaves to its right in standardized distribution. If $t = 1.5$, the probability that the real NPV will be lower than the PPV is 6.681%, and the probability that it will be higher is 93.319%. Therefore, it is acceptable to consider the NPV safe enough to base decisions on. The decision maker can take higher t values in order to increase the probability—which is higher than 90%—close to 100%, but that decision would hardly be justifiable, as there is so much aversion to risk, for the higher t is, the more we penalize risky projects.

Taking all this into account, if the NPV has a normal distribution and if we establish its parameters μ and σ, once the value t has been settled (which I presume must be located between 0 and 2, although it depends on many factors, as it has already been discussed), we can apply Equation (3) so that the problem can be solved. On the other hand, it is quite usual to presuppose the normality of NPV distribution (according to the central limit theorem).

The problem is that use of the normal distribution implies that we have to define its parameters μ and σ; many people who are not acquainted with statistics have difficulty in finding μ values, even if they are dealing with a known problem. The situation becomes more complicated when we must find a value for σ. A possible simplification is what follows: Calculate the maximum NPV (which we call b) and the minimum NPV (which we call a), suppose that there are 6 standard deviations between a and b (rejecting a .00270 probability), and act as if it is a normal:

$$\mu = \frac{a + b}{2} \tag{4}$$

$$\sigma = \frac{b - a}{6} \tag{5}$$

For $t = 1.5$,

$$PPV = \frac{a + b}{2} - \frac{1.5(b - a)}{6}$$

$$PPV = \frac{(3a + b)}{4} = 0.75a + 0.25b \tag{6}$$

The calculus of a and b values can be done merely by supposing an optimistic situation and a pessimistic one. We shall next see that the normal, as it has been treated here, is just a particular case within beta distribution when symmetry occurs.

V. BETA DISTRIBUTION

The aforementioned difficulty in defining the normal distribution μ and σ parameters has led many to adopt a simpler distribution, the incomplete beta function or beta distribution (see Kendall and Stuart, 1958, p. 151), even though it may be subject to increased criticism from the theoretical point of view. In this way, asymmetry can appear, which makes the decision based on a μ and σ basis more difficult, except for some particular cases [as, for example, with the quadratic utility function—see Gómez-Bezares (1987, pp. 316–317)]. We cannot justify its use either, as we did with the normal distribution, on the basis of the central limit theorem. All this assumed, use of beta distribution has become very popular, because of its simplicity when making estimations and its flexibility when taking asymmetry into account. These are the main reasons for frequent use of the incomplete beta function in operations research and decision theory. Program evaluation and review technique (PERT) and simulation are some specific examples of the frequent use of beta distribution, and we will see that it also makes it easier to solve investment problems when risk is involved.

Beta distribution can be defined as follows:

$$f(X) = \frac{X^{m-1}(1 - X)^{n-1}}{\beta(m, n)} \qquad (m > 0, n > 0, 0 < X < 1) \tag{7}$$

To clarify, we convert the variable X, which takes values between 0 and 1, into Y so that $a < Y < b$; $Y = a + (b - a)X$. Hence,

$$f(Y) = \frac{(Y - a)^{m-1}(b - Y)^{n-1}}{\beta(m, n)(b - a)^{m+n-1}} \tag{8}$$

where the parameters that interest us are

$$\mu = \frac{an + bm}{m + n} \tag{9}$$

$$M \text{ (mode)} = \frac{a(n - 1) + b(m - 1)}{m + n - 2} \tag{10}$$

$$\sigma^2 = \frac{(b - a)^2 mn}{(m + n + 1)(m + n)^2} \tag{11}$$

[We assume $m > 1, n > 1$. If both m and n are <1, M gives a minimum or an antimode—see Rahman (1968, pp. 127–132).]

This distribution may be defined by four parameters (a, b, m, and n), although its interest lies in its ability to be defined by attributing values to the a, b, and M parameters. Obviously, anyone conversant with a variable can give the maximum value b, the minimum a, and the mode M. If the reader will consider his or her income for the coming year, the amount to be spent on holidays, and so on, there should be no difficulty in attributing the a, b, and M values to these variables.

To define the beta distribution with only three parameters, certain assumptions need to be made. Let $m = 3 + \alpha$ and $n = 3 - \alpha$ (see Chacón, 1973, pp. 229–231). As values a, b, and M are known, α can be found, whereupon the distribution is defined. In the case being considered here,

$$\mu = \frac{a + b + 4M}{6} \tag{12}$$

Some authors simplify even further and give α just two possible values: $-\sqrt{2}$ and $+\sqrt{2}$ [refer to PERT; see Hillier and Lieberman (1967, pp. 225–234)]. In this case, the parameters are

$$M = \frac{a(2 + \sqrt{2}) + b(2 - \sqrt{2})}{4} \tag{13}$$

or

$$M = \frac{a(2 - \sqrt{2}) + b(2 + \sqrt{2})}{4} \tag{14}$$

and

$$\sigma = \frac{b - a}{6} \tag{15}$$

If we opt for this system, it will in fact only be necessary to attribute values to parameters a and b in order to define the distribution and then choose whether the skewness is positive or negative.

A further possibility is to assume $m = A + \alpha$ and $n = A - \alpha$, whereupon Equations (9) through (11) become

$$\mu = \frac{[a(A - \alpha) + b(A + \alpha)]}{2A}$$

Therefore

$$\mu = \frac{a + b}{2} + \frac{\alpha(b - a)}{2A}$$

$$M = \frac{a(A - \alpha - 1) + b(A + \alpha - 1)}{2A - 2} \tag{16}$$

Therefore

$$M = \frac{a + b}{2} + \frac{\alpha(b - a)}{2A - 2} \tag{17}$$

$$\sigma^2 = \frac{(b - a)^2(A^2 - \alpha^2)}{(2A + 1)(2A)^2} \tag{18}$$

If the value of A is greater than 1, skewness will depend on the value of α, and where $\alpha = 0$, dispersion will be dependent on A. In order to attribute values to A and α, we need to attribute a value to the mode and make certain assumptions as to the concentration. One possible assumption is to say that $\sigma = (b - a)/6$ when $\alpha = 0 \Rightarrow 8A + 4 = 36, A = 4$.

The most accurate course of action would be to define a, b, M, and σ^2, but this is hardly feasible. The usual practice is to take a, b, and M as data for the purpose of attributing a value for A (e.g., 3) and then find α.

Assuming the beta distribution is thus revised, we can now suppose that NPV follows this distribution and that the PPV distribution leaves a 6.681% probability to its left ($t = 1.5$ in the standardized normal distribution). Simple models may be like the following three (where values for a and b are assumed):

1. Positive skewness, $m = 3 - \sqrt{2}$, $n = 3 + \sqrt{2}$. The mode is

$$M = \frac{a(2 + \sqrt{2}) + b(2 - \sqrt{2})}{4} \tag{19}$$

If this mode is regarded as being sufficiently accurate, by referring to the tables for this beta distribution,

$$\text{PPV} \approx a + 0.05(b - a) = 0.95a + 0.05b \tag{20}$$

2. Negative skewness, $m = 3 + \sqrt{2}$, $n = 3 - \sqrt{2}$. The mode is

$$M = \frac{a(2 - \sqrt{2}) + b(2 + \sqrt{2})}{4} \tag{21}$$

Again, if this mode is regarded as being sufficiently accurate, by referring to the tables for this beta distribution,

$$\text{PPV} \approx a + 0.45(b - a) = 0.55a + 0.45b \tag{22}$$

In either case, $\sigma = (b - a)/6$, as we have seen in Equation (15). If the same concentration is maintained, in the case of symmetric distribution, we have $A = 4$.

3. Symmetric, $m = n = 4$. The mode is in the center. By referring to the tables for this beta distribution,

$$\text{PPV} \approx a + 0.25(b - a) = 0.75a + 0.25b \tag{23}$$

This is the same as the case for the normal distribution [Equation (6)].

VI. PRACTICAL CONCLUSIONS AND AN EXAMPLE

Assuming the NPV criterion to be applicable, whatever distributions as may be deemed relevant may be taken for fund generation and the NPV distribution found (one way of achieving this is by simulation). If the final distribution is normal (or practically normal) and a linear penalization is admitted, Equation (3) may be applied:

$$\text{PPV} = \mu - t\sigma \tag{3}$$

Then, if $t = 1.5$, $\text{PPV} = \mu - 1.5\sigma$.

Simpler still is to attribute a maximum value b and a minimum value a for the NPV and then, on the basis of the asymmetry, select one or another of the three following equations:

$$M = \frac{a + b}{2} \qquad\qquad \text{PPV} = \frac{3a + b}{4} = 0.75a + 0.25b \tag{6}$$

$$M = \frac{a(2 + \sqrt{2}) + b(2 - \sqrt{2})}{4} \qquad \text{PPV} = 0.95a + 0.05b \tag{20}$$

$$M = \frac{a(2 - \sqrt{2}) + b(2 + \sqrt{2})}{4} \qquad \text{PPV} = 0.55a + 0.45b \tag{22}$$

Consider a project where, depending on fund generation, the NPV ranges between \$500,000 and −\$50,000 (the former being the most optimistic expectation and the latter being the least optimistic). To evaluate this as described above, we ask the experts to try and estimate its mode (around what value will the greatest probabilities exist?), and we offer three alternatives (figures in thousands):

$$M = (500 - 50)/2 = 225$$

$$M = [-50(2 + \sqrt{2}) + 500(2 - \sqrt{2})]/4 = 30.55$$

$$M = [-50(2 - \sqrt{2}) + 500(2 + \sqrt{2})]/4 = 419.45$$

If the first one is selected, PPV $= -50 \times 0.75 + 500 \times 0.25 = 87.5$. If the second one is selected, PPV $= -50 \times 0.95 + 500 \times 0.05 = -22.5$. If the third one is selected, PPV $= -50 \times 0.55 + 500 \times 0.45 = 197.5$.

Therefore, the project is found to be of interest in the first and the third of the above cases.

VII. THEORETICAL EPILOGUE

Starting from the Markowitz model, the usual procedure is to assume upsloping indifference curves with increasing slope (Tobin, 1958). If we assume indifference straight lines (as pieces into which curves are divided), we reach the decision criterion $\mu - t\sigma$.

When we assume normal distributions of the results, the meaning of the t parameter is obvious, and its estimation, although subjective, is relatively simple. On the other hand, the use of normal distributions makes it easier to justify the decision based on the (μ, σ) binomial.

If we know only the maximum and minimum values of the distributions, we can still assume (approximate) normality and estimate σ.

When considering the asymmetry, it is difficult to make a decision by taking into account only μ and σ. But if we accept it, the formulations based on the beta distribution can be very useful (with different possibilities for the different assumptions).

When taking into account a new project in an investment portfolio, the problem becomes more complicated, although it can be accurately treated with an adequate variation of the t parameter.

REFERENCES

CHACÓN, E. (1973). *Teoría de los Grafos* (Madrid: Ibérico-Europea)

COPELAND, T. E., and J. F. WESTON (1988). *Financial Theory and Corporate Policy*, (Reading, Mass.: Addison-Wesley).

GÓMEZ-BEZARES, F. (1987). "Criterios de Selección de Inversiones con Riesgo," *Boletín de Estudios Económicos*, 42, pp. 287–321.

GÓMEZ-BEZARES, F. (1988). "Decisioni di Investimento con Rischio," *L'Industria* 9, pp. 637–648.

GÓMEZ-BEZARES, F. (1989). *Dirección Financiera* (Bilbao: Desclée de Brouwer).

HALEY, C. W., and L. D. SCHALL (1979). *The Theory of Financial Decisions* (London: McGraw-Hill).

HILLIER, F. S., and G. J. LIEBERMAN (1967). *Introduction to Operations Research* (San Francisco: Holden-Day).

KENDALL, M. G., and A. STUART. *The Advanced Theory of Statistics*, vol. 1 (London: Griffin).

MARKOWITZ, H. (1952). "Portfolio Selection," *Journal of Finance* 7, pp. 77–91.

MARKOWITZ, H. (1959). *Portfolio Selection: Efficient Diversification of Investments* (New York: Wiley).

MARKOWITZ, H. (1987). *Mean-Variance Analysis in Portfolio Choice and Capital Markets* (Oxford: Basil Blackwell).

RAHMAN, N. A. (1958). *A Course in Theoretical Statistics* (London: Griffin).

TOBIN, J. (1958). "Liquidity Preference as Behavior Towards Risk," *Review of Economic Studies* 26, pp. 65–86.

VAN HORNE, J. C. (1986). *Financial Management and Policy* (Englewood Cliffs, N.J.: Prentice-Hall).

6

The Application
of the Lognormal Distribution
to Risk Analysis

Moon H. Lee*

ABSTRACT

This article explains the use of the lognormal probability distribution in Hertz's model of risk analysis. It describes a procedure for fitting a three-parameter lognormal distribution to three-level forecasts of an input variable. Behavioral support for the lognormal model is given. The differences between the output distribution generated by the lognormal model and Hertz's results are discussed.

I. INTRODUCTION

A recent survey by Pike (1989) reports that firms use a variety of techniques in analyzing risky capital projects, and that the trend is toward the use of sophisticated capital budgeting approaches over time.[1] He finds that there is a significant positive association between the application of sophisticated project evaluation techniques in practice and managers' assessments of the effectiveness of capital budgeting tools. Pike's survey results show that the wide assortment of capital budgeting tools

*I thank the referees and the editor for helpful comments.

used by firms ranges from simple methods of payback and average accounting rate of return to spreadsheet techniques (internal rate of return, net present value, adjustment of the hurdle rate for risk, and sensitivity analysis) and management science techniques such as computer simulation and probability analysis. While the above-mentioned simple capital budgeting tools and spreadsheet techniques remained popular, 40% of the firms in a sample of 100 firms used computer simulation to analyze project risks.

The simulation approach to project evaluation, which is known today as risk analysis, was originally developed by Hertz in 1964 in an article that has since become a *Harvard Business Review* reprint classic. Hayes (1975) observes that many management consulting firms offer risk analysis as one of their featured services. Projects that lend themselves to risk analysis tend to be large, strategic investments where the risks involved in undertaking them are substantial. Risk analysis has been applied to both private and public investments. Kalymon (1981) and Hertz and Thomas (1983, 1984) identify some application areas where risk analysis has been used. Because of the complexities of the risks involved, investment projects in the energy, defense, mining, high-technology, and manufacturing industries, and projects in the public sector of the economy, are prime candidates for analysis by simulation.

To use Hertz's simulation approach, the manager first identifies the input variables that affect cash flows, such as the size of the market for the product, the firm's market share, the product price, and variable and fixed costs of production. The manager then assigns subjective probabilities to possible values of these input data. Various random values of these data are then drawn and combined to give a probability distribution of rates of return on investment. Interdependencies, like the inverse relationship between product price and the quantity demanded, can be built into the simulation model.

Everett (1986) simplifies Hertz's approach by replacing the task of obtaining management's estimates of subjective probabilities with the use of the normal probability distribution to characterize the uncertainties of input variables. The normal probability distribution assumes that the random changes in a variable such as cost and quantity are additive. While the normal probability distribution is a good approximation in many situations where errors are distributed additively, a better probability distribution for describing financial and economic variables is the lognormal probability distribution. This probability distribution is derived for a process in which the observed value is a random proportion of the previous value of the variable, and so the changes in the variable are driven by a multiplicative process. It is a common phenomenon that the magnitude of a change in price or quantity demanded of a product is larger at a higher price or volume than the corresponding change when the price or volume is small. The price or quantity change tends to be proportional to the previous level of the price or quantity demanded of the product. Asset prices also seem to possess this property of the lognormal distribution, that is, the property of proportional effects.[2] Because of this desirable property, the lognormal distribution is frequently used in finance and economics. Financial researchers and economists have employed the lognormal probability distribution in cost-volume-profit analysis, cost and production functions, asset and option pricing models, portfolio selection models, and insurance claims analysis.

This article introduces use of the lognormal probability distribution in risk analysis. This distribution is chosen because of its economic rationale (it obeys the law of proportional effects) and because it is the most frequently cited distribution in the finance and economics literature. In Section II, a review of the finance and economics literature that employs the lognormal distribution is given. The theory and procedure for fitting a three-parameter lognormal probability function to three-level forecasts of input variables for use in risk analysis is described. The use of the lognormal probability distribution in risk analysis is illustrated with the case project analyzed by Hertz in Section III. The output distribution from this simulation is compared with the results obtained by Hertz. The differences in results are discussed, with particular attention paid to explaining why a continuous lognormal probability distribution is a better distribution to use than a subjectively assessed probability distribution in risk analysis. In Section IV a review is made of the literature that discusses the circumstances when the simulation approach to project risk appraisal is appropriate and the limitations of the use of the capital asset pricing model in project evaluation. Concluding remarks appear in Section V.

II. CHARACTERIZATION OF BUSINESS UNCERTAINTY

It is known that many real processes approximate certain standard theoretical probability distributions. In this section we discuss the justification for adopting the lognormal probability distribution to describe random processes that generate business data. We then develop the theory for fitting the three-parameter lognormal probability distribution to three-level forecasts of a random variable. An algorithm for estimating the lognormal parameters by a numerical method is described.

A. Practical Uses of the Lognormal Distribution

If a variable x is affected by many random causes, each of which produces a small effect proportional to x itself, the natural logarithm of x is approximately normal and x is distributed lognormally. This property of the lognormal distribution, that is, the law of proportional effects, is the reason why early authors found the lognormal distribution useful in modeling the variability of product prices and sales.

Aitchison and Brown (1957) cite many examples of use of the lognormal distribution to describe income statistics and physical and industrial processes. With respect to the applicability of the distribution to describe price data, they note (p. 102) that, "Expenditures on particular commodities, or the prices paid per unit of a commodity by individual families, are often approximately lognormal". Several other early authors have recorded their observations on the test of fit of the lognormal function to sales. Holt et al. (1960), for example, find the lognormal fit for sales data for electrical motor parts and cooking utensils to be good and conclude: "On the whole the evidence we have analyzed suggests that the lognormal distribution holds considerable promise as a useful approximation to the distribution of sales for many products, and this conclusion is supported by other investigators."[3] They offer practical reasons for the observed goodness-of-fit of the lognormal distribution to sales data as they note that "for the *a priori* considerations, it is not implausible to suppose that sales to any one customer in a period of time might be determined by the product rather than the sum of a great many different random factors."

The lognormal probability distribution is the distributional assumption for the popular translog cost function and the well-known Cobb-Douglas production function. Many empirical studies of cost and production functions have employed the translog and Cobb-Douglas cost functions and the Cobb-Douglas production function. These are the standard econometric forms for cost and production functions that are discussed in most economics texts as, for example, in Varian (1978). In a recent application, Banker, Conrad, and Strauss (1986) employ the translog cost function to make inferences about hospital costs. Marlin (1984) discusses the fit of the lognormal distribution to insurance claims data.

More contemporary authors have used the lognormal distribution to construct business decision-making, asset pricing, and portfolio selection models. Hilliard and Leitch (1975) employ the lognormal distribution to describe product prices, sales, and costs in a cost-volume-profit analysis. Lee and Rao (1988) derive a capital asset pricing model in a lognormally distributed securities market. Hilliard and Clayton (1982) discuss the expected geometric mean criterion in ranking investments which has its foundation in the lognormal distribution. The seminal paper on contingent claims pricing of Black and Scholes (1973) assumes stock prices follow a lognormal or geometric diffusion process. Lee, Rao, and Auchmuty (1981) derive an option pricing model that allows for discrete trading in a lognormal securities market. More recently, Naik and Lee (1989) price a stock index option in a jump-diffusion economy, where again the lognormal assumption is found to be useful. Last, Kroll and Levy (1986) find the lognormal probability function to be particularly attractive in formulating stochastic dominance rules for making asset choices. The many practical and analytical applications of the lognormal distribution in finance and economics make it a natural choice for use in analyzing risky capital projects.

B. Transformation of Skew Distributions

The lognormal distribution, like many probability distributions, is basically skew. It is theoretically possible to find a normal function z of a variable x, the distribution of which is skew. The skew distribution can then be transformed into a normal distribution. The cumulative distribution function $P(x)$ of the skew distribution may be written as

$$P(x) = \frac{1}{(2\pi)^{1/2}} \int_{-\infty}^{z} exp\left(\frac{-v^2}{2}\right) dv \tag{1}$$

$$= F(z)$$

where z is a function of x and v is a variable of integration.

The first derivative of Equation (1) gives the probability density function:

$$p(x) = \frac{1}{(2\pi)^{1/2}} exp\left(\frac{-z^2}{2}\right) dz \tag{2}$$

One practical form of z is given by

$$z = \frac{g(x) - m}{s} \tag{3}$$

where the transformation function $g(x)$ is normally distributed about a constant m with standard deviation s. The transformation function $g(x) = \ln(x - t)$, where t is another constant, is used in the derivation of the probability density function for the three-parameter lognormal distribution.

C. Three-Parameter Lognormal Distribution

Consider a random variable x such that a simple displacement of x, $x' = x - t$, is lognormally distributed. The range of x is $t < x < \infty$, where the location parameter t defines the lower bound value for x. Assume that the natural logarithm of $x - t$, that is, $\ln(x - t)$, is normally distributed with mean m and standard deviation s. Using the transformation function $g(x) = \ln(x - t)$, the cumulative distribution function is given by

$$P(x) = F(z) \qquad t \leq x < \infty \tag{4}$$

where $z = [\ln(x - t) - m]/s$.

The first derivative of Equation (4) with respect to x gives the probability density function:

$$p(x) = \frac{1}{s(x - t)\,(2\pi)^{1/2}}\, exp\left[\frac{\{-ln(x - t) - m\}^2}{2s^2}\right] \tag{5}$$

The density function is roughly depicted in Figure 6.1. The variable x has a positively skew, unimodal, continuous distribution which is completely specified by the three parameters m (scale parameter), s (shape parameter), and t (location parameter).

The lognormal fractiles of order j are obtained from

$$x_j = \exp(m + z_j s) + t \tag{6}$$

where z_j is the standard normal variate.

For example, the 0.1 and 0.9 lognormal fractiles are given by

$$x_{0.1} = \exp(m - 1.28s) + t$$

and

$$x_{0.9} = \exp(m + 1.28s) + t$$

Figure 6.1

The Lognormal Distribution.

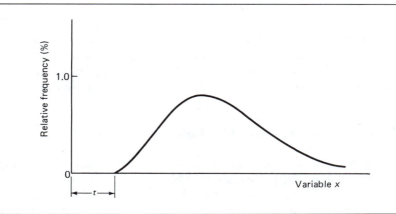

Equation (6) provides the basis for generating the three-parameter lognormal variate in simulation studies. In Appendix A we derive the equations for estimating m, s, and t from management's forecasts of a random variable, say product price, at three levels of accuracy: the most likely price and the pessimistic and the optimistic prices. An algorithm for solving numerically the three estimating equations is suggested in Appendix B.

III. A CASE EXAMPLE

The basic data used in the simulation runs were drawn from Hertz's article (1964) and are also found in Hertz and Thomas (1983); they are shown in Table 6.1. The project under study was a proposal to consider a $10 million extension to the existing facilities of a chemical processing plant for a medium-sized industrial chemical producer. The basic data can be grouped under three categories:

1. Market analyses, which gave forecasts of the total market size, the market growth rate, the firm's share of the market, and the selling price. These forecasts were subject to errors, as their values depended on future anticipations of consumer acceptance of the product.
2. Investment cost analyses, which gave estimates of the total investment required, the economic life of the facilities, and the salvage value of the facilities. These analyses took into account the service life and operating cost characteristics expected in the future, which were subject to error and uncertainty.
3. Operating and fixed cost analyses, which gave estimates of variable costs and overhead expenses, which were also subject to uncertainty.

Hertz's study was replicated with the lognormal distribution replacing subjective probabilities in quantifying the uncertainties in project variables. The algorithm shown in Appendix B was employed to estimate the values of the scale, shape, and location parameters of the lognormal distribution for the project variables shown in Table 1. Initial guesses of 0.1 and 0.2 for the shape parameter were used. The average number of iterations used to reduce the error function f_k to within 0.0001 was between five and nine. It took a few seconds of computer time to find the lognormal parameters for the nine input variables.

In this study 3600 simulated discounted cash flow computations were carried out. Hertz performed the same number of simulations. The computer CPU time required to perform this number of simulations is

TABLE 6.1   Basic Input Data[a]

INPUT VARIABLES	MOST LIKELY FORECASTS	PESSIMISTIC FORECASTS	OPTIMISTIC FORECASTS
Market size (tons)	250,000	100,000	340,000
Selling price ($/ton)	510	385	575
Market growth rate (per year)	0.03	0	0.06
Share of market	0.12	0.03	0.17
Total investment (million $)	9.5	7	10.5
Useful life of facilities (years)	10	5	15
Residual value (million $)	4.5	3.5	5
Variable costs ($/ton)	435	370	545
Fixed costs (thousand $)	300	250	375

[a] Pessimistic and optimistic forecasts represent approximately 1 to 99% probabilities; that is, there is a 1-in-100 chance that the value actually achieved will be less than the pessimistic forecast or greater than the optimistic forecast.

Source: Hertz (1964) and Hertz and Thomas (1983).

very modest on today's high-speed computers. The probability distribution of the simulated internal rates of return is shown in columns 1 and 2 in Table 6.2, and the distribution obtained by Hertz is shown in column 3. The distribution of lognormal-produced rates of return is plotted in Figure 6.2, and Hertz's results are plotted in Figure 6.3.

As can be seen from the two histograms in Figure 6.2 and 6.3, the distributions are dramatically different. The lognormal-produced distribution of internal rates of return is smooth and unimodal. These are desirable properties of a probability distribution. With a distribution of

TABLE 6.2   Probability Distribution of Rates of Return

PERCENT RETURN	RELATIVE FREQUENCY (%)	
	Lognormal Inputs	Hertz's Results[a]
0	8.1	3.5
5	13.3	15.9
10	21.9	5.4
15	22.4	21.4
20	16.4	10.8
25	10.5	30.4
30	4.7	12.6
>30	2.7	0.0

[a] The figures in column 3 are from Hertz (1964) and are also found in Hertz and Thomas (1983).

Figure 6.2

Histogram of rates of return (lognormal inputs).

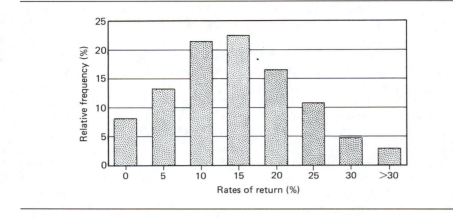

regular shape, it is meaningful to compute means, variances, and other parameters of the distribution. This histogram is skew to the right and has the general shape of a lognormal distribution. Since the majority of asset pricing models assume lognormality of security returns, and securities represent claims on the underlying real investments, it is important that the returns on real capital assets have the same distributional form

Figure 6.3

Histogram of rates of returns (Hertz's results).

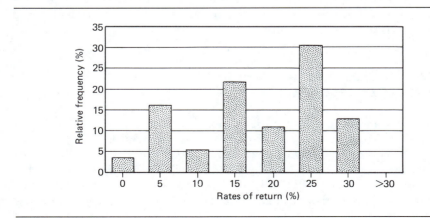

as the returns on securities. The lognormality of rates of return on investment has been found to be consistent with accepted theories of choice in asset selection. Hilliard and Clayton (1982) show that the portfolio that maximizes the expected geometric rate of return is optimal for investors with logarithmic utility. This utility function is widely employed in the literature on asset pricing. Kroll and Levy (1986) establish a lognormal efficient frontier in the application of stochastic dominance rules to portfolio decisions. The lognormal distributional assumption is consistent with the model of random walk. Wise (1966) points out the resemblance between the lognormal model and the random walk model. This establishes an interesting link between the lognormal distribution and efficient markets, since there is a close parallel between the concept of efficient capital markets and the random walk model.

In contrast, Hertz's distribution of internal rates of return shown in Figure 6.3 is lumpy and negatively skew. The distribution is multimodal. An arbitrary distribution of rates of return on investment obtained from simulation is not unexpected, since the distributional forms of input variables gathered from diverse sources are arbitrary and can take on odd shapes.[4] The subjectively assessed distributions for input variables often lack a consistent economic or theoretical foundation. A lumpy distribution of rates of return that is skew to the left is not supported by empirical evidence on returns on marketable assets. On other hand, the smooth, unimodal distribution in Figure 6.2 is a result of the use of a continuous well-behaved distribution function for input variables. The choice of the lognormal distribution for input variables is based on a behavioral rationale (the law of proportional effects), and the output distribution from the stimulation study resembles the distribution of security returns postulated by asset pricing models. For these reasons, it is felt that the lognormal probability distribution is a better distribution to employ in risk analysis than subjective probability distributions which are open to arbitrariness, a source of error that may change the output distribution significantly.

IV. THE MEASUREMENT OF RISK IN PROJECT EVALUATION

The measurement of risk in project appraisal is an unsettled issue. The relevant risk measure may be project-specific as well as being dependent on the other assets held by the firm's shareholders. A good discussion of these issues is provided by Kalymon (1981) and by Miller (1988). Kalymon first shows analytically that large-scale energy projects have very low systematic risk (a negative beta) in an oil-importing economy, while for an energy-self-sufficient economy energy projects have a beta risk of around 1. In examining the increasing dependence of the countries in the western world on oil imports, Kalymon argues that the importance of systematic risk in oil investments appears to have diminished and that nonsystematic risks as defined by the capital asset pricing model (CAPM) that arise from extraneous factors such as cartel oil pricing practices and government tax and subsidy policies cannot be ignored. The nonsystematic risk in the strict CAPM sense of energy projects may not in practice be eliminated by investors through portfolio diversification. He constructs a simulation model to show the impact of oil reserves, competition, and government taxation on nonsystematic risk. The nonsystematic risk is shown to be large and is highly influenced by a diverse set of technological, political, and market forces. The risk premium demanded by investors for energy investments is high if the nonsystematic risk or total project risk exposure is large. However, if investor behavior is guided by systematic risk as defined by the CAPM, investments in energy projects should be perceived to be of low risk, and, consequently, the rates of return required to induce energy investments should be quite low.

Miller (1988) considers first the case of a family-owned firm whose owners have no outside investments. He defines corporate risk as the degree of correlation of the returns from a capacity-expansion project with the returns from the capacity already owned. He argues that a family-owned firm will reject a profitable capacity-expanding investment if corporate risk is high. If the demand shrinks after the expansion is made, not only will the new investment be unprofitable, but the established business will be worth less. So the family will rationally choose not to expand. Miller next considers the case of a large corporation with owners who have optimally diversified. The risk to the shareholders of expansion by the firm depends on how the returns on the new investment correlate with the returns on the other investments owned by the stockholders. This depends partly on the competitive strength of the firm in the product market. If the firm's product market position is strong, so that there is little uncertainty about the capacity expansion being utilized, both the total risk and the systematic risk are small. If the firm has a weak market position, the sales from the capacity expansion are sensitive to general economic conditions. Such an investment has a high systematic risk.

In simulation or risk analysis, the usual presumption is that project or business risk is relevant to project value. The role of nonsystematic and systematic risks in value determination has not been completely resolved. Empirically, it is well known that security prices of firms traded on stock exchanges fail to support the CAPM. This implies that the unsystematic risk in the CAPM sense, either in part or in whole, of new investments undertaken by exchange-listed companies is priced in the capital market. We have discussed above a number of factors that can change the relative importance of systematic and unsystematic risks, described the relevance of these measures of risks to investor behavior, and drawn attention to the lack of an acceptable theory of valuation. Given this discussion, risk analysis is likely to be relevant to publicly traded corporations as well as to family-owned businesses.

V. CONCLUSION

The evaluation of risky projects is one of the principal corporate functions. Consequently, in this chapter we described a procedure for incorporating the lognormal distribution into Hertz's risk analysis model. We provided behavioral support for the use of this distribution and reviewed an extensive literature that has applied the lognormal distribution to the estimation of cost and production functions, the pricing of securities and derivative assets, and the derivation of optimal rules of choice. We reanalyzed the capital project described by Hertz and compared the resulting distribution of rates of return on investment with the distribution obtained by Hertz. We discussed the differences in the two distributions and supported our contention that it is preferable to use the lognormal distribution in project simulation than a subjectively determined distribution.

APPENDIX A: ESTIMATION OF THE PARAMETERS OF THE THREE-PARAMETER LOGNORMAL DISTRIBUTION

Consider two fractiles:

$$x_i = \exp(m + z_i s) + t$$

and

$$x_j = \exp(m + z_j s) + t$$

where $x_i < x_j$.

Then,

$$\frac{\ln(x_i - t) - m}{z_i} = \frac{\ln(x_j - t) - m}{z_j}$$

so that

$$m = \frac{z_j \ln(x_i - t) - z_i \ln(x_j - t)}{z_j - z_i} \tag{A1}$$

Since

$$\ln(x_i - t) - z_i s = \ln(x_j - t) - z_j s$$

then

$$s = \frac{\ln(x_j - t) - \ln(x_i - t)}{z_j - z_i} \tag{A2}$$

From Equation (A2),

$$t = \frac{x_j - x_i \exp[(z_j - z_i)s]}{1 - \exp[(z_j - z_i)s]} \tag{A3}$$

Now the mode of the lognormal distribution is given by

$$x_0 = \exp(m - s^2) + t \tag{A4}$$

Extracting m from Equation (A4), we have

$$m = \ln(x_0 - t) + s^2 \tag{A5}$$

Eliminating m from Equations (A1) and (A5) gives

$$s^2 = \frac{z_j \ln(x_i - t) - z_i \ln(x_j - t)}{(z_j - z_i) - \ln(x_0 - t)} \tag{A6}$$

For symmetric fractiles Equations (A3) and (A6) reduce to

$$t = x_i - x_{1-i} \exp(2zs)$$

and

$$s^2 = \frac{\ln(x_i - t) + \ln(x_{1-i} - t)}{2 - \ln(x_0 - t)}$$

where

$$z_j = -z_i = |z|$$

and

$$x_j = x_{1-i}$$

APPENDIX B: A NUMERICAL ALGORITHM

Assume that the most likely estimate x_0 and two outboard values x_i, the pessimistic estimate, and x_j, the optimistic estimate, of a variable are known.

The steps for the determination of m, s, and t by the Newton-Raphson iterative procedure are as follows:

1. Obtain the values of the standard normal variates z_i and z_j from a table of the standard normal distribution, corresponding to their cumulative probability values of i and j.
2. Make an initial guess of the value of s, say $s_1 = 0.1$.
3. With the assumed value s_1, compute t_1 from Equation (A3).
4. Left-hand side (LHS) of Equation (A6) = s_1^2.
5. Compute the right-hand side (RHS) of Equation (A6).
6. Define $f_1 = \text{RHS}_1 - \text{LHS}_1$.
7. Select another value of s, say $s_2 = 0.2$.
8. Repeat steps 3 through 6 and define $f_2 = \text{RHS}_2 - \text{LHS}_2$.
9. Use the Newton-Raphson method to select a better approximation of s:

$$s_{k+1} = \frac{s_k - f_k(s_k - s_{k-1})}{f_k - f_{k-1}}$$

10. Continue iterating until f_k is made as small as desired, say 0.0001.
11. With the final values of s and t, compute m from Equation (A5). Thus the Equations (A3), (A5), and (A6) have been numerically solved for m, s, and t.

NOTES

1. For references on other surveys on the use of capital budgeting tools in practice, see the bibliography given in Pike (1989) and Aggarwal (1980).
2. Theoretical probability distributions are derived on the basis of a behavioral assumption about the variable of interest. For example, the beta probability distribution permits representation of a random variable that takes on values over an identifiable interval with known upper and lower bounds. Therefore, the beta distribution is a useful probability model for describing the estimated time required to complete a project phase in PERT-CPM network scheduling or the proportion of defective units on a production line (0 to 1 interval). Even though the beta distribution can take on many shapes (symmetric, left or right skew), it lacks behavioral support for its use in risk analysis. There does not seem to be any literature on use of the beta distribution in other areas of finance or in economics.
3. See also Beckmann and Bobkoski (1958) and Food and Agriculture Organization (1960).
4. The experience of Kryzanowski, Lusztig, and Schwab (1972) in gathering subjective probabilities shows that business executives' perception of an expanding input variable is one for which the distribution is skew to the right.

REFERENCES

AGGARWAL, R. (1980). "Corporate Use of Sophisticated Capital Budgeting Techniques: A Strategic Perspective and a Critique of Survey Results," *Interfaces* 10 (April), pp. 31–34.

AGGARWAL, R., and L. A. SOENEN (1989). "Project Exit Value as a Measure of Flexibility and Risk Exposure," *Engineering Economist* 35 (Fall), pp. 39–54.

AITCHISON, J., and J. A. C. BROWN (1957). *The Lognormal Distribution* (Cambridge: Cambridge University Press).

BANKER, R. D., R. F. CONRAD, and R. P. STRAUSS (1986). "A Comparative Application of Data Envelopment Analysis and Translog Methods: An Illustrative Study of Hospital Production," *Management Science* 32 (January), pp. 30–44.

BECKMANN, M. J., and F. BOBKOSKI (1958). "Airline Demand: An Analysis of Some Frequency Distributions," *Naval Research Logistics Quarterly* 5 (March), pp. 43–51.

EVERETT, M. D. (1986). "A Simplified Guide to Capital Investment Risk Analysis," *Planning Review* 14 (July), pp. 32–36.

FOOD AND AGRICULTURE ORGANIZATION, UNITED NATIONS (1960). *World Demand for Paper to 1975* (Rome: United Nations).

HAHN, G. J., and S. S. SHAPIRO (1967). *Statistical Models in Engineering* (New York: Wiley).

HAYES, R. H. (1975). "Incorporating Risk Aversion into Risk Analysis," *Engineering Economist* 20 (Winter), pp. 99–121.

HERTZ, D. B. (1964). "Risk Analysis in Capital Investment," *Harvard Business Review*, 32 (January–February), pp. 95–106.

HERTZ, D. B. (1968). "Investment Policies That Pay Off," *Harvard Business Review*, 36 (January–February), pp. 96–108.

HERTZ, D. B., and H. THOMAS (1983). *Risk Analysis and Its Applications* (New York: Wiley).

HERTZ, D. B., and H. THOMAS (1984). *Practical Risk Analysis: An Approach Through Case Histories* (New York: Wiley).

HILLIARD, J. E., and R. J. CLAYTON (1982). "Obtaining and Parameterizing Multiperiod Portfolios with Desirable Characteristics Under Lognormal Returns," *Decision Sciences* 13 (April), pp. 240–250.

HILLIARD, J. E., and R. A. LEITCH (1975). "Cost-Volume-Profit Analysis Under Uncertainty: A Log Normal Approach," *Accounting Review* 50 (January), pp. 69–80.

HOLT, C. C., ET AL. (1960). *Planning Production, Inventories, and Work Force* (Englewood Cliffs: Prentice-Hall).

HULL, J. C. (1977). "The Input to and Output from Risk Evaluation Models," *European Journal of Operational Research* 1 (November), pp. 368–375.

JOHNSON, N. I., and S. KOTZ (1970). *Continuous Univariate Distributions*, 1 and 2 (Boston: Houghton Mifflin).

Kalymon, B. A. (1981). "Methods of Large Project Assessment Given Uncertainty in Future Energy Pricing," *Management Science* 27 (April), pp. 377–395.

Kroll, Y., and H. Levy (1986). "A Parametric Approach to Stochastic Dominance: The Lognormal Case," *Management Science* 32 (March), pp. 283–288.

Kryzanowski, L., P. Lusztig, and B. Schwab (1972). "Monte Carlo Simulation and Capital Expenditure Decisions—A Case Study," *Engineering Economist* 18 (Fall), pp. 31–48.

Kunz, K. S. (1957). *Numerical Analysis* (New York: McGraw-Hill).

Lee, C. F. (1985). *Financial Analysis and Planning: Theory and Application* (Reading, Mass.: Addison-Wesley).

Lee, M. H. (1967). "Statistical Transformation of Probabilistic Information." Master's Thesis, University of British Columbia.

Lee, W. Y., and R. K. S. Rao (1988). "Mean Lower Partial Moment Valuation and Lognormally Distributed Returns," *Management Science* 34 (April), pp. 446–453.

Lee, W. Y., R. K. S. Rao, and J. F. G. Auchmuty (1981) "Option Pricing in a Lognormal Securities Market with Discrete Trading," *Journal of Financial Economics* 9 (March), pp. 75–101.

Linter, J. (1965). "The Valuation of Risk Assets and the Selection of Risky Investments in Stock Portfolios and Capital Budgets," *Review of Economics and Statistics*, 47 (February), pp. 13–37.

Marlin, P. (1984). "Fitting the Log-Normal Distribution to Loss Data Subject to Multiple Deductibles," *Journal of Risk and Insurance* 51 (December), pp. 687–701.

Marshall, W. (1981). "The Capital Market Value of a Multiperiod Investment with the Option of Premature Abandonment," *Decision Sciences* 12 (October), pp. 612–622.

Miller, E. M. (1988). "On the Systematic Risk of Expansion Investment," *Quarterly Review of Economics and Business* 28 (Autumn), pp. 67–77.

Mullins, D. W., Jr. (1982). "Does the Capital Asset Pricing Model Work?," *Harvard Business Review* 60 (January–February), pp. 105–115.

Naik, V., and M. Lee. (1989). "General Equilibrium Pricing of Options on the Market Portfolio With Discontinuous Returns," Unpublished manuscript, Faculty of Commerce and Business Administration, University of British Columbia.

Naylor, T., et al. (1966). *Computer Simulation Techniques* (New York: Wiley).

Olkin, I., L. J. Gleser, and C. Derman (1978). *Probability Models and Applications* (New York: Macmillan).

Patel, J. K., C. H. Kapadia, and D. B. Owen (1976). *Handbook of Statistical Distributions* (New York: Dekker).

Pike, R. (1989). "Do Sophisticated Capital Budgeting Approaches Improve Investment Decision-Making Effectiveness?" *Engineering Economist* 34 (Winter), pp. 149–161.

Roll, R., and S. A. Ross (1984). "The Arbitrage Pricing Theory Approach to Strategic Portfolio Planning," *Financial Analysts Journal* (May–June) pp. 14–26.

Ross, S. A. (1976). "The Arbitrage Theory of Capital Asset Pricing," *Journal of Economic Theory* 13 (December), pp. 341–360.

Sharpe, W. F. (1964). "Capital Asset Prices: A Theory of Market Equilibrium Under Conditions of Risk," *Journal of Finance,* 19 (September), pp. 425–442.

Varian, H. R. (1978). *Microeconomic Analysis* (New York: Norton).

Wise, M. E. (1966). "Tracer Dilution Curves in Cardiology and Random Walk and Lognormal Distributions," *Acta Physiologica et Pharmacologica Neerlandica* 14, pp. 175–204.

7

Managerial Risk Preferences and Investment Decisions Under Uncertainty: A Gamma Preference Framework

BARRY N. STEDMAN AND YONG H. KIM

ABSTRACT

A classic problem confronted by any decision maker is incomplete knowledge regarding the outcome of a particular investment. While the capital asset pricing model and the efficient market theory suggest that risky investments can be evaluated by using the systematic risk and expected return of the investment, there may be sufficient caveats in some situations to require an analysis of total risk. In such cases the decision maker can evaluate different investments by comparing their distributions of return, but it is often impossible to make investment decisions without resorting to subjective utility functions or other complex measures of determining risk preference. Further, it is not possible to evaluate a single investment in isolation without resorting to comparisons with criteria developed from references to other investments or utility functions. This article proposes that the gamma distribution can be interpreted as a model that captures a manager's perspectives or an individual's risk preferences. It can be used as a benchmark in selecting a single investment in isolation or from among several mutually exclusive investments, or even to select the most effective strategies for accomplishing a specific invest-

ment. Thus the decision maker does not have to resort to utility functions when selecting among risky investments.

I. INTRODUCTION

The decision to invest in an asset whose actual return is unknown is a familiar subject in both financial theory and financial practice. There exist numerous models for decision making under risk and uncertainty; but all have distinct limitations in theory, in practice, or in both. Most decision models and criteria assume that at least two mutually exclusive assets are under consideration. That is, the assets will consume part (or all) of the same resources, and the decision maker will select the invest- ment yielding the highest level of utility given the cost of the resources to be consumed. If the principle of Fisher separation holds, investment decisions regarding production and financing are simplified greatly into a two-step process with an objective market criterion of maximizing wealth that does not consider an individual's subjective preferences. This condition occurs only if capital markets are efficient to the extent that transaction costs are negligible and the borrowing rate is equal to the lending rate. The implication is that production/investment deci- sions of firms can be delegated to managers since all will make the same decision regardless of the shape of each individual's indifference curve. If transaction costs are nontrivial, the principle of Fisher separation is invalidated and the individual's indifference curve (and therefore utility function) becomes important. Thus while the theory of finance and in- vestment decision making is simplified by assuming that the necessary market conditions exist for the separation principle to hold, this assump- tion may not be valid in the real world.

If markets are frictionless in that transaction costs are trivial, the capital market line can be formulated as a linear, efficient set of assets. Other assumptions about the divisibility and marketability of assets, ho- mogeneous opportunity sets for all investors, and maximization of ex- pected utility of wealth by investors permit development of the capital asset pricing model (CAPM). In this model the only relevant risk in determining the value of an asset is its systematic risk or covariability with the performance of the market as a whole. The total risk of the asset does not need to be considered if the unsystematic (nondiversifiable) risks are small and partly offsetting, or if these risks can be reduced to a negligible level by contractual means. For example, when a firm insures capital assets against noneconomic outcomes (earthquakes, fires, floods, etc.) or hedges commodity prices that might vary as a function of weather conditions, the firm is engaging in total risk considerations. By reducing or eliminating these significant noneconomic risks, the firm is able to consider systematic risk as the only relevant measure of market value. If a firm believed that only systematic risk is relevant to value, it would never purchase insurance or engage in any form of hedging, because unsystematic risks could be diversified away more effectively by the firm's shareholders. The substantial activity in commodity and insurance markets suggests that firms do reduce large, unsystematic risks (not only catastrophic events but also outcomes that cause substantial variations in profitability).

The importance of total risk also holds for an individual manager who may control only one or a few major investment projects in a firm with a fully diversified portfolio of many assets. It has been shown, both theoretically and empirically (Fama, 1976), that the standard deviation of returns of a portfolio of securities decreases asymptotically to the average covariance of all securities as the number of securities increases, and that most diversification benefits can be obtained with only 10 to 15 securities. With only a few assets, the manager is presented with an investment portfolio whose total variance is comprised of a significant proportion of individual asset variances; and in this situation the total variance of each asset becomes more important. If the manager's performance is measured by the performance of the few assets under his or her control, it may be reasonable to expect investment decisions to be aimed at maximizing his or her own utility by considering risks other than systematic risk.

For a firm with only a few major assets, the relevant risk may be total risk. The firm could well be bankrupted or severely disrupted by unsystematic risk—a chance that no manager would willingly take solely on the basis of a financial theory that argues that individual investors can diversify unsystematic risk away more efficiently than the firm. The presence of real agency costs supports this hypothesis.

Lessard and Shapiro (1985) have proposed that systematic risk may not be the appropriate measure of risk for multinational corporations. For these firms, total risk is the relevant measure because diversifiable risks may be so extensive as to have a significant influence on the expected level of cash flow. This variability can affect access to credit as well as the long-term operation of the firm since managers are reluctant to take advantage of opportunities. Lessard and Shapiro "rewrite" the objective functions of some multinational firms to include a penalty factor so that the value of the firm declines as the variability of the cash flow increases. They observe that a firm might reduce unsystematic risk by insuring and hedging its operations to eliminate major risk variables: for example, changes in commodity prices or foreign exchange rates. These hedging contracts and insurance would be priced efficiently according to the CAPM and would reduce the total risk by decreasing the penalty factor.

Determining the benefits of some risk management strategies requires analysis of total risk in a risk preference framework. Even though unsystematic risk can be diversified away by individual investors, the efficiency of market-priced insurance and hedging may be superior. Risk management strategies reduce the risk of an investment, but the decision to pursue such a course of action depends entirely on the relationship between the cost of reducing the total risk and the risk premium the individual decision maker is prepared to pay. Determining the risk premium for an individual requires knowledge of that individual's utility function.

In all these situations, we are concerned with total risk and the risk preference of either the firm or an individual investment manager. Problems arise as to the nature of subjective preferences for risk and the form of the utility function that facilitates the reconciliation of risk and return. Attempts to specify utility functions have not been very successful for two reasons: The shapes of these functions varying from one individual to another, and difficulty in describing the trade-off between wealth and utility.

In addition, the existing decision framework does not adequately address the problem of investing in projects that arise over time. For example, a project may arise at one point in time, and the decision may have to be made either to invest in the project or to "bank" the resources until a superior project comes along. This is not to imply capital rationing; but there will always be other investments, and the decision maker should have a technique for considering a single project in isolation, apart from the decision to invest or bank the resources. These decisions are generally made using techniques that employ evaluation benchmarks such as a minimum-hurdle rate of return or a net present value (after discounting at an appropriate required rate) greater than or equal to zero.

Assets with uncertain returns can be evaluated by using summary measures of the distribution of returns. However, using the measures of expected value and standard deviation (or the mean-variance approach of Markowitz) in isolation implicitly assumes that the distribution of returns is normal or that utility curves are quadratic. In all other cases, these two summary measures do not evaluate fully the level of risk over the range of returns because they do not describe the distribution completely. The addition of higher-order moments, including skewness, creates several problems such as difficulties in interpretation and communication of these measures to upper-level management (Rosenthal, 1978). The limitations of mean-variance approaches are pronounced when the distributions are highly skewed or multimodal. In these situations the entire distribution must be evaluated. Some other techniques of analyzing investments with uncertain returns are second-order (and third-order) stochastic dominance, the $\alpha - t$ model[1] developed by Fishburn (1977), and the three-parameter risk measure of Stone (1973). While these techniques reflect utility theory and evaluate the form of the distribution, only the models of Fishburn (e.g., McKenna and Kim, 1986) and Stone can consider many different attitudes toward risk.[2] However, these models consider only downside risk below a target or specified level of return.

Yet another approach is that used by Buck and Askin (1986). They have suggested that risk has two dimensions: exposure, which is measured by the probability of encountering undesirable consequences, and the nature of the undesirable consequences. They employ a partial mean as a measure of downside risk, where the partial mean is the expected value of a random variable conditioned on its falling in a specified range.

It should be possible to evaluate a project's distribution of possible returns with respect to a desired profile (a preferred distribution) of returns established by the individual decision maker or imposed as corporate policy. The desired profile of returns is a benchmark (not unlike a minimum-hurdle rate of return) that can be compared to the estimated profile of risky investments and evaluated by using a technique such as stochastic dominance. The objective of this chapter is to provide such a model so that decisions can be made for projects arising over time, or for selection among mutually exclusive projects without direct recourse to utility functions. Capital budgeting decisions can then be made by fully evaluating the entire distribution of returns on an investment in the context of a specific risk preference profile.

Section II employs a heuristic approach in examining the risk preferences of decision makers, given the incentive structures confronting them, and proposes the gamma function as a robust model for a risk-averse decision maker's risk preference profile. However, it should be noted that other distributional forms also can be used as models of the risk preference profile. Section III reviews some of the specific properties of the gamma distribution, and Section IV examines techniques for evaluating the gamma preference function model and the distribution of returns for an investment. Section V illustrates the use of the gamma preference function in a hypothetical decision to invest in a capital asset such as real property. The conclusion and avenues for further exploration are presented in Section VI.

II. RISK PREFERENCE

This section is applicable to both the individual investor and the manager of a firm who may be considering investing in financial or real assets. It accepts the proposition that there exist real agency costs and that decision makers act so as to maximize the wealth of shareholders, subject to their own behavioral constraints. As a result, there is a system of incentives and disincentives that motivate people in deciding to invest. It includes not only direct rewards and punishments of monetary value but also changes in status as perceived by others and changes in the individual's self-esteem. The structure of this retribution system and the value or utility placed on different incentives and disincentives help to determine managerial (or individual) perspectives on investment decisions.

In the real world, decision makers act within the constraints placed on them so as to maximize their individual utilities. The utility function of managers is a function of wealth, and wealth is a function of penalties and bonuses that result from performance. Although the appropriate incentive can convert non-wealth-maximizing managers to wealth-maximizing managers, it assumes that all incentives are valued identically by all managers and that all have the incentive necessary to motivate them to wealth-maximizing performances. Assuming complete homogeneity of managers is unrealistic; therefore, agency costs vary from one individual to the next. If these agency costs did not exist, there would be no need to recognize outstanding performances or to penalize failures. However, the prevalence of bonuses for managers suggests that their investment decisions are made in response to the perceived retribution structure of the organization.

If a manager believes that an investment achieving an actual return less than some target amount will result in some form of personal penalty from the firm, such as a loss of status or a transfer, then the investment will be assigned a low level of utility. On the other hand, if an investment achieving a return in excess of some specified amount will produce a reward, perhaps in the form of direct remuneration (such as a bonus) or acknowledgment of outstanding performance, then it will be assigned a higher level of utility. At some level of return, there is neither reward nor penalty, and the decision maker is indifferent. The investment decisions of a firm are a direct consequence of the incentives (both positive and negative) for performance and the personal utility functions of its managers. For the individual investor, the opportunities for direct gains and losses in wealth provide the incentives that motivate investment decisions.

The actual levels of utility assigned by the decision maker depend on that individual's utility function. Concave, convex, linear, or S-shaped utility functions modify the response to a specific reward or punishment. To suggest that a decision maker is concerned only with downside risk as embodied in risk measures such as the semivariance and the $\alpha - t$ model means that the decision maker is considering segments of the utility function relating to the portion of the distribution of possible outcomes below a target level. This implies a primary concern for trying to avoid the punishment or loss of wealth resulting from a failure to attain the target or required level of return. Clearly, this is not so, since the opportunity to receive rewards that accrue from outstanding performance is also a significant driving force behind the actions of most decision makers. The decision to invest is therefore a trade-off between the potential for loss and gain of utility; and for most decision makers, the trade-off reflects risk-averse behavior. Accordingly, we are concerned with developing a risk preference function for risk-averse individuals. However, since the degree of risk-averse behavior varies from one individual to another, it is necessary for the risk preference function to be adaptable in order to reflect different trade-off relationships.

The indifferent return is the level of return a decision maker can achieve without incurring a loss or receiving a reward. It is the target return. Returns below this level yield increasing dissatisfaction, while those above it yield increasing satisfaction. The preference for (or the utility derived from) different levels of return can be seen as the desired probability of obtaining specific returns. Over all possible returns, the preferences or probabilities generate a distribution that implicitly reflects both the individual's utility function and the incentives available. This relationship will be referred to as the preference function.

If the marginal utility of wealth is positive but decreasing, returns above the indifference level will reflect marginally decreasing desirability. At all times, a higher return is preferred to a lower one, assuming that higher levels of performance are continuously reinforced by the system of incentives. If human wants can never be satisfied completely, all returns above the indifference level will be desirable to some degree. That is, the preference function is asymptotic and unbounded on the right-hand side of the target return (if the firm is not restricted in its ability to reward the individual manager).

While the assumption of diminishing marginal utility of returns for values greater than the target or indifference level simplifies the form of the upper segment of the preference function, the form of the lower segment of the preference function is more difficult to substantiate. Assumptions about the utility function and the individual's subjective response to disincentives are critical. The individual's ability to accept failure, loss of status and economic position, and even humiliation is important. While the general conditions of positive but decreasing marginal utility also apply to returns below the indifference level, the preference function may not be asymptotic and unbounded on the left-hand side.

There are several possible scenarios that can be employed. In the first scenario, the decision maker can experience diminishing marginal utility throughout the range of all possible returns. The implication of this scenario is that the decision maker not only prefers more wealth (or reward) to less but also abhors failure in an ever-increasing manner.

Most alternatives to this scenario reflect changes in the rate at which the individual's utility or disutility declines. For example, a manager with a low tolerance for failure experiences a greater decline in utility for returns below the target level than a manager with a high tolerance for failure. It may be that for some (high-achieving) individuals, any retrograde step is totally unacceptable. In this case, the decision maker prefers an investment whose distribution of returns is truncated at the target level.

Finally, the decision maker may consider returns below the target down to a specified level; that is, a minimum return level exists below which it does not matter if investment returns fall. If a firm is restricted in its ability to punish a manager for failure to achieve a specified rate of return, for a rate of return below this level there is no disincentive, and no utility or preference can be assigned to it. For the individual investor, the minimum return is limited to the extent of the resources invested (implying a return of -100%), although some risk-averse decision makers resist any loss of resources. This does not mean that an investment with a distribution that is partly below the minimum level will not be accepted. It does mean that investment returns less than the minimum level will be assigned a zero value in the preference function and will bias against the selection of that investment.

The rate of decline of the preference function on either side of the target return depends on the incentive system for performance and the utility function of the individual, so that it may not be unimodal. For example, if a manager believes that success in a particular venture, evidenced by achieving a specified rate of return, leads to a highly prized promotion, the corresponding return will be accorded a higher probability or desirability of occurrence. This may be equated to an S-shaped utility function; but for our purposes we will be concerned only with monotonic, decreasing marginal utility. It can be argued that for institutional decision makers the preference function may be discontinuous, the steps representing the various levels of incentives provided by the organization. However, we will assume that incentives are "divisible" in order to obtain a continuous preference function.

The preference function is a direct reflection of the individual's utility function because the utilities associated with each level of return and the corresponding incentive have been considered in the assignment of probability values to different levels of returns.

The model proposed in this article identifies three decision criteria that confront the individual in making the decision to proceed with an investment:

1. What is the minimum return that can be accepted? Returns less than this amount will have a probability or desirability of occurrence of 0%.
2. What is the target return on investments of this risk type? This return must occur most frequently and is defined as the mode of the preference function.
3. What is the probability or desirability that returns can fall below or should exceed the target return?

These three criteria are necessary and sufficient to describe the risk preference function if it is assumed to take the form of the gamma distribution. The criteria directly consider the risk preference of the individual decision maker and reflect his or her response to incentive/retribution. Consider, for example, two people who have the same target return but different levels of risk aversion. A high aversion to risk is identified by a high probability of (or preference for) returns occurring at and around the target level. The individual who is more risk-averse has a higher minimum return and therefore a smaller range between the minimum return and the target return. A decision maker who is more ambitious and less risk-averse has a greater desire that returns exceed the target level and is less averse to the possibility of a lower minimum return.

A recent empirical study of risk taking by managers identifies two focal values that are frequently mentioned as requiring attention (March and Shapira, 1987). The target level for performance (or breakeven point) is the same as the target level or indifference return used in this model. The other value is a survival level which can be equated to the minimum level of return. March and Shapira observe that "these two reference points partition possible states into three: success, failure, and extinction. . . ."

The observation is valid for the gamma preference function wherein returns below the minimum result in extinction, returns between the target and the minimum return represent economic failure, and returns that exceed the target indicate success of the investment. March and Shapira also consider an additional factor: the desire to succeed (or avoid failure) given the position of indifference as essential for understanding the behavior of most managers in undertaking investments having uncertain outcomes. This value corresponds to the probability or desirability that returns exceed the target level in the gamma preference function.

It should be noted that the gamma distribution is not the only distribution that fulfills these criteria. While many distributions with three parameters will suffice (e.g., the Weibull distribution), the gamma distribution has two advantages: First, it is parsimonious in its parameters; and second, it is very flexible in form and is able to represent a wide range of individual investment behavior.[3] Adding more parameters may improve the goodness of fit of the function to be used as a model of investment behavior, but it does not necessarily justify the added complexity. The gamma distribution meets the minimum criteria for decision making as revealed by real management experiences (March and Shapira, 1987).

III. THE GAMMA DISTRIBUTION

The probability density function generated by the gamma-type random variable has the form

$$f(y) = \begin{cases} \dfrac{y^{\alpha-1}e^{-y/\beta}}{\beta^{\alpha}\Gamma(\alpha)} & \text{for } \alpha, \beta > 0.0, \\ 0.0 \text{ elsewhere} & 0.0 \leqq y < \infty \end{cases} \tag{1}$$

where α = shape parameter and β = scale parameter. The expression $\Gamma(\alpha)$ is the gamma function:

$$\Gamma(\alpha) = \int_0^{\infty} y^{\alpha-1}e^{-y}\,dy$$

If α is an integer, $\Gamma(\alpha)$ is equal to $\alpha - 1$.

This distribution has a skewed unimodal form with the majority of the area under the function located close to the origin. As y increases after the mode, the right-hand tail becomes asymptotic. The distribution has the ability to acquire a varied form by modifying the shape parameter α and the scale parameter β. The location of the distribution can be varied by including a third parameter or by simply transforming the distribution to have the origin at $y = 0.0$.

The form of the distribution determined by the three decision criteria established in the preceding section is unique; that is, these criteria are the only constraints that must be considered in generating a specific gamma preference function that represents the risk return preferences of the decision maker.

The first constraint, the minimum level of return, establishes the origin of the distribution. The distribution can be transformed to have the origin at 0.0 simply by adding or subtracting this value.

The second constraint, the target return, is the mode of the distribution. The mode measures the location of the return value that occurs most frequently and is the maximum ordinate of the gamma distribution. This value is used to generate the scale parameter β according to the formula

$$\beta = \frac{\text{mode (or target)}}{\alpha - 1.0}$$

The third constraint is the cumulative probability (or desirability) that returns fall below the target level or, alternatively, the probability that returns exceed the target level. The probability value is used to generate the shape parameter α. Because the integral does not exist in closed form, determining the value of the shape parameter requires complex calculations involving an iterative process for the gamma distribution. This third constraint is defined within the limits

$$0.0 \leq \Pr(y) \leq 0.5$$

In a practical application of the gamma distribution to the risk preference function, the limits are even more restrictive. The gamma density function [Equation (1)] value is very sensitive to changes in the shape parameter, increasing dramatically as the value of the shape parameter increases. The physical limits of the computer being used restrict the value of the shape parameter, so that the maximum probability level is somewhat less than .5. As the probability level approaches .5, the shape parameter approaches infinity and the form of the distribution approaches the normal distribution. The shape parameter also depends on the position of the mode or target level. The shape parameters for different probability levels are shown in Table 7.1 for a scale parameter held constant at 1.0. Figure 7.1 indicates shape parameters for varying levels of the mode, and Figure 7.2 indicates the scale parameters for varying levels of the mode.

TABLE 7.1 α Values and Cumulative Probabilities From the Origin to the Mode

α (SHAPE)	β (SCALE)	MODE (TARGET)	CUMULATIVE PROBABILITY OF y < MODE	ORDINATE
1.0	1.0	0.0	.0	1.0
2.0	1.0	1.0	.2715	0.367
3.0	1.0	2.0	.3287	0.270
4.0	1.0	3.0	.3572	0.224
5.0	1.0	4.0	.3751	0.195

Figure 7.1

Model parameters. α values (for probability 2.5 to 35%, mode = 1, 2, 3).

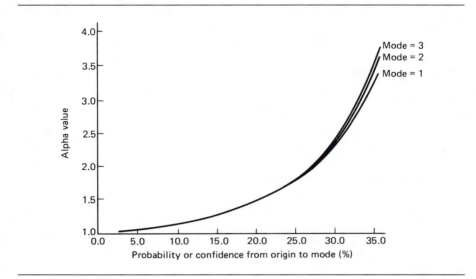

Figure 7.2

Model parameters. β values (for probability 2.5 to 35%, mode = 1, 2, 3).

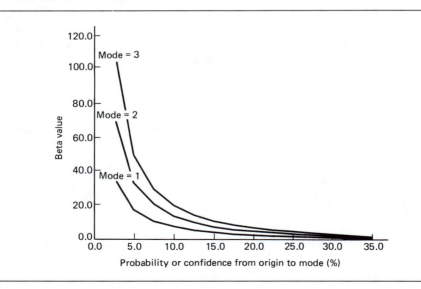

IV. EVALUATION

The evaluation of an estimated distribution of returns for an investment in the framework of the gamma preference function requires techniques that evaluate the distributions over a relevant range for the investment. Some possible techniques may include high-order moments to capture the effect of skewness, or stochastic dominance to evaluate the entire distribution. Stochastic dominance techniques also can be used for evaluating a risky investment when the gamma preference function is considered a benchmark distribution. However, in a gamma preference function framework, no further adjustment is required to capture the effects of differing degrees of risk aversion since the function captures an individual's preferences for different levels of returns. Accordingly, the conditions of stochastic dominance may not have to be satisfied entirely. The investment will be accepted if its cumulative distribution F is "superior" to that of the gamma preference function G.

The two distributions are evaluated up to an extreme limit on the right-hand side. Tests of the gamma preference function have produced consistent results when the limit is established at a point where 99.9% of one distribution has accumulated.[4] A decision rule that selects the distribution that stochastically dominates the other by having the lowest accumulated area under the cumulative probability distribution to the extreme limit has been studied in preliminary tests of the gamma preference function. This criterion is not that of second-order stochastic dominance, which requires the total area of $F(x) - G(x)$ to the left of any point to be nonpositive for the distribution of the investment to dominate the gamma preference function and, therefore, be preferred by the decision maker. That is, for the distribution of the investment to dominate (or be accepted), the gamma preference function by second-order stochastic dominance at some specified level a must be positive, that is

$$\int_{-\infty}^{a} [F(x) - G(x)] \, dx \leq 0.0$$

where the strong inequality must hold for some value of x.

If the distributions cross once, then for G to dominate F, the expected value of G must be greater than or equal to F (Vickson, 1975). But if the graphs of the cumulative probability distributions cross more than once, the conditions may not hold and higher-order forms of stochastic dominance may be required to evaluate the distributions. The gamma preference function may eliminate[5] this constraint, so that the test becomes

$$\int_{-\infty}^{x} F(x) - G(x) \, dx > 0.0$$

where x is the extreme limit of the distributions.

The value of this test indicates the relative preference for the investment and can be compared to the values generated by evaluating other assets using the same benchmark.

V. ANALYSIS USING THE GAMMA PREFERENCE FUNCTION

The ability of the gamma preference function to select among risky assets is demonstrated using the following hypothetical investment in real property. Stochastic dominance is utilized to evaluate the investment using the gamma preference function as a benchmark.

A firm is considering real property as an investment and uses the decision criteria of an expected rate of return of about 13% and a maximum total risk level or standard deviation of 3%. The firm has established a minimum rate of return of 5% for any investment, reflecting a high level of risk aversion. It would like to see at least 60% of its projects exceed the target rate of return of 12%. These three latter criteria establish the form of the gamma (or risk) preference function illustrated in Figure 7.3.

Figure 7.3

Distribution for a hypothetical project.

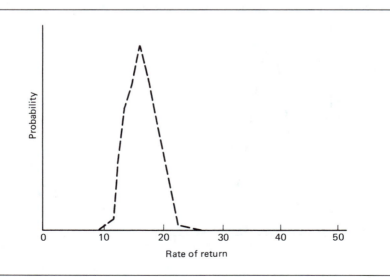

Monte Carlo simulation was used to obtain the distribution of rates of return shown in Figure 7.4. About 50% of the time, the return on the investment will be less than or equal to the most frequently obtained rate of return of 16.5%. The mean of the distribution is 16.0%, and the standard deviation is 1.6%.

The results of first-order and second-order stochastic dominance analysis are illustrated in Figure 7.5. This investment can be accepted by the first-order stochastic dominance criterion. If the firm wants a higher percentage of its projects to exceed the target return, for example, 70% instead of 60% (Figure 7.6), neither first-order nor second-order stochastic dominance conditions hold; and the investment cannot be accepted. If the risk preference of the decision maker is such that the minimum return is 0.0%, the target is 12.0%, and 60% exceeded the target (Figure 7.7), first-order stochastic dominance does not hold. Under these decision conditions, the firm has a desired expected return of about 13.8% and a standard deviation of about 4.2%. Second-order stochastic dominance does not hold through the range of returns, although the investment project dominates the gamma preference function at all return levels above approximately 16%. At the extreme limit, the investment project is marginally dominant. The results of these decision conditions are shown in Figure 7.8.

Figure 7.4

Gamma preference function. Minimum, 5%; target, 12%; probability, 40%.

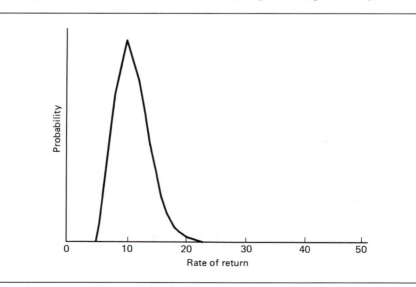

Figure 7.5

Stochastic dominance analysis. Gamma preference function: Minimum, 5%; target, 12%; probability, 40%.

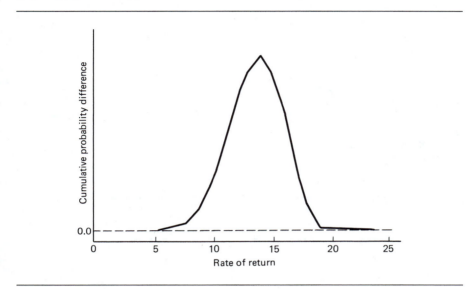

Figure 7.6

Gamma preference function. Minimum, 5%; target, 12%; probability, 30%.

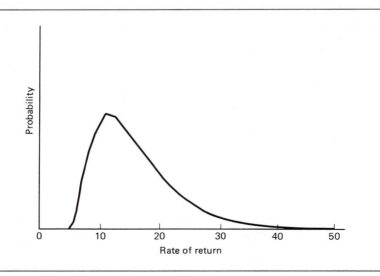

Figure 7.7

Gamma preference function. Minimum, 0%; target, 12%; probability, 40%.

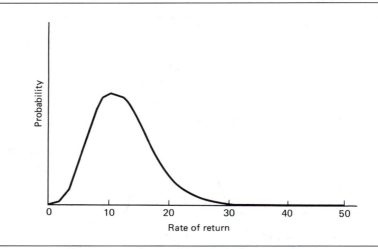

Figure 7.8

Stochastic dominance analysis. Gamma preference function: Minimum, 5%; target, 12%; probability, 30%.

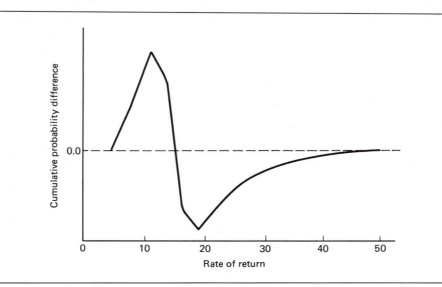

VI. CONCLUSION

The gamma preference function can be employed as a model of a risk-averse decision maker's risk preference. In a nonportfolio context, it represents the desired profile or ideal distribution of returns for any project. The distribution of returns for an investment, when obtained through a method of analysis such as simulation, can then be compared to the gamma preference function by using an analytical tool such as stochastic dominance to determine the acceptability of the project.

The gamma preference function discussed in this chapter has been restricted to the examination of total risk and has not been explored from the perspective of portfolio theory. It has not been the intention here to contradict standard finance theory of portfolio diversification but rather to suggest a direction for further exploration. Additional research is required in this area if the gamma preference function is to be applied comprehensively to the selection of investments. In this regard, Lee and Rao (1988) have explored the valuation of uncertain investments in a capital asset pricing model context, measuring risk as semideviation or semivariance for second-order and third-order stochastic dominance models, respectively. Their mean lower-partial-moment model might be applied to the gamma preference function framework to avoid the computational difficulties of stochastic dominance rules in portfolio choice problems.

Unlike other decision models, the gamma preference function does not require two or more projects to be evaluated at the same point in time. The technique can consider a single project in isolation since it depends only on the individual's (or the manager's preferences for returns. It provides a benchmark for the comparison and ranking of investments. All that is required is knowledge about the *minimum acceptable return, the return preferred to occur most often, and the desirability (or probability) of returns falling below or exceeding this desired return.* The gamma preference function is a decision technique that reflects more information on the decision maker's attitudes toward risk and return. It is intuitively appealing and operationally promising.

NOTES

1. The $\alpha - t$ model developed by Fishburn quantifies the risk (as semivariance) below a specified target return by weighting the deviations by a measure α of the decision maker's risk preference. If α is greater than 1.0, then the decision maker is risk-averse, while a value less than 1.0 is identified with risk-seeking behavior. The model has the form

$$\int_{-\infty}^{t} (x_n - t)^\alpha \, d_n$$

where t = target and α = measure of risk preference.

2. For a risk-averse decision maker, if one asset has second-order stochastic dominance, then it will be preferred to the other(s) regardless of the specific form of the utility function. However, second-order stochastic dominance does not consider degrees of risk-averse behavior.

3. For a discussion of other distributional forms, see Johnson and Katz (1970).

4. The limit of 99.9% is used because the gamma preference function is unbounded on the right-hand side, while the estimated distribution of the investment is contained within a fixed range resulting from the simulation process.

5. We have undertaken some testing of the gamma preference function and have determined that this condition holds. However, additional research must be undertaken to ascertain the validity of the test as demonstrated here.

REFERENCES

BUCK, JAMES R., and RONALD G. ASKIN (1986). "Partial Means in the Economic Risk Analysis of Projects," *Engineering Economist* 23, pp. 189–212.

FAMA, E. F. (1976). *Foundations of Finance* (New York: Basic Books.

FISHBURN, PETER C. (1987). "Generalization of Expected Utility Theories: A Survey of Recent Proposals," adapted from Peter C. Fishburn, *Nonlinear Preference and Utility Theory* (Baltimore: Johns Hopkins University Press).

FISHBURN, PETER C. (1977). "Mean-Risk Analysis With Risk Associated With Below-Target Returns," *American Economic Review* 67, No. 2 (March), pp. 116–126.

JEAN, WILLIAM (1975). "Comparison of Moment and Stochastic Dominance Ranking Methods," *Journal of Financial and Quantitative Analysis* 10 (March), pp. 151–161.

JOHNSON, NORMAN L., and SAMUEL KATZ (1970). *Continuous Univariate Distributions* (Boston: Houghton Mifflin).

KHAMIS, S. H., and W. RUDERT (1965). *Tables of the Incomplete Gamma Function Ratio* (Darmstadt: Justus Von Leibit Verlag).

LEE, WAYNE L., and RAMESH K. S. RAO (1988). "Mean Lower Partial Moment Valuation and Lognormally Distributed Returns," *Management Science* 34, No. 4 (April), pp. 446–453.

LESSARD, DONALD R., and ALAN C. SHAPIRO (1985), "Guidelines for Global Financing Choices," *International Financial Management Theory and Application*, Donald R. Lessard (ed.), (New York: Wiley).

MARCH, G. J., and Z. SHAPIRA (1987). "Managerial Perspectives on Risk and Risk Taking," *Management Science* 33, No. 11 (November), pp. 1404–1418.

McKENNA, F. W., and Y. H. KIM (1986). "Managerial Risk Preferences, Real Pension Costs and Long Run Corporate Pension Fund Investment Policy," *Journal of Risk and Insurance* 53, No. 1 (March) pp. 29–48.

MARKOWITZ, HARRY (1959). *Portfolio Selection* (New Haven: Yale University Press).

PEARSON, KARL (1934). *Tables of the Incomplete* Γ *Function* (Cambridge: Cambridge University Press).

PORTER, R. BURR (1974). "Semivariance and Stochastic Dominance: A Comparison," *American Economic Review* 64, No. 1, (March), pp. 200–204.

ROSENTHAL, R. E. (1978). "The Variance of Present Work of Cash Flows Under Uncertain Timing," *Engineering Economist* 31, No. 3, pp. 163–170.

STONE, BERNELL K. (1973). "A General Class of Three-Parameter Risk Measures," *Journal of Finance* 28 (June), pp. 675–685.

VICKSON, R. G. (1975). "Stochastic Dominance for Decreasing Absolute Risk Aversion," *Journal of Financial and Quantitative Analysis* 10 (December), pp. 799–811.

WHITMORE, G. A. (1970). Third-Degree Stochastic Dominance," *American Economic Review* 60 (June), pp. 457–459.

8

An Application of
the Box-Jenkins Methodology
to Capital Budgeting
Under Uncertainty

PAUL FALLONE AND CARMELO GIACCOTTO

ABSTRACT

This chapter presents Box-Jenkins methodology-based procedures to value capital expenditure projects that have serially correlated cash flows. While it is intuitively clear that project risk should be a function of such correlation, this chapter shows that mean expected project NPV is also dependent on time-series correlations among project cash flows. These results have important implications for capital budgeting theory and practice as they relate to projects with serially correlated cash flows.

I. INTRODUCTION

Capital budgeting is a fundamental area of interest within financial management, and decisions to accept or reject projects are among the most important faced by managers. Over the past 20 years the concept of relevant risk measurement of a project has shifted, at least in theory, from total project risk, as first introduced by Hillier (1963) from net present value (NPV) methodology, to only the risk contribution of the project to systematic firm risk, as in a strict (portfolios are the "market") capital asset pricing method (CAPM) framework. However, in an excellent study of the relevant risk associated with project hurdle rates, Findlay, Gooding, and Weaver (1976) point out that the relevant project risk probably lies somewhere between these extremes. For, although assumptions about firm goals, the nature of the project, capital markets, and relevant portfolios yield a resolution in theory, this resolution is seldom borne out unambiguously in empirical studies. Chen and Moore (1982) modify the Hillier value risk analysis to include possible uncertainty in the parameters of the cash flow distributions and, in the same paper, arguing from a general CAPM framework as in Levy (1980) and citing the work of Myers and Turnbull (1977), conclude that ". . . while the Hillier approach yields analytic results that are not identical to those under the CAPM, the disparities ordinarily should not be significant."

In any case, perhaps for these reasons or others, the Hillier methodology remains a fundamental tool for working managers. There has been more recent work (e.g., Fuller and Kim, 1980) that begins to introduce less restrictive intertemporal (auto-) correlations between cash flows than those originally introduced by Hillier. This article is another step in that direction, and the importance of incorporating autocorrelation into NPV analysis as demonstrated here underscores the conclusion of Bey and Singleton (1978) in a different context: "The assumption of intertemporally independent cash flows almost invariably will cause the financial manager to select a nonoptimal portfolio of capital assets."

In the following sections, we derive simple exact expressions for the mean and variance of a project when the cash flows, or their first differences, follow general autoregressive moving-average processes as popularized by Box and Jenkins (1976). Such models have been used successfully in forecasting quarterly and annual corporate earnings [see, for example, Khumawala, Polhemus, and Liao (1981), Lorek (1979), or Hopwood and Mckeown (1981)], and they are often the appropriate models for describing a time series in which observations above or below the mean are followed by similar observations, as is quite often the case with cash flows from a capital investment. The results for stationary processes are presented in Section II, Equations (8) and (11), and for nonstationary processes in Section III, Equations (20) and (23). Section IV provides examples, demonstrates the role of utility functions in the decision process, and describes an application of the basic equations to the determination of an IRR in certain cases. The conclusion and direction for future research appear in Section V.

II. CASH FLOWS FOLLOWING STATIONARY PROCESSES

For each integer $1 \leqq t \leqq T$ let the random variable $\tilde{c}_t$ be the cash flow generated at time t by a capital investment with expected life T and let $\tilde{e}_t$ be a normal variate with mean 0, variance v, and $\text{cov}[\tilde{e}_s, \tilde{e}_t] = 0$, $s \neq t$. Assume $\tilde{c}_t$ is given by the following stationary autoregressive moving average process of order (p, q) [ARMA (p, q) process]:

$$\tilde{c}_t = d + a_1\tilde{c}_{t-1} + \cdots + a_p\tilde{c}_{t-p} + \tilde{e}_t - b_1\tilde{e}_{t-1} - \cdots - b_q\tilde{e}_{t-q} \qquad (1)$$

where $\tilde{c}_k = 0$ and $\tilde{e}_k = 0$ with certainty if $k < 1$.

We rewrite Equation (1) in matrix form as[1]

$$P\tilde{C} = d\mathbf{1} + Q\tilde{F} \qquad (2)$$

where

$$P = \begin{Bmatrix}
1 & 0 & 0 & \cdots & 0 & 0 & 0 & \cdots & 0 \\
-a_1 & 1 & 0 & \cdots & 0 & 0 & 0 & \cdots & 0 \\
-a_2 & -a_1 & 1 & \cdots & 0 & 0 & 0 & \cdots & 0 \\
\cdot & -a_2 & -a_1 & \cdots & 0 & 0 & 0 & \cdots & 0 \\
\cdot & \cdot & -a_2 & \cdots & 1 & 0 & 0 & \cdots & 0 \\
-a_p & -a_{p-1} & \cdot & \cdots & -a_1 & 1 & 0 & \cdots & 0 \\
0 & -a_p & \cdot & \cdots & -a_2 & -a_1 & 1 & \cdots & 0 \\
0 & 0 & -a_p & \cdots & \cdot & \cdot & -a_1 & \cdots & 0 \\
0 & 0 & 0 & \cdots & -a_{p-1} & -a_{p-2} & \cdot & \cdots & 0 \\
0 & 0 & 0 & \cdots & -a_p & -a_{p-1} & -a_{p-2} & \cdots & 1
\end{Bmatrix}$$

is the $T \times T$ matrix of autoregressive coefficients,

$$Q = \begin{Bmatrix}
1 & 0 & 0 & \cdots & 0 & 0 & 0 & \cdots & 0 \\
-b_1 & 1 & 0 & \cdots & 0 & 0 & 0 & \cdots & 0 \\
-b_2 & -b_1 & 1 & \cdots & 0 & 0 & 0 & \cdots & 0 \\
\cdot & -b_2 & -b_1 & \cdots & 0 & 0 & 0 & \cdots & 0 \\
\cdot & \cdot & -b_2 & \cdots & 1 & 0 & 0 & \cdots & 0 \\
-b_q & -b_{q-1} & \cdot & \cdots & -b_1 & 1 & 0 & \cdots & 0 \\
0 & -b_q & \cdot & \cdots & -b_2 & -b_1 & 1 & \cdots & 0 \\
0 & 0 & -b_q & \cdots & \cdot & \cdot & -b_1 & \cdots & 0 \\
0 & 0 & 0 & \cdots & -b_{q-1} & -b_{q-2} & 1 & \cdots & 0 \\
0 & 0 & 0 & \cdots & -b_q & -b_{q-1} & -b_{q-2} & \cdots & 1
\end{Bmatrix}$$

is the $T \times T$ matrix containing the moving average coefficients,

$$\tilde{C}' = (\tilde{c}_1, \ldots, \tilde{c}_T)$$

is the vector of cash flows over the life of the investment,

$$\tilde{F}' = (\tilde{e}_1, \ldots, \tilde{e}_T)$$

is the vector of disturbance terms, and

$$1' = (1, \ldots, 1)$$

Equation (2) yields

$$\tilde{C} = dP^{-1} + P^{-1}Q\tilde{F}$$

and the first two moments of $\tilde{C}$ are

$$E(\tilde{C}) = dP^{-1}1 \tag{3}$$

and

$$\text{var}(\tilde{C}) = vP^{-1}QQ'(P^{-1})' \tag{4}$$

where $'$ denotes transpose.

Let r denote the risk-free rate of interest,[2] K the vector of discount factors,

$$K = [(1 + r)^{-1}, (1 + r)^{-2}, \ldots, (1 + r)^{-T}]$$

and I the initial capital investment. The net present value of the investment, $\widetilde{NPV}$, is given by

$$\widetilde{NPV} = K'\tilde{C} - I$$

and it follows that its expected value and variance are given by

$$E(\widetilde{NPV}) = K'E(\tilde{C}) - I = dK'P^{-1}1 - I \tag{5}$$

and

$$\text{var}(\widetilde{NPV}) = vK'P^{-1}QQ'(P^{-1})'K \tag{6}$$

Equations (5) and (6) may be written more concisely and without the need to invert the matrix P by the following technique:[3] Let $X' = (x_1, \ldots, x_T) = (P^{-1})'K$. Then,

$$K'P = K'$$

and for $1 \leq t \leq T$,

$$x_t - a_1 x_{t-1} - \cdots - a_p x_{t-p} = (1 + r)^{-t}$$

holds where $x = 0$ if $k > T$. Hence

$$x_t = a_1 x_{t+1} + \cdots + a_p x_{t+p} + (1 + r)^{-t} \tag{7}$$

computes the entries of X recursively beginning with x_T, then x_{T-1}, and so on.

Since $X = K'P^{-1}$, substitution into Equations (5) and (6) yields

$$E(\widetilde{NPV}) = dX'1 - I = d \sum_{1}^{T} x_t - I \tag{8}$$

and

$$\text{var}(\widetilde{NPV}) = vX'QQ'X \tag{9}$$

However, another application of the recursive technique used above simplifies Equation (9) further. Let $Y = Q'X$. Then, for $1 \leq t \leq T$,

$$y_t = x_t - b_1 x_{t+1} - \cdots - b_q x_{t+q} \tag{10}$$

where, again, $x_k = 0$ if $k > T$. Then Equation (10) calculates y_t recursively, beginning with y_T, then y_{T-1}, and so on. The substitution of Y into Equation (9) yields

$$\text{var}(\widetilde{NPV}) = vYY' = v \sum_{1}^{T} y_t^2 \tag{11}$$

Finally note that since $\tilde{c}_t$ is normally distributed for all t, $\widetilde{NPV}$ is normally distributed with mean and variance given by Equations (8) and (11) and note that $E(\widetilde{NPV})$ is not a function of $b_1, b_2, \ldots, b_q$.

III. CASH FLOWS FOLLOWING NONSTATIONARY PROCESSES

As pointed out by, for example, Nelson (1973) many business and economic time series that do not follow a stationary ARMA (p, q) process have the property that the first differences between consecutive observations, first differences, do follow such a process. Hence, using the notation developed in Section II, for $1 \leq t \leq T$ we define

$$\tilde{w}_t = \tilde{c}_t - \tilde{c}_{t-1} \tag{12}$$

and assume that $\tilde{w}_t$, in place of $\tilde{c}_t$, follows the stationary ARMA (p, q) process [Equation (1)] of Section II. With $W' = (\tilde{w}_1, \ldots, \tilde{w}_T)$ we have the first two moments of $\tilde{W}$ as

$$E(\tilde{W}) = dP^{-1}1 \tag{13}$$

and

$$\text{var}(\tilde{W}) = vP^{-1}QQ'(P^{-1})' \tag{14}$$

In order to bring the results of this section back to the cash flows, that is, $\tilde{C}$, we define the $T \times T$ matrix

$$U = \begin{pmatrix} 1 & 0 & 0 & \cdots & 0 \\ 1 & 1 & 0 & \cdots & 0 \\ 1 & 1 & 1 & \cdots & 1 \end{pmatrix}$$

and note that

$$\tilde{C} = U\tilde{W}$$

Hence,

$$E(\tilde{C}) = UE(\tilde{W}) = dUP^{-1}1 \tag{15}$$

and

$$\text{var}(\tilde{C}) = U \,\text{var}(\tilde{W})U' = vUP^{-1}QQ'(P^{-1})'U' \tag{16}$$

give the expected value and variance of $\tilde{C}$ in this nonstationary case.

Since $\widetilde{\text{NPV}} = K'\tilde{C} - I$, we have the expected $\widetilde{\text{NPV}}$ and its variance given by

$$E(\widetilde{\text{NPV}}) = K'E(\tilde{C}) - I = dK'UP^{-1}1 - I \tag{17}$$

and

$$\text{var}(\widetilde{\text{NPV}}) = K' \,\text{var}(\tilde{C})K = vK'UP^{-1}QQ'(P^{-1})'U'K \tag{18}$$

Again, using the recursive procedure of Section II, we demonstrate that there is no need to invert the matrix P.

Define the matrix $Z = (z_1, \ldots, z_T) = (P^{-1})'U'K$. Then

$$Z'P = K'U$$

and for $1 \le t \le T$ this gives

$$z_t - a_1 z_{t+1} - \cdots - a_p z_{t+p}$$
$$= (1 + r)^{-t} + (1 + r)^{-(t+1)} + \cdots + (1 + r)^{-T} \tag{19}$$

where $z_k = 0$ if $k > T$. The latter equation may be used to compute the entries of Z recursively beginning with z_T, then z_{T-1}, and so on. We then have

$$E(\widetilde{\text{NPV}}) = dZ'1 - I = d \sum_1^T z_t - I \tag{20}$$

and

$$\text{var}(\widetilde{\text{NPV}}) = vZ'QQ'Z \tag{21}$$

(Again note that the expected net present value is a function of only d, a_1, ..., a_p, and r, *but* these (except for r) are the parameters of a first-difference model and *do not* have the same interpretations as in Section II.)

Finally, Equation (21) may be further simplified as follows: Define the matrix $S = (s_1, \ldots, s_T) = Q'Z$. Then for $1 \leq t \leq T$ we have

$$s_t = z_t - b_1 z_{t+1} - \cdots - b_q z_{t+q} \tag{22}$$

where $z_k = 0$ if $k > T$. The latter equation may be used to calculate the entries of S recursively beginning with s_T, then s_{T-1}, and so on. Equation (21) then becomes

$$\text{var}(\widetilde{\text{NPV}}) = vS'S = v \sum_1^T s_t^2 \tag{23}$$

Since $\tilde{w}_t$ and $\tilde{c}_t$ are normally distributed for all t, it follows then that $\widetilde{\text{NPV}}$ is normally distributed with mean and variance given by Equations (20) and (22).

Table 8.1 provides a convenient summary of the main results of Sections II and III, and Figure 8.1 gives the (continuous) progress of expected cash flows for a few simple time series.

Figure 8.1

Examples of cash flow variations over time.

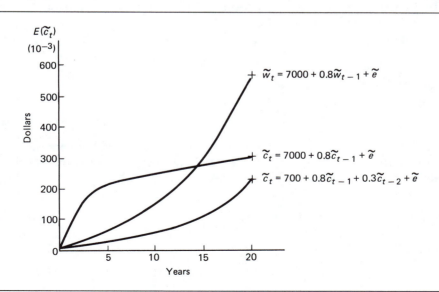

TABLE 8.1.　Cash Flows for Stationary and Nonstationary Processes

CASH FLOW FOLLOWS A STATIONARY PROCESS	CASH FLOW FOLLOWS A NONSTATIONARY PROCESS
$\widetilde{NPV}$ is normally distributed.	$\widetilde{NPV}$ is normally distributed.
$E(\widetilde{NPV}) = d \sum_1^T x_t - I$	$E(\widetilde{NPV}) = d \sum_1^T z_t - I$
$\text{var}(\widetilde{NPV}) = v \sum_1^T y_t^2$	$\text{var}(\widetilde{NPV}) = v \sum_1^T s_t^2$
$x_t = a_1 x_{t+1} + \cdots + a_p x_{t+p} + (1 + r)^{-t}$	$z_t = a_1 z_{t+1} + \cdots + a_p z_{t+p} + (1 + r)^{-t}$ $+ (1 + r)^{-(t+1)} + \cdots + (1 + r)^{-T}$
$y_t = x_t - b_1 x_{t+1} - \cdots - b_q x_{t+q}$	$s_t = z_t - b_1 z_{t+1} - \cdots - b_q z_{t+q}$

IV.　EXAMPLES AND INTERPRETATIONS

To illustrate the use of Equations (19), (20), (22), and (23) consider a capital investment with a stream of cash flows whose first differences follow a stationary ARMA (1, 1) process for which the following values hold:

$$I = \$200,000 \qquad\qquad r = 0.08$$
$$d = \$7000 \qquad\qquad\quad a_1 = 0.8$$
$$v = \$13,450 \qquad\qquad b_1 = 0.4$$
$$T = 10 \text{ years}$$

From Equations (19) and (22),

$$z_t = 0.8 z_{t+1} + \sum_{j=t}^{10} (1.08)^{-j}$$

and

$$s_t = z_t - 0.4 z_{t+1}$$

Then, from Equations (20) and (23),

$$E(\widetilde{NPV}) = 7000 \sum_1^{10} z_t - 200,000 = \$384,737$$

and

$$\text{var}(\widetilde{NPV}) = 13,450 \sum_1^{10} s_t^2 = \$304,139$$

The probability that $\widetilde{NPV} > 0$, $\text{Pr}(\widetilde{NPV} > 0)$, is approximately .9.

Next we provide a table that shows how $E(\widetilde{NPV})$, $\text{var}(\widetilde{NPV})$, and $\Pr(\widetilde{NPV} > 0)$ change as a_1 and b_1 assume different admissible values (see Box and Jenkins, 1976).

Since $E(\widetilde{NPV}) < 0$ for the projects in rows 1 and 2 of Table 8.2, they will not be acceptable to a manager. To interpret the remaining projects in Table 8.2 we assume a negative exponential utility function

$$U(x) = 1 - \exp(-\alpha x)$$

for the relevant manager, with $\alpha > 0$ the coefficient of risk aversion. [Risk-averse utility functions in conjunction with normal distributions are treated extensively in Norgaard and Killeen (1980), and the reader is referred to that article for the motivation behind this selection for $U(x)$.] It follows (see Norgaard and Killeen, 1980) that

$$E[U(\widetilde{NPV})] = 1 - \exp[-\alpha E(\widetilde{NPV}) + \alpha^2 \, \text{var}(\widetilde{NPV})/2]$$

and, consequently, with $\alpha = 0.9$ for illustration, the first four projects in row 3 and the first two projects in row 4 are not acceptable since $E[U(\widetilde{NPV})] < 0$ for these projects. Now let the remaining projects be numbered as follows:

```
. .   . .    . .    . .    . .

. .   . .    . .    . .    . .

. .   . .    . .    . .     1

. .   . .     2      3      4

  5     6     7      8      9
```

TABLE 8.2.   Expected Present Values and Risks With Changes in a_1 and b_1

		$b_1 = -0.8$	$b_1 = -0.4$	$b_1 = 0$	$b_1 = 0.4$	$b_1 = 0.8$
$a_1 = -0.8$	$E(\widetilde{NPV})$	−60,588	−60,588	−60,588	−60,588	−60,588
	$\text{var}(\widetilde{NPV})$	162,810	130,155	97,538	65,013	32,861
	$\Pr(\widetilde{NPV} > 0)$	.35	.32	.27	.18	.03
$a_1 = -0.4$	$E(\widetilde{NPV})$	−26,593	−26,593	−26,593	−26,593	−26,593
	$\text{var}(\widetilde{NPV})$	203,569	162,811	122,085	81,440	41,119
	$\Pr(\widetilde{NPV} > 0)$	.45	.44	.41	.37	.26
$a_1 = 0$	$E(\widetilde{NPV})$	28,809	28,809	28.809	28,809	28,809
	$\text{var}(\widetilde{NPV})$	271,056	216,913	162,811	108,807	55,197
	$\Pr(\widetilde{NPV} > 0)$	.54	.55	.57	.60	.70
$a_1 = 0.4$	$E(\widetilde{NPV})$	133,733	133,733	133,733	133,733	133,733
	$\text{var}(\widetilde{NPV})$	402,220	322,332	242,500	162,811	83,662
	$\Pr(\widetilde{NPV} > 0)$	.63	.66	.71	.79	.95
$a_1 = 0.8$	$E(\widetilde{NPV})$	384,737	384,737	384,737	384,737	384,737
	$\text{var}(\widetilde{NPV})$	730,882	588,507	446,219	304,139	162,811
	$\Pr(\widetilde{NPV} > 0)$	.70	.74	.81	.90	.99

It further follows from $U(x)$ that project i will be preferred to project j if

$$[E(\widetilde{NPV_i}) - E(\widetilde{NPV_j})] - \frac{\alpha}{2}[\text{var}(\widetilde{NPV_i}) - \text{var}(\widetilde{NPV_j})] > 0$$

Hence, again with $\alpha = 0.9$, the order of preference of the acceptable projects in Table 2 (from "most" to "least") is 9, 8, 7, 6, 4, 5, 3, 2, 1.

In certain cases, Equations (7) and (8) may be used to obtain a value for r that will cause the $E(\widetilde{NPV})$ of Equation (8) to equal 0. For example, consider a model of cash flows as follows:

$$\tilde{c}_t = d + a\tilde{c}_{t-1} + \text{noise}$$

If these flows proceed from time 1 to T ($\tilde{c}_k = 0, k < 1$), the expected net present value is given by Equation (8), where the x_t's are given recursively by

$$x_t = ax_{t+1} + (1 + \rho)^{-t}$$

Here ρ represents a *to-be-determined* discount rate. The following table shows the scheme of correct coefficients for the x_t's:

x_T:	1				
x_{T-1}:	a	1			
x_{T-2}:	a^2	a	1		
$\cdots$	$\cdots$	$\cdots$	$\cdots$	$\cdots$	
x_{T-n}:	a^n	a^{n-1}	a^{n-2}	$\cdots$	a 1

That is,

$$x_{T-n} = a^n(1+\rho)^{-T} + a^{n-1}(1+\rho)^{-(T-1)} + \cdots$$
$$+ a(1+\rho)^{-(T-n+1)} + (1+\rho)^{-(T-n)}$$

Then clearly,

$$\sum_1^T x_t = (a^{T-1} + a^{T-2} + \cdots + a + 1)(1+\rho)^{-T}$$
$$+ (a^{T-2} + a^{T-3} + \cdots + a + 1)(1+\rho)^{-(T-1)}$$
$$+ \cdots + (a + 1)(1+\rho)^{-2} + (1+\rho)^{-1}$$

Hence, $E(\widetilde{NPV}) = 0$ only if

$$\frac{I}{d}(1+\rho)^T - (1+\rho)^{T-1} - (a+1)(1+\rho)^{T-2}$$
$$- \cdots - (a^{T-2} + a^{T-3} + \cdots + a + 1)(1+\rho)$$
$$- (a^{T-1} + a^{T-2} + \cdots + a + 1) = 0$$

For illustration, suppose $d = \$7000$, $I = \$200,000$, $T = 10$ years, and $a = 0.8$. Then the above equation becomes

$$28.571(1 + \rho)^{10} - (1 + \rho)^9 - 2.8(1 + \rho)^8 - 5.24(1 + \rho)^7$$
$$- 8.192(1 + \rho)^6 - 11.553(1 + \rho)^5 - 15.242(1 + \rho)^4$$
$$- 19.193(1 + \rho)^3 - 23.354(1 + \rho)^2 - 27.683(1 + \rho) - 32.146 = 0$$

This equation may be solved using standard techniques (e.g., bisection sign) to yield in this case

$$\rho \doteq 0.270052 \doteq 27\%$$

As another example of the above technique but utilizing Equations (19) and (20), consider the following first-difference model of cash flow generation:

$$\tilde{c}_t - \tilde{c}_{t-1} = d + a(\tilde{c}_{t-1} + \tilde{c}_{t-2}) + \text{noise}$$

or, equivalently,

$$\tilde{c}_t = d + (a + 1)\tilde{c}_{t-1} - a\tilde{c}_{t-2} + \text{noise}$$

The following scheme gives the coefficients for the x_t's:

x_T:	1		
x_{T-1}:	$a + 1$	1	
x_{T-2}:	$a^2 + a + 1$	$a + 1$	1
x_{T-3}:	$a^3 + a^2 + a + 1$	$a^2 + a + 1$	$a + 1$ 1
$\cdots$	$\cdots$	$\cdots$	$\cdots$ $\cdots$
x_{T-n}:	$a^n + a^{n-1} + \cdots + a + 1$	$a^{n-1} + a^{n-2} + \cdots + a + 1$	$a + 1$ 1

That is,

$$x_{T-n} = (a^n + a^{n-1} + \cdots + a + 1)(1 + \rho)^{-T} + (a^{n-1} + a^{n-2} + \cdots$$
$$+ a + 1)(1 + \rho)^{-(T-1)} + \cdots + (a + 1)(1 + \rho)^{-(T-n+1)} + (1 + \rho)^{-(T-n)}$$

Then,

$$\sum_1^T x_t = [a^{T-1} + 2a^{T-2} + 3a^{T-3} + \cdots + (T - 1)a + T](1 + \rho)^{-T}$$
$$+ [a^{T-2} + 2a^{T-3} + 3a^{T-4} + \cdots + (T - 2)a + (T - 1)](1 + \rho)^{-(T-1)}$$
$$+ \cdots + [a + 1](1 + \rho)^{-2} + (1 + \rho)^{-1}$$

Hence, $E(\widehat{NPV}) = 0$ only if

$$\frac{I}{d}(1 + \rho)^T - (1 + \rho)^{T-1} - [a + 1](1 + \rho)^{T-2}$$

$$- \cdots - [a^{T-2} + 2a^{T-3} + 3a^{T-4} + \cdots + (T - 2)a + (T - 1)](1 + \rho)$$

$$- [a^{T-1} + 2a^{T-2} + 3a^{T-3} + \cdots + (T - 1)a + T] = 0$$

Again consider the case where $d = \$7000$, $I = \$200,000$, $T = 10$ years, and $a = 0.4$. Then the above equation becomes

$$28.571(1 + \rho)^{10} - (1 + \rho)^9 - 1.4(1 + \rho)^8 - 2.96(1 + \rho)^7$$

$$- 5.584(1 + \rho)^6 - 7.234(1 + \rho)^5 - 8.893(1 + \rho)^4 - 10.557(1 + \rho)^3$$

$$- 12.223(1 + \rho)^2 - 13.889(1 + \rho) - 15.569 = 0$$

This solves to yield an approximate ρ of

$$\rho \doteq 0.16025 = 16\%$$

V. CONCLUSION

The analysis of risk in a capital budgeting context has a long history dating back to Hillier's seminal article. His methodology for independently distributed cash flows is routinely presented in financial management texts such as Brigham (1983) and Van Horne (1983). If the condition of independence does not hold, both texts suggest the use of simulation techniques.

In contrast, in this article we have presented an analytical solution to the problem of selecting a project with serially correlated cash flows, and the procedure is general enough to accommodate both stationary and nonstationary flows. The examples not only validate the intuitive notion that a project's risk is a function of cash flow interdependence, but they also demonstrate an important impact on $E(\widehat{NPV})$ of this interdependence. In fact, cash flow correlation may affect this mean more than the variance of $\widehat{NPV}$. This point seems to have gone unnoticed over the years; certainly the two texts cited above give no hint to the reader that such a relationship exists.

Future research should be directed toward developing appropriate models and parameters. An approach that might prove useful in this regard is the "pure play" technique used by Fuller and Kerr (1981) to estimate divisional betas. Essentially, one matches an anticipated project with a similar one already existing or with a business with a product line similar to the project. Once such a pure play has been identified, a sample of cash flows can be used to estimate the appropriate model.

NOTES

1. See Box-Jenkins (1976) for a complete description of stationary ARMA (p, q) models, in particular, restrictions on coefficients.
2. See Van Horn (1983) for the appropriate interest rate to be used in this context.
3. See Ali (1977) for a discussion of this approach in time series analysis.

REFERENCES

Ali, M. (1977). "Analysis of Autoregressive-Moving Average Models: Estimation and Prediction," *Biometrika*, pp. 535–545.

Bey, R. P., and J. C. Singleton (1978). "Autocorrelated Cash Flows and the Selection of a Portfolio of Capital Assets," *Decision Science*, pp. 640–657.

Box, G., and G. Jenkins (1976). *Time Series Analysis: Forecasting and Control* (San Francisco: Calif.: Holden-Day).

Brigham, E. (1983). *Financial Management: Theory and Practice* (New York: Dryden Press).

Chen, S., and W. Moore (1982). "Investment Decision Under Uncertainty: Application of Estimation Risk in the Hillier Approach" *Journal of Financial and Quantitative Analysis*, Vol. 17 No. 3 pp. 425–440.

Findlay, M. C., A. E. Gooding, and W. Q. Weaver (1976). "On the Relevant Risk for Determining Capital Expenditure Hurdle Rates," *Financial Management* 5 (Winter), pp. 9–16.

Fuller, R., and S. Kim (1980). "Inter-Temporal Correlation of Cash Flows and the Risk of Multi-Period Investment Projects," *Journal of Financial and Quantitative Analysis*, Vol. 15 No. 5 pp. 1149–1162.

Fuller, R., and H. Kerr (1981). "Estimating the Divisional Cost of Capital: An Analysis of the Pure-Play Technique," *Journal of Finance*, Vol. 36 No. 5 pp. 997–1009.

Hillier, F. (1963). "The Derivation of Probabilistic Information for the Evaluation of Risky Investments," *Management Science*, pp. 443–457.

Hopwood, W. S., and J. C. McKeown (1981). "An Evaluation of Univariate Time-Series Earnings Models and Their Generalization to a Single Input Transfer Function," *Journal of Accounting Research*, pp. 313–322.

Khumawala, S., N. Polhemus, and W. Liao (1981). "The Predictability of Quarterly Cash Flows," *Journal of Business Finance and Accounting*, Vol. 8 No. 4 pp. 493–510.

Levy, H. (1980). "The CAPM and Beta in an Imperfect Market" *Journal of Portfolio Management* 6 (Winter), pp. 5–11.

Lorek, K. S. (1979). "Predicting Annual Net Earnings With Quarterly Earnings Time-Series Models," *Journal of Accounting Research*, pp. 190–203.

Meyers, S. C., and S. M. Turnbull (1977). "Capital Budgeting and the Capital Asset Pricing Model: Good News and Bad News," *Journal of Finance*, Vol. 32 No. 2 pp. 321–333.

Nelson, C. (1973). *Applied Time Series Analysis for Managerial Forecasting* (San Francisco, Calif.: Holden-Day).

Norgaard, R., and T. Killeen (1980). "Expected Utility and the Truncated Normal Distribution," *Management Science*, pp. 901–909.

Van Horne, J. (1983). *Financial Management and Policy* (Englewood Cliffs, N.J.: Prentice-Hall).

9

Capital Budgeting
and the
Learning Curve Phenomenon

M. ANDREW FIELDS

ABSTRACT

This chapter examines the affects of the learning curve on the attractiveness of capital expenditure projects. Learning curve effects influence the size, timing, and riskiness of project cash flows. Ignoring these learning curve effects by using average costs can lead to erroneous capital budgeting decisions for projects where cash flows are influenced by learning.

I. INTRODUCTION

Repetition of human activity tends to cause a certain amount of learning to occur. This learning curve (LC) effect has been widely discussed in the business literature and appears to be applicable in many diverse settings (e.g., see Belkaoui, 1983; Imhoff, 1978; Yelle, 1979). Many years ago companies in the aircraft industry discovered that certain repetitive processes could be described mathematically and that such models could be used to estimate the amount of time necessary to complete a task as it is repeated. It was determined that the more complex the activity, the greater the potential to achieve decreases in the time necessary to complete each succeeding unit of production.

In this chapter we consider the effect of the learning curve on operating costs and the impact these costs have on the amount and timing of cash flows from new investment opportunities. Consideration of only average per-unit cost can be misleading because of the potential impact of the LC. Operating costs are very high during production of the early units but decline rapidly as production continues. Of course, part of such a decrease in costs may be due to economies of scale. However, the LC effect is important also. Furthermore, many authors have described the hazards and lost opportunities experienced by those who ignore the impact of learning. For example, according to Hirschmann (1964), "Further improvements are always possible over time so long as people are encouraged, or even ordered, to seek them." In evaluating capital investment projects, it is important for the analyst to incorporate the LC effect into the estimation of cash flows and to be aware of the impact this effect can have on project risk and acceptance.

The chapter is organized in the following manner. Section II provides a brief introduction to the basic LC model. Section III presents a capital budgeting example which will be used throughout the remainder of the chapter. Section IV describes the effect of the learning curve on capital budgeting, and Section V explains the impact on project risk. Section VI provides the summary and conclusions.

II. LEARNING CURVE MODEL

The learning curve underlying any particular process can be expressed mathematically as

$$Y = TX^b \tag{1}$$

where Y = cumulative average time per unit when producing X units
$\quad\ \ X$ = number of units to be produced
$\quad\ \ T$ = estimated time needed to complete the first unit
$\quad\ \ b$ = index of the rate of learning

The b parameter is expressed by the relationship

$$b = \frac{\log(\text{rate of learning})}{\log 2} \tag{2}$$

In order to solve for Y, the cumulative average time per unit, Equation (1) can be expressed in log form as

$$\log Y = \log T + b \log X \tag{3}$$

This transformation results in a linear relationship that is useful in determining the amount of learning that will occur in any given situation.

As an example of the learning curve, assume that $T = 100$ hours, that X is estimated to be 4, and that the learning rate is 80%. In this case, Y equals 64 hours and is an estimate of the average time necessary to produce each of the four units. The total time is 256 hours, consisting of 100 hours for the first unit, 60 hours for the second unit, 50.63 hours for the third unit, and only 45.37 hours for the fourth unit. Note that the estimate of average time declines according to the percentage rate of learning each time the number of units produced (X) is doubled (i.e., 100 for one, 80 for two, and 64 for four).

The LC model requires that estimates of b, T, and X be made before Y can be determined. Baloff and Kennelly (1967, p. 135) state that in many early applications it was assumed that a single rate of learning would "be experienced in all start-ups. Unfortunately, significant variations among different start-ups have been reported by most empirical studies. . . ." Billon (1966) reports that firms with experience from previous products of a similar nature encountered significant variations in their rates of learning. Previous experience with similar products and processes helps to provide an accurate estimate, as does information concerning the experience of other companies in related situations, if available. Baloff (1967) illustrates how a company can use its prior experience to develop parameter estimates. However, in many instances this parameter is the most critical variable and it is important to consider the impact of the uncertainty associated with the estimate.

The estimated time needed to complete the first unit T may be a critical variable depending on its level of uncertainty. Often, this variable is ignored in the analysis, but doing so can be a mistake. If the situation or application is familiar, the estimate may be quite accurate and it will cause very little uncertainty. However, in many situations, such as when there is little prior experience or information, it is difficult to form an accurate estimate, in which case T may become an important consideration.

The total number of units to be produced is an important element in most capital budgeting evaluations. Unlike b and T, it is not a parameter of the LC model, but it is an important variable in Equation (1). This interaction with the LC results in an additional impact on project cash flow estimates. However, the estimate of X may be a relatively unimportant variable for two reasons. First, the number of units to be produced may be set explicitly by contract in some cases. However, in other situations there may be uncertainty concerning the final number of units. Second, the LC is relatively insensitive to changes in total production for large numbers of products. Morse (1972) reports that a large change in X is needed to affect results dramatically. However, for lower values of X, a small change may be critical. A significant level of uncertainty in the estimate of X may affect cash flows to the same extent that it does for estimates of the learning rate and time required to complete the first unit.

The amount of uncertainty related to each of these three variables depends on the specific situation. However, the impact that deviations in these estimates have on project acceptability can be anticipated and studied before management commits capital and/or talent to the project. This will be discussed after introducing an example.

III. PROJECT EXAMPLE

Assume that XYZ Company is considering investing in a new project that will involve the production of a newly designed industrial robot for one of the firm's customers. The proposed project calls for one robot to be produced each year for the next 8 years. The project will not result in any new asset investment, as the company presently has the facilities to produce the product. The only initial outlay necessary is $23,616 to pay for training production crews.

The company estimates that it will take 100 days to produce the first unit. In addition, the production department feels that an 80% learning rate is appropriate based on the company's past experience. The material cost for the robots is estimated to be fixed at $100,000 per unit. Direct labor will   cost $1000 per day. The company has enough contracts to keep its lines busy with other products during the rest of the year. The tentative price per unit has been set at $164,575.

Table 9.1 indicates the average and marginal time needed to produce each unit. The average time required for each of eight units is 51.2 days, with the first unit requiring 100 days and the eighth unit only 35.46 days. Table 9.2 lists the projected annual cash flows to be generated by the project. The direct labor cost is $100,000 ($1000 × 100 days) initially

TABLE 9.1   Marginal Time Required to Produce Each Unit (Eight units)

UNITS	TOTAL TIME (DAYS)	AVERAGE TIME (DAYS)	MARGINAL TIME (DAYS)
1	100.00	100.00	100.00
2	160.00	80.00	60.00
3	210.63	70.21	50.63
4	256.00	64.00	45.37
5	297.82	59.56	41.82
6	337.01	56.17	39.19
7	374.14	53.45	37.13
8	409.60	51.20	35.46

TABLE 9.2 LC Project Annual Cash Flows and Average Cash Flow

	YEAR 1	YEAR 2	YEAR 3	YEAR 4	YEAR 5	YEAR 6	YEAR 7	YEAR 8	AVERAGE ANNUAL CASH FLOW
Revenues	$164,575	$164,575	$164,575	$164,575	$164,575	$164,575	$164,575	$164,575	$164,575
Material, $100,000/unit	(100,000)	(100,000)	(100,000)	(100,000)	(100,000)	(100,000)	(100,000)	(100,000)	(100,000)
Direct labor, $1000/day	(100,000)	(60,000)	(50,631)	(45,369)	(41,819)	(39,191)	(37,133)	(35,457)	(51,200)
Total cost	(200,000)	(160,000)	(150,631)	(145,369)	(141,819)	(139,191)	(137,133)	(135,457)	(151,200)
Cash flow	($35,425)	$4,575	$13,944	$19,206	$22,756	$25,384	$27,442	$29,118	$13,375

but declines to \$35,457 with the eighth unit. Because revenue and material cost per unit are fixed, cash flows rise as the direct labor cost declines, with the first unit causing a cash outflow of \$35,425 and the last unit providing a cash inflow of \$29,118. The average total cost is \$151,200, and this results in an average cash flow estimate of \$13,375.

IV. LC PROJECT CASH FLOW ESTIMATION AND EVALUATION

Because cash operating costs decline and net cash flows increase over time, cash flow patterns from projects that experience a learning curve (hereafter called LC projects) may differ from normal capital investment projects. Consider the LC project example presented in Table 9.2. Cash flow is negative initially, but it becomes positive in year 2 and increases each period for the duration of the project. Compare this to the case where project cash flows equal the average cash flow each year. The present value of the LC project cash flows is lower than if the project has level costs and cash flows—less value is placed on the positive inflows because they occur farther into the future. Table 9.3 presents the cumulative present value of annual cash flows for the LC project and normal projects A and B. All three projects have the same initial outlay. Project A has an annual cash flow of \$13,375, equaling the average LC project cash flow, and a net present value (NPV) of \$47,739 at a discount rate of 10%. This is much higher than the \$27,679 NPV of the LC project.[1] Thus holding other factors constant, a project that is affected by the LC will be less valuable.

For standard costing purposes, many firms employ the average cost as a basis for estimation. However, for capital budgeting purposes, the actual timing of the cash flows should be used so that the project may be evaluated properly. The potential problem for a LC project occurs when estimates of average cost and cash flow are substituted for the actual annual amounts. As can be seen from comparing the LC project and project A in Table 9.3, this understates the present value of costs and overstates the NPV estimate.

A second potential problem for a LC project is that its cash flow pattern may cause differences in the ranking of projects (provided by alternative capital budgeting evaluation techniques) to become more pronounced. Table 9.3 indicates that the LC project is acceptable as an investment (NPV > 0). Consider project B which also has a NPV of \$27,679 and will provide a cash flow annuity of \$9615 for 8 years. Both projects are equivalent according to this measure. However, two other common methods of evaluation give project B a higher ranking, as can be seen in the accompanying table. This disagreement between the NPV

TABLE 9.3   NPV at 10% for LC Project and Normal Projects A and B

YEAR	LC Project[a]	CUMULATIVE PRESENT VALUE OF ANNUAL CASH FLOWS Project A[b] ($)	Project B[c]
Initial outlay	($23,616)	($23,616)	($23,616)
1	(55,821)	(11,457)	(14,875)
2	(52,040)	(403)	(6,929)
3	(41,563)	9,646	295
4	(28,445)	18,781	6,862
5	(14,315)	27,086	12,832
6	13	34,636	18,260
7	14,095	41,499	23,194
8 (NPV)	$27,679	$47,739	$27,679

[a] The annual cash flows for the LC project are provided in Table 9.2.

[b] The cash flow for project A is $13,375 each year for 8 years. This is the average cash flow presented in Table 9.2.

[c] The cash flow for project B is $9615 each year. This is the 8-year annuity that provides a NPV equal to that of the LC project NPV.

method and the internal rate of return (IRR) and payback methods causes a problem only when acceptable projects need to be ranked. However, if either of these measures is used instead of NPV, project B appears to be superior even though both projects have equivalent NPVs.

	INTERNAL RATE OF RETURN (%)	PAYBACK (YEARS)
LC project	21.0	4.9
Project B	36.5	2.5

It is the difference between projects in the timing of cash flow that causes the ranking disparity in this situation. Figure 9.1 presents the marginal contribution to NPV of the present value of annual cash flow for each of the first 30 years (one unit per year) for the LC project and for project B. The normal project has a steady decline in the marginal contribution but, as indicated before, the LC project initially has a negative cash flow. This becomes positive very quickly, and the project continues to receive large marginal positive cash flows for several years. However, because of the time factor and the decreasing advantage from learning, the marginal contribution to NPV each year begins to decline after year 6.

Figure. 9.1

Marginal present value of cash flows—LC project and project B.

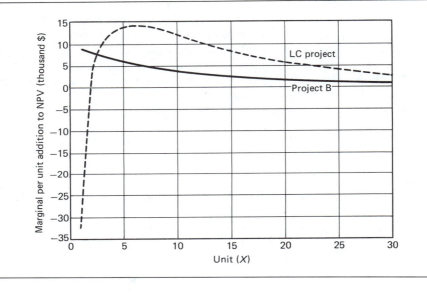

Differences in the timing of cash flows causes a ranking discrep-ancy between the NPV and the IRR because of the reinvestment rate assumption each method implicitly makes (e.g., see Brigham and Ga-penski, 1987). NPV assumes that cash flows are reinvested at the cost of capital, while IRR assumes that the appropriate rate is the project's own IRR. A project must have an IRR greater than the cost of capital to be acceptable. There are larger differences between the reinvestment rate assumptions for projects with high IRRs. As the discount (reinvestment) rate moves upward, the IRR method places more and more emphasis on early cash flows. NPV is superior and should be used in order to provide a fair evaluation of projects because its reinvestment rate assumption has more validity, both in general and with respect to the specific impact of the learning curve.

V. EFFECT OF THE LC ON PROJECT RISK

Projects that are affected by learning curve pose another potential prob-lem for capital budgeting analysis—project risk increases. As indicated previously, there is uncertainty present in the estimates of cash flow arising from variance in b, X, and T, which is in addition to the general uncertainty that all projects may share. As a result, consideration should be given to the impact of this variation on project risk and acceptability. For example, Harvey (1976) illustrates the effect on the IRR for both positive and negative percentage changes in the values of b and X. However, there is one particular aspect of this problem that is extremely important in capital budgeting analysis—the amount of error that would have to occur before the project accept/reject decision is reversed. Therefore, the analyst is immediately more concerned with changes in this direction. The NPV technique is utilized in order to develop an approach to aid in the evaluation of this uncertainty.

The NPV and LC formulations can be combined and expressed as

$$I_0 = \sum_{j=1}^{X} \frac{P - [T(j)^{b+1} - T(j-1)^{b+1}]DL - F}{(1 + i)^j} \qquad (4)$$

where I_0 = initial outlay
X = cumulative number of units (periods)^2
P = price
T = time necessary to complete the first unit
DL = cost per direct labor day
F = fixed cost per unit
i = cost of capital

This formulation determines where the present value of cash flows is equal to the initial outlay (NVP = 0). This is the indifference point for the accept/reject decision. Equation (4) can be used to determine this indifference point for the learning rate, the time required to produce the first unit, or the total number of units to be produced.

A. The Learning Rate Estimate

The effect of variance in the learning rate estimate is an important consideration in capital budgeting. As noted previously, this may be a very critical factor since a small change in the rate may cause a large change in the amount and timing of costs. The learning rate indifference point can be determined utilizing Equation (4) and compared to the actual estimate of b. With this information, it is possible to assess the probability of underestimating the learning rate and accepting a poor project or overestimating the rate and rejecting a profitable investment. When the time needed to produce the first unit is 100 days and $X = 8$, the learning rate must move above 82.8% before the project results in a negative NPV. Thus a 3.5% increase over the original estimate of 80% will have a critical impact on the project's NPV.

In order to evaluate the impact of variance in the learning rate on project risk completely, it is necessary to consider the sensitivity of the

NPV estimate to changes in the rate of learning and the other factors jointly. For example, Figure 9.2 presents the impact of changes in the learning rate on the NPV of the LC project (assuming $X = 8$), with b varying from 76% to 84%. This represents a range of ±5% from the original estimate of 80%. The impact on NPV from changes in the learning rate when T is 95 and 105 days (also ±5%) is presented in Figure 9.2 as well. Here the learning rate indifference points occur at 84.4% and 81.3%, respectively.

Table 9.4 provides a numerical comparison of project NPVs over a range of estimates for these two factors. As can be seen, a learning rate of 81% provides a negative NPV if T is 106 days or longer. This drops to 103, 100, and 97 days with rates of 82%, 83%, and 84%, respectively. A basic spreadsheet program is ideal to use for this analysis. For this project, it is apparent that variance in the rate of learning has a much greater impact on the estimate of NPV than variance in T.

B. Total Number of Units

The total number of units to be produced may be an important factor in the capital budgeting decision. The indifference point for X occurs at about six units—it is necessary to produce and sell six units to break

Figure 9.2

Learning rate indifference points for $T = 95$, 100, and 105 days.

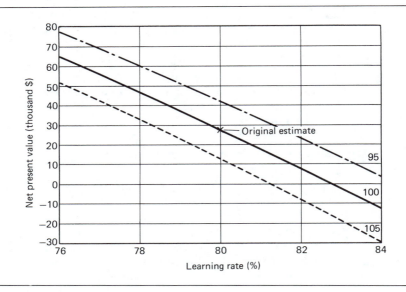

TABLE 9.4   Sensitivity Analysis for Learning Rate and *T*

FIRST-UNIT PRODUCTION TIME, T	NET PRESENT VALUE (THOUSAND $) LEARNING RATE (b)			
	b = 81%	b = 82%	b = 83%	b = 84%
96	30,030	20,441	10,636	614
97	27,001	17,311	7,404	−2,722
98	23,971	14,182	4,173	−6,058
99	20,941	11,052	941	−9,394
100	17,911	7,922	−2,291	−12,731
101	14,882	4,793	−5,523	−16,067
102	11,852	1,663	−8,754	−19,403
103	8,822	−1,467	−11,986	−22,739
104	5,792	−4,596	−15,218	−26,075
105	2,763	−7,726	−18,450	−29,412
106	−267	−10,855	−21,682	−32,748

even on a time-adjusted basis. This can be seen in Table 9.3 since the project has an NPV of just $13 in year 6. If the number of units sold falls below six, the project will incur a loss in value. With this information, it is possible to determine the risk associated with lower-than-expected total production in the case of an acceptable project, as well as the amount needed and the likely probability of additional production in the case of a rejected project.

Figure 9.3 illustrates the impact of variance in X jointly with that of the rate of learning. The NPVs provided from sales of up to 11 units are presented for learning rates of 75%, 80%, 85%, and 90%. Just over 4 units need to be sold in order to break even with a 75% learning rate; 6 and 11 units are needed with 80% and 85% rates, respectively. The project NPV is never positive when the learning rate is 90%. It is apparent from the graph that the impact of variance in X is affected by the rate of learning. At a rate of 90%, NPV is very insensitive to changes in X. However, when the rate is 75%, variance in X has a noticeable impact. With an 80% rate, variance in X has an impact on project NPV, but it is much smaller than the impact of variance in the learning rate itself.

C. The Time Required to Produce the First Unit

The impact of variance in the estimate of the time required to produce the first unit can be examined in a similar manner. The value of T needs to rise to about 109 days before the project NPV becomes negative. Figure 9.4 presents the project NPV for a range of T from 90 to 110 days. This represents a range of ±10% from the original estimate of 100 days. The impact of changes in T when the learning rate is 72% and 88% (also ±10%) is presented in Figure 9.4 as well. The figure indicates that vari-

Figure 9.3

Unit (X) indifference points for $b = 75\%$, 80%, 85%, and 90%.

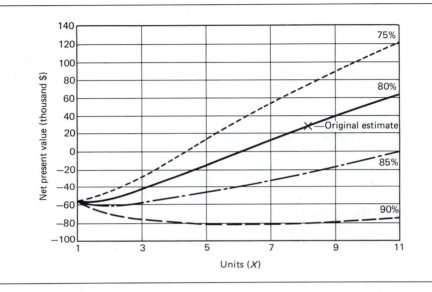

Figure 9.4

First-unit (T) indifference points for $b = 72\%$, 80%, and 88%.

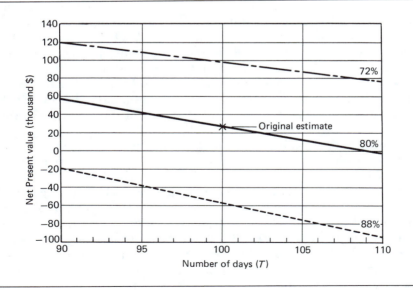

ance in the estimate of T has a similar effect at various rates of learning. However, as is the case with X, the impact on NPV of variance in T is much less than that of variance in the learning rate.

The previous discussion indicates that variance in the estimates of X and T will have an impact on the project's NPV, but estimating the rate of learning is much more critical and should be given greater attention. As can be seen from this example, the impact of the LC on the uncertainty of project cash flow estimates can be anticipated and incorporated directly into the capital budgeting evaluation process.

VI. SUMMARY AND CONCLUSIONS

The learning curve interacts with the capital budgeting process in three important ways. First, the LC has a substantial impact on project cash flows. Early cash flows are lower than average, very possibly negative, because of the substantial cost required to produce the early units of production. These cash costs decrease rapidly as the effects of learning occur, but the marginal contribution of learning eventually becomes much less significant. It is important that the timing and amount of cash flows be incorporated directly into the evaluation of a project. The use of average cost upwardly biases the estimate of project profitability.

Second, alternative capital budgeting techniques may yield conflicting rankings when a project affected by the learning curve is compared to other acceptable projects. This difference in ranking is caused by the impact of the learning curve on the timing and amount of project cash flows and the different reinvestment rate assumptions underlying the net present value and the internal rate of return evaluation techniques. The internal rate of return places heavier emphasis on earlier cash flows since it assumes a higher rate of reinvestment with an acceptable project. The NPV technique should be used to provide a fair evaluation of projects because its reinvestment rate assumption has more validity, both in general and with respect to the specific impact of the learning curve.

Third, projects affected by the learning curve have additional uncertainty present in their cash flows estimates. It is necessary to analyze the impact that this additional uncertainty has on project risk and acceptability. An examination of the impact of variance in the learning rate, the time required to produce the first unit, and the total number of units to be produced helps to determine the importance of each of these three estimates. Of particular interest is the amount of change that needs to occur in each of these variables before the accept/reject decision is reversed. Sensitivity analysis, including calculation of these indifference points, helps to provide this insight. It is important to consider this analysis explicitly because of the unique circumstances that the LC introduces into the capital budgeting process.

NOTES

1. This assumes that all cash flows occur at year end. While this may be somewhat unrealistic, it does not materially affect the example. A more complex situation can be implemented easily.
2. To aid the presentation, it has been assumed that one unit will be produced each year. Thus periods and units are equivalent. This can be adapted to a more realistic situation easily.

REFERENCES

ABERNATHY, W. J., and K. WAYNE (1974). "Limits of the Learning Curve," *Harvard Business Review* 42 (September–October), pp. 109–119.

BALOFF, N. (1967). "Estimating the Parameters of the Start-up Model—An Empirical Approach," *Journal of Industrial Engineering* (April), pp. 248–253.

BALOFF, N., and J. W. KENNELLY (1967). "Accounting Implications of Product and Process Start-Ups," *Journal of Accounting Research* 5 (Autumn), pp. 131–143.

BELKAOUI, A. (1983). *The Learning Curve: A Management Accounting Tool* (Westport, Conn.: Quorum Books).

BILLON, S. A. (1966). Industrial Learning Curves and Forecasting," *Management International Review* 6 (No. 1), pp. 65–79.

BRIGHAM, E. F., and L. C. GAPENSKI (1987). *Intermediate Financial Management,* 2nd ed. (New York: Dryden Press).

BUMP, E. A. (1974). "Effects of Learning on Cost Projections," *Management Accounting* 55 (May), pp. 19–24.

GILLESPIE, J. F. (1981). "An Application of Learning Curves to Standard Costing," *Management Accounting* 63 (September), pp. 63–65.

HARRIS, L. C., and W. L. STEPHENS (1978). "The Learning Curve: A Case Study," *Management Accounting* 59 (February), pp. 47–54.

HARVEY, D. W. (1978). "Financial Planning Information for Production Start-Ups," *Accounting Review* 53 (October), pp. 838–845.

HIRSCHMANN, W. R. (1964). "Profit From the Learning Curve," *Harvard Business Review* 32 (January–February), pp. 125–139.

HOUSE, W. C. (1967). "Use of Sensitivity Analysis in Capital Budgeting," *Management Services* (September–October), pp. 37–40.

IMHOFF, E. A., JR. (1978). "The Learning Curve and Its Applications," *Management Accounting* 59 (February), pp. 44–46.

MORSE, W. J. (1972). "Reporting Production Costs That Follow the Learning Curve Phenomenon," *Accounting Review* 47 (October), pp. 761–773.

Rappaport, A. (1967). "Sensitivity Analysis in Decision Making," *Accounting Review* 42 (July), pp. 441–456.

Summers, E. L., and G. A. Welsch (1970). "How Learning Curve Models Can Be Applied to Profit Planning," *Management Services* (March–April), pp. 45–50.

Voyda, T. G. (1972). "How to Use the Learning Curve for Planning and Control," *Cost and Management* (July–August), pp. 25–32.

Yelle, L. E. (1979). "The Learning Curve: Historical Review and Comprehensive Survey," *Decision Sciences* 10 (Spring), pp. 302–324.

10

Some Implications of Competition for Capital Investment

JAMES S. ANG AND STEPHEN P. DUKAS

ABSTRACT

This chapter examines capital budgeting decision in a competitive environment. It is shown that in such cases the NPV is a function of competitive intensity and project duration. Ignoring either factor will result in erroneous estimates of project value in a competitive setting.

I. INTRODUCTION

The net present value (NPV) criterion of project evaluation has traditionally been accepted (Copeland and Weston, 1988) as the theoretically superior capital budgeting technique because of its concordance with the principle of value maximization. Several authors have criticized the application of this criterion in that it understates the true value of an investment by ignoring (1) strategic growth opportunities (Kester, 1984), (2) the fact that management can discontinue the project before the end of its economic life (Mason and Merton, 1985), (3) the ability of management to delay the investment decision (MacDonald and Siegel, 1986), (4) the arrival of information throughout the life of the project (Majd and Pindyck, 1987), and (5) management's option to temporarily shut down the production process (MacDonald and Siegel, 1985). Through these omissions, it has been asserted that the use of net present value criteria[1] has undermined the levels of real investment in the United States and stunted economic growth (Hayes and Garvin, 1982).

While the above criticisms are justified in their attempts to quantify factors affecting value, a crucial and often ignored fact is that a firm typically makes investment decisions in a competitive environment. Recognition of the possibility of entry by competitors brings out the quasirent nature of capital budgeting projects. In a competitive environment firms have only a temporary advantage in technology, product concepts, production, and marketing skills. Forecasted cash flows can be reduced or eliminated by competitive entry, yet, apart from the use of certain ad hoc risk adjustment procedures, the presence of competitors is usually not explicitly considered in the capital budgeting process or in the theoretical development of capital budgeting models.

Trigeorgis (1986) examines the capital budgeting decision with competition in a contingent claims analytical framework by modeling an industry as a collection of firms holding (call) options to enter the market. He considers various formulations of random competitive arrivals and equates the impact of competition to the effect of "dividends" in the call option pricing problem. An assumption made in Trigeorgis' analysis is that all firms in the competitive model have the same information set. If all firms in a competitive industry are informationally identical, the market for new product introductions is dichotomous. In other words, either no firm enters the market or all firms in the industry enter the market at the same time. This assumption of informationally symmetric markets is not relevant for most industries, and it eliminates a primary justification for the belief that positive NPVs exist in the first place. Informational asymmetry is an essential feature of an industry exhibiting projects with positive NPVs.

Miller (1988) cites the economic result that if a competitive industry's return on investment is limited to a normal return (zero economic profit), then truly positive NPV projects are rare for any firm in the industry. If this is true, Miller's insight is that there are many more bad projects (negative NPV) that good ones (positive NPV), which results in biased NPV forecasts.[2]

This study develops capital budgeting decision models that incorporate both competition and asymmetric information. It will be shown, using a probabilistic model of competitive entry, that ignoring competition in the valuation process can seriously overstate the value of an investment and lead to incorrect investment decisions. When competition is considered, the net present value of an investment is a monotonically decreasing function of both the level of competitive intensity in the market and the duration (Boardman, Reinhart, and Celec, 1982; Copeland and Weston, 1988) of the project's cash flows, which implies that, unlike the noncompetitive case, the pattern of discounted cash flows matters in the capital budgeting problem. In order to demonstrate these results, this chapter is organized as follows. Section II develops the competitive model for net present value and discusses the impact of competitive intensity and duration on project value. Section III reports the simulation effects of changing the parameters of the model on net present value, the internal rate of return (IRR) and the discount rate. Section IV discusses possible extensions of the model and its empirical implementation, and Section V summarizes and concludes the study.

II. THE MODEL

This section compares the net present value of a project under both noncompetitive and competitive conditions. The noncompetitive capital budgeting decision criterion using the NPV method of cash flow evaluation, NPV_n, is

Invest if $NPV_n > 0$, otherwise reject the project

where $NPV_n = C - I$

$\quad C$ = present value of all future cash flows generated by the project from immediately after the time of the initial investment to the project termination date T

$\quad I$ = initial investment

Assume that cash flows from the proposed investment are continuous[3] and that T, the terminal date of the project, is 1; then the economic life of the project can be mapped onto the half-open interval $t(0, 1)$ without loss of generality.

The viewpoint of this investigation is that of a firm with the technological capability to introduce a new product or innovation into the market (firm 1). Firm 1, the "innovator," possesses technological information that the other firms in the industry do not have. At t_0 firm 1 faces n competitors, the "followers," all of which lag firm 1 in their ability to introduce a competing product. Assume that probabilistic entry by one of the n competitors at any date t^*, $0 < t^* < 1$, will eliminate firm 1's subsequent estimated cash flows.[4] Because of the possibility of competitive entry, firm 1 faces a stochastic project termination date; that is, $T = t^*$ [the time interval $(0, t^*)$ is the expected duration of firm 1's competitive advantage]. In contrast, in a noncompetitive environment, $T = 1$ (i.e., the project will not be interrupted). Firm 1's problem, then, is to estimate competitive net present value, NPV_c which is possible if the stochastic process underlying the waiting time for competitive entry is assumed to be known.

Here it is assumed that the waiting time for a competitive arrival follows a Poisson process, which implies that the probability of competitive entry before a given time t is defined by the exponential distribution with parameter θ. We can think of the next competitive entrant from the pool of competitors, firm 2, as being the first in line in the quene for obtaining superior technological information. Firm 2 is able to influence the parameter of the exponential distribution through, for example, the amount of its research and development expenditures. In effect, θ measures the effectiveness and the intensity of the competitor's effort. The larger the value of θ, the greater the probability of competitive entry relative to a given time period. Note that in this scenario, the next most competitive entrant, firm 2, is naive in that it does not consider the competitive environment in its own evaluation of capital investments.[5]

Given θ, competitive NPV for firm 1 is defined as

$$\text{NPV}_c = C \int_0^1 \frac{\delta g(t, \alpha)}{\delta t} F(t:\theta) \, dt - I$$

$$= \alpha C \int_0^1 t^{\alpha-1} e^{-\theta t} \, dt - I$$

(1)

where $F(t:\theta)$ is the probability that a competitive entrant will arrive after a given time t. In other words, $F(t:\theta) = 1 - p(t^* < t)$, the probability density function of the exponential distribution. $g(t, \alpha) = t^\alpha$, $a > 0$, is the cumulative proportion of the present value of the total cash inflows C that has been received by firm 1 as of time t, and $\delta g(t, \alpha)/\delta \alpha = t^\alpha \ln(t) < 0$ for $0 < t < T$.[6]

Since $\delta g(t, \alpha)/\delta a < 0$, the larger the value of α, the smaller the proportion of the total present value cash inflows C received by firm 1 at any point in time t. Note that if $\alpha = 1$, then Ct^α, the present value of the cash flows received up until t, is directly proportional to t, and the present value cash flows are received equally over the life of the project, implying that the unadjusted cash flows grow at the discount rate (i.e., $g = k$). If $\alpha < 1$, the growth rate is initially greater than k but declines as t increases. If $\alpha > 1$, the reverse holds, and the growth rate g is initially close to zero but increases as t increases. In other words, for $\alpha < 1$, $\delta g/\delta t > 0$ and $\delta^2 g/\delta t^2 < 0$, and for $\alpha > 1$, $\delta g/\delta t > 0$ and $\delta^2 g/\delta t^2 > 0$. The parameter α is used in this analysis to describe the discounted cash flow pattern of the cumulative present value cash inflows.[7] As a result, α provides a convenient characterization of the growth patterns of both the unadjusted and the present value cash inflows at any time t and thus serves as a proxy for the duration of the project's cash flows.[8] Figure 10.1 shows Ct^α for $\alpha = 0.25$, $\alpha = 0.50$, $\alpha = 1.00$, and $\alpha = 2.00$. Since the termination date T, in the noncompetitive case equals 1 (i.e., a noncompetitive project enjoys its full life), NPV$_n$ is invariant with respect to changes in α. In other words, $Ct^\alpha = C$ for all values of α and the time pattern of discounted cash flows does not affect noncompetitive net present value. This is not true if there is a possibility of competitive entry. With competition, the premature termination of a project resulting from competitive entry at any time t^* will result in greater present value losses, the larger the value of α (the discounted cash flows occurring later in time). In Figure 10.1, the present value losses due to premature termination at t^* are shown as the vertical distance between the noncompetitive present value cash inflows (the horizontal line $Ct^\alpha = 1$) and the graphs of Ct^α. As can be seen, at any time t, except for $t = 1$, $Ct^{0.25} > Ct^{0.5} > Ct > Ct^2$; therefore, $1 - Ct^{0.25} < 1 - Ct^{0.5} < Ct < Ct^2$, and present value losses are a positive function of α. This is summarized as

Proposition I:
In a competitive environment, not only does the timing of undiscounted cash flows matter because of the time value of money, but the timing of discounted cash flows matters because of the possibility of premature project termination.

Having gained an understanding of the cash flow patterns described by α and the significance of the timing of discounted cash flows to competitive net present value, we can more easily investigate the

Figure 10.1

Cumulative present values cash flows.

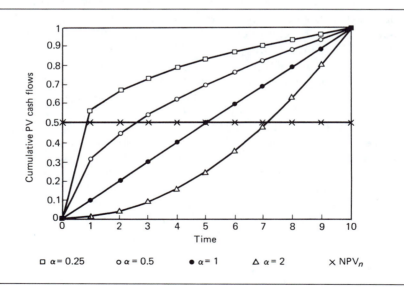

□ $\alpha = 0.25$ o $\alpha = 0.5$ ● $\alpha = 1$ △ $\alpha = 2$ × NPV_n

marginal effect of competitive intensity θ on the investment decision. For nonintegral values of α, a finite expression for Equation (1) (NPV$_c$) does not exist. For the moment, assume $\alpha = 1$, and then a simplified form of Equation (1) can be derived.

$$\text{NPV}_c = \frac{C}{\theta} - \frac{C}{\theta e^\theta - I} \tag{2}$$

with $\alpha = 1$ and

$$\frac{\delta \text{NPV}_c}{\delta \theta} = C \left(\frac{1}{\theta e^\theta} + \frac{1}{\theta^2 e^\theta} - \frac{1}{\theta^2} \right) \tag{3}$$

Equation (3) is less than 0 if $e^\theta > 1 + \theta$, which is true for all θ relevant to this analysis, since $\theta > 0$. Equation (3) demonstrates

Proposition II:
NPV$_c$ will decline, given an increase in the degree of competitive intensity.

Examining the difference between competitive and noncompetitive NPV confirms this result.

$$\text{NPV}_n - \text{NPV}_c = C - I - \frac{C}{\theta} + \frac{C}{\theta e^\theta + I}$$

$$= C \left(1 - \frac{1 - 1/e^\theta}{\theta} \right) \tag{4}$$

Equation (4) is greater than zero if $1/e^\theta > 1 - \theta$, which is true for all θ not equal to zero and thus true for all relevant θ in this analysis. An increase in firm 2's competitive effort decreases NPV$_c$ from the standpoint of firm 1. Ignoring the presence of the degree of competitiveness in the market can cause net present value to be overstated and can increase the possibility of investing erroneously. Equation (4) demonstrates that competitors reduce the value of a capital investment from what it would be in a noncompetitive setting and should thus be explicitly considered in the capital budgeting decision.

We asserted previously that, contrary to the valuation process in a noncompetitive environment, the timing of discounted cash flows matters. This can be further demonstrated in this simplified NPV setting. Increasing α from 1.00 to 2.00 results in the following formulation for NPV:

$$\text{NPV}_{c2} = \frac{2C}{\theta(1/\theta - 1/e\theta - 1/\theta e^\theta) - I} \tag{5}$$

$$\text{NPV}_{c2} - \text{NPV}_c = \frac{2C}{\theta^2(1 - 1/e^\theta) - C/\theta(1 + 1/e^\theta)} \tag{6}$$

Equation (6), the difference between competitive net present values when α increases from 1.00 to 2.00, is <0 if $(2 - \theta)e^{\theta} < 2 + \theta$, which is true for all relevant θ. Therefore, an increase in α from 1 to 2 decreases NPV_c. Given the direct relationship between duration and α cited before, and the inverse association between α and NPV_c, we can conclude that in a competitive situation the duration of a project's cash flows is inversely related to its net present value, confirming the result that the timing of discounted as well as undiscounted cash flows is important in a competitive environment. Increasing the duration of a project (holding NPV_n constant) reduces NPV_c because more of the present value cash flows are concentrated farther away in time, and the firm facing the investment problem thus has more to lose in the event of competitive entry. Thus two projects having the same noncompetitive net present value may not have the same value under rivalry. We have shown

Corollary II.1
If the durations of two projects' cash flows differ, the project with the shorter duration will have a higher NPV_c, even if their noncompetitive profitability index and NPV are the same.

The results of this section indicate that serious errors can occur in the valuation of an investment if the competitive environment and the timing of the investment's present value cash flows are neglected. Contrary to the situation in the noncompetitive case, an increase in either the degree of competitive intensity of the market or the duration of the investment causes a reduction in competitive net present value.

III. SIMULATION RESULTS

Simulations were performed in order to demonstrate the sensitivity of the NPV and internal rate of return criteria to changes in competitive intensity θ and the timing of present value cash flows α. Since point estimates of the parameters θ and α are imprecise, simulation results can provide the practitioner with information on the sensitivity of the results to the choice of θ and α. The simulation algorithm used in this section is as follows.

The following variables were held constant throughout the simulation exercise:

$C = \$120{,}000$

$I = $ initial investment $= \$100{,}000$

$\text{NPV}_n = \$20,000$

k = required rate of return in a noncompetitive setting = 0.15

T = project's economic life = 10 years.

In order to derive an expression for competitive NPV, it is assumed that cash inflows occur at the end of each year. The discrete analog for NPV_c [Equation (4)] is developed as follows:

$C(t_j)\alpha$ = cumulative present value cash flow in year j ($j = 1, T$)

$Zj = C(t_j^\alpha - C(t_{j-1})^\alpha$, present value cash flow in year j

$Xj = Zj(1 + k)^j$, undiscounted cash flow in year j.

Competitive net present value in the discrete case is

$$\text{NPV}_c = \sum_{j=1}^{T} \frac{X_j}{(1 + k)^j e^{-\theta t(j)} - I} \tag{7}$$

where k = cost of capital in a noncompetitive environment
$t_j = j/T$, the mapping of T into the interval $(0, 1)$
$e^{-\theta t(j)}$ = probability that competitive entry will occur after year j

In addition to NPV_c, three other variables are of interest:

IRR_c = competitive IRR, the interest rate solution to $\text{NPV}_c = 0$

k_c = competitive required rate of return, the interest rate that equates the noncompetitive undiscounted cash flows with NPV_c

$D = \Sigma(j = 1, T)jZj/C$, the duration measure for the investment.

Four values of α (0.25, 0.50, 1.00, 2.00) reflecting increasing duration are used as inputs to Equation (7). For each value of α, 16 values of θ^9 corresponding to increasing competitive intensity are examined, resulting in a total of 64 simulations.

Figures 10.2 and 10.3 plot NPV_c and IRR_c against competitive intensity θ. In Figure 10.3, NPV_n is represented as the horizontal line extending from \$20,000. The reduction in NPV resulting from increasing competitive intensity is measured as the vertical distance between NPV_n and the relevant graph of NPV_c. For example, at $\alpha = 0.25$, as θ increases, NPV_c declines from \$20,000 to \$9208.31, a decrease of \$10,791.69. Note that increasing α has the effect of rotating the NPV_c curve downward. At $\alpha = 2$, as θ increases, NPV_c declines to $-\$7373.33$ for a total decrease of $-\$27,373.33$.

Figure 10.2

NPV$_c$ versus competitive intensity.

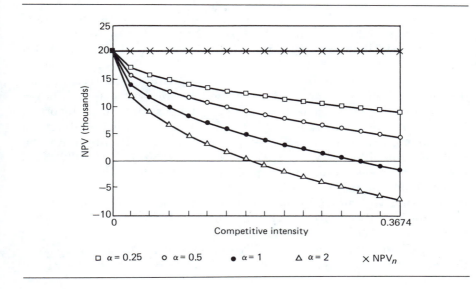

Figure 10.3

IRR$_c$ versus competitive intensity.

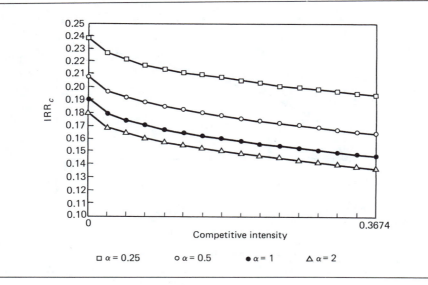

The same relationships hold in Figure 10.4, which compares competitive intensity to the competitive internal rate of return IRR_c. As θ increases, IRR_c declines monotonically for all levels of α. At $\alpha = 0.25$, increasing the marginal competitive intensity causes a 4.47% decline in IRR_c from 23.85% to 19.38%. Once again, increasing α causes a downward rotation in the IRR_c curve. When $\alpha = 2$, and with θ increasing, IRR_c declines from 18.00% to 13.75%, a total decrease of 4.25%. As determined in Section II, Figures 10.3 and 10.4 show that an increase in either competitive intensity or duration (as proxied by α) results in a decrease in both NPV_c and IRR_c. For long-duration projects (α is large) and highly competitive markets (θ is large), the possibility of an incorrect investment decision increases. What looks like a plausible investment in a noncompetitive context ($NPV_n = \$20,000$) can actually turn out to be quite unprofitable ($NPV_c = \$7373.33$ for $\theta = 0.3674$, $\alpha = 2.00$). This result emphasizes the need to explicitly consider the competitive environment and the pattern of discounted cash flows in the capital budgeting decision and indicates that to the degree that these factors are ignored in the NPV_n analysis, NPV_n can be overstated, resulting in more projects being accepted than might be warranted.

In Figure 10.4, the competitive opportunity cost of capital k_c is plotted against the level of competitive intensity; k_n is shown as the

Figure 10.4

k_c versus competitive intensity.

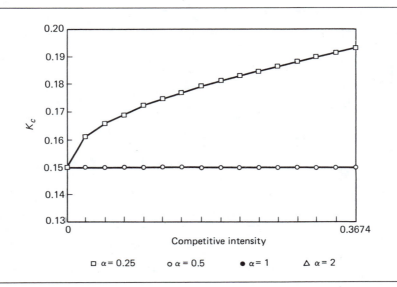

Competitive intensity

□ $\alpha = 0.25$ ○ $\alpha = 0.5$ ● $\alpha = 1$ △ $\alpha = 2$

horizontal line extending from 0.15. As θ increases, k_c increases from 15% to 19.31%, or 4.31%. Note that k_c is invariant to changes in α; this is because changes in α affect the level of expected returns, not their risk. This is an interesting result, especially from the standpoint of the interpretation of α as a proxy for duration, because traditionally D is normally thought of as proxy for (interest rate) risk. In this simulation, changing the duration of an investment, holding NPV constant, leaves risk unchanged but reduces NPV_c because of a decline in expected return.

IV. EXTENSIONS OF THE MODEL

A. Changing the Assumption of the Impact of Competitive Entry on Present Value Cash Flows

The assumption that competitive entry eliminates all future cash flows after t^* can be relaxed to incorporate partial reductions in cash flows. Let β be the proportionate reduction in cash flows after t^* due to the arrival of a competitor, and then the general competitive net present value model is

$$\text{NVP}_c' = \sum_{j=1}^{T} \{Z_j e^{-\theta t(j)} + (1 - \beta)Z_j - (1 - \beta)Z_j e^{-\theta t(j)}\} - I \qquad (8)$$

with β defined on the interval $[0, 1]$. If $\beta = 1$, all cash flows after t^* are eliminated as a result of competitive entry, and we have competitive NPV, NPV_c, as discussed in Section III. If $\beta = 0$, then competitive entry has no effect, and we are left with the middle term in Equation (10), $\Sigma(j = 1, T)Z_j$, and thus NPV_c' is equal to noncompetitive net present value, NPV_n. NPV_c' is bounded above by NPV_n and below by NPV_c. The simulation results in Section III are thus a worse case scenario and are mitigated slightly if the generalized formula is used. The use of Equation (8) does not, however, change the implications of Sections II and III. Only in the case of $\beta = 0$ is it true that the intensity of competitive effort and the duration of the project's cash flows will have no effect on net present value.

B. Empirical Estimation of θ

The usefulness of NPV_c and NPV_c' as a practical decision methodology is maximized when the firm conducting the analysis has some past experience with the typical delay involved in the entry of the next best competitor. If the firm has historical data on these waiting times, then maximum likelihood estimation techniques can be used to estimate θ. This methodology has an advantage over the option pricing technique discussed earlier and other ad hoc methods of risk adjustment in that it injects an element of objectivity into the analysis. A more important case, however, involves new projects with which the firm has had no prior technical experience (a "high-tech" project, for example). If this is the capital budgeting situation of firm 1, its technical staff and market research department must estimate θ using technological forecasting methods. In either situation, it appears that firm 1 can successfully confront the problem of measuring the degree of market competitive intensity.

C. Relaxation of the Assumption That the Next Competitive Entrant, Firm 2, Is Competitively Naive

In this section we relax the assumption that firm 2 is competitively naive. Consider a capital budgeting project with perpetual cash flows in each period equal to C. In the absence of competition, the net present value of the project to firm 1, the innovator, is

$$\text{NPV} = \frac{C}{k} - I \tag{9}$$

where k is the discount rate and I is the initial investment, as before.

If competition is present, then, as discussed above, the noncompetitive NPV, $C/k - I$, overstates the competitive NPV. This overstatement is a function of both when the competitor enters and the cash flow reduction that results when the competitor forces firm 1 to share its economic rents. If there is more than one potential competitor in the market, the situation becomes more complicated, in that each firm must weigh its decision to invest based not only on their own evaluation of the project but also on those of all other firms in the industry. The question of which firm will enter first and the patterns of competitive entries must then be used as input to firm 1's investment decision.

In order to simplify this problem somewhat, consider a three-firm industry, with firm 1 the innovator and firms 2 and 3 possible competitors. The following assumptions are assumed to hold:

1. The initial investment opportunity being evaluated is a perpetuity with initial investment I and constant cash flow C.
2. Firm 1 has the ability to start the project immediately.
3. All three firms have the same initial investment I and cost of capital k. If any firm decides to invest, the initial investment must be made immediately (i.e., at time 0).
4. Firm 3 lags firm 2 in its ability to install the project. In terms of Section III, this implies that $\theta_1 > \theta_2 > \theta_3$. Since θ is a function of

research and development expense R, this implies that firm 1 can make more efficient use of its research and development expenditures than firm 2 and that firm 2 is more efficient than firm 3 [i.e., for any level of r, $\theta_1 = f_1(R) > \theta_2 = f_2(R) > \theta_3 = f_3(R)$].

5. If firm 2 enters the market, the constant cash flow C will be proportionately reduced by β_1, and if firm 3 subsequently enters the market, C will be further reduced by β_2.

6. Firms 1, 2, and 3 are risk-neutral.

Given these assumptions, firm 1's evaluation of the project is based on three possibilities: firm 2 and firm 3 both enter the market, firm 2 alone enters the market, and neither of the competitors enter. These three cases are examined below.

Case 1.1: Cash Flow to Firm 1 If Both Firms 1 and 2 Enter the Market

If both competing firms enter the market, the cash flows accruing to firm 1 will be proportionately reduced at times t^*_1 and t^*_2 (the times at which firms 2 and 3 enter the market, respectively). Since competitive arrivals are assumed to follow a Poisson process, the expected time of competitive arrival, or t^*, is a function of θ. In particular, since the waiting time for competitive arrival follows an exponential distribution, the expected arrival time is equal to $1/\theta$ and thus t^*_1 (or t^*_2), for the purposes of this example, is equal to the end of the time period in which $1/\theta_1$ or $1/\theta_2$) occurs. Given this definition of t^*_1 and t^*_2, the competitive net present value to firm 1 for this case is

$$\sum_{t=1}^{t^*_1-1} \frac{C}{(1+k)^t} + \sum_{t=t^*_1}^{t^*_2-1} \frac{C(1-\beta_1)}{(1+k)^t} + \frac{C(1-\beta_1-\beta_2)}{k(1+k)^{t^*_2-1}} - I \tag{10}$$

The first expression in Equation (10) is the present value of the noncompetitive cash flows up until the time of the first competitive entry, the second expression is the present value of the noncompetitive cash flows reduced by β_1 as a result of the entry of the first competitor, and the third expression is the present value of the perpetuity, where the perpetual cash flows $C - \beta_1 - \beta_2$ are net after both firms 1 and 2 have entered the market.

Case 1.2: Cash Flow to Firm 1 If Firm 2 Alone Enters the Market

If only firm 2 decides to invest in the project, then firm 1's evaluation of the project should be based on the following equation:

$$\sum_{t=1}^{t^*_1-1} \frac{C}{(1+k)^t} + \frac{C(1-\beta_1)}{k(1+k)^{t^*_1-1}} - I \tag{11}$$

As in Equation (12), the first expression is the present value of the cash flows up until the time at which firm 2 enters the market. The second expression in Equation (11) corresponds to the third expression in Equation (10) and represents the present value of the perpetuity, where the constant cash flow is net of the reduction caused by firm 2's arrival.

Case 1.3: Cash Flow to Firm 1 If Neither Firm 1 or 2 Enters the Market
    If firm 1 does not face any competition, then the net present value problem reduces to Equation (9), the noncompetitive case.
    Firm 1's decision as to which model to use must be based on the alternatives facing firms 2 and 3, and the analysis of firm 2's possible decisions must also be based on its perception of firm 3's investment decision. For firm 2, the investment decision is based on one of two alternatives, which depend on whether or not firm 3 enters the market.

Case 2.1: Cash Flow to Firm 2 If Firm 3 Enters the Market
    If firm 2 is facing the possible entry of a competitor, then its analysis of the prospective investment should be based on

$$\sum_{t=t_1^*}^{t_2^*-1} \frac{C(1 - \beta_1)^t}{1 + k} + \frac{C(1 - \beta_1 - \beta_2)}{k(1 + k)^{t_2^*-1}} - I \tag{12}$$

where the first expression is the present value of the net cash flows to firm 2 before firm 3 enters the market and the second expression is the present value of the perpetuity to firm 2, where the constant cash flow is reduced to reflect the competitive effects of the presence of firms 1 and 2 in the market.

Case 2.2: Cash Flow to Firm 2 If Firm 3 Fails To Enter the Market
    In this case, the value of the capital investment to firm 2 is equal to the value of a perpetuity with constant cash flows $C - \beta_1$ beginning in the year t^*_1:

$$\frac{C(1 - \beta_1)}{k(1 + k)^{t_1^*-1}} - I \tag{13}$$

Case 3: Cash Flow to Firm 3 If It Enters the Market
    In choosing which model to use to evaluate the proposed investment, firm 2 must consider firm 3's decision, which in turn derives from an analysis of the perpetual cash flows after time t^*_2:

$$\frac{C(1 - \beta_1 - \beta_2)}{k(1 + k)^{t_1^*-1}} - I \tag{14}$$

The alternative cash inflows in this three-firm world are represented as

Period	1	2	3	...	t^*_1	...	t^*_2	...
Firm 1:								
Case 1.1	C	C	C	...	$C(1 - \beta_1)$	...	$C(1 - \beta_1 - \beta_2)$	...
Case 1.2	C	C	C	...	$C(1 - \beta_1)$	...		...
Case 1.3	C	C	C	...		...		...
Firm 2:								
Case 2.1	0	0	0	...	$C(1 - \beta_1)$	...	$C(1 - \beta_1 - \beta_2)$	...
Case 2.2	0	0	0	...	$C(1 - \beta_1)$	...		...
Firm 3:								
Case 3	0	0	0	...		...	...	$C(1 - \beta_1 - \beta_2)$	...

Note that since competition works to eliminate economic rents, this imposes an upper limit on the sum $\beta_1 + \beta_2$. This limit arises from the standpoint of firm 1, where $C[1 - (\beta_1 + \beta_2)]/k = I$ if no economic rents are earned. Thus $\beta_1 + \beta_2 < 1 - Ik/C$. This, along with the analysis above, results in the following conclusions:

1. As expected, economic rents, and thus the probability of competitive entry, are a positive function of the constant cash flow C and a negative function of the initial investment I and the cost of capital k.

2. As in the case of the naive competitor, noncompetitive NPV overstates the true NPV. This overstatement is magnified as the estimated (noncompetitive) economic rents increase, because the probability of competitive entry is positively related to the magnitude of (estimated) economic rents.

3. It is possible that under a certain combination of parameter values, the NPV to firm 1 is greater when both firms 2 and 3 exist than when only firm 2 exists. This is because the threat of firm 3 entering would either stop or delay firm 2 from entering.

4. The net present value to firm 1 is negatively related to the magnitude of β_1 and β_2. Paradoxically, if β_1 is large enough, overall NPV to firm 1 may increase, because the possibility exists that firm 2 may enter the market, whereas firm 3 will now find it unprofitable to invest (i.e., a switch from Case 1.1 to Case 1.2), and thus the present value of the overall cash flow reduction to firm 1 may be less. Thus there is an incentive for the most efficient firm in the industry to collude, justifying governmental regulation. Note that in this scenario, there is also an incentive for firm 1 to voluntarily reduce its constant cash flow C by some factor α, so that other firms with

similar production technologies will find it unprofitable to invest. This can be a viable strategy for the most efficient firm in the industry as long as $\alpha < \beta_1 + \beta_2$.

5. An implication of item 3 is that a better strategy for the less efficient firms in the industry is to compete through the use of alternate production technologies. This relaxes the assumption of a constant initial investment I for all firms in the industry. Effectively, the objective for each firm in the industry is to become the front runner.

6. Relaxation of the assumption of risk neutrality would not change the general results in this section. Assuming risk aversion would, however, make the optimal solution considerably more complex, as mathematical programming techniques would have to be used.

V. SUMMARY AND CONCLUSION

This chapter has investigated the capital budgeting decision in a competitive environment characterized by asymmetric information. The presence of competitors alters the relevant set of variables in the valuation of capital assets. It has been shown that, contrary to the situation in the noncompetitive case, competitive net present value is a function of the degree of competitive intensity in the market and the duration of the investment's cash flows. Thus, in a competitive setting, the timing of discounted cash flows is relevant to the valuation problem. A ranking rule such as, "For a given noncompetitive NPV choose the project with the shortest duration or the shortest (discounted) payback period" maximizes firm value above and beyond any role using the NPV or profitability index alone. Serious errors in the estimation of a project's value can occur if the presence of competitors is ignored in the analysis of net present value. The decrease in NPV and IRR associated with an increase in either competitive intensity or duration implies that these variables should be explicitly incorporated into most analyses of capital budgeting problems.

NOTES

1. Use of the internal rate of return (IRR) method is subject to the same criticisms.

2. Using Bayesian analysis, Miller shows that the implication of the preponderance of bad projects is that NPV forecasts will be biased because of the uncertainty surrounding the prior distribution of investment projects, even if forecasters are unbiased in their cash flow estimates. His insight that positive biases exist in a competitive environment has been supported with

survey data (Mills, 1988) and behavioral experiments (Trigeorgis, 1986). Failure to take into account the nonuniform prior distribution of possible projects in a competitive industry can lead to serious economic consequences for firms using traditional capital budgeting techniques.

3. This assumption is relaxed in Section III.

4. This assumption is relaxed in Section IV.

5. Firm 2 does not incorporate the possibility of the arrival of firm 3 into its capital budgeting decision, firm 3 does not consider firm 4, and so on. This has the effect of intensifying firm 2's competitive effort. Firm 2 is willing to commit more resources toward eliminating firm 1's informational advantage because its own estimate of project net present value is overstated.

6. The following results assume that the probability of competitive entry is a positive function of time. These results can be generalized to any probability distribution for which the distribution function of competitive entry is positively related to the length of time after the first competitive arrival.

7. α can also be modeled as a function of time without loss of generality. This would allow S-shaped cash flow patterns in Figure 10.1 and would expand the relevant set of present value cash flow patterns to all those whose first derivative with respect to time is continuous and positive on the interval (O, T)

8. The duration D of an investment project in this competitive environment can be defined as

$$D = \frac{\int_0^1 \delta/\delta t[C(t)^\alpha]t \, dt}{C} = \frac{\alpha}{\alpha + 1}$$

with $dD/d\alpha = 1/(\alpha + 1)^2$. This demonstrates a positive relationship between the duration of the project cash flows and α. As α approaches 0, the cumulative present value cash flows become increasingly concentrated toward time 0; thus the project returns its average present value very quickly, and its duration is very short. When $\alpha = 1$, the average present value is returned at the midpoint of the economic life of the project ($t = 0.5$); as a α approaches ∞, the cumulative discounted cash flows are concentrated toward the end of the project's economic life, and its duration approaches the terminal date of the project ($t = 1.0$). As is evident from both the equation above and Figure 10.1, duration is a direct function of α.

9. The values of θ used in simulations are computed as follows: $\theta = 0.003(x^{1/2})$, where x takes on the values 0, 1000, 2000, . . . , 14,000, 15,000. This assumes a diminishing marginal return to competitive effort and results in values of θ ranging from 0 to 0.3674.

REFERENCES

BOARDMAN, C. M., W. J. REINHART, and S. E. CELEC (1982). "The Role of the Payback Period in the Theory and Application of Duration to Capital Budgeting," *Journal of Business Finance and Accounting* 9, pp. 511–522.

BUTLER, J. S., and BARRY SCHACHTER (1989). "The Investment Decision: Estimation Risk and Risk Adjusted Discount Rates," *Financial Management* 18 (Winter), pp. 13–22.

COPELAND, T. E., and J. F. WESTON (1988). *Financial Theory and Corporate Policy*, 3rd ed. (Reading, Mass.: Addison-Wesley), chaps. 2–3.

GILBERT, R. J., and R. G. HARRIS (1984). "Competition with Lumpy Investment," *Rand Journal of Economics* 15, pp. 197–212.

HAYES, R. H., and D. A. GARVIN (1982). "Managing as If Tomorrow Mattered," *Harvard Business Review* 60 (May–June), pp. 70–79.

KESTER, W. C. (1984). "Today's Options for Tomorrow's Growth," *Harvard Business Review*, 58 (March–April), pp. 153–160.

MACAULAY, F. R. (1938). *Some Theoretical Problems Suggested by the Movements of Interest Rates, Bond Yields, and Stock Prices in the United States Since 1856.* New York: National Bureau of Economic Research), pp. 44–53.

MACDONALD, R. L., and D. R. SIEGEL (1985). "Investment and the Valuation of Firms When There Is An Option to Shut Down," *International Economic Review* 26, pp. 331–349.

MACDONALD, R. L., and D. R. SIEGEL (1986). "The Value of Waiting to Invest," *Quarterly Journal of Economics* 401 (November), pp. 707–727.

MAJD, S., and R. S. PINDYCK (1987). "Time to Build, Option Value, and Investment Decisions," *Journal of Financial Economics* 18, pp. 7–27.

MASON, S. P., and R. C. MERTON (1985). "The Role of Contingent Claims Analysis in Corporate Finance," in E. Altman and M. Subrahmanyam (eds.), *Recent Advances in Corporate Finance* (Homewood, Ill.: Richard D. Irwin).

MILLER, E. M. (1988). "Safety Margins and Capital Budgeting Criteria," *Managerial Finance*, Special Issue on the Capital Budgeting Process Theory and Practice, 14(2/3).

MILLS, D. E. (1988). "Preemptive Investment Timing," *Rand Journal of Economics* 19, pp. 114–122.

PRUITT, S. W., and L. J. GITMAN (1987). "Capital Budgeting Forecast Biases: Evidence From the Fortune 500," *Financial Management* 16 (Spring), pp. 46–51.

TRIGEORGIS, L. (1986). "Valuing the Impact of Uncertain Competitive Arrivals on Deferrable Real Investment Opportunities." Unpublished working paper, Harvard Business School.

STATMAN, M., and T. T. TYEBJEE (1985). "Optimistic Capital Budgeting Forecasts: An Experiment," *Financial Management* 14 (Autumn), pp. 27–33.

11

Turning Growth Options
Into Real Assets

W. CARL KESTER

ABSTRACT

This chapter reviews the contingent claims approach to the valuation of capital expenditure proposals. The problem of timing future investments is examined when competitive advantage is eroding and when learning results from earlier projects.

A traditional approach to capital budgeting generally treats projects as isolated investment opportunities about which an accept/reject decision must be made immediately. Some type of discounted cash flow criterion is usually recommended as the basis for decision making.

In practice, however, many proposed projects are not isolated efforts. They are part of a larger capital expenditure program, or "cluster," of related projects to be implemented over a long span of time. They often require large, irreversible commitments of funds; contain projects that can be undertaken, altered, or abandoned at various points in time; and, importantly, have the potential to create valuable new investment opportunities for the firm in the future. These features impart strategic significance to an investment program and raise a number of important tactical issues. Beside the question of whether or not to invest, a company must decide *how* it will execute the program, especially as concerns the timing of the investment.

Because of their strategic implications, investment timing decisions are deemed by many practitioners to be beyond the scope of financial analysis. However, recent advances in the application of contingent claims analysis to capital budgeting problems give rise to the possibility that this view will be overturned. Indeed, these advances hold the promise of integrating strategic and financial analyses of projects by simultaneously overcoming deficiencies in the treatment of uncertainty inherent in ordinary discounted cash flow analysis and imparting rigor to the assessment of operating flexibilities embedded in long-lived capital expenditure programs.[1]

This article furthers this integration by analyzing from a contingent claims perspective two common practical problems of investment decision making: the timing of capital commitments in a competitive environment and the sequencing of project execution within the context of a larger capital expenditure program extending over many periods. In focusing on these particular problems, it is shown generally that many of the strategic and tactical considerations that practitioners (correctly) claim are beyond the scope of ordinary net present value (NPV) analysis can still be reconciled with the traditional financial objective of maximizing shareholder value. We need only expand our perspective on what constitutes value and how investment decisions can affect this value over time.

Section I of this chapter describes briefly a contingent claims approach to capital budgeting and summarizes some important implications of this approach. Section II focuses on the specific problem of timing future capital commitments. This problem is examined under conditions where competitive advantage is eroding and under conditions where learning results from early projects undertaken within a broader capital expenditure program. Further insights are developed by use of several numerical examples in Section III. General conclusions are drawn in Section IV.

I. A CONTINGENT CLAIMS APPROACH TO CAPITAL BUDGETING

Departures from conventional capital budgeting prescriptions such as "Maximize net present value" and "Accept all projects with an internal rate of return greater than the cost of capital" are commonplace observations among clinical researchers of large, modern corporations. Sometimes this variance can be explained simply as misapplications of otherwise correct capital budgeting tools. However, even in organizations where formal capital budgeting criteria are well understood, some of the most critical resource allocation decisions are made through a less formal process of deriving a consensus among top corporate executives, placing heavy reliance on "competitive" or "strategic" considerations.

Unfortunately, the lack of rigor in such a process can lead to situations in which weak projects are justified on an ad hoc basis, all in the name of strategy. A more appropriate framework for such projects is one that overcomes the restrictiveness of ordinary net present value analysis *and* the lack of analytic discipline that so often characterizes qualitative evauation. Contingent claims analysis presents such a framework.

In a contingent claims framework, discretionary investment opportunities are considered to be analogous to call options on securities. The "security" underlying the discretionary investment opportunity—hereinafter, *growth option*—is actually the bundle of assets, tangible and/or intangible, that constitutes the opportunity in question. The growth option's "exercise price" is the cash outlay necessary to acquire the assets.

This analogy compels one to consider how the various determinants of a call option's value might influence the value of future investment opportunities and thus the firm's capital budgeting decisions. But the analogy also prompts one to draw a distinction between two basic components of an investment's value:

1. That attributable to cash flows resulting from ownership and operation of real assets, and
2. That attributable to new options for future investment also made available to the firm as a consequence of real asset ownership and operation.

With regard to the second component of value, some capital investment projects may be perceived as being similar to a "compound option," that is, an option whose exercise brings forth additional options as well as possibly generating cash flows. Research and development projects, a decision to enter a new market, or the acquisition of a company are all examples of discretionary investment opportunities that are likely to open the door to still more investment opportunities as well as cash flows.

The casting of investment opportunities as call options on assets, and the distinction between assets in place and growth options as components of value, yield a number of important implications for capital budgeting. These have been discussed at length in an earlier paper (Kester 1984) and are summarized briefly as follows:

1. *It may be rational to invest in a business activity beyond the point justified by conventional discounted cash flow analysis* (i.e., to "overinvest") *if the investment is viewed as a "purchase" of valuable growth options.* In principle, option-creating investments should be subjected to an expanded net present value test in which

both components of value—that stemming from cash flows and that from new growth options—are analyzed. Projects with negative net present value may be worth accepting if they yield new growth options whose value more than offsets that lost because of the project's direct cash flow consequences. Investment decisions made on this basis are familiar to many practitioners who often refer to them as "expense investing" or "loss-leader" investments.

2. *Overinvestment may appear most acute in volatile industry environments.* This results from the positive effect that risk has on an option's value, other things held constant.[2] Because heightened risk can increase the value of growth options, projects that represent compound growth options in volatile markets have a comparative advantage in the capital budgeting process over comparable projects yielding only cash flows or new options in less risky environments.

3. *Overinvestment may also appear most acute during periods of tight capital and high interest rates, other things being equal.* This results from the positive effect that increases in the interest rate have on an option's value.[3] Just as heightened risk can create a comparative advantage for compound growth options, so too can higher interest rates create a comparative advantage for compound growth options in the capital budgeting process. This advantage could be sufficient to cause value-maximizing companies facing high capital costs to shift the mix of their capital expenditures toward projects generating valuable new growth options rather than toward primarily cash generating projects.

4. *Firms should find long-lived growth options* (i.e., deferrable investment opportunities) *to be more valuable than short-lived options and should avoid exercising them any sooner than necessary.* This arises from the fact that an option's value increases as the length of time before expiration increases (Figure 11.1). The more time available before one has to commit capital, the better one's opportunity to capitalize on large gains in a project's value or to avoid damaging losses due to adverse future events. Because more time before having to commit capital makes a growth option more valuable, managers avoid sacrificing value needlessly by deferring final accept/reject decisions about a project as long as practically possible.

This last implication is particularly noteworthy. The value enhancement that arises from deferrability gives rise to an important but somewhat counterintuitive result: An *option* to invest will be actually worth *more* than the net present value of the underlying project. Figure 11.2 illustrates this relationship between the value of a deterrable

Figure 11.1

The relation between growth option value and the length of time projects can be deferred. The value of growth options rises as the length of time projects can be deferred increases.

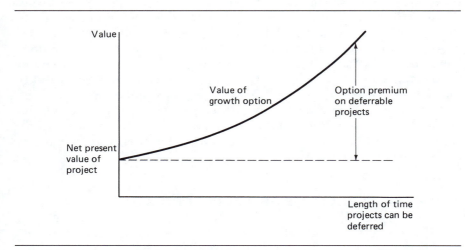

Figure 11.2

The relationship between growth option value and a project's net present value. X, Project's capital outlay; VV, net present value of project corresponding to various asset values; GG, Growth option value corresponding to various asset values.

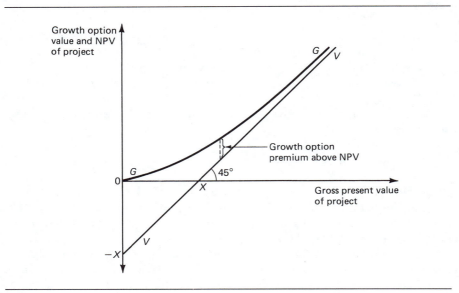

growth option at a given point in time and the net present value of the investment if the underlying asset were put in place immediately. As the gross present value of the project increases, so too does the project's net present value and the value of the option to invest. Note, however, that the option's value (shown by line GG) always remains above the net present value of the project (shown by line VV). Indeed, growth options have positive value even if the underlying project has a negative net present value at a given point in time, provided there exists a possibility that future developments will render the project more valuable. The vertical distance between the growth option value curve and the net present value line in Figure 11.2 represents the value premium attributable to deferrability that would be sacrificed if capital were committed any sooner than necessary.

II. TIMING THE EXERCISE OF GROWTH OPTIONS

The logic underlying the deferral of capital expenditures as long as possible is inescapable within the context of the preceding simple analogy between discretionary investment opportunities and call options. However, even a cursory examination of actual practice makes clear the fact that capital is often committed earlier than absolutely necessary. The sacrifice in growth option value that this entails may be justified provided an offsetting gain, or the avoidance of an even greater loss, is generated in the process. Two common situations in which such a justification might exist are

1. An ability to preempt competitive investment that would otherwise erode a growth option's value, and
2. An ability to learn or gather relevant information so that future investments might possibly be made under more favorable terms.

Each of these motives for the early commitment of capital is explored in detail below.

A. Preemptive Investment

The holder of a call option on a security has the luxury of an exclusive right to the exercise of his or her particular option. The right cannot be abrogated legally by others. Competition for the investment opportunity held by the call option owner is nonexistent.

In contrast, such a fully protected right to exercise a particular investment opportunity is not generally available to the holder of a growth option. Some growth options, such as those involving new capacity to produce a unique, patented product or involving a new production technology that cannot be duplicated by others, might reasonably be considered proprietary in nature. But other investment opportunities might effectively be owned by more than one industry participant. For example, opportunities to enter a new market or to build new production facilities in a particular location are likely to be at the disposal of more than one company. Such growth options are of a shared variety and are more accurately thought of as "collective" opportunities of the industry.[4]

A second important discrepancy between growth options and ordinary call options on securities is that growth options are not likely to be tradable at low cost in an efficient market. Certain proprietary growth options might be purchased or sold by means of patents or licensing agreements but usually involve significant costs in the way of legal expenses and ongoing monitoring costs. Shared growth options may not be tradable at all, since they are by definition already owned by other industry participants and potential entrants.

Many other growth options may have to be bought or sold only in conjunction with specific real assets, or even specific individuals, to which they may be "attached." They might be attached in the sense that their value is dependent on some competitive advantage afforded by those assets or individuals. For example, options to expand production of items whose unit costs, and thus profit contributions, are heavily dependent on experience curve effects have different values depending on the cumulative production experience of the firm possessing them. A capacity expansion option may be quite valuable in the hands of a large-volume producer but be of little or no value to a potential new entrant with no production experience.

These characteristics of growth options are significant because they imply that (1) the value of some growth options can be eroded by competitors' actions and, more importantly, (2) a firm cannot easily escape such erosions by selling the option to others. Effectively, the response to anticipated erosion in growth option value may be limited to simply an early commitment of capital designed to *preempt* competitors' investments. The low-cost producer of a chemical commodity might prevent capacity expansion on the part of competitors by quickly adding new capacity in response to an increase in demand despite a desire to wait and observe future developments in the market. This alternative may be preferable to trying to preserve a shared growth option whose value could erode rapidly.

An early, preemptive commitment of capital may be the only available response to unavoidable erosion of value at the hands of competitors, but is it always desirable? Not necessarily, if one approaches the problem from a growth option perspective. Consider the comparative statics analysis depicted in Figure 11.3. As before, each graph specifies

Figure 11.3

Determining conditions for the early exercise of growth options.

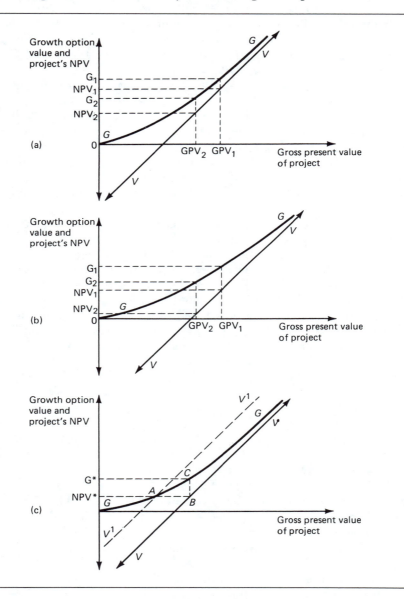

the relationship between a project's gross present value at a given point in time and (1) its net present value as a set of real assets in place (line VV), and (2) its value as an unexpired growth option (line GG).

Early investment is justified in the case depicted in Figure 11.3a. If a reduction in the project's gross present value from GPV_1 to GPV_2 is anticipated, then the firm owning the growth option will suffer a loss in value of $G_1 - G_2$. However, if the firm is able to prevent the loss through an early commitment of capital, it will sustain a loss of only $G_1 - NPV_1$. Because the cost of "killing" the growth option early is less than the erosion of value that would otherwise occur, the firm is better off committing capital early.

The opposite situation is shown in Figure 11.3b. A decline in the gross present value of a project equivalent to that shown in Figure 11.3a does *not* justify killing the growth option early. The loss in growth option value that would be sustained at the hands of competitors ($G_1 - G_2$) is less than the premium for deferrability ($G_1 - NPV_1$) that would be sacrificed if the growth option were exercised prematurely.

As a general rule, one can conclude that early commitments of capital to preempt competitors is justified only if the cost of killing the growth option is equal to or less than the loss of growth option value that would otherwise transpire. The precise point of indifference between committing capital early and retaining the project as a growth option (despite expected erosion of value of a given amount) is shown graphically in Figure 11.3c. The anticipated erosion in the gross present value of the project is represented by the dotted line $V'V'$. The breakeven point in a project's growth option value, above which it should be exercised early and below which it should be retained as a growth option, is shown as G^* in Figure 11.3c.

It bears emphasizing that *what matters in the timing of preemptive moves is the before and after effects of competitive investments on a project's growth option value, not such effects on its net present value per se.* That is, it is not sufficient for the anticipated decline in a project's net present value only to equal the cost of killing the growth option in order to justify an early commitment of capital. Rather, the savings in a project's net present value resulting from preemptive investment must actually *exceed* the cost of killing the growth option. This result may be confirmed in Figure 11.3c by noting that the length of line segment AB, the anticipted loss in the project's net present value, exceeds that of BC, the cost of killing the growth option.

The conditions under which a growth option should be exercised early for preemptive purposes varies from one situation to another. However, several key characteristics can be specified to help discriminate between growth options that are suitable for early exercise and those that are not. In general, growth options should be exercised early rather than be allowed to erode in value at the hands of competitors whenever the growth option is shared, the anticipated decline in value is large, the net present value of the underlying project is high, and the riskiness of the project is low. A stronger preference for implementing a project early also exists during periods of low interest rates. When interest rates are high, companies should be more inclined to hold projects as unexercised growth options.

B. Sequential Investment in Capital Expenditure Programs

The discussion so far has focused on the timing of capital commitments for a single, deferrable project considered in isolation. A more complex situation is encountered when dealing with a capital expenditure *program* made up of many related projects to be implemented over a long period of time.

An example of this more complex type of investment problem is that faced by a large manufacturer of consumer products. The company was considering entry into the market for personal care items and had a number of new products in various stages of development. Not only did it have to decide whether or not to go forward with the entry decision, it also had to decide when to make its move, how big its capital commitment ought to be, and the rapidity with which new products should be introduced. Should the company introduce products sequentially or take a "shotgun" approach to breaking into the market? If a sequenced approch proved desirable, which product (or products) should be introduced first and which later? A separate but related issue was the possibility of exiting from this business if long-run profitability did not seem viable. How long should the company endure losses before abandoning its venture in this market?

The company's decisions would be straightforward if the various new products in development were completely independent projects. Provided they were free of competitive threats, they could be held as a portfolio of growth options, each being exercised when it was perceived to have matured. Alternatively, if competitive threats did exist and conditions justified an early commitment of capital, then a rapid, simultaneous exercise of all these growth options would be appropriate.

However, in the actual situation, the new products clearly were not purely independent projects. The successful launching of any given personal care item would depend in part on the brand name image created by the company in this new category and on dealer support. Because consumer habits and tastes regarding personal care items were only vaguely understood by this company and because new channels of distribution were involved, it was evident that the company's ability to manage future product introduction would depend critically on the experience it gained in the early introductions. Moreover, early successes or failures would in and of themselves influence future trade support, consumer acceptance, and competitors' behavior in this market.

Because of such project interdependence and the capacity to learn from early product introductions, neither a shotgun approach to entry nor a series of independent accept/reject decisions for each product as it was readied for national rollout would have been optimal. Rather, a planned sequence of introductions was the appropriate means for the company to maximize value over time. The previously cited conditions that could justify the early exercise of an option can be used to determine the optimal sequence. Specifically, the optimal sequence was that obtained by exercising first those options believed to have the smallest premium above net present value. Again, these are generally growth options that are deeply "in the money" (i.e., have high net present values), have low risk, and are shared with competitors or are maturing quickly.

III. SEQUENCING INVESTMENTS USING THE GROWTH OPTION FRAMEWORK

A numerical example can illustrate the solution to the above project-sequencing problem. Consider the five interrelated projects described in Table 11.1. They are characterized by the capital outlay required and the present value of expected future cash inflows. All are assumed to be deferrable for as many as 5 years except project E, which must be undertaken within the next 2 years or be foregone entirely. Capital outlays are assumed to remain constant over time at the levels shown in column 2 of Table 11.1. For simplicity, it is also assumed that each project imple-

TABLE 11.1.   Characteristics of Five Interrelated Projects

Project[a]	Capital Outlays (million $)	Present Value of Expected Cash Inflows (million $)	Gain in Present Value from a Prior Success (%)	Loss in Present Value from a Prior Failure (%)
A	50	80	20	−20
B	75	65	20	−20
C	75	80	100	−50
D	75	80	5	− 5
E	75	80	20	−20

[a] All projects are deferrable for 5 years except project E, which is deferrable for only 2 years.

mented will meet with only one of two outcomes: success or failure. In each outcome, the net present value of the project is assumed to be known with certainty. Thus the only uncertainty involved is with respect to the success or failure of each new project.

If a project is a success, it has the side benefit of increasing the present value of all the *unexercised* projects. A failure has the opposite result. The percentages shown in columns 4 and 5 of Table 11.1 indicate how each project's gross present value is assumed to change (with certainty) in response to a prior success or failure, respectively. It is in this sense that the five projects may be considered interrelated within the context of this example. Paralleling the consumer products company's situation, these changes in value might be associated with heightened or diminished trade support, consumer acceptance, and so on, following a prior success or failure.

Figure 11.4 provides an illustration of how a project's worth can rise or fall depending on prior events. Figure 11.4a shows the pattern of project B's *net* present value, given all possible combinations of prior successes and failures. As one may observe, project B has negative net present value at the outset but can rise in value considerably if a number of previously implemented projects meet with success. On the other hand, more than one failure will only cause its value to diminish further.

A. A Simple Option Valuation Formula

An advantage of characterizing a project's outcome as either a success or a failure is that a simple two-state option pricing formula can be used to value each project as a growth option (see the Appendix for a complete description of the formula). Again, project B is used to illustrate the application of this formula. Its value as a growth option is shown in Figure 11.4b for every possible combination of prior successes and failures of other projects.

Two points are worth noting about project B as a growth option. First, consistent with the discussion in Section II of this article, project B's growth option value exceeds its corresponding net present value as an implemented project at every stage except the last. Even where project B has a negative net present value, its growth option value remains greater than or equal to zero. This difference is the premium attributable to project deferrability referred to earlier.

Second, in the fifth and final stage of deferral, project B's growth option value is equal to the greater of its net present value or zero. That is, when the project cannot be deferred any longer, its value as a growth option becomes identical to its net present value *if the net present value is positive*. If its net present value is negative, the project will simply be abandoned and its value will become zero.

Figure 11.4

The net present value and growth option value of project B subsequent to the outcomes of earlier projects. (A riskless rate of return of 5% was assumed in these calculations.) (a) Project B's net present value pattern. (b) Project B's growth option value pattern.

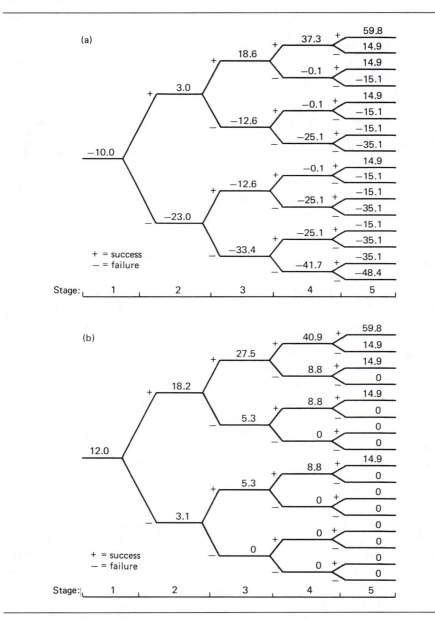

B. Determining the Optimal Sequence

Returning to Table 11.1 the problem to be solved is how best to implement the capital expenditure program represented by the five designated projects. It should be evident that implementing all five at once, either in the present or at any point during the 5-year time horizon, will not be appropriate. The reason is that simultaneous execution provides no opportunity for important events to occur or information to be learned that could enhance the projects' present values (note, once again, the potential improvement in the value of project B if successful projects are introduced ahead of it). Thus the best way to implement the program is sequentially. The problem then becomes one of determining which order of project execution is best.

The optimal sequence is shown in Figure 11.5a. It is derived by valuing each project as a growth option using a two-state option pricing formula. Starting at the beginning of the expanding chain of success and failures, the project exhibiting the smallest difference between its value as a growth option and as a set of assets in place (i.e., the smallest deferral premium) is exercised first. The same sort of calculation, comparison, and choice is made at the next stage, and so on, throughout the entire lattice. The total present value for this particular sequence is $109.7 million.[5]

The optimal sequence of project execution is consistent with the preceding analysis of conditions under which growth options should be exercised early. Specifically, one may note that the "deep-in-the-money" growth option (project A), the low-risk growth option (project D), and the short-lived growth option (project E) are all exercised within the first three periods. For each of these projects, there is relatively little value to be gained through deferral. Hence relatively little value is lost by early exercise.

In contrast, the high-risk growth option (project C) and the "out-of-the-money" growth option (project D) are retained as options until the end of the investment program. For these two projects, the deferral premium is relatively large, making it unattractive to exercise them early.

C. A Myopic Sequence

For purposes of comparison, a myopic sequence is shown in Figure 11.5b. The myopic sequence is derived by starting at the beginning of the chain of successes and failures and executing at each stage that project with the highest net present value. The total value of this sequence is estimated to be $102.3 million—nearly 10% less than that of the optimal sequence.

The myopic sequence differs from the optimal one in two major

Figure 11.5

Alternative sequences of project introductions. (a) Optimal sequence. (Assumes a riskless rate of 5%.) (b) Myopic sequence.

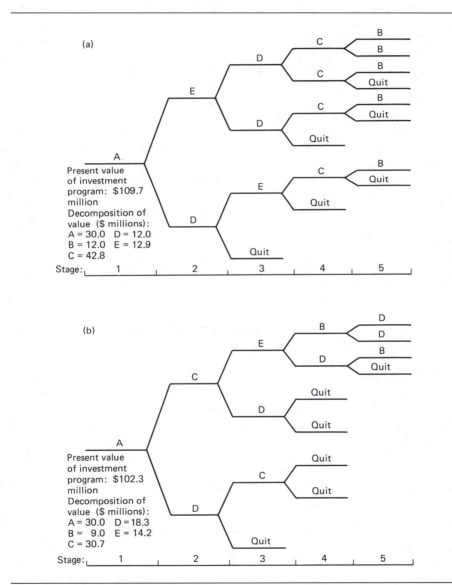

(a)

Present value of investment program: $109.7 million
Decomposition of value ($ millions):
A = 30.0   D = 12.0
B = 12.0   E = 12.9
C = 42.8

Stage: 1   2   3   4   5

(b)

Present value of investment program: $102.3 million
Decomposition of value ($ millions):
A = 30.0   D = 18.3
B = 9.0   E = 14.2
C = 30.7

Stage: 1   2   3   4   5

respects. First, the risky project (C) is executed much earlier in the sequence—in fact, immediately after the first success—while the low-risk project (D) is retained until the end as long as the investment program meets with favorable outcomes. This reversal relative to the optimal sequence arises because net present values analysis assigns no value to an ability to defer project execution. Consequently, the positive impact of risk on a growth option's value, and the incentive it creates to retain projects as growth options rather than as assets in place, is not captured in the analysis.

Second, the investing company will be inclined to abandon its investment program too soon if a sequential application of net present value analysis is used. The proximate cause of this tendency is that project E, the short-lived growth option, is allowed to expire worthless in some situations so that a higher net present value project can be adopted in its place. This in turn forecloses opportunities for project B's net present value to rise above zero.

The root cause for early abandonment, however, is that net present value analysis simply fails to capture the additional value that exists whenever a project can be deferred and executed at some future date, possibly under more favorable circumstances. When an investment program is analyzed from a growth options perspective, this additional value is recognized and investment decisions are made to preserve that value as long as possible.

D. Declining Competitive Advantage and the Role of Growth Options as Exit Barriers

The above example may be extended by assuming that there is a cost to deferring a project. This cost can be modeled as an erosion of competitive advantage resulting in higher capital outlays to implement a project. For example, let us now assume that the outlays for the projects shown in Table 11.1 rise by 5% each year. All other conditions remain the same.

Both the optimal and myopic sequences of projects in this extended example are shown in Figure 11.6. The optimal sequence produces a total value for the program of $89.2 million, while the myopic sequence has a value of $80.3 million.

In this example, the tendency to abandon the investment program prematurely is even more pronounced.[6] Indeed, in the myopic case, a failure at any point in the chain of events results in a decision to quit. Quite the opposite is true in the optimal sequence. In fact, the optimal sequence includes the possibility of exercising project E with a *negative* net present value (−$5.9 million)! Although counterintuitive, this decision is rational in light of the relatively high value of project C (the high-risk project) as a growth option. The value lost by exercising project E is

Figure 11.6

Alternative sequences of project introduction with the erosion of competitive advantage. (A) Optimal sequence. (Assumes an annual riskless rate of 5%.) (B) Myopic sequence. In both cases the erosion of competitive advantage is captured by assuming that capital outlay increases by 5% a year.

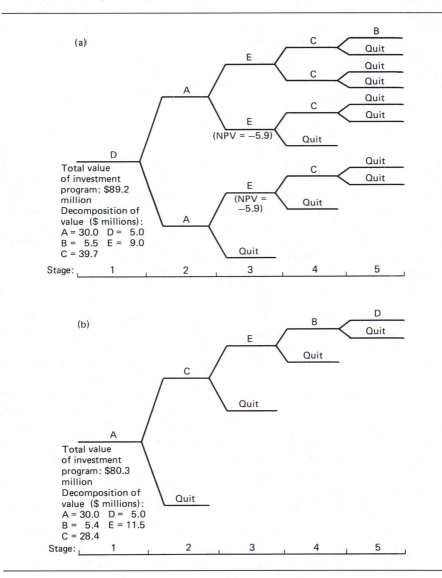

more than offset by the value preserved in holding project C one more year as a growth option.

From the perspective of conventional net present value analysis, this latter outcome suggests that growth options can operate as a type of "exit barrier." That is, although the operation of certain real assets may not be profitable in and of itself, the dependence of other growth options on these assets may cause a company to continue their operation and even to persist in making further investments in their support. The objective of doing so is simply to preserve the value of these other growth options.

IV. CONCLUSION

A common criticism of modern management is that it is supposedly preoccupied with financial rather than strategic considerations and that it focuses on near-term profitability at the expense of long-term growth. Among other factors, routine discounted cash flow analysis is commonly cited as contributing to this state of affairs.

While both the causes and the extent of this problem may be overstated, the analysis presented here suggests that there is some validity to the criticism. An exclusive reliance on ordinary net present value analysis can lead to inappropriate investment decisions. Specifically, individual projects may be undervalued and/or executed at inappropriate times. Furthermore, entire investment programs may even be abandoned prematurely, or not initiated at all, on the basis of net present value analysis.

The solution to this problem presented here is to think of discretionary investment opportunities as contingent claims on real assets or growth options. The payoff from adopting this new perspective can be substantial. At the individual *project* level, it helps us recognize that the value to be gained from an investment extends beyond directly attributable cash flows to include future investment opportunities as well. It also provides a logical framework for identifying and appreciating those characteristics of projects (i.e., risk, deferrability, etc.) that make them particularly valuable growth options.

At the investment *program* level, a growth option perspective can help coordinate individual project executions. Furthermore, it helps mitigate the tendency to forego a potentially valuable future because of adverse developments in the present. Indeed, even the acceptance of a project with negative net present value may be justified if its purpose is to create valuable new growth options or to preserve the value of existing ones.

Many executives doubtlessly already make investment decisions in a sophisticated way as far as strategy and timing are concerned. Thus, where capital budgeting is already done well, the insights presented here will seem familiar and will be implicit in the investment decisions made. The contribution of the growth option framework is that these insights can be made explicit and explained in a manner consistent with the traditional objective of maximizing shareholder value.

APPENDIX: A SIMPLE OPTION VALUATION FORMULA

A project whose value can be expected to be higher or lower by a certain amount at the end of a year can be valued as a growth option using the following simple formula.[7]

$$G_t = \frac{G_{t+1}^+(1 + r_f - R_{t+1}^-) + G_{t+1}^-(R_{t+1}^+ - 1 - r_f)}{(1 + r_f)(R_{t+1}^+ - R_{t+1}^-)}$$

where G_t = value of growth option in the current period

G_{t+1}^+ = value of growth option in the next period, assuming that the underlying asset has risen in value

G_{t+1}^- = value of growth option in the next period, assuming that the underlying assets have fallen in value

R_{t+1}^+ = factor by which value of underlying assets will rise under favorable conditions (e.g., a 20% increase in value would be represented as 1.2)

R_{t+1}^- = factor by which value of underlying assets will fall under unfavorable conditions (e.g., a 20% decline in value would be represented as 0.8)

r_f = risk-free, one-period rate of return expressed as a fraction

For a project with only one period before expiration, G_{t+1}^+ and G_{t+1}^- are the project's net present value one period hence under favorable and unfavorable conditions, respectively. In states of the world in which net present value is negative, the project will be abandoned and the value zero used for G_{t+1} in the above formula.

For projects with several years before expiration, the above formula can be applied recursively to arrive at a growth option value in the present. This has been done for project B in Figure 11.4. By starting at the end of the diagram in Figure 11.4b, the value of the project as a one-period growth option has been calculated for each possible state in stage 4. These values are then used in the option pricing formula to calculate the value of project B as a growth option in stage 3. This process is repeated until the current period is reached.

NOTES

1. For a clear, concise treatment of these advances, see Brealey and Myers (1988). Also, see Kester (1986) for a broad survey of the literature and applications of contingent claims analysis to corporate finance. Myers (1984) elaborates on the potential for using option pricing theory to bridge the gap between finance theory and strategic planning.

2. Heightened risk can increase an option's value because the option holder has the right, *but not the obligation,* to exercise the option. This allows the option holder to benefit fully from any potential increases in the underlying assets' value while avoiding the full range of potential losses. He or she does so by simply not exercising the option so long as the value of the asset is below the exercise price. Because of this ability, increases in the volatility surrounding an asset's value (other things held constant) has the asymmetric effect of increasing an option holder's chance of realizing a large gain without equally increasing his or her chances of realizing a large loss. This asymmetry is the source of the positive risk effect on an option's value.

3. As interest rates rise, the present value of future cash outlays required to exercise an option fall. Other things remaining constant, this decline will increase the current value of an option.

4. Broadly interpreted, most growth options can probably be considered shared options. But one must take care not to be too categorical in this regard. The distinction between proprietary and shared options is actually more one of degree than of kind. Because of such factors as brand-name awareness, locational advantages, experience curve effects, economies of scale, and so on, different owners of a given growth option may face very different exercise prices. In some cases, the differences may be so substantial as to eliminate the possibility that the shared option will be exercised by more than one or two owners.

5. The same sequence and total present value can be obtained by proceeding *backward* through the chain of successes and failures. Starting at the end, a value is assigned to all possible investment decisions in each state (where "state" is defined as the number and order of prior successes and failures). The value is obtained by adding together the net present value of the projects implemented and the option value of any unexercised options. The investment decision providing the greatest value for a given state is selected as the optimal choice. The value-maximizing decision for each state of the prior stage is then calculated, and so on, until the beginning is reached.

6. A second point to note is the advancement of project D to the start of the optimal sequence in place of project A. This happens because project D's capital outlay increases each period by an amount roughly equivalent to the increase in its present value following a success. Consequently, project D has very little upside potential and therefore is worth very little as a growth option.

7. Detailed descriptions of this formula's development are provided in Cox, Ross, and Rubinstein (1979) and in Rendleman and Bartter (1979).

REFERENCES

BREALEY, RICHARD A., and STEWART C. MYERS (1988). *Principles of Corporate Finance, 3rd ed. (New York: McGraw-Hill), pp. 495–519.*

COX, JOHN C., STEPHEN A. ROSS, and MARK RUBINSTEIN (1979). "Option Pricing: A Simplified Approach," *Journal of Financial Economics* 7 No. 3 (September, pp. 229–263.

KESTER, W. CARL (1984). "Today's Options for Tomorrow's Growth," *Harvard Business Review* (March–April), pp. 153–160.

KESTER, W. CARL (1986). "An Options Approach to Corporate Finance," in Edward I. Altman (ed.), *Handbook of Corporate Finance* (New York: Wiley), pp. 5.1–5.35.

MYERS, STEWART C. (1984). "Finance Theory and Financial Strategy," *Interfaces* 14 (January–February), pp. 126–137.

RENDLEMAN, RICHARD J., and BRITT J. BARTTER (1979). "Two-State Option Pricing," *Journal of Finance* (December), pp. 1093–1110.

12

Flexibility, Synergy, and Control in Strategic Investment Planning

EERO KASANEN AND LENOS TRIGEORGIS*

ABSTRACT

This article presents an integrated options-based strategic investment planning and control framework. This integrated approach is able to quantify various "strategic" sources of value, such as the flexibility embedded in real options, the synergy between groups of parallel projects, and interdependencies among projects over time (growth options). It also provides a rationale for the use of accounting-based controls, which are bypassed in traditional finance. It discusses how to design proper controls consistent with the value-maximizing strategy and conditional on the exercise of major future options.

* We express our gratitude to Professors Richard F. Meyer and Scott P. Mason of Harvard University, who supervised our respective theses. This article is partly the result of integrating some of our thesis ideas. We also wish to thank Carliss Baldwin, Pei-Rong Chiang, Michelle Hamer, John Minahan, Krishna Palepu, and Satish Thosar for helpful comments.

I. INTRODUCTION

Managerial practice deviates from standard capital budgeting theory in a number of respects. For example, managers often undertake projects that have negative net present value (NPV) (e.g., research and development investments), justifying their actions with vague concepts such as flexibility, synergy, and strategic positioning. Furthermore, managers continue to use accounting-based measures in capital budgeting even though every respectable textbook argues that NPV is the only correct valuation measure.

In fact, managers may have been intuitively trying all along to act according to the value-maximizing paradigm, even when textbook capital budgeting methods have been unable to incorporate all the sources of (especially, strategic) value. Managers and strategists have always struggled intuitively with a variety of strategic concerns, even though they might have been unable to properly quantify them. Consider the following examples:

1. In light of uncertainty in the external environment, perceptive managers recognize that various projects may have built-in flexibility allowing them to react to changing conditions, as opposed to the view portrayed by a fixed scenario of cash flows under passive management. In reality, as time goes by and uncertainty is resolved, projects can be deferred, abandoned, expanded, contracted, or otherwise modified. These operating real options provide a vehicle for active managerial intervention at different stages in the lives of projects. The existence and potential exercise of operating options, dictated by the future needs of unpredictably changing market conditions, are a source of additional value beyond that captured by traditional NPV.

2. Unlike the simplistic view that each project can be valued independently of others, good managers appreciate the existence of interactions among various projects. For example, managers see synergies between parallel projects undertaken simultaneously or interdependencies among projects over time (growth options). In such cases, whole sets of interacting projects need to be valued collectively.

3. Internally, although managers may agree that firm value maximization is their primary task and NPV the proper evaluation measure, they have to live with the fact that managerial incentive and control schemes are typically tied to observable, short-term accounting measures. Such incentives and controls are needed to induce and monitor adherence to the desired strategy. But if the controls are not properly designed, satisfying the control cutoff levels [e.g., Re-

turn on Assets (ROA) $\geq x\%$, growth rate $\geq y\%$) or achieving the best possible results may not necessarily promote the desired objectives. The real challenge then is to select the control levels (x, y) in a way that is consistent with and enforces the value-maximizing strategy.

In this chapter we integrate an options-based approach to capital budgeting with a strategic investment planning framework linked through properly designed controls. The integrated model can quantify various strategic components of value, such as the flexibility embedded in real options, the synergy between groups of projects undertaken simultaneously, and interdependencies among projects over time (growth options).

This article also offers some justification for using short-term accounting-based controls in practice, even though they have been mostly ignored in traditional finance. The chapter shows how to set appropriate control cutoff levels consistent with the value-maximizing strategy, which should be revised conditional on the exercise of major future options or occurrence of other major market developments.

The rest of the article is structured around the three main phases of capital budgeting. Section II deals with the valuation of (collections of) projects under an expanded or strategic NPV framework. It presents the strategic investment-mix and options approaches to capital budgeting and illustrates how they can be used to assess the value of operating real options, of project synergies, and of project interdependencies over time. Section III describes how to design control targets compatible with value maximization. The active management of projects over time is discussed in Section IV, and implications and concluding remarks are presented in Section V.

II. CHOOSING THE RIGHT PROJECTS: A STRATEGIC NPV FRAMEWORK

Finance theory prescribes choosing projects that have positive net present value of expected cash flows, or if projects are mutually exclusive, the ones that have the highest NPV. Broadly defined, the value-maximizing paradigm is, of course, the only sound basis for rational business decisions. However, the standard methods in capital budgeting neglect or cannot properly handle many sources of economic value. Specifically, the following sources of strategic value have been difficult to capture in a standard capital budgeting framework:

- Managerial operating flexibility—seen as a collection of operating real options
- Synergies between projects undertaken simultaneously
- Growth opportunities and interdependencies among projects over time.

We subsequently present two methods, a strategic investment-mix model and an options-based approach that we have employed in actual business situations, whose integration may provide the quantitative tools needed to capture a larger portion of strategic value.

The strategic investment-mix approach is an integrated strategic planning and control model based on the ideas of R. Meyer.[1] The principles underlying this approach are as follows:

- Corporate strategic planning, capital budgeting, incentive schemes, and control mechanisms should form an integrated system promoting the primary goal of firm value maximization (Figure 12.1).
- The selection of proper control targets is seen as an essential practical feature in the implementation and monitoring of the value-maximizing strategy.
- A crucial task of strategic investment is to create and manage a collection of profitable future investment opportunities.[2]

Figure 12.1

An integrated planning/incentives/control approach to capital budgeting.

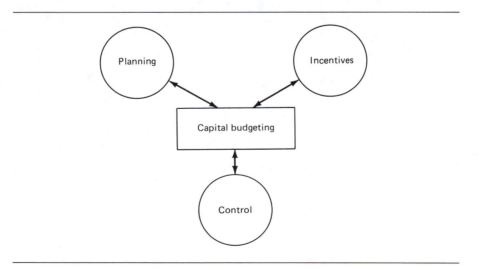

Figure 12.2

Strategic capital budgeting.

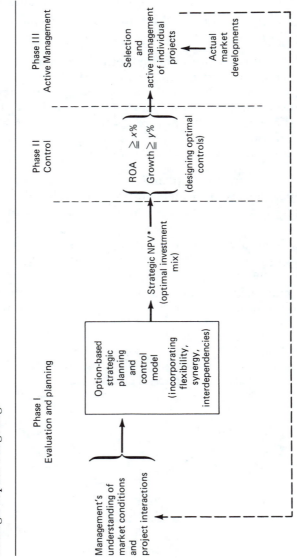

As shown in Figure 12.2, the key elements in the strategic investment model are (1) the explicit modeling of management's understanding of market conditions and of the interactions among individual projects, and (2) the subsequent modeling of whole investment categories. Examples of such investment categories are cost reduction, maintenance, market development or capacity expansion, research and development, and new product introduction.

This strategic investment-mix approach is a vehicle for building an integrated corporate model for strategic discussions. The actual model structure should be tailored to the business unit and market situation. The formation of competitive power, the impact on costs, and the production capacity can be explicitly taken into account as model inputs (see Kasanen, 1986). Any known or anticipated project interactions, both parallel and across time, should also be factored into the model. The result is the value-maximizing strategy (NPV*) or growth path, which indicates how much should be invested in each project category (Figure 12.3).

During the next phase, a set of accounting-based targets (e.g., ROA and growth rate) can be designed so as to induce and help monitor adherence to the value-maximizing strategy previously identified. Such controls can help in the selection and active management of individual projects, contingent on market developments. This feeds back into the next planning cycle, and so on (Figure 12.2).

Figure 12.3

The optimal investment mix along the growth path.

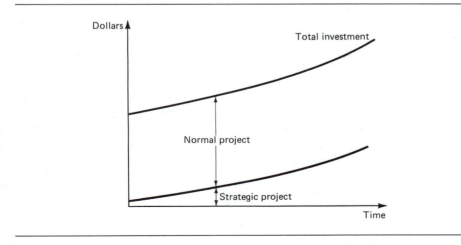

Strategic investment planning should also take advantage of option valuation tools. Unlike traditional discounted cash flow (DCF) techniques, an options-based valuation approach may be able to properly quantify the operating flexibility, synergy, and certain strategic aspects of project value. Investment opportunities can be seen as collections of options on real assets or real options. Strategic planning can then be viewed as the explicit recognition, creation, and management (optimal exercise) of the portfolio of real options associated with the firm's collection of current and future projects. An options approach to capital budgeting should thus be interwoven with and supportive of the firm's strategic planning.

We subsequently illustrate three sources of value that managers have been struggling with qualitatively but which may now be quantified using an integrated options-based strategic planning approach.

A. The Value of Flexibility (Operating Real Options)

There is a close, though not exact, similarity between operating real and financial options. For example, the holder of an American call option on a stock has a right, but no obligation, to buy the stock by paying a specified price prior to its given maturity. The option is exercised if the associated benefits exceed the cost involved, otherwise it is allowed to expire worthless. Similarly, the management of a firm having a discretionary investment opportunity has the right, but no obligation, to acquire the project's benefits if they exceed the required investment outlay (the exercise price) before the opportunity disappears (on the expiration date). The underlying "asset" in this case, V, is the (gross) present value of expected cash flows to be generated from the implemented project, excluding any required outlays.

Consider first the option to defer undertaking a project such as drilling for oil, extracting a mineral, or developing a new product as afforded by a lease, property rights, or a patent, respectively. Even if immediate initiation of the project has a negative NPV of cash flows, such an option empowers management with the flexibility to wait and invest (i.e., exercise) only in case future project benefits V rise above the then associated costs I. Just before the opportunity ceases (e.g., when the lease or patent expires), management obtains $\max(V - I, 0)$. The option to defer investment can thus be seen as a call option on the project (or, more generally, on the project value V and any subsequent real options). The option to delay investment has been analyzed by McDonald and Siegel (1986) and in the case of offshore petroleum leases by Siegel, Smith, and Paddock (1987). Also, Majd and Pindyck (1987) value the flexibility to delay the construction schedule of projects with sequential investment.

The option to expand a project's scale (e.g., plant capacity) in the future by a given percentage $e\%$ by incurring an extra cost I_E can also be seen as a call option but on part, $e\%$, of the project. The investment opportunity with the option to expand can thus be viewed as the base scale project plus a call option on future (proportionate) investment, that is, $V + \max(eV - I_E, 0)$. Under uncertain market conditions, it may be prudent, for example, to build excess production capacity (slack) that would allow enlarged, faster, or prolonged production in case future demand develops beyond expectations. This may place the firm in an advantageous competitive position and become a source of strategic value.

Similarly, the option to shrink a project's scale by $c\%$ by, say, cutting planned advertising or operating costs I_C, can be valued as a put option on $c\%$ of the project with the exercise price equal to the variable cost savings I_C, that is, $\max(I_C - cV, 0)$. It may thus be justified, for example, to design a plant with higher variable costs (and lower fixed costs) for the flexibility to cut operating costs if the demand for a new product does not follow expectations. The above options are analyzed in Trigeorgis and Mason (1987).

In certain projects such as oil drilling and mineral extraction, management may have the flexibility to cease operations in a given year if revenues cannot cover variable operating costs; each year's operation can thus be viewed as a call option on that year's cash revenue R having as exercise price the variable operating costs I_V, that is, $\max(R - I_V, 0)$. The option to temporarily cease operations has been analyzed by McDonald and Siegel (1985) and by Brennan and Schwartz (1985) in the case of mining operations.

Management may also have the flexibility to switch investment from the current to its best future alternative use. This may take the form of switching from a current input to using a cheaper future substitute, or redeploying assets from producing a current output to a more profitable future alternative. At an extreme, if future prospects turn sour, management may exercise its option to abandon the project altogether, selling its assets in the second-hand market for their salvage value. (The project can even be abandoned during construction by foregoing a coming planned outlay if it exceeds the value from continuing the project.) The option to switch use can be valued as an American put option on the current project value V with the exercise price the best future alternative use value S, entitling management to receive $V + \max(S - V, 0)$ or $\max(S, V)$. The option to exchange one commodity for another is analyzed by Kensinger (1987), while the option to permanently abandon is examined by Myers and Majd (1989).

Ignoring the value of these operating real options can significantly undervalue investment opportunities. By improving profit potential while limiting losses through active management under uncertainty, these options cause a beneficial asymmetry in the probability distribution of project value (or NPV) that can be captured only through an expanded (strategic) NPV criterion (NPV*):

Expanded (strategic) NPV*

= traditional (passive) NPV of expected cash flows

+ value of operating options from active management

+ interaction effects (synergy, interproject dependence)

It should be noted that valuing each operating real option separately and summing these individual results may overstate the combined value of flexibility since multiple real options within a given project may interact. The presence of subsequent real options results in a higher effective underlying asset for prior options. Furthermore, the exercise of certain prior real options (e.g., to expand or contract a project) may change the underlying asset and value of later options on it. Interactions among various real options are examined by Trigeorgis (1986), and an application is presented in Trigeorgis (1989).

In addition to interactions among operating real options within a single project, there can be interaction effects of synergy among groups of simultaneously undertaken projects and of interproject dependence across time (spawning or growth options). These interactions constitute true ingredients of strategic value and are examined further later. Because of such interactions, the combined value of these operating and strategic real options can be captured correctly only through options-based numerical analysis valuation techniques within an integrated strategic investment planning framework [see Trigeorgis (1988) for a numerical analysis approach]. We next examine the value of synergy and project interdependencies.

B. Synergy Between Projects (Taken Together or in Parallel)

Suppose a mature business unit is expected to produce the following financial results if the base scale operation is maintained:

Present Value of:	Base Case (Maintenance)
Sales, S	100
Operating costs, C	(80)
Net cash flows,[3] V	20

Consider two new investment opportunities that come along. (1) An I_E = \$11 million advertising expenditure in new market development (market expansion) that would expand sales by e = 50%, and (2) an I_C = \$10 million cost reduction investment that would cut unit costs by c = 10% regardless of production scale. Under traditional valuation, taking each project separately gives the following results:

Present Value of:	Market Expansion	Cost Reduction
Sales, S	150	100
Operating costs, C	(120)	(72)
Investment , I_E, I_C	(11)	(10)
Net cash flows, V	19	18

The incremental cash flows from either project are negative. Standard cash flow analysis therefore suggests that either project would decrease the value of the business unit and should be rejected.

In fact, each of these opportunities can be seen as an option. The market expansion project can be viewed as a call option on V with the exercise price the extra cost I_E, so that the value of the business unit becomes

$$V' = V + \max(eV - I_E, 0) = 20 + \max(0.50 \times 20 - 11, 0)$$
$$= 20 + \max(-1, 0)$$

If exercised, the expansion in scale would be worth -1, and so this project would not be implemented by itself under present market conditions.

Similarly, the cost reduction opportunity can be seen as a call option on the cost savings ($c\%$ of C) with exercise price I_C, so

$$V' = V + \max(cC - I_C, 0) = 20 + \max(0.10 \times 80 - 10, 0)$$
$$= 20 + \max(-2, 0)$$

Again, it is not worth exercising the cost reduction option by itself, as it would reduce business unit value by 2.

Consider, however, taking both projects together. If it is assumed that the unit cost reduction does not depend on whether you expand or not, the combined results are now encouraging:

Present Value of:	Market Expansion and Cost Reduction
Sales, S	150
Operating costs, C	(108)[4]
Investment, $I_E + I_C$	(21)
Net cash flows, V	21

Viewed as options, the combined market expansion and cost reduction investments taken together result in

$$V' = V = \max[eV - I_E + c(1 + e)C - I_C, 0]$$
$$= 20 + \max[0.50 \times 20 - 11 + 0.10(1 + 0.50) \times 80 - 10, 0]$$
$$= 20 + \max[+1, 0]$$

The strategic source of value $(+1)$ in this example comes from the synergy between the projects taken together. The value of synergy, which went unnoticed in the standard analysis, can alternatively be modeled in a strategic planning framework.[5] For example,

$$\max V' = S' - C' - (d_E I_E + d_C I_C) \qquad d_E \in \{0, 1\}; d_C \in \{0, 1\})$$

where $S' = \begin{cases} S & \text{if } d_E = 0 \text{ (no expansion)} \\ (1 + e)S & \text{if } d_E = 1 \text{ (expansion)} \end{cases}$

$C' = \begin{cases} aS' & \text{if } d_C = 0 \text{ (no cost reduction)} \\ a(1 - c)S' & \text{if } d_C = 1 \text{ (cost reduction)} \end{cases}$

with $S = 100$, $a = 0.8$,[6] $e = 0.5$, $c = 0.1$, $I_E = 11$, $I_C = 10$. Alternatively, the problem can be written in compact form:

$$\max V' = (1 + ed_E)S[1 - a(1 - cd_C)]$$
$$- (d_E I_E + d_C I_C) \qquad (d_E, d_C \in \{0, 1\})$$

The 0-1 decision variables are needed to capture the asymmetry introduced by active management under uncertainty. The expected value-maximizing strategy can be searched for, even if there are hundreds of similar market and cost equations in the model. The important point is to capture the complicated network of interdependencies caused by market feedback from outside the company and cash flow generation inside the company. The decision variables are the investments in various project categories, and the outcome is the optimal investment mix.

C. Sequential Project Interdependencies Over Time (Growth Options or Spawning)

Consider the typical practice of classifying investment opportunities as normal or as strategic. Normal investment typically refers to the production and selling of existing products, while strategic investment mainly refers to new market and product development commitments (e.g., research and development). Assume the standard cash flow profile of each type of project for the business unit is as follows:

Normal Project

Time	0	1	2	3
Book value of assets	21.0	14.0	7.0	0.0
Sales		30.0	40.0	50.0
Minus costs		21.0	29.0	34.9
Minus depreciation[7]		7.0	7.0	7.0
Pretax profit		2.0	4.0	8.1
Minus tax (50%)		1.0	2.0	4.0
Profit after tax		1.0	2.0	4.0
Investment	(21.0)			
Net cash flow	(21.0)	8.0	9.0	11.0
NPV_N (at 10%) = +2.0				

Assuming the risk-adjusted cost of capital is 10%, the NPV of expected cash flows for the normal project is +2.0. The normal project is worth undertaking because its NPV is positive.

Strategic Project

Time	0	1	2	3
Book value of assets	3.0	2.0	1.0	0.0
Sales		2.0	3.0	4.0
Minus costs		2.0	2.0	1.5
Minus depreciation		1.0	1.0	1.0
Pretax profit		(1.0)	0.0	1.5
Minus tax (50%)		(0.5)	0.0	0.75
Profit after tax		(0.5)	0.0	0.75
Investment	(3.0)			
Net cash flow	(3.0)	0.5	1.0	1.75
NPV_S (at 10%) = −0.4				

Assuming again that the risk-adjusted cost of capital is 10%,[8] the NPV of expected cash flows for the strategic project is −0.4. Thus standard NPV analysis leads to rejection of this strategic investment. If, however, the strategic project can generate future growth opportunities, this standard analysis is myopic.

Suppose, for example, that investing in the strategic project now generates the opportunity to invest in a normal project, such as the one above, during the next period. Then, in a deterministic world (or with perfect forecasting ability), the true value of the strategic project is given by $NPV_S + NPV_N/(1 + k)$ or $-0.4 + 2.0/1.1 = 1.4$. Even in the absence of uncertainty, the interaction effect across time, that is, opening up the opportunity to invest in the future, creates a strategic source of value.[9]

More generally, not only strategic projects generate subsequent investment opportunities, but certain normal projects may do so as well (e.g., creative ideas for new products generated during the normal manufacturing process of existing products). This interdependency can be illustrated with a spawning (interdependence) matrix.

Spawning (Interdependence) Matrix

FROM	TO	
	Strategic	Normal
Strategic	1.05	1.03
Normal	0.02	0.30

For example, the number 1.03 in the matrix means that if you invest one unit (base scale) in the strategic project this year, next year you will have the option to invest up to 1.03 units (3% above base scale) in the normal project. If such spawning relationships continue in the future, there will be a dynamic system or chain of interdependent projects.

In a perpetual deterministic system of such interdependent projects, it would be optimal to invest as much as is feasible in both investment categories each period. The value-maximizing growth path approaches a steady state where, in this example, the optimal investment mix consists of 9.7% investment in the strategic project category and 90.3% in the normal one (see Kasanen, 1986). This optimal steady-state investment mix is a key output of this strategic planning model.[10]

If there is uncertainty in the future project value, the strategic investment is even more valuable since it creates an option to invest in the normal project next year if the project does well but not if it does poorly. For example, suppose that the normal project's present value of expected cash inflows, currently $V = 23$, is expected to move up or down by 20% next year (to $V^+ = 27.6$ or to $V^- = 18.4$) with equal probability ($p = .5$). The required investment of $I_N = 21$ should only be made next year if the project does well (V^+), but not otherwise (V^-). Thus the total value resulting from this strategic investment is

$$\text{NPV}_S + \frac{p \max(V^+ - I, 0) + (1 - p) \max(V^- - I, 0)}{1 + k}$$

$$= -0.4 + \frac{0.5 \max(27.6 - 21, 0) + 0.5 \max(18.4 - 21, 0)}{1 + 0.10}$$

$$= -0.4 + [0.5 \; 6.6 + 0]/1.10$$

$$= +2.6$$

This result is in contrast to the earlier one of $+1.4$ obtained from calculating strict expected values under passive management.[11]

The source of strategic value here is found in the interdependencies among projects across time. A dynamic model of investment opportunity generation can help analyze the ramifications of these spawning effects. Under uncertainty, the strategic value of such project interdependencies is higher because of the discretionary option element. In fact, an earlier investment in a chain of such interdependent projects can be seen as a call option on the next investment, and so on (a compound call option situation). The strategic option value of the follow-up investment may far exceed its own NPV (which might even be negative). But even if the NPV of both projects is negative, high future uncertainty may make the strategic option to take the follow-up investment, under favorable conditions, even more valuable, and the negative NPV strategic investment worth taking.

III. VALUE-MAXIMIZING CONTROLS

Once the value-maximizing strategy, broadly defined to incorporate the value of flexibility, synergy, and project interdependencies (NPV*) has been identified, a compatible control system to help implement this strategy must be designed. Again, it is crucial that the capital budgeting process, incentive schemes, and control mechanisms be in harmony with the intended strategy. If the managerial actions required to implement the strategy cannot survive the actual resource allocation bargaining, or if they are in contradiction with the manager's personal incentives, the strategy will never come to fruition (Figure 12.1). Anthony and Dearden (1980), as well as Kaplan (1982), provide good summaries and surveys on management controls. Merchant (1982) and Ruefli and Sarrazin (1981) also discuss the role and characteristics of good controls.

A. Need for Incentives and Controls

Even a perfect value-maximizing strategy may not achieve satisfactory results if the actual organizational incentives and controls lead managerial decisions away from the chosen strategy. Incentives and observable controls are needed to guarantee that the overall business strategy is in the interest of the managers to implement as well. Arrow (1964, p. 400) provides helpful insight into this matter: "The top management can never, strictly speaking, know if the activity manager's objective function has been maximized; instead, their enforcement rules should be such as to encourage him to increase the value of the objective function as much as possible."

The problem of designing proper incentive and control measures arises even in the strict value-maximizing paradigm, because NPV is neither an ideal short-term incentive nor an effective control measure. The very features that make NPV the best criterion for project selection and planning make it unsuitable for short-term control purposes. NPV is unobservable in the short term, and its realization is revealed only through time. Accounting-based measures are almost immediately observable and, properly selected and used, can offer useful practical guidance.

Short-term measurable indicators of performance are needed because managers rotate, organizational boundaries change, and agreements are (specified and) changed. Since short-term measures are revealed each year, they allow incentive contracts to be renegotiated periodically, giving management valuable flexibility. Also, normal short-term indicators are often easier to understand and manage than most long-term contracts.[12]

Yet, not even a perfect NPV-maximizing strategy, along with appropriate incentive schemes that match that strategy, can guarantee good results. Even competent managers need concrete short-term targets to let them know where they stand—not to mention managers who may be incompetent, dishonest, or burned out and not even acting according to incentive schemes serving their own interests. For whatever reason, even with the best intentions, the business unit may deviate from the optimal strategy. It is therefore of paramount importance to be able to discern this early, when corrective actions can still be taken.

For many managers control is not just a secondary implementation issue.[13] Planning, incentives, and control should form an integrated system, the purpose of which is to guide managers in the chosen direction. In traditional finance, controls have been bypassed almost completely. Nevertheless, controls can play a useful role in implementation of the desired strategy. Arbitrarily set (e.g., as a result of an internal political process) control targets may be dysfunctional. However, if properly derived from and consistent with the value-maximizing strategy, controls can help guide the organization toward the desired goals.

B. Design of a Value-Maximizing Set of Control Targets

Consider an actual situation found in many companies where business strategy calls for growth and product leadership, research and development is expensed in internal calculations, while managers are rewarded on the basis of return on investment (ROI). This seems to constitute a contradiction of objectives, measurement, and incentives.

The design of control targets should be based on the value-maximizing strategy, not on the maximum levels achievable. It may be possible, for example, to increase ROA if investment is cut, or to increase market share if the profit margin is cut. But these actions do not necessarily promote value maximization. Because optimal target levels are typically lower than their highest feasible levels, the concept of managerial slack becomes relevant. Managerial slack for a control target is defined here as the set of decisions that will meet or better the target.

Consider a typical control target, such as ROA $\geq x\%$, taken alone. There are many sets of investment decisions, in addition to the value-maximizing strategy, that can meet this target. Some of these decisions may even be contrary to the desired strategic direction. Consider, however, adding a second target, for example, growth rate $\geq y\%$. Then there are fewer investment choices that satisfy both constraints simultaneously.

As the managerial slack for each control target determined according to the value-maximizing strategy contains the value-maximizing investment mix (NPV*), their intersection narrows down the desired strategy. A typical set of control targets with opposing or contradictory managerial slacks pushing toward the desired strategy can include ROA, growth rate, and a budget constraint,[14,15] as illustrated in Figure 12.4.

Figure 12.4

The value-maximizing strategy (NPV*) determined by the intersection of the managerial slacks of a set of different control targets (ROA, growth, budget constraint).

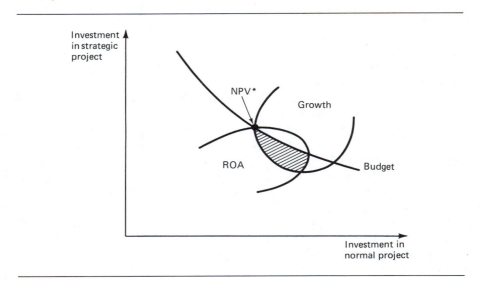

In essence, the original optimization problem under value maximization is transformed for implementation and control purposes into an equivalent set of satisficing constraints (control targets) whose intersection contains the optimum strategy. Maximizing value and satisficing a set of control constraints can be made economically equivalent, provided the control target cutoff levels are properly chosen.

The tightness of control targets, or the amount of managerial slack around the value-maximizing strategy, may depend on the amount of external uncertainty and the quality of management. Creative and competent managers with a proven track record may be trusted with more managerial slack so that they can take advantage of unexpected developments in a more uncertain market.[16]

If the realized value of the strategy is contingent on the exercise of major future options or on other major market developments, a set of conditional control targets should also be made available to lower-level managers. For example, conditional on exercising a major option to expand or a growth option, the growth target may be increased while the ROA cutoff levels are decreased appropriately.

C. An Illustration

Revisiting the earlier example on project interdependencies across time in Section II,C from the control point of view, we find that setting the ROA and growth rate targets at the particular levels ROA = 13.5% and growth rate = 7.7% is consistent with the value-maximizing strategy.

We can also examine whether investment in each project category will make managerial incentive schemes look good or bad in the future, relative to no investing. In this case, it can be shown that the ROA target by itself leads to a negative impact on incentives for the early years, while the growth rate leads to positive incentives for all the years. But set at the optimal levels and used in combination, this pair of controls supports the desired strategy.

Let us further suppose that the business unit manager, for whatever reason, underinvests (e.g., invests only 75% of the optimum amount in each project). An interesting question is, How long will it take for top management to detect this deviation from the value-maximizing strategy? Again, it can be shown that the ROA completely fails to detect this deviation from the value-maximizing path. Instead, it shows a consistent improvement in the control target as a result of underinvestment. This represents just another case where ROA rewards the dismantling of the business, supporting the popular belief that ROA and growth are conflicting objectives.[17] On the other hand, the growth target in this case would immediately detect the deviation from the optimal growth path (see Kasanen, 1986).

Since NPV cannot be used as a relevant short-term control measure, it is useful to know how to construct a proper set of observable, short-term control targets and incentives to guide managers toward the value-maximizing strategy.

IV. ACTIVE MANAGEMENT OF INVESTMENT PROJECTS OVER TIME

The value of active management and project interactions is not captured in the standard accept/reject decision and postaudit framework. In a turbulent business environment, new opportunities arise and old plans have to be revised or abandoned. Option pricing, dynamic strategic planning, and control models are better able to capture these sources of value.

Active management of investment opportunities means that managers constantly look for opportunities to exercise the built-in options in investment projects or create new ones. If major changes in the environment occur, or important options are exercised or created that will change the remaining alternatives, the initial value-maximizing strategy has to be modified. Similarly, a set of conditional control targets should be made available to lower-level managers, contingent on the exercising of such major options.

Long-term strategic plans and the search for the value-maximizing strategy should be seen as an ongoing process where the investment-mix and control targets are periodically revised as managers actively try to benefit from new business opportunities or modify old ones. The purpose of strategic planning and the use of proper control targets is to pursue this value-maximizing strategic path as it evolves through time.

Not only does the corporate strategy have to be flexible and evolve over time, but the control targets compatible with that strategy naturally have to be reevaluated whenever the strategy itself is changed. For example, the growth and ROA target levels must reflect the most recent understanding of the value-maximizing strategy (Figure 12.5).

Thus developments in the external environment should be reflected in the active management of investments and in a regular fine-tuning of organizational control targets.[18] The allowed managerial slack should also be a function of the uncertainty in the business environment. In a tranquil environment, for example, the set of targets managers have to meet can be tight and detailed. In a turbulent environment, on the other hand, creative managers may need fewer targets and greater slack or flexibility, so that they can react more swiftly to changing conditions. As shown in Figure 12.6, if there is no or little uncertainty, the optimal strategy is a single solution (point) and control targets can be defined

Figure 12.5

Following-up and revising the value-maximizing strategy (NPV*) and the set of compatible controls over time.

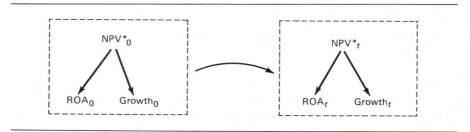

Figure 12.6

The tightness of controls (managerial slack) should be inversely related to the amount of uncertainty.

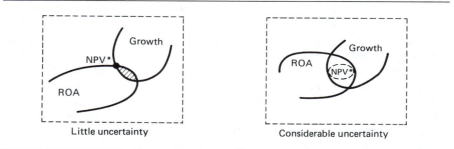

tightly. If there is considerable uncertainty, however, the value-maximizing strategy may consist of a larger set (region) of near-optimal solutions, allowing more managerial slack.

V. IMPLICATIONS AND CONCLUSION

A mechanistic determination of the standard NPV of expected cash flows from a single project treated in isolation may overlook several sources of strategic value intuitively grasped by skillful managers. For example, project synergies between parallel projects and interdependencies among projects across time create strong interaction effects. Operating options and growth opportunities are major sources of strategic value in an uncertain business environment.

These sources of strategic value can be properly quantified using an integrated strategic planning and control model that incorporates option features. Options-based valuation techniques can be used for pricing both the strategic and operating options embedded in projects (e.g., the options to expand, abandon, modify, or delay a project).

Furthermore, even if value maximization is "king," it should not govern alone. Strategic NPV is the ideal, the standard against which practical remuneration and control systems should be calibrated. In the capital budgeting process, measures for planning, incentives, and control need to be used simultaneously. It is not necessarily incompatible to search for the value (NPV*)-maximizing strategy while at the same time using short-term indicators and performance measures.

For practical implementation purposes, it may be useful to use several control measures in capital budgeting, as is widely practiced, including a capital budget constraint.[19] However, these measures must be derived from and be attuned to the value-maximizing strategy. Naturally, the more uncertainty there is in the environment, the more valuable the option features become and the more managerial slack in control is needed for active and creative managers.

Capital budgeting should thus not be treated as a static, mechanistic accept/reject lower-level staff function but should instead be integrated with the strategic planning and control system. Business strategy should involve selection of the investment mix that leads to the value-maximizing path. Top management should actively and continually be involved in shaping the desired investment strategy and setting proper control targets to guide the organization toward the chosen strategy.

In an uncertain business environment, the value-maximizing strategy is not simply a fixed set of decisions made upfront, but a direction that must be modified when conditions change. Management should periodically examine whether its current organizational control targets are compatible with the new strategic thrust. It should also constantly look for opportunities to optimally exercise existing investment options or to create future ones. In this effort, a set of conditional controls, contingent on the exercise of such major future options, may prove useful to managers.

This chapter has offered an integrated options-based strategic investment planning and control framework which can capture various strategic sources of value (e.g., flexibility, synergy, and project interdependencies). It has also provided a rationale for the use of accounting-based controls and shown how to design proper controls consistent with the value-maximizing strategy.

NOTES

1. This is described in "General Meter Corporation," Harvard Business School case 4-176-113 (1976).
2. The true bottleneck in growth is the lack of profitable investment opportunities, not the lack of funds.
3. For simplicity, depreciation, taxes, and changes in working capital are ignored here.
4. Assumes that I_C = $10 million will cut unit costs by the same percentage (c = 10%) whether we expand or not.
5. In a deterministic world, the strategic planning formulation and the option model give identical results. Under uncertainty (say, in V), the strategic planning formulation performed in a backward dynamic programming fashion with repeated iterations and built-in contingent decision variables is in principle correct if the right discount rate can be identified. The option approach can be seen as a transformation of this problem that overcomes the discount rate pitfall by transforming the probabilities (into risk-neutral ones) so as to allow risk-free discounting.
6. The cost here is assumed for simplicity to be a constant proportion (80%) of sales, but any deterministic cost function can be handled by the model.
7. Assumes straight-line depreciation on initial investment (asset book value) of 3.
8. For simplicity, we keep the same discount rate as for the normal project; in reality, it can be higher.
9. Under uncertainty, even if the combined NPV is negative, the strategic growth option value may make the strategic commitment worthwhile.
10. The total NPV of the business unit with perpetual spawning is given by the following input-output relationship:

$$V = (-0.4, 2) \begin{pmatrix} 1-1.05/1.1 & -1.03/1.1 \\ -0.02/1.1 & 1-0.3/1.1 \end{pmatrix}^{-1} \begin{pmatrix} s \\ n \end{pmatrix}$$

where s is the initial investment in the strategic project and n is initial investment in the normal project. For example, if s = 1 and n = 0, the value of the business unit will be +99. Contrast this with the value of each project taken alone: +2.0 for the normal project and 0 for the strategic one (as the latter would not be exercised (because of its negative NPV). Even if the normal project can spawn itself (i.e., generate future normal investment opportunities), according to the coefficient 0.3 in the matrix, the value of the normal project category will be only 2.75. [For details see Kasanen (1986, pp. 63–67).]
11. This calculation bypasses the discount rate problem, which in option situations such as this one changes in a complex way (i.e., is not constant). Option pricing, which is the proper methodology to use here, can be seen as a version of this analysis with transformed risk-neutral probabilities (p') that enable discounting at the riskless rate (see Trigeorgis and Mason, 1987). Here, if r = 6%, p' = .65, giving an NPV of +3.65 (rather than +2.6).

12. Value-based measures can and should be used in designing long-term managerial incentive schemes. If the shares of the business unit are traded, it may be possible to design sophisticated "performance shares" schemes. However, there are many problemtic issues in the implementation of long-term binding managerial contracts, especially if the business unit shares are not traded. For example, what happens if the manager is fired or leaves the company? What if the business unit is reorganized or taken over? What if the bonus according to the current incentive scheme turns negative in the future?

13. As controls are the ultimate vehicle for communicating what top management really wants and what the strategy implies, several authors on management control put control first and view planning as the necessary groundwork for the determination of controls and targets. Michael (1980, p. 37) even goes as far as to state that planning is a technique of feedforward control.

14. It may not matter that much which particular set of measures is used as control targets, as long as they are derived from the value-maximizing strategy and there are enough opposing targets pushing toward the chosen strategy. In particular, the choice of depreciation schedule is not especially important if a battery of different targets is used.

15. The number of required control targets can be reduced by choosing control measures of different orientation, that is, with managerial slack regions on different sides of the value-maximizing strategy. For example, ROA and growth rate could form a good couple as ROA punishes overinvestment while high growth deters underinvestment.

16. In an uncertain business environment, the value-maximizing strategy is not a fixed set of decisions but rather an expected abstract ideal to be followed which should be continually revised contingent on future developments.

17. See Dearden's (1965) classic case against ROI-based control.

18. Merchant (1982, p. 44) also emphasizes the desirable future orientation of controls: "First, control is future-oriented: the goal is to have no unpleasant surprised in the future." (In the value-maximizing paradigm, the surprises refer to deviations from the value-maximizing strategy.) Ruefli and Sarrazin (1981, p. 116) also see the role of controls as not looking back and dwelling on the correctness of past decisions but as giving future guidance: "The point is not to bring to light past errors but to identify needed corrections to steer the corporation in the desired direction."

19. Under the value-maximizing paradigm, budget constraints should not be used in strategic planning. The corporation can and should raise the required amount of funds for undertaking all profitable projects. Nevertheless, the budget constraint may serve as a good control measure since it is measurable, objective, practical, and informative. Combined with other control targets (e.g., ROA and growth), it can provide a good guide for driving the business unit toward the chosen strategy.

   The confusion about the need for budget constraints can be resolved by focusing on the proper role of the budget constraint. It should not be related to the amount of funds available in capital markets but rather to the amount of funds that can be used profitably in product markets. Thus the budget constraint should be an output of strategic planning that can be used for operating planning and control. Furthermore, it forces business units and divisions to set internal priorities, thereby reducing managerial biases. The widespread managerial use of budgets can be attributed to these attractive features of budgets as controls and self-screening devices.

REFERENCES

ANTHONY, ROBERT, and JOHN DEARDEN (1980). *Management Control Systems* (Homewood, Ill.: Richard D. Irwin)

ARROW, KENNETH J. "Control in Large Organizations," *Management Science* 10, pp. 397–408.

BRENNAN, MICHAEL, and EDUARDO SCHWARTZ (1985). "Evaluating Natural Resource Investments," *Journal of Business* 58, pp. 135–157.

DEARDEN, JOHN (1969). "The Case Against ROI Control," *Harvard Business Review* 47 (May–June pp. 124–135.

KAPLAN, ROBERT S. (1982). *Advanced Management Accounting* (Englewood Cliffs: Prentice-Hall).

KASANEN, EERO (1986). "Capital Budgeting and the Control of Business Unit Growth." Doctoral Thesis, Harvard University.

KENSINGER, JOHN W. (1987). "Adding the Value of Active Management into the Capital Budgeting Equation," *Midland Corporate Finance Journal* 5 (Spring), pp. 31–42.

MAJD, SAMAN, and ROBERT PINDYCK (1987). "Time to Build, Option Value, and Investment Decisions," *Journal of Financial Economics* 18 (March), pp. 7–27.

MASON, SCOTT P., and ROBERT C. MERTON (1985). "The Role of Contingent Claims Analysis in Corporate Finance," in E. Altman and M. Subrahmanyam (eds.), *Recent Advances in Corporate Finance* (Homewood, Ill.: Richard D. Irwin).

MCDONALD, ROBERT, and DANIEL SIEGEL (1985). "Investment and the Valuation of Firms When There Is an Option to Shut Down," *International Economic Review* 26 (June), pp. 331–349.

MCDONALD, ROBERT, and DANIEL SIEGEL (1986). "The Value of Waiting to Invest," *Quarterly Journal of Economics* 101 (November), pp. 707–727.

MERCHANT, KENNETH A. (1982). "The Control Function of Management," *Sloan Management Review* 23, pp. 43–55.

MICHAEL, STEPHEN R. (1980). "Feedforward Versus Feedback Controls in Planning." *Managerial Planning* 6 (November–December), pp. 34–38.

MYERS, STEWART C. (1987). "Finance Theory and Financial Strategy," *Midland Corporate Finance Journal* 5 (Spring) pp. 6–13.

MYERS, STEWART C., and SAMAN MAJD (1989). "Abandonment Value and Project Life," *Advances in Futures and Options Research* 6, pp. 121–143.

RUEFLI, TIMOTHY, and JACQUES SARRAZIN (1981). "Strategic Control of Corporate Development Under Ambiguous Circumstances," *Management Science* 27, pp. 1158–1170.

SIEGEL, DAN, JAMES SMITH, and JAMES PADOCK (1987). "Valuing Offshore Oil Properties with Option Pricing Models." *Midland Corporate Finance Journal* 5 (Spring), pp. 22–30.

TRIGEORGIS, LENOS (1986). "Valuing Real Investment Opportunities: An Options Approach to Strategic Capital Budgeting." Ph.D. Thesis, Harvard University.

TRIGEORGIS, LENOS, and SCOTT P. MASON (1987). "Valuing Managerial Flexibility." *Midland Corporate Finance Journal* 5 (Spring), pp. 14–21.

TRIGEORGIS, LENOS (1988). "A Conceptual Options Framework for Capital Budgeting." *Advances in Futures and Options Research* 3, pp. 145–167.

TRIGEORGIS, LENOS (1990). "A Real Options Application in Natural Resource Investments," *Advances in Futures and Options Research* 4, pp. 152–164.

TRIGEORGIS, LENOS, (1991). "A Log-transformed Binomial Numerical Analysis Method for Valuing Complex Multi-option Investments." *Journal of Financial and Quantitative Analysis* 26 (September), pp. 309–326.

13

Capital Budgeting and the Utilization of Full Information: Performance Evaluation and the Exercise of Real Options

Tamir Agmon*

ABSTRACT

This chapter considers the role of contingent claims analyses in managing and evaluating ongoing capital projects. It is shown that the inability to identify and assess events that provide truly new information can lead to incorrect capital budgeting decisions.

I. INTRODUCTION

Recently there has been new interest in capital budgeting which can be traced to two sources: (1) lack of satisfaction with the way that standard net present value (NPV) procedures perform, and (2) development of new financial techniques and their application to corporate finance, no-

* In writing this article I have benefited from the comments of my colleagues at the University of Southern California Los Angeles and in Tel Aviv, Israel. I am also grateful for the comments of Raj Aggarwal and an anonymous referee.

tably the application of option pricing models. The first source creates the demand for a critical reevaluation of the accepted procedures of capital budgeting, and the second provides the means for such an evaluation.

The two dimensions of the criticism are expressed in an article by Trigeorgis and Mason (1987). They indicate that traditional NPV procedures ignore management ability to revise its strategies based on actual outcomes during the life of the project while options-based analyses can recognize this managerial flexibility.[1]

In a more recent article Aggarwal and Soenen (1989) deal with a specific case of management flexibility, the ability to exit a project over its life. They design a procedure that integrates this ability into the NPV calculation. This is somewhat similar to evaluation of the degree of specificity of a given project and its effect on the net present value of the project. [Agmon and Wihlborg (1989) provide a discussion of project specificity in the context of international investment.]

Trigeorgis and Mason and Aggarwal and Soenen, as well as other reseachers, are correct in their criticism.[2] They also provide interesting and useful solutions for specific problems. It is also important, however, to place these criticisms in a general characterization of the accepted model of capital budgeting.

The traditional NPV approach is a one-period model of a perfect capital market. Uncertainty is treated by adding a risk premium based on specific assumptions with regard to the distributions of the cash flows and/or the nature of the utility functions. Once a decision has been made, time expires. In the next period everything starts anew. This model cannot accommodate the complexity of real-life situations where the decision is a dynamic process of periodic adjustment and where management can use the complete information at any point of adjustment rather than summary variables like the expected value, the variance, and the resulting risk premium.

This chapter addresses one specific issue within this framework: how to make the NPV approach more responsive to the full set of information available at the time of the investment decision. The responsiveness is measured by the adjustment process which can be described in terms of a vector of real options. (The exit option discussed by Aggarwal and Soenen is one example.) Utilization of the full set of available information is both practical and important. It is practical because all the information is available and the procedure for using it is quite simple. It is important in the sense that if it is not done, the result may be value-reducing.

It is important to realize that the procedure described here does not depend on the arrival of new information. Indeed, it is assumed throughout that the probability distribution of the relevant events is stationary over time. (In this aspect the model is consistent with the standard body of assumptions in financial economics.)

The plan of this chapter is as follows: The general model is presented in Section II. The main message is that the full set of information has to be tested against current events as part of the dynamic process of reevaluating the project. The general approach is illustrated in Section III by presenting a case study. This vehicle was chosen to provide a realistic assessment of what is involved in applying the model to real data. In the last section of the paper, Section IV, the question of when to exercise real options based on realizing the information at the initial decision time is discussed.

II. A DYNAMIC EVENT-CONTINGENT NPV MODEL

Corporate investment decisions are made in an environment of uncertainty and over multiperiod horizons. Traditionally the uncertainty is handled by first estimating the probability distribution of the periodic cash flows and then summarizing the probability distributions by some summary statistics. The time element is handled by discounting. The two issues are related by the interdependency of the choice of the summary statistics and the discounting factor. Whichever technique is used, the end result is a vector of cash flow representations discounted to provide an estimate of the NPV.

This system is appropriate if the investment decision is a static, one-time decision. Although some investment decisions may be characterized as such, the general case involves a sequence of decisions over time. In other words, the accept/reject decision is followed by other decisions with regard to the investment project. These decisions are made in later time periods after the initial decision has been made. The simplest case is where management can decide to abandon the project at given time periods between its inception and its conclusion. In other cases management may allow changes, be they changes in scale, in technology, or in the product, or a combination of these. In each of these cases, the decision whether to abandon the project or not, or whether to change some of the parameters, maybe by exercising an operational option, should be based on a performance evaluation of the project to date. Such a performance evaluation should be based on the full set of relevant information and not on the expected value or some other representation of the probability distribution of the cash flows. Before presenting a general model, let us illustrate this point with a simple numerical example.

Suppose that a firm is considering an investment project with the following probability distribution of cash flows:

Annual Cash Flow	Probability
(100)	.5
1100	.5

The probability distribution of the cash flows is assumed to be stationary over the life of the project which is 5 years. The investment outlay for this project is 1000, and it is certain. The firm is using a risk-adjusted discounted cash flow (DCF) model. Accordingly, the periodical cash flows are represented by the expected value of the cash flows, and a risk-adjusted discount rate is used to discount the periodic expected values. If the NPV is greater than zero, then the project is acceptable and the investment takes place. Given the information above, the project can be presented in the standard way as

$$(1000) \quad 500 \quad 500 \quad 500 \quad 500 \quad 500$$

Given a risk-adjusted discount rate of 20% (in real terms), the discount factor is 2.991 and the NPV of the project is 495.5. The project is acceptable and the investment takes place.

Assume now that after the investment has taken place management evaluates the project once every period. The purpose of the evaluation is to decide whether to continue with the project or to abandon it. [The term "abandonment" is taken from Brealey and Myers (1984). It is used to include selling the assets in place.] Given the nature of the generating function of the cash flows and the attendant probability distribution of the cash flows, we know that management will observe either a loss of 100 for the period or a profit of 1100. Assume further that the two cases, (100) and 1100, can be associated with two externally observed events A and B. The events may be natural, like the amount of rainfall, or market-related, like the price of copper. Clearly the performance evaluation should be done relative to the event that has occurred rather than relative to the expected value of the cash flows, which in this case are unattainable in any one period. If the latter is used as the benchmark, then observing a loss of 100 rather than a profit (expected) of 500, management may decide to abandon the project—a value-reducing decision, given the simple case described above. This is unlikely to happen in our simple example, but as is illustrated in the next section, unjustified and value-reducing abandonments like the one described above do take place.

The solution to this problem is to design a performance evaluation mechanism that will be consistent with the structure of the information set used for the initial decision. (We maintain the assumption that no new information becomes available between the investment and the performance evaluation periods.) A system like this is described in Figure 13.1.

Figure 13.1

Expected versus actual project cash flows.

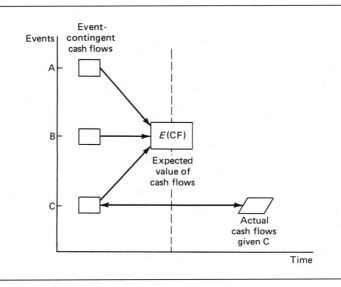

The simple example described above can be generalized in a simple model. The model is discrete to make its application easier. (A continuous version will not affect the results.)

Let $CF_i t$ be the probability distribution of the cash flows for time t. $CF_i t$ is dependent on i, where $i = 1, 2, \ldots , n$ is a vector of mutually exclusive and all-inclusive events. Each event i has a probability p_i, where $0 > p_i < 1$ and $\Sigma p_i = 1$.

Following the standard capital budgeting model, the NPV associated with a given investment project can be written as NPV $= E(CF_i)t/ (1 + k)$, where k is the risk-adjusted discount rate. Given a positive NPV, the performance evaluation has to be done by comparing the actual cash flows ACF_t generated by the project in a given period t to the event-dependent expected cash flows, that is, to $CF t$ with $a = a$, where i denotes the event that has actually taken place in period t. As illustrated in the simple example above, comparing the actual cash flows to the expected value of the cash flows is theoretically wrong and potentially value-reducing. However, real cases are never as simple as the example above. In order to examine the practicality and the importance of the general model presented above, a realistic case study is presented and analyzed in the next section.

III. AN EXAMINATION OF THE EVENT-DEPENDENT PERFORMANCE EVALUATION MODEL FOR CAPITAL BUDGETING—THE CASE OF BEST SOUPS

At the beginning of 1979 the manager of the canned foods division at Associated Manufacturers heard that the owners of Best Soups were interested in selling their factory. Best Soups was at the time a privately owned medium-sized factory for specialty canned soups. It was a rarity in the sense that most of the production in the industry was controlled by three large, diversified conglomerates. The food products group of Associated Manufacturers, itself a large, diversified industrial conglomerate, was one of the two largest organizations that controlled most of the production in this field. The canned foods division was part of the food products group of Associated Manufacturers.

The division manager approached the president of the food products group and asked for permission to enter into negotiations with the owners of Best Soups in order to acquire part or all of their shares. It was agreed that the group would buy the shares if, when viewed as an investment project, the purchase met the standard conditions, that is, the investment had a positive net present value.

Following this understanding, the division manager appointed a task force to evaluate the acquisition of Best Soups as a capital budgeting decision. In the negotiations with the owners of Best Soups it was tentatively agreed that the food products group of Associated Manufacturers would buy 50% of the controlling shares of Best Soups for the sum of $13 million. It was also agreed that after 3 years one of the parties would buy the shares of the other party, following the "You cut, I choose" method. At that time one party would make a proposal, and the other party would have the right to purchase the shares of the proposing party at the price specified in the proposal. If it refused to do so, than it would have to accept the proposal and sell its 50% of the shares.

The task force recommended to top management acceptance of the project including the above-mentioned stipulation. The recommendation of the task force was based on calculation of the net present value of the project as an independent project. It was argued that if the project was acceptable on its own, there would be no need to explore synergism and other positive externalities.

The calculated cash flows of the investment (acquisition of 50% of the controlling shares of Best Soups) and the net present value of the investment are summarized in Table 13.1.

The high discount rate reflects the relatively high risk of the project. The risk emanates from the large amount of competition in the market, as well as from possible technological and production problems in the transfer of Best Soups to a joint venture with the division. For

TABLE 13.1.   Calculated Cash Flows and the Net Present Value

Year	1978	1979	1980	1981	1982	1983	1984
Cash flow (million $)	(13,000)	(300)	3,400	8,750	9,500	10,900	10,900
Present value at 20% (million $)	(13,000)	(250)	2,360	5,066	4,579	3,651	3,041

example, the agreement left some management positions at the discretion of the original owners of Best Soups, and the task force felt that this might create problems in the future. For these reasons the task force figured a negative cash flow of $300,000 in the first year of operations in addition to the original investment of $13 million. It was assumed that the investment had a 6-year horizon and that the cash flows would cease in 1985. The residual value was estimated at zero. Given these assumptions, the net present value of the proposed project was $5,447,000. The project was acceptable even as an independent project. Although the reported cash flows represented some probability distribution of actual cash flows, the distributions were not specified in the feasibility study. We will see later that the failure to do so created a problem in the performance evaluation. However, the use of a relatively high discount rate, 20% in real terms, indicated uncertain cash flows.

The investment was approved in 1978, and the joint venture began operations in 1979. The reported financial results of the first 2 years were disappointing. In the first year of operations the reported loss was $1,639,456. In the second year the reported loss of Best Soups was significantly greater at $3,494,342. This was compared to an expected loss of $600,000 for the operation as a whole in 1979 and expected gross profits of $6.8 million in 1980. During the third year a process of negotiations with the original owners of Best Soups began. Given what was evaluated by the canned foods division as very poor results, the division offered a very low price for the 50% shares that the original owners of Best Soups held. The original owners decided to exercise their option to buy back the 50% of the shares they had sold 2 years earlier. Following that, they sold their entire holdings to another conglomerate. In the next 5 years Best Soups performed very well. In retrospect the management of the canned foods division of Associated Manufacturers felt that making a low bid for the remaining 50% of the shares of Best Soups was a mistake. Yet, based on the poor performance of the unit, it seemed a good decision at the time. Or was it?

A lot of what transpired in the third year was dependent on evaluation of the financial results for the first 2 years. The way that the management of the division, indeed the management of Associated Manufacturers, viewed the situation seems quite straightforward. According to the plan, the division share in the cash flows [based on Earnings Before Interest and Taxes (EBIT)] should have been a loss of $300,000 in 1979 and a profit of $3.4 million in 1980. These numbers translate to a loss of $600,000 and a profit (on an EBIT basis) of $6.8 million for the whole operation in 1979 and 1980, respectively. Not only was, the actual loss in 1979 much bigger than expected, but the loss situation became worse in 1980. That led management to reevaluate the project at a significantly lower level than the original feasibility study and to tender a low proposal for the remaining 50% of the shares. However, the reported results for 1979 and 1980 should have been evaluated based on an event-contingent dynamic approach as described in Section II. This procedure would have produced a totally different picture.

The first step in evaluating the reported results of Best Soups for the years 1979 and 1980 is to go back to the feasibility study to ascertain how the expected cash flows for those 2 years were generated and to recalculate the cash flows given the events that took place in 1979 and 1980. Given this information, a new vector of event-dependent cash flows can be computed. These cash flows will be compared to the actual results as a basis for deciding on the value of the project from 1981 on.

This last step was of particular importance in the case of Best Soups, as the management of the division of canned foods had to come up with an offer to purchase the 50% shares of stock held by the original owners. Given the nature of the agreement between the original owners and the division, the offer should have reflected the best estimate of the true value at the beginning of 1981.

The data for comparison of the results are presented in Table 13.2.

An examination of the data shows that according to the plan, the plant should have produced at a low level in the first year after the acquisition, 1979, and it should have moved into a higher level of production in the second year, 1980. In retrospect, the level of production in the first year was about one-half of the planned level, and the level of production in 1980 resembled the planned level of production for 1979. In financial terms, the lag in production caused a loss in 1979, gross profits of -19.3%. The possibility of such a loss should have been part of the probability distribution of the cash flows for 1979, as it reflects the ability of the new joint venture to overcome the initial problems in

TABLE 13.2.   Comparison of Plan to Actual Results, 1979–1980

	1979 Plan	1979 Actual	1980 Plan	1980 Actual
Sales (thousand cases)	2600	1472	3900	2560
Cost of production (%)	72.5	119.3	71.5	63.7
Gross profit (%)	27.5	(19.3)	28.5	36.3

setting up the operations. Given the common simulation approach to capital budgeting under uncertainty introduced many years ago by Hertz (1964), such a factor could be captured by varying the production levels in the first 2 years. The different levels of production could have been associated with externally observed states of nature. This would have allowed a coupling of the actual result with the estimated result, given the state of nature that occurred.

Another way to present the same argument involves the probability distribution of the length of the "break-in" period. The planned production numbers represent the expected value of the length of this period, expressed in units of production; it can, and did, vary. In this case it was longer than expected and therefore costlier. It is important to realize that all the information was available at the time of the decision and that no new information arrived between decision time and performance evaluation time. The only difference between the two time periods is that in the latter, management knew which one of the alternative states of nature included in the probability distribution of the cash flows in the first period actually happened. As management knew that only one state would occur, the fact that one specific state of nature did occur does not alter the validity of the probability distribution or the assumption about their stationarity.

A closer look at the actual production data suggests that, given what happened, the whole plan should have been adjusted by adding one more year to the break-in period and the production spread over time accordingly. The additional loss during the first year should then have been added to the investment and the net present value recalculated.

Failure to recognize the nature of the reported results as a reflection of a longer break-in period, which is part of the investment, was the cause of another mistake made by the division management that evaluated the performance of Best Soups. There is no place to charge interest to the part of the loss that is an additional investment. After all, the interest is a return for capital employed, and thus it is part of the present value of the project. In other words, by discounting the cash flows by 20% per year, a return on the capital employed has been charged already. Charging any part of the implicit or explicit investment with interest is like asking for return on the capital twice. Recalculating the NPV, as is done below, provides a return for all capital employed. Part of this return is paid in the form of interest.

We can now estimate the additional investment due to the delay in production. In doing so it is assumed that the production plan was moved back 1 year. The reported loss in 1979 was $1,639,456, and in 1980 it was $3,494,342. Estimation of the additional investment is presented in Table 13.3. (All the data have been adjusted for inflation.)

TABLE 13.3. Estimation of the Additional Investment, 1979–1980 (in 1978 prices)

	1979 ($)	1980 ($)
Reported loss	1,639,456	3,494,342
Minus interest cost	175,656	524,151
Net of interest	1,463,800	2,970,190
In 1978 prices	1,300,000	2,393,670
Planned loss	600,000	—
Additional investment	700,000	2,393,670

The additional expenditures in 1979 and 1980 cannot be explained solely on the basis of a delay in the break-in process. The data presented in Table 13.2 indicated that the gross profits in 1980 were higher than expected. In other words, the cost of production was as expected, or better. Given the actual level of production in 1980, the results should have been similar to the expected results for 1979, that is to say, a loss of about $600,000 for the operation as a whole. Yet even after the adjustment for financing cost and for inflation during that period, the actual loss was $2,393,670.

The additional cost can be traced to a deviation from the expected value in the cost of marketing. Data on the expected levels and on the actual cost of marketing, finance, and administration are presented in Table 13.4. As the costs are expressed in percentage of sales, some of the deviations from the planned items are explained by the delayed production plan. The cost of financing was already accounted for by adjusting the interest cost and inflation. The higher-than-planned cost of marketing in 1980 may represent a larger-than-expected investment in setting up a marketing infrastructure for the product. Again, the estimated expenditure for this item represented the expected value over a number of possibilities. One has to go back to the feasibility study to examine the assumptions with regard to the marketing expenditure and to contrast them with what actually happened. Only then can a meaningful evaluation be made.

TABLE 13.4. Comparison of Plan to Actual Results, 1979–1980 (% of sales)

	1979 Plan	1979 Actual	1980 Plan	1980 Actual
Marketing	11.6	19.4	12.0	40.0
Administration	6.5	22.7	6.3	10.4
Finance	4.4	18.5	4.4	23.0

For the purpose of our analysis we will assume that all additional expenditures, adjusted for interest and inflation, should be treated as investments. One possible way to evaluate the project is to recalculate the net present value on a 1978 basis, given what actually happened. As the original evaluation was done for the 50% share of Associated Manufacturers, the reevaluation is done on the same basis. The data are presented in Table 13.5.

The net present value of this specific scenario is still positive at $2,326,000. This calculation is an example of the efficient use of information as time unfolds. In other words, this calculation is based on a process that turns probability distributions into deterministic numbers. In some sense there is no new information as time moves on, as the state that has happened and the associated cash flows were part of the probability distribution used in the original decision. In this case a set of events less favorable than these, which were represented by the expected values of the cash flows, have occurred. The project still has a positive net present value, using the actual results for 1978 and 1979 and the expected values of the cash flows (adjusted for the less-then-expected production) from there on.

There is no reason to abandon the project. It is not even clear that the NPV of the project should be changed at all if the events reported above are consistent with the probability distribution of the cash flows assumed in the original feasibility study. The high rate of discount, 20% in real terms, is an indication that the decision makers thought that the probability distribution of events and cash flows was very wide. Therefore one may assume that better-than-expected results may occur in the future and that the NPV of the project over its lifetime will stay as expected.

In the case of Best Soups the sets of probable events do not lend themselves to a clear and externally measurable way to denote which event did take place. Indeed, the actual set of events was constructed from the reported results. In the simplistic case presented earlier, it was very easy to define a set of mutually exclusive events and to decide ex post which event had occurred. There are a number of more realistic cases where it is possible to define events on an external basis and to decide after the fact which set of events has taken place.

TABLE 13.5.   Calculated Cash Flows and the Net Present Value: A Specific Set of Events (Actual)

Year	1978	1979	1980	1981	1982	1983	1984
Cash flow (million $)	(13,000)	(650)	(1,197)	3,400	8,750	9,500	10,900
Present value at 20% (million $)	(13,000)	(541)	(831)	1,969	4,218	3,819	3,651

One such case is where the financial result depends to a great extent on the price of one input, like copper, oil, or any other commodity. A less obvious example is where the outcome is strongly dependent on the business cycle in the market. A case in point is the domestic airlines industry. Other cases may be closer to the case of Best Soups. But even in these cases the principle of evaluation can and should be the same.

IV. REALIZATION OF EXISTING INFORMATION, NEW INFORMATION, AND THE EXERCISE OF REAL OPTIONS

The application of option pricing models to capital budgeting is a natural extension of the recent developments in capital markets theory. A necessary condition for a useful application of the theory, and its practice, is an understanding of some basic differences between a financial option traded in a capital market and a real or operational option implicit in an investment project. Kensinger (1987) provides a description of different types of real options and how they might be evaluated. Missing from his analysis, as well as from some of the studies referred to in his article, is a discussion of when to exercise the option. That this is an issue at all is already a difference between financial options and real options. In financial markets the difference between the market price and the exercise price of the option provides all the necessary information on whether to exercise the option or to let it expire. This is not the case with real options. Management should maintain and evaluate the set of information available at the time of the original investment in order to make a decision whether to exercise a real option, such as abandonment, change in input, or any other change, or not to exercise it. The difference in the triggering of the two types of options stems from the different decision processes of financial investors relative to management of a corporation, as well as from the American nature of the real option since most financial options are European.

To illustrate and clarify the different nature of the two options and to relate the argument to the efficient use of information discussed in Sections II and III, let us consider a currency option relative to the ability of management to change the source of an input, used in a certain project, from one country to another and therefore from one currency to another. The real option is similar to the currency option in providing a possibility of moving from one currency to another.

The first option is a standard financial option. With a call currency option for deutsche marks the owner of the option has the right to buy a given amount of deutsche marks for a prespecified amount of U.S. dollars on a given date. The mechanism of triggering the option is quite simple.

If at the exercise date the deutsche mark–dollar exchange rate is lower than the option-specific exchange rate, the owner will exercise the option, otherwise the owner will let the option expire. Note that this is a one-period decision and that the option is either exercised at a given date or not exercised at all. The real option is more complicated. Assume that in a certain project an input is bought in Germany in deutsche marks. Given the current and the expected volatility in exchange rates, the management plans a contingency source for this input in the United States, where the input can be bought in U.S. dollars. Assume further that with regard to this input the purchasing power parity is not holding.

A change in the exchange rate that suggests a transition from one supplier to another is not a sufficient condition for a switch. The benefits of a cheaper source, measured in U.S. dollars, should be compared to the cost of the switch, including future costs like the possibility of retaliation in the future by the German supplier. In doing so, it is important to assess whether the change in the exchange rate is a transitory or a long-term change. Short-term, transitory changes may not justify a change in suppliers.[3] In order to assess the nature of the change in the exchange rate, management may want to examine the information with regard to the probability distribution of the exchange rate available at the time of the original investment decision. If the observed change is well within the random volatility of the exchange rate assumed at the time of the original investment decision, the real option may not be exercised. Whereas a financial option, a currency option, will be exercised even if the change in the exchange rate is a fleeting fluke.

If we consider organizational inertia and personal considerations, in addition to the possibility of exercising the option later because of its American nature, it is easily seen that the decision whether to exercise a real option, and when to do so, is not a simple one. An important consideration in the decision whether to exercise the option or not is whether there is new information that justifies the change via the option. For example, in the case described in Section III, the question could be phrased as follows: Is there any new information that justifies exercising the option of selling the 50% of the shares of Best Soups and thus abandoning the project? One way of abandoning the project is by bidding low for the 50% of the shares still owned by the original owners.

In summary, it is clear that the inability to distinguish between new information versus the realization of an event, or a series of events, already taken into account in the expected value that was the basis of the original investment decision, can and does lead to incorrect capital budgeting decisions. Thus, it is important that the management of capital projects involves an ongoing ability to assess and identify events that provide truly new information.

NOTES

1. Trigeorgis and Mason (1987, p. 15).
2. See, for example, Hayes and Abernathy (1980) and Hodder and Riggs (1985).
3. Johansson (1987) provides evidence on the reluctance of major Japanese companies to change their domestic suppliers in the face of a substantial decline in the dollar–yen exchange rate.

REFERENCES

AGGARWAL, R., and L. A. SOENEN (1989). "Project Exit Value as a Measure of Flexibility and Risk Exposure," *Engineering Economist* 35 (Fall) pp. 39–54.

BREALEY, R., and S. MYERS (1984). *Principles of Corporate Finance*, 2nd ed. (New York: McGraw-Hill).

HAYES, R., and W. ABERNATHY (1980). "Managing Our Way to Economic Decline," *Harvard Business Review* 48 (July–August) pp. 67–77.

HERTZ, D. B. (1964). "Risk Analysis in Capital Investment," *Harvard Business Review* 32 (January–February) pp. 95–106.

HODDER, J., and H. RIGGS (1985). "Pitfalls in Evaluating Risky Assets," *Harvard Business Review* 53 (January–February) pp. 128–135.

JOHANSSON, J. (1987). "Marketing Policies of Japanese Firms in a Stronger Yen World." Paper presented at the First Annual IBEAR Research and Management Conferernce, University of Southern California, Los Angeles April 2–4.

KENSINGER, J. W. (1987). "Adding the Value of Active Management Into the Capital Budgeting Equation," *Midland Corporate Finance Journal*, 5 (Spring) pp. 33–42.

TRIGEORGIS, L., and S. P. MASON (1987). "Valuing Managerial Flexibility," *Midland Corporate Finance Journal* 5 (Spring) pp. 14–21.

14

Capital Budgeting for Replacements With Unequal Remaining Life

LeRoy D. Brooks

ABSTRACT

A capital budgeting decision procedure appropriate for choosing the continuance, replacement, or abandonment of an asset in place is examined. The optimal replacement decision on an asset already in service requires simultaneous consideration of project life, project chaining, and possible abandonment points for both the asset in place and the replacement asset. The additional information required for the suggested procedure compared to the traditional replacement procedure is generally manageable, and a practical solution procedure is feasible.

I. INTRODUCTION

Machinery and equipment replacements are involved in most of the capital budgeting decisions for many firms and in many of the decisions for most firms. Surprisingly, a limited amount of material in the financial literature concerns replacement of assets already owned by the firm. The topic should be of practical appeal to decision makers. A greater delineation of adopted assumptions and the resulting impact on modeling to achieve wealth-maximizing objectives should be of interest to academicians and practitioners. This chapter reviews current recommended practices and attempts to enhance the building of a more comprehensive approach to evaluating project replacements.

Most recent finance texts that mention the replacement issue adopt the assumption that the old equipment will have a life equal to the life of the new equipment. For example, this assumption is adopted in problem solutions shown in Block and Hirt (1987), Brigham (1986), and Schall and Haley (1983). These authors are not faulted for their overly restrictive assumption since introductory texts are already sufficiently burdened with other essential information. Most advanced texts in the capital budgeting area, however, fail to reconsider the replacement issue. Articles in prominent finance journals tend to discuss specific facets involved in the replacement issue rather than examine the entire decision framework.

In the traditional approach to the replacement issue, an assumption is generally adopted that the replacement asset has the same useful life as the remaining service life of the equipment now in use. This equal-life assumption is fraught with potential pitfalls and should be used only with extreme caution when making actual decisions. First, a mutually exclusive alternative of abandonment that automatically exists when considering a replacement decision is excluded from direct consideration, and the exclusion may lead to faulty decisions. A mutually exclusive decision to abandon the old equipment and not take on a replacement is always an available option coincident to any replacement decision. The standard replacement evaluation procedure examines the marginal cash flows from operating the new versus the old equipment and the salvage value from the period-zero disposal of the old equipment. This is a marginal evaluation of the old versus the new that fails to directly consider the alternative of abandonment of old without replacement with new. In some decision situations, it may be obvious that abandonment without replacement is a large wealth loss alternative. Thus an implicit rejection of this evaluation that is inherent in the traditional replacement evaluation may be acceptable in some instances.

Second, consideration of mutually exclusive later replacement dates is also avoided with the traditional replacement analysis. When all possible replacement dates are considered, the solution procedure becomes one of selecting the optimal remaining life of the old equipment. Bierman and Smidt (1988) and Levy and Sarnat (1986) evaluate an optimal life determination for new equipment. A later section will indicate how their suggested modeling can be adjusted to accommodate the optimal replacement or abandonment time horizon for existing equipment. Thus the traditional replacement analysis may often be unsound and may not lead to wealth-maximizing decisions because of a failure to adequately consider mutually exclusive alternative replacement or abandonment dates (Aggarwal and Soenen, 1989).

Third, a potential bias toward favoring a replacement also exists with the traditional replacement analysis. To lengthen the life of the old equipment to match the new, additional costs are added to the cost of operating the old equipment in adequate service. The additional costs include additional repairs, maintenance, component replacements, re-building, and opportunity losses relative to the new equipment resulting from less reliability and greater expected downtime. Since alternative mutually exclusive replacement and abandonment dates are not being considered, extension of the ending life of the older equipment beyond its optimal cessation date to the life of new equipment commonly results in excessive costs in maintaining the old equipment in service. With the traditional procedure employing incremental costs between the new and old, the relative position of the new equipment is enhanced. A bias toward excessive replacement is invoked.

The traditional approach to evaluating replacements may serve as a useful pedagogical device for the novice to capital budgeting. Limitations inherent in the approach should lead to its rejection in practice. Yet in discussions with capital budgeting decision makers, widespread use of the procedure appears to exist.

The replacement decision entails simultaneous consideration of the abandonment decision, optimal equipment life, and optimal project chaining. The most comprehensive analysis of the two last-mentioned issues, with respect to the replacement decision, is provided by Thuesen and Fabrycky (1989, pp. 264–279). Their approach is similar to the one provided here. Howe and McCabe (1983) also consider a finite-chain replacement problem where the optimal lives of the assets in the chain need not be equal. Their procedure is particularly appropriate when the equal-life assumption does not hold. The literature on the abandonment issue is extensive and has a direct bearing on the replacement issue. An option to abandon at any given time rather than continue or replace should be explicitly considered when evaluating a replacement problem. Robichek and Van Horne (1967) suggest abandonment when the present value of future cash flows does not exceed abandonment value, while Dyl and Long (1969) extend the analysis to consider all possible future abandonment opportunities. Bonini (1977) provides a dynamic programming model that expands on the earlier works by considering different abandonment possibilities and uncertain cash flows. Alternatively, Howe and McCabe (1983) combine the abandonment issue with replacement chaining but do not explicitly consider an initial asset in place, as do Thuesen and Fabrycky (1989), who do not completely consider the abandonment issue. Thuesen and Fabrycky examine the replacement problem by assuming that either the old or the new equipment *must* be used. Abandonment of both is not an available option. An evaluation of abandonment of the asset in place without replacement is allowed and is considered in this chapter.

Journal articles and the Thuesen and Fabrycky text have extended analysis of the replacement decision well beyond the traditional replacement analysis employed by many practitioners. Here we consider the earlier developments and provide an initial step in integrating the various issues that impact replacement decisions.

II. MODELS AND ENVIRONMENTS

The remainder of this article describes alternative replacement decision models and the type of decision environment that gives rise to the appropriate use of each model. Central to each model is the explicit recognition that each period gives rise to the mutually exclusive options of abandonment, continuance, and replacement. A second dimension of the environment considers whether a decision is replicable or unique and thereby cannot be repeated. The third dimension concerns the existence of either a discrete or an infinite time horizon. The use of incremental versus total cash flows is also evaluated.

A. Unique Replacement With Equal Finite Project Life

This is the traditional approach discussed above and is provided here to allow comparisons with the alternative evaluation criteria provided later. The solution is nearly exclusively shown on an incremental cash flow basis in the literature. An incremental cash flow ΔC_{ijm} is the difference in cash flow $C_{jn} - C_{in}$ that occurs at point n in time between the new project j and the old project i. Incremental net present value is easily computed as

$$\Delta \text{NPV}_{ij} = \sum_{n=0}^{N} \frac{\Delta C_{ijn}}{(1 + k)^n} \tag{1}$$

where N is the common terminal life of both equipments and k is a constant cost of funds. For a going concern with an expected life far exceeding N periods, the above procedure is accurate only when the optimal remaining life of the old equipment and the optimal life of the new equipment are both equal to N. An additional restriction imposed by the incremental approach comes from requiring that both projects be in the same risk class, where k is the appropriate discount rate. This assertion is probably reasonable in most circumstances but should not necessarily be accepted out of hand without due consideration.

The use of total cash flows for both the old and the new projects can avoid some of the shortcomings of the incremental approach, but at a greater cost imposed by requiring more, and possibly not readily available, information. With the total cash flow approach, the NPV_i and the NPV_j are derived separately with the standard NPV model.

$$NPV_h = \sum_{n=0}^{N} \frac{C_{hn}}{(1 + k_h)^n} \qquad (2)$$

for $h = i, j$. The C_{i0} for the old project is the opportunity loss cash flow foregone by not selling the equipment at its residual point-zero value. Two of the potential shortcomings of the incremental approach are avoided. First, the mutually exclusive decision to abandon the old without replacement is provided. If the NPV_i and the NPV_j are both less than zero, abandonment without replacement is required. Second, if the analyst is convinced that the projects are in different risk classes, a project-specific discount rate k_h can be used.

The total cash flow procedure does require additional information on the total per-period cash flows originating from the old equipment. Once equipment is integrated into the operations of a company, it may be difficult to separate out all of its specific cash flow impacts. A thorough evaluation of the replacement problem that includes consideration of the abandonment option is, however, dependent on determining total cash flows. If the cost of obtaining the required information is prohibitive or the information is not obtainable, the recognizably flawed traditional incremental approach may be required.

B. Unique Replacement With Unequal Project Life and a Finite Time Horizon

This approach requires determination of the optimal abandonment or replacement timing subject to a given time horizon constraint. The decision is essentially one of finding the joint optimal life of both the old and the new equipment constrained by a fixed terminal date. Using a planning horizon of N, where for convenience in notation no more than one replacement will be considered,

$$NPV_{i_{M1}, j_{M2}} = \sum_{n=1}^{N} \frac{C_{i_{M1}, j_{M2}, n}}{(1 + k)^n} + \frac{S_{i_{M1}}}{(1 + k)^{M1}} - \frac{I_{j_{M1}}}{(1 + k)^{M1}} + \frac{S_{j_{M2}}}{(1 + k)^{M2}} \qquad (3)$$

where $C_{i_{M1}, j_{M2}, n}$ is the cash flow at point n with the conditions that

$$C_{i_{M1}j_{M2},n} = \begin{cases} C_{in} & \text{if } n \leq M1 \\ C_{jn} & \text{if } M1 < n \leq M2 \\ 0 & \text{if } M2 < n \leq N \end{cases}$$

and $M1$ is the date of discontinuance of the old equipment project i and initiation date of the new project j, while $M2$ is the abandonment date for the new equipment. In the current analysis, we are not allowing intervening periods of time when project i is abandoned and project j is purchased at a future point in time later than $M1$. The notation can be easily modified to reflect this condition.

The $C_{i_{M1}j_{M2},n}$ is a period net operating flow arriving at point n. Changes in period investment flows associated with both the new and the old equipment other than in the replacement year are also included in $C_{i_{M1}j_{M2},n}$. For example, this includes incremental changes in inventory balances, receivables, and rebuilding costs. $S_{i_{M1}}$ represents the end of life, point $M1$, cash flows from the old equipment, including salvage value, tax consequences from disposal, and working capital investment changes initiated by the retirement. $S_{j_{M2}}$ represents the comparable end-of-life effects on the replacement equipment occurring at $M2$. $I_{j_{M1}}$ represents the investment flows on the new equipment at point $M1$. The new equipment is to be used for a period of no more than $N - M1$. Since $M2$ can be less than or equal to N, abandonment of the new equipment before the time horizon of N is permitted.

The complete set of possible mutually exclusive alternatives needs to be considered before the maximum $\text{NPV}_{i_{M1},j_{M2}}$ can be derived. The first alternative is immediate abandonment of the old without a new replacement. Equation (3) reduces to $\text{NPV}_{i_0j_0} = S_{i_0}$ in this instance. Next, $\text{NPV}_{i_{M1},j_{M2}}$ is calculated for the remaining mutually exclusive alternatives. $M2 = 1, 2, \ldots, N$, for every $M1 = 0, 1, \ldots, N$ subject to the additional conditions that $M1 \leq M2$ and $M2 \leq N$. Thus there are $\sum_{n=1}^{N+1} n$ possible mutually exclusive alternatives in an N-period planning horizon when including the N possible abandonment dates for the old equipment without replacement by the new (when $M1 = M2$, no purchase of new equipment occurs). With long-life assets and time horizons, extensive computational requirements are necessary to isolate the optimal decision. The final decision is to select the maximum $\text{NPV}_{i_{M1},j_{M2}}$ from the set of $\sum_{n=1}^{N+1} n$ alternatives.

The suggested algorithm considers abandonment without replacement in every period, replacement in all possible periods by the new equipment, and abandonment of the new equipment in all possible periods. This addresses the concerns in using the traditional incremental replacement evaluation discussed earlier except for the inability to consider the old and the new projects at different risk-adjusted discount rates. Equation (3) is easily modified to accommodate this condition:

$$
\mathrm{NPV}_{i_{M1}, j_{M2}} = \sum_{n=1}^{M1} \frac{C_{i_{m1}, n}}{(1 + k_i)^n} + \sum_{n=M1+1}^{M2} \left[\frac{C_{j_{m2}, n}}{(1 + k_j)^n} - \frac{C_{i_{m1}, n}}{(1 + k_i)^n} \right]
$$
$$
+ \frac{S_{i_{M1}}}{(1 + k_i)^{M1}} - \frac{I_{j_{M1}}}{(1 + k_j)^{M1}} + \frac{S_{j_{M2}}}{(1 + k_j)^{M2}} \tag{4}
$$

Implementation of the suggested approach is constrained by additional computational and informational requirements not found in the traditional incremental cash flow replacement analysis. An exhaustive analysis of the entire set of mutually exclusive alternatives is necessary to isolate both the optimal replacement point and the holding-time horizon of the new replacement equipment. Information requirements are also much more extensive. The traditional procedure typically examines only a current point-zero replacement and replacement equipment held for its generally subjectively estimated useful life. Incremental cash flows are required for only one NPV evaluation. Since $\sum_{n=1}^{N+1} n$ mutually exclusive evaluations are required with the proposed procedure, total cash flows per period are required for each set of evaluations. The requirement may not be as onerous as initially suspected. At a minimum, cash flow estimates are required for a maximum of N possible periods for both the old equipment and the new equipment, salvage values are required for each possible abandonment point, and the investment in the new equipment is required. This is $(3N + 1)$ observations, and only about three times the information needed in the traditional replacement analysis. If the distribution of real costs over the life of the new equipment is invariant to the acquisition date, no additional information is required. More cash flow estimates are required if this assumption cannot be adopted.

Practical implementation of the model is not very difficult if the set of possible observations is restricted to the $(3N + 1)$ observations. A standard optimal life PC spreadsheet template is fairly easily modified to accommodate the requirements of Equation (4) or (5). To exhaustively examine all possible combinations, $(N + 1)$ spreadsheets are required, one for each possible $M1$ date. A total of $(N - M1 + 1)$ projects are evaluated on each spreadsheet. For example, with $N = 10$ years and the spreadsheet for the $M1 = 4$ date, abandonment values of the asset-in place for year 4 are determined as the first mutually exclusive possible decision. The continuance of the old project to year 4 together with the holding of the new project for $M2 = 5, 6, \ldots, 10$ comprises the remaining six mutually exclusive alternatives evaluated on the spreadsheet for $M1 = 4$.[1]

The recommended approach is not exhaustive of the set of mutually exclusive alternatives that should be investigated if an earlier simplify-ing assumption is dropped. For convenience, a time horizon N was adopted when no more than one replacement was considered. By allow-ing additional replacements, a still higher NPV may be achieved be-cause of the availability of additional combinations of projects over time. For example, assume that $N = 5$ and that projects i and j (and replace-ments of project j) have a maximum possible life of 5. One possible alternative, not considered previously, is to abandon at zero and buy a new project j each period for $n = 0, 1, \ldots, 4$. Another is to abandon the old at zero, hold the first project j for three periods, and purchase a second project j for the remaining two periods. A computer algorithm can be built to consider all feasible combinations. As long as the information requirements do not explode, because of loss of the independence be-tween acquisition date and cost distributions assumption, for example, the optimal NPV is achievable.

Consideration needs to also be directed toward specification of the time horizon N and the impact that this choice of a finite time horizon has on the analysis and results. The decision to specify a finite time horizon is appropriate in a venture where termination of the venture is pre-scribed. Almost any other explanation that forces the time horizon con-straint onto the decision structure is suspect. A fairly strong case could be argued for accepting a terminal date if the rate of technological change is uncertain. This can lead to unexpected substantive changes in estimated cash flows where the potential changes increase rapidly as a function of time. A reluctance to consider replacements chained through time to infinity may rightfully occur. The N may then reasonably be set equal to the maximum of the chained sum of the potential life of the old and the new equipment. An alternative optimal solution procedure is suggested in this situation. Since the N date no longer represents a "bailout" date, as in the venture case, a going-concern assumption seems more appropriate. Under this condition, the maximum equal annuity equivalent (EAE), calculated on the $M2$ date, is consistent with wealth maximization.

$$EAE_{iM1\,jM2} = \frac{kNPV_{iM1\,jM2}}{1 - (1 - k)^{-M2}} \qquad (5)$$

A separate $EAE_{iM1\,jM2}$ is needed for every $M2 = 1, 2, \ldots, N$ and for every $M1 = 0, 1, \ldots, N$ subject to the constraints $M1 \leq M2$ and $M2 \leq N$. Now N represents the sum of the remaining maximum feasible life of the old equipment plus the anticipated possible life of the new equipment. Again, the information needed for solution may be as few as $(3N + 1)$ observations.

The rationale leading to the EAE procedure is consistent with any decision on mutually exlcusive decisions of unequal time horizons. The

EAE procedure is widely used in optimal-life decisions where a going concern or company with an expected long life is a reasonable assumption to adopt. Again, a practical implementation of the model under the above conditions is fairly easily achieved by modifying a standard optimal life PC spreadsheet template.

In the replacement case just considered, the optimal replacement point and optimal life decision on the two equipments remain joint and inseparable. A constraint on the analysis time horizon is adopted because of curtailment of further acceptable forecasting beyond the anticipated life of the two pieces of equipment. This is why there was no resort to chaining identical new equipments to an infinite time horizon in determining an alternative EAE measure.

C. Replacement With Replicable Projects and an Infinite Time Horizon

In the absence of technological change, and with a product and company with an infinite anticipated life, an infinite chaining approach is recommended. With an infinite chaining approach, the $\text{NPV}_{i_{M1}}$ must first be derived for the possible life $M1$ of the old equipment for $M1 = 0, 1, \ldots,$ N where N now refers to the maximum possible life of the old project. Next, the optimal life of equipment j needs to be derived independent of considering replacement of the old equipment. This is a standard EAE calculation based on each possible life of the new equipment. The procedure can be found in Bierman and Smidt (1988), Copeland and Weston (1988), Levy and Sarnat (1986), Schall and Haley (1983), and Thuesen and Fabrycky (1989). Next, the present value of the perpetuity of the maximum EAE_j starting at $M1 + 1$ is derived. The total NVP_{M1} is symbolically

$$\text{NPV}_{M1} = \sum_{n=1}^{M1} \frac{C_{i_{M1},n}}{(1 + k_i)^n} + \frac{S_{i_{M1}}}{(1 + k_i)^{M1}} + \frac{\text{EAE}_{j*}}{k_j(1 + k_j)^{M1}} \tag{6}$$

where terms are as defined previously and max (NPV_{M1}) for $M1 = 0,$ $1, \ldots, N$ determines the wealth-maximizing strategy. The information required for the solution is the same as the prior cases, and a practical solution procedure can be farily easily incorporated into a standardized PC spreadsheet template.

III. CONCLUSIONS AND DISCUSSIONS

Bierman and Smidt (1988, p. 287), recognize the necessity for a replacement decision to consider estimates of the economic values of its anticipated future replacements. Their discussion considers the additional costs of carrying the old equipment for one period and the obtained benefit of delaying the costs of acquiring and operating all future replacements for one period. Their procedure is designed for a condition where the future replacements will perform the same function and generate the same revenue stream. Thus their approach reduces to a net present cost minimization criterion.

The procedures recommended in this article draw on their insight into the replacement problem and go on to consider a broadened set of conditions. First, the set of mutually exclusive decisions that are always at least implicitly available when considering a replacement problem are described and considered. Second, the definitions of cash flow information are broadened so that revenue changes induced by replacement equipment can be accommodated in the suggested NPV and EAE derivations. Third, the impact on modeling arising from the selected time horizon assumption is described. The appropriate NPV procedure for a venture resulting in Equation (3) or (4) is materially different from the EAE approach of Equation (5) or (6). Fourth, in an information-constrained environment the procedure of Equation (5) provides a manageable solution, while Equation (6) is more appropriate in an unchanging environment of identical replacements and infinite time horizons. Fifth, and possibly most importantly, further examination of the replacement decision leads to serious concerns for the traditional replacement evaluation, where only replacement at point zero is considered and where only one possible life of the new replacement asset is considered.

The topic seems of sufficient economic importance to justify use of the more comprehensive replacement analysis by actual decision makers. The modeling is quite straightforward and simple. The additional information required to implement the proposed procedures is feasible and practical if some reasonably realistic assumptions can be adopted. Shortcomings of the traditional replacement procedure lead to non-wealth-maximizing decisions that can be averted with the suggested procedures.

This preliminary examination of the replacement issue leaves much room for refinement in many areas. First, algorithms for narrowing the set of mutually exclusive alternatives that need to be considered, and programming procedures that minimize the iterations needed to derive an optimal solution, are obtainable. Restrictions on the functional form of the cash flows over time on both the old equipment and its replacement would probably be required. The development of these methods would increase the practical usefulness of the procedures in this article that now require substantial numbers of mutually exclusive alternative comparisons. Second, the rates of expected technological change and variance in technological change can be explicitly endogenized in the modeling. The decision to subjectively limit the time horizon to some ad hoc selected period N in Equations (3) through (5) implicitly assumes no technological changes within the planning horizon and complete uncertainty about technological change beyond this horizon. Third, the analytical framework changes materially if explicit consideration of the level of diversification of the investors is considered. Covariance of the replacement decision cash flows with other projects, the domestic economy, or the world economy might be needed in deriving the appropriate discount rates k_i and k_j within the model. In like manner, the models can be modified to explicitly consider adjustment for inflation and nonconstant costs of funds over time. Clearly, much is left to be done by practitioners and academicians in providing more operationally efficient replacement decision algorithms.

NOTES

1. An example Lotus 1-2-3 spreadsheet is available from the author on request.

REFERENCES

AGGARWAL, RAJ, and LUC A. SOENEN (1989). "Project Exit Values as a Measure of Flexibility and Risk Exposure," *Engineering Economist* 35 (Fall), pp. 39–54.

BIERMAN, HAROLD JR., and SEYMOUR SMIDT (1989). *The Capital Budgeting Decision*, 7th ed. (New York: Macmillan).

BLOCK, STANLEY B., and GEOFFREY A. HIRT (1987). *Foundations of Financial Management*, 4th ed. (Homewood, Ill.: Richard D. Irwin).

BONINI, CHARLES P. (1977). "Capital Investment Under Uncertainty with Abandonment Options," *Journal of Financial and Quantitative Analysis* 12 (No. 1, March), pp. 39–54.

BRIGHMAN, EUGENE F. (1986). *Fundamentals of Financial Management*, 4th ed. (Chicago: Dyrden Press).

COPELAND, THOMAS E., and J. FRED WESTON (1988). *Financial Theory and Corporate Policy*, 3rd ed. (Reading, Mass.: Addison-Wesley).

DYL, EDWARD A., and HUGH W. LONG (1969). "Abandonment Value and Capital Budgeting." *Journal of Finance* 24 (No. 1, March), pp. 88–95.

HOWE, KEITH M., and GEORGE M. McCABE (1983). "On Optimal Asset Abandonment and Replacement," *Journal of Financial and Quantitative Analysis* 18 (No. 3, September), pp. 295–305.

LEVY, HAIM, and MARSHALL SARNAT (1986). *Capital Investment and Financial Decisions*, 3rd ed. (Englewood Cliffs, N.J.: Prentice-Hall).

ROBICHEK, ALEXANDER A., and JAMES C. VAN HORNE (1967). "Abandonment Value and Capital Budgeting," *Journal of Finance* 22, (No. 4, December), pp. 577–589).

Schall, Lawrence D., and Charles W. Haley (1983). *Financial Management,* 3rd ed. (New York: McGraw-Hill).

Thuesen, G. J., and W. J. Fabrycky (1989). *Engineering Economy,* 7th ed. (Englewood Cliffs, N.J.: Prentice-Hall).

15

The Make or Buy Decision in Capital Budgeting

MOSHE BEN-HORIN AND LATHA SHANKER

ABSTRACT

This article approaches the make-or-buy managerial decision from a capital budgeting point of view. It derives a breakeven quantity point above which the firm should prefer the "make" to the "buy" alternative for the case of full equity financing as well as the case for financing through borrowing. When borrowing is allowed, the make alternative becomes relatively more advantageous. Finally, it examines the make-or-buy decision under fully anticipated inflation and concludes that with accelerated depreciation as allowed under the 1986 tax bill the likelihood is that anticipated inflation will give the make alternative a further advantage.

I. INTRODUCTION

The make-or-buy decision is a capital budgeting decision of considerable importance to many firms. As Jauch and Wilson (1979) emphasize, the decision is not a routine procedure but rather a strategic decision that must involve the attention of top management. The make-or-buy decision is an important one, and previous authors have addressed it in different contexts. A number of authors have provided quantitative frameworks for objective analysis of the make-or-buy decision. For example, Baker and Taylor (1979) employ linear programming in a cost-minimization framework to determine if external acquisition of services would be optimal. Raunick and Fischer (1972) input probability distributions of uncertain input factors into a Monte Carlo simulation. They arrive at a cumulative probability distribution of the capitalization rate whose median is compared with the market rate of return to arrive at the optimal decision. Levy and Sarnat (1976) consider the make-or-buy decision in a capital budgeting context. Teresko (1978) makes the point that new issues force the make-or-buy decision in the auto industry. Government regulations that dictate the performance of cars (average 27.5 miles per gallon) and stringent automobile emission standards favor buying. Firms' policies of having full employment, resistance to having employment go up or down at will, and rapid technological advancements also favor buying.

Gambino (1980) examines the financial and nonfinancial considerations that affect the make-or-buy decision. The financial considerations are costs (which depend on fixed costs, variable costs, and production capacity) and investments. The nonfinancial considerations are level of activity at a plant, quality of the item, and quantity and dependability of supply. Weston (1981) states that instead of considering the make-or-buy decision for each product separately and independently, the firm should make this decision in a multiple-product framework. Thus the make-or-buy decision may be optimized, because consideration of the interrelationship between the costs of making the different products allows trade-offs between levels of production or purchasing of different products.

Dale and Cunningham (1983) analyze the sequence of events by which a make-or-buy decision was resolved at a medium-sized British engineering and fabrication firm and the management levels and financial factors influencing the outcome, paying special attention to the purchasing-manufacturing interface.

Butler and Carney (1983) use a transactions cost analysis to examine different cases under which the make-or-buy decision becomes important. The cases examined involved either a low-cost supplier or a supplier with expertise or capital investment in making the equipment.

Kobert (1984) states that the make-or-buy decision may be used to reduce hedge inventories when the firm is faced with irregular demand. The firm's inventory carrying costs may be high if a dominant or erratic supplier forces the firm to take a greater quantity than required, or if the supplier offers attractively low prices during a recession.

Anderson and Weitz (1986) examine the marketing functions such as advertising, sales force management, and distribution and how they may be performed more efficiently through vertical integration (make rather than buy).

Walker and Weber (1987) report the effect on the make-or-buy decision of the interaction between competition among suppliers and of uncertainty regarding a buyer's future requirements of the item and uncertainty regarding technological changes.

This chapter examines the make-or-buy decision in a capital budgeting context, with special attention to quantity uncertainty, through sensitivity analysis and breakeven analysis.

Justification for examining the make-or-buy decision may itself be examined. One of the financial considerations involved in the make-or-buy decision are the variable costs to make the item versus the variable costs to purchase the item. The variable costs under the "make" decision are raw material, labor, incremental factory overhead, managerial, purchasing, and inventory carrying costs. The variable costs under the "buy" decision are purchase price, transportation and receiving, and inspection costs (Gambino, 1980, p. 22). These variable costs can be quite different under the make and the buy alternatives. For instance, competition among suppliers could cause the purchase price to the firm to be lower than the cost to make the product in-house. In times of recession, suppliers may offer large discounts. If the supplier firm is a monopoly, the price charged may be so high that the firm may find it cheaper to make the part. Large buyers may also be able to reduce the price to themselves through large-quantity discounts. In the case of changes in the quality standards of the item, suppliers may add a premium to the price charged. The firm's labor union agreements may make it more costly for the firm to manufacture the part.

Financial considerations also involve investment in the equipment required to make the item and tax credits and tax shelters following from investment, such as the investment tax credit and depreciation tax savings. These may be of different magnitudes for the supplier and the firm making the make-or-buy decision because of differences in tax rates.

In short, financial considerations involved in make-or-buy decisions becomes important in imperfect product and capital markets.

If there is uncertainty regarding the volume (quantity) of the item required by the firm, consideration of the make-or-buy decision becomes even more important. For instance, if the firm's quantity requirements are uncertain, the firm may be unprotected in a market with a single supplier and no alternative suppliers because contracts with the supplier generally specify the quantity. Again, if the quantity requirements for the item increase, the contract with the supplier will have to be rewritten, thus increasing the transaction costs involved in purchasing. The make alternative may become more attractive under the circumstances.

Hsiao and Smith (1978), Durway (1979), Thal (1982), and Evans (1984) all advocate the use of sensitivity analysis in making decisions.

Hsiao and Smith and Durway, and Thal, are especially interested in the application of sensitivity analysis to capital budgeting decisions. A capital budgeting decision such as a make-or-buy decision takes place in an uncertain environment. A major source of this uncertainty arises from the fact that estimates used in the decision, such as quantity estimates, are likely to be less than perfect. Therefore, sensitivity analysis can be used to analyze the effect of imperfect estimation on the profitability of a project. Sensitivity analysis can identify the variables that have a significant impact on the decision. It can also be used to quantify risk in such a way that projects can be compared. Leamer (1985) points out that sensitivity analysis is needed for all empirical studies to test how sturdy their inferences are in light of possible errors in variables. It seems clear, therefore, that sensitivity analysis is an extremely valuable tool to use in quantifying risk because of uncertainty in the demand for the item and the effect of this uncertainty on the optimal choice.

We examine the use of sensitivity analysis in the make-or-buy decision and show how it may be appropriately applied.

Breakeven analysis has been examined by Kotts and Lau (1978), Levine (1978), Shih (1979), Patterson (1980), and Dhavale and Wilson (1980). The consensus is that it is a useful decision-making tool. Strischek (1983) examines the use of breakeven analysis by a commercial banker to assess the risks involved in lending to a manufacturer. The analysis involves estimating the sales necessary for the manufacturer to break even and the sensitivity of profits to a change in sales. Das (1984) examines breakeven analysis in the context of a developing country. Morely and Glendinning (1987) point out that determination of the breakeven point is extremely important and that the concept is valid and useful. Ames and Hlavacek (1989) suggest that, especially in an industry that is in a maturity phase, the price charged by suppliers becomes very important in deciding whether to purchase. This depends on the quantity purchased. Ames and Hlaveck are of the opinion that some of the information the company cannot do without includes what the present breakeven point is, how it relates to capacity, and how much volume can be increased without changing capacity.

The above articles provide support for the valuable information supplied by a breakeven analysis. In addition, since contracts with suppliers have to specify the quantity required, and the price charged generally depends on the quantity required, it is extremely important that the firm compute the breakeven point at which the make and the buy decisions are equally preferred. We, therefore, examine this analysis. We also examine the effect of inflation on the choice between the two alternatives.

II. THE MAKE-OR-BUY DECISION IN THE FRAMEWORK OF CAPITAL BUDGETING

Following Levy and Sarnat (1976), we assume that a firm is producing a certain product for which it requires a certain input component. The firm can either buy the component from an external supplier at a cost of P dollars per unit or decide to undertake production of the component at an initial capital cost of I dollars per unit and a subsequent variable cost of C dollars per unit. The initial investment is fully depreciable using (for simplicity but without loss of generality) the straight-line method of depreciation. The net present value (NPV) of the cost of the components assuming the decision is to buy it from the outside supplier is given by

$$\text{NPV}_B = -\sum_{t=1}^{n} \frac{(1 - T)PQ}{(1 + k)^t} \tag{1}$$

where T = tax rate

Q = quantity of components demanded per year, which is uncertain

k = capitalization rate application to the uncertain cash flow $(1 - T)PQ$

n = project's lifetime in years

t = index for the year

The NPV of the decision to make the component is given by

$$\text{NPV}_M = -I - \sum_{t=1}^{n} \frac{(1 - T)CQ}{(1 + k)^t} + \sum_{t=1}^{n} \frac{TD}{(1 + r)^t} \tag{2}$$

where D denotes the annual depreciation expense and r is the riskless rate of return.

Note that in Equation (2) we discount the depreciation tax shield at the riskless rate of return. This is based on an assumption that the firm's taxable income is large enough to absorb the depreciation tax shield. If there is uncertainty regarding whether the firm's taxable income is high enough to absorb the depreciation tax shield, the depreciation tax shield is discounted using k, the capitalization rate applicable to the uncertain cash flow.

We make the simplifying assumption that the depreciation tax shield is certain, since the objective of this article is to focus on the uncertainty in the demand for the product Q.

Subtracting Equation (1) from Equation (2), we obtain

$$\text{NPV}_{M-B} = -I + \sum_{t=1}^{n} \frac{(1 - T)(P - C)Q}{(1 + k)^t} + \sum_{t=1}^{n} \frac{TD}{(1 + r)^t} \tag{3}$$

Equation (3) provides the key to the decision to make rather than buy. If NPV_{M-B} is positive, the optimal decision should be to make the component. If the NPV is negative, the decision should be to buy it from the outside supplier.

NPV_{M-B} is an increasing linear function of Q.[1] However, Q, the demand for the component, is uncertain. Levy and Sarnat (1976) have observed that if Q is uncertain (but all the other variables are known with certainty), one can deal with the uncertainty in Q by examining the value of NPV_{M-B} for different values of Q and thus the sensitivity of NPV_{M-B} to changes in the value of Q for different values of Q can be assessed.

However, this attempt to deal with the uncertainty in Q double-counts for the risk inherent in Q. Since the capitalization rate k applied to the uncertain cash flow $(1 - T)(P - C)Q$ includes a risk premium, only the expected value of Q, $E(Q)$, should be used in Equation (3) to calculate NPV_{M-B}, and no sensitivity analysis is required. This stems from the rationale of using the risk-adjusted discount rate in the NPV formula. An alternative procedure is to discount the entire *expected* cash flow at the riskless rate of return

$$NPV_{M-B} = -I + \sum_{t=1}^{n} \frac{(1 - T)(P - C)Q + TD}{(1 + r)^t} \tag{4}$$

and then conduct a sensitivity analysis, computing NPV_{M-B} in Equation (4) for alternative values of Q. This procedure accounts for the risk only once.

Note that in Equation (3), $E(Q)$, the expected value of Q, is used in place of Q and risk is accounted for by using the risk-adjusted capitalization rate k. Equation (4) is used in conjunction with a sensitivity analysis to account for risk. Therefore, uncertain estimates of the value of Q are used in place of Q in Equation (4).

To clarify this argument, consider the following example. Assume that

$I = \$10,000$	$r = 0.05$
$P = \$10$	$k = 0.15$
$C = \$8$	$n = 4$
$T = 0.5$	

The distribution of Q is assumed to be uniform over the range 1700 units to 2300 units. The assumption of a uniform distribution does not impair the generality of the example. It is assumed only because the following argument is easier to set forth with this distribution, rather than with, for example, the normal distribution. Calculating NPV_{M-B} for different values of Q using Equation (3), we obtain the following results:

Q (units)	NPV_{M-B} ($)
1700	−714.10
2000	142.40
2300	998.89

Considering the above results, we should argue that though the firm expects to sell 2000 units on the average with a resultant NPV_{M-B} of $142.40, the firm must consider the danger of low demand ($Q = 1700$ units) with a resulting NPV_{M-B} of −$714.10, which would negate the decision to make.

However, let us consider the worst possible situation—that of the demand falling to its lowest value, 1700 units. Substituting 1700 units for Q in the cash flow formula is equivalent to removing all the risk of the project. After all, the assumed probability distribution of Q shows that Q cannot fall below 1700 units, which implies that NPV_{M-B} evaluated at $Q = 1700$ is the NPV_{M-B} in the worst state of the world, and it possesses no additional risk. Therefore, the capitalization rate applicable to the value of Q in the worst case is the riskless cost of capital $r = 0.05$. At a 5% cost of capital we have $NPV_{M-B} = \$460.56$. This amply demonstrates that using a risky cost of capital *in addition to* performing a sensitivity analysis constitutes double-counting for the risk.

It may be seen from the above that our numerical example assumed that the values of $I, P, C, T,$ and D are given and that the only uncertainty arises from uncertainty in Q. Our assumption of the probability distribution of Q as a uniform distribution implicitly assumes Q is independent of the other variables. However, it is quite likely that some or all of the variables $I, P, C, T, D,$ and Q are interrelated. The interrelationships can be captured by specifying joint probability distributions of these variables from which random selections of variable values are made to conduct the sensitivity analysis. The advantage of using a sensitivity analysis is that it is flexible enough to allow analysis of simple as well as extremely complicated situations with interdependencies among all variables.

III. THE BREAKEVEN QUANTITY

Given Equation (3), a breakeven quantity Q^* can be easily derived (see Levy and Sarnat, 1976) such that if the quantity the firm expects to sell exceeds the breakeven point, the make alternative will be more desirable than the buy alternative. By setting NPV_{M-B} to zero and solving for Q, we obtain

$$Q^* = \frac{I - \sum_{t=1}^{n} \dfrac{TD}{(1 + r)^t}}{\sum_{t=1}^{n} \dfrac{(1 - T)(P - C)}{(1 + k)^t}} \tag{5}$$

In our example, the breakeven point is $Q^* = 1950$ units. This means that if the *expected* level of Q exceeds Q^*, the make alternative will be preferred.

One can also derive a breakeven quantity Q_{min} for the minimum value of Q. This quantity applies in the case in which the firm can specify a minimum quantity to be produced every year. Such a possibility exists, for example, if the firm contracts for a delivery of a certain number of units per year. The breakeven quantity can be derived as follows:

$$Q_{min} = \frac{I - \sum_{t=1}^{n} \dfrac{TD}{(1 + r)^t}}{\sum_{t=1}^{n} \dfrac{(1 - T)(P - C)}{(1 + r)^t}} \tag{6}$$

where r is, as before, the riskless rate of interest. In our example, $Q_{min} = 1570$ units. Thus if the quantity anticipated by the firm *definitely* exceeds 1570 units (i.e., even at the most pessimistic forecast), the make alternative will be preferred.

Note, however, that while the buy alternative requires an after-tax cash outflow of $(1 - T)PQ$ per year, the make alternative requires a smaller annual cash outflow: $(1 - T)CQ - TD$. Thus the make decision involves a smaller cash outflow every year.

The difference between the cash flows is $(1 - T)(P - C)Q + TD$, and if the quantity Q is uncertain, the differential cash flow is a random variable. However, if a minimum quantity Q_{min} can be specified, it is clear that the differential cash flow will at least be equal to $(1 - T)(P - C)Q_{min} + TD$. This means that by choosing to buy rather than make, the firm will *surely* be foregoing a cash flow of at least $(1 - T)(P - C)Q_{min} + TD$.

In order to create a *parity* between the alternatives considered, the firm should consider borrowing (at the riskless rate of interest) the amount required to finance the purchase of the assets necessary for the make alternative such that the annual interest and principal repayment will equal $(1 - T)(P - C)Q_{min} + TD$. The Appendix contains a detailed explanation of the analysis used. This builds on the analysis of the "lease-versus-buy" decision analyzed in Levy and Sarnat (1979). Specifically, the make-versus-buy alternative now requires a cash outflow of

$$(1 - T)(P - C)Q + TD + TX \tag{7}$$

where X is the interest payment on the loan. To solve for the breakeven quantity taking the interest tax subsidy into account, we find the value of Q that satisfies

$$I = \sum_{t=1}^{n} \frac{(1 - T)(P - C)Q + TD_t + TX_t}{(1 + r)^t} \tag{8}$$

Equation (8) may be written as[2]

$$I = \sum_{t=1}^{n} \frac{(1 - T)(P - C)Q + TD_t}{[1 + (1 - T)r]^t} \tag{9}$$

Equation (8) is the same as Equation (A9), and Equation (9) is the same as Equation (A11) in the Appendix.

Note that this analysis takes into account principal payments on the loan. It may also be adjusted to incorporate salvage values of the assets in the make decision. The salvage value is then added to the numerator of the term with $t = n$ on the right-hand side of Equation (9).

Thus the new breakeven quantity (denoted Q_{min}^L, for minimum quantity with leverage is

$$Q_{min}^L = \frac{I - \sum_{t=1}^{n} \dfrac{TD_t}{[1 + (1 - T)r]^t}}{\sum_{t=1}^{n} \dfrac{(1 - T)(P - C)}{[1 + (1 - T)r]^t}} \tag{10}$$

In our example we have

$$Q_{min}^L = 1340 \text{ units}$$

If sales reach 1340 units per year, a loan can be taken out to finance the acquisition of the assets, giving the firm an added interest tax subsidy which will cause the make alternative to be preferred to the buy alternative, while the financial risk of the make alternative is not greater.

IV. THE MAKE-OR-BUY DECISION UNDER INFLATION

We shall address three effects of inflation on the make-or-buy decision. The first is the change in the cost values P and C, the second is the reduced value of the depreciation tax shelter, and the third is the increase in the real value of the interest tax subsidy.

We first analyze the effect of inflation on the rate of interest on corporate bonds. Following Miller's (1977) analysis, we assume that the rate of interest paid on tax-exempt bonds r_0 is exogenously determined. Given the personal tax rate T_p, the rate of interest that must be offered on corporate bonds is $r_c = r_0/(1 - T_p)$. This rate is the minimum rate that will entice an investor with a personal tax rate T_p to purchase corporate bonds, since the rate of interest net of personal taxes is $r_c(1 - T_p)$, which is equal to r_0: $r_c(1 - T_p) = r_0$. The real after-tax cost of borrowing is $r_c(1 - T)$.

Assuming a rate of inflation h, the nominal tax-exempt rate changes, according to Fisher's equation, to $R_0 = (1 + r_0)(1 + h) - 1$. If there is no change in the personal tax rate, the relationship between the rate of interest on tax-exempt bonds and the rate of interest on corporate bonds is maintained. Hence, if the rate on corporate bonds changes to R_c, the following relationship must hold: $R_c = R_0/(1 - T_p)$. The firm's real after-tax cost of borrowed funds is equal to $[1 + R_c(1 - T)]/(1 + h) - 1$.

If we assume that the values of both P and C are adjusted proportionally to the rate of inflation so that in year t the cost per unit from the external source is $P(1 + h)^t$ and the cost per unit for the make alternative is $C(1 + h)^t$, their real values will be $P(1 + h)^t/(1 + h)^t = P$ and $C(1 + h)^t/(1 + h)^t = C$, respectively. In this case, when we apply the real discount rate to real cash flow in Equation (10) we obtain

$$Q_{min}^L = \frac{I - \sum_{t=1}^{n} \dfrac{TD_t/(1 + h)^t}{[1 + R_c(1 - T)]^t/(1 + h)^t}}{\sum_{t=1}^{n} \dfrac{(1 - T)(P - C)}{\{[1 + R_c(1 - T)]/(1 + h)^t\}}}$$

$$= \frac{I - \sum_{t=1}^{n} \dfrac{TD_t}{[1 + R_c(1 - T)]^t}}{\sum_{t=1}^{n} \dfrac{(1 - T)(P - C)}{\{[1 + R_c(1 - T)]/(1 + h)\}^t}} \qquad (11)$$

Both the numerator and denominator of Equation (11) are clearly greater for $h > 0$ than for $h = 0$, hence the effect of inflation on the numerator is not clear. Consequently, the effect of inflation on Q_{min}^L is unclear. The value of the minimum breakeven point Q_{min}^L depends on the interaction between the reduction in the real after-tax cost of borrowing and the fall in the real value of the depreciation tax shelter. If, however, the investment is a relatively long-term investment and the accelerated depreciation as allowed by the 1986 tax law is used, the effect of inflation on the real value of depreciation can be relatively moderate compared to the effect of the reduced real value of the cost of capital.[3] If this happens, the breakeven point Q_{min}^L is reduced by inflation.

Another factor that can contribute to Q_{min}^L being lower with anticipated inflation compared with the no-inflation state is that the adjustment of P and C to inflation might not be the same. If the firm that adopts the make decision is able to control the increase in the cost per unit C better than it can control the price adjustment of the external supplier, then we expect that the difference in real terms between P and C will increase with inflation, a factor that will make the denominator of Equation (11) larger and the value of Q_{min}^L even smaller.

V. CONCLUDING REMARKS

This chapter examined the make-or-buy decision in capital budgeting. We developed a way to conduct a sensitivity analysis that avoids double-counting for the risk. Furthermore, we compared the make decision and the buy decision after neutralizing the difference in the financial risks of the two alternatives. We showed that when this is done, the make decision has a greater comparative advantage over the buy alternative. Finally, we examined the decision under anticipated inflation and developed the breakeven point for preferring the make alternative to the buy alternative. With highly accelerated depreciation as allowed by the 1986 tax law, the effect of inflation on the real value of depreciation is relatively small, and the likelihood is that inflation will reduce the breakeven point at which the make alternative is preferred.

APPENDIX

This appendix shows the annual cash outflows under the buy alternative and the make alternative and the conditions under which a firm would be indifferent between the two alternatives. It is based on a similar analysis of the lease-or-buy decision in Levy and Sarnat (1979). Under the buy alternative,

$$\text{Cash outflow} = (1 - T)PQ \qquad (A1)$$

Under the make alternative,

$$\text{Cash outflow} = (1 - T)CQ - TD \qquad (A2)$$

If $P > C$, the cash outflow is higher for the buy alternative. Therefore, the buy alternative has higher financial risk to shareholders. In order to equate the riskiness of the make and the buy alternatives, if the firm decides to make the product, it should do so by buying assets by borrowing in such a way that the annual cash outflows under the make alternative inclusive of principle and after-tax interest payments equal the annual cash outflows under the buy alternative.

Neutralization of the differential risk in year t implies that the following relationship holds:

$$B_{t-1} - B_t + (1 - T)rB_{t-1} + (1 - T)CQ - TD = (1 - T)PQ \quad \text{(A3)}$$

where
B_t = principal outstanding at time t
r = interest rate charged to the firm or rate of interest on corporate borrowing assumed equal to the risk-free rate
$B_{t-1} - B_t$ = principal repaid at time t
$(1 - T)rB_{t-1}$ = after-tax interest payment at time t

From Equation (A3) we obtain

$$B_{t-1} = \frac{(1 - T)(P - C)Q + TD + rTB_{t-1} + B_t}{1 + r} \quad \text{(A4)}$$

Since by definition $B_n = 0$, we obtain for $t = n$,

$$B_{n-1} = \frac{(1 - T)(P - C)Q + TD + rTB_{n-1}}{1 + r} \quad \text{(A5)}$$

Using Equations (A4) and (A5), we have

$$
\begin{aligned}
B_{n-2} &= \frac{(1 - T)(P - C)Q + TD + rTB_{n-2} + B_{n-1}}{1 + r} \\
&= \frac{(1 - T)(P - C)Q + TD + rTB_{n-2}}{1 + r} \\
&\quad + \frac{(1 - T)(P - C)Q + TD + rTB_{n-1}}{(1 + r)^2} \\
&= \sum_{t=n-1}^{n} \frac{(1 - T)(P - C)Q + TD + rTB_{n-1}}{(1 + r)^{t-(n-2)}}
\end{aligned}
\quad \text{(A6)}
$$

Continuing this substitution procedure, we obtain

$$B_0 = \sum_{t=1}^{n} \frac{(1 - T)(P - C)Q + TD + rTB_{t-1}}{(1 + r)^t} \quad \text{(A7)}$$

The firm will be indifferent between the make or the buy alternative if

$$I = \sum_{t=1}^{n} \frac{(1 - T)(P - C)Q + TD + rTB_{t-1}}{(1 + r)^t} \quad \text{(A8)}$$

Since $rB_{t-1} = X_t$ = interest payment at time t, the firm will be indifferent between make or buy if

$$I = \sum_{t=1}^{n} \frac{(1 - T)(P - C)Q + TD + TX_t}{(1 + r)^t} \quad \text{(A9)}$$

From Equation (A3) we can write B_{t-1} as

$$B_{t-1} = \frac{(1 - T)(P - C)Q + TD + B_t}{1 + (1 - T)r} \tag{A10}$$

Proceeding in a similar way as above, we can show that the firm will be indifferent between the make or buy alternative if

$$B_0 = I = \sum_{t=1}^{n} \frac{(1 - T)(P - C)Q + TD}{[1 + (1 - T)r]^t} \tag{A11}$$

If we assume that the assets the firm purchases for the make decision have a salvage value, this is easily incorporated into the analysis. This is a cash inflow under the make alternative and, therefore, a cash outflow or cash flow lost under the buy alternative. This salvage value will be added to the numerators of Equations (A7) through (A9), and (A11) for values of $t = n$.

NOTES

1. We assume, of course, that P is greater than C since otherwise it is clear that the decision should be to buy the component.
2. See, for example, Lewellen and Emery (1980) and Levy and Sarnat (1979) for a proof of this argument.
3. For details see Ben-Horim (1981), Cross (1980), and Jaffe (1978).

REFERENCES

AMES, B. C., and J. D. HLAVACEK (1989). "Numbers You Can't Do Without," *Sales and Marketing Management* 141 (March), pp. 54–57.

ANDERSON, E., and B. A. WEITZ (1986). "Make or Buy Decisions: Vertical Integration and Marketing Productivity," *Sloan Management Review* 27 (Spring), pp. 3–19.

BAKER, K. R., and R. E. TAYLOR (1979). "A Linear Programming Framework for Cost Allocation and External Acquisition When Reciprocal Services Exist," *Accounting Review* 54 (October), pp. 784–790.

BEN-HORIM, MOSHE (1981). "Cost of Capital, Capital Budgeting and Inflation," Working Paper 378, Hebrew University, Jerusalem.

BUTLER, R., and M. G. CARNEY (1983). "Managing Markets: Implications for the Make-Buy Decision," *Journal of Management Studies* (April), pp. 213–231.

CROSS, S. M. (1980). "A Note on Inflation, Taxation and Investment Returns," *Journal of Finance* 35 (March), pp. 177–180.

DALE, B. G., and M. T. CUNNINGHAM (1983). "The Purchasing/Manufacturing Interface in the Make or Buy Decision," *Journal of Purchasing and Materials Management* (Spring), pp. 11–18.

DAS, C. (1984). "A Unified Approach to the Price-Break Economic Order Quantity (EOQ) Problem (Developing Countries)," *Decision Science* 15 (Summer), pp. 350–358.

DHAVALE, D. G., and H. G. WILSON (1980). "Breakeven Analysis with Inflationary Cost and Prices," *Engineering Economist* 25 (Winter), pp. 107–121.

DOWST, S. (1976). "Make or Buy: Delivery Problems Can Tip the Scales," *Purchasing* (September).

DURWAY, J. W. (1979). "Evaluating Risk: Sensitivity Analysis and Simulation," *Infosystems* (May), pp. 70–71.

EVANS, J. R. (1984). "Sensitivity Analysis in Decision Theory," *Decision Science* 15 (Spring), pp. 239–247.

FRAND, E. A. (1981). "Make or Buy?," *Industrial Research and Development* (March), pp. 23–25.

GAMBINO, A. J. (1980). "Make or Buy Decisions," *Management Accounting* 62 (December), pp. 55–56.

GOLLAND, M. L. (1978). "Buying or Making the Software Package That Is Best for You," *Journal of Systems Management* 29 (August), pp. 48–51.

HSIAO, F. S. T., and W. J. SMITH (1978). "Analytical Approach to Sensitivity Analysis of the Internal Rate of Return Model," *Journal of Finance* 33 (May), pp. 645–649.

JAFFE, J. F. (1978). "A Note on Taxation and Investment," *Journal of Finance* 33 (December), pp. 1439–1445.

JAUCH, L. R., and H. K. WILSON (1979). "A Strategic Perspective for Make or Buy Decisions," *Long Range Planning* 12 (December), pp. 56–61.

KETZ, J. EDWARD (1978). "Software Packages—Should a Firm Make or Buy Them?," *Cost and Management* (July–August), pp. 43–46.

KOBERT, N. (1984). "How Make-or-Buy Decisions Can Affect Hedge Inventories," *Purchasing* (October 18), p. 63.

KOTTS, J. F., and H. LAU (1978). "Stochastic Breakeven Analysis," *Journal of the Operations Research Society* (March), pp. 251–257.

LEAMER, E. E. (1985). "Sensitivity Analysis Would Help," *American Economic Review* 75 (June), pp. 308–313.

LEVI, M. D., and J. H. MAKIN (1979). "Fisher, Philips, Friedman and the Measured Impact of Inflation on Interest," *Journal of Finance* 34 (March), pp. 35–52.

LEVINE, J. B. (1978). "Examining the Breakeven Analysis," *Management Accounting* 59 (June), pp. 35–39.

LEVY, HAIM, and MARSHALL SARNAT (1976). "The Make or Buy Decision," *Journal of General Management* (Autumn), pp. 46–50.

LEVY, HAIM, and MARSHALL SARNAT (1979). "On Leasing, Borrowing and Financial Risk," *Financial Management* 9 (Winter), pp. 47–54.

LEWELLEN, W. G., and D. R. EMERY (1980). "On the Matter of Parity Among Financial Obligations," *The Journal of Finance* 35 (March), pp. 97–111.

MACKINNIS, FRANK R. (1980). "Benefits of In-House Manufacturing vs. Outside

Purchasing—Make vs. Buy," *Production and Inventory Management* (Third Quarter), pp. 23–28.

MILLER, M. H. (1977). "Debt and Taxes," *Journal of Finance* 32 (May), pp. 261–297.

MORELY, D., and R. GLENDINNING (1987). "Costing (Standard Costing, Selling Pricing and Breakeven Point)," *Management Decision*, 25 (No. 5), pp. 42–47.

PATTERSON, R. T. (1980). "Breakeven Analysis: Decision Making Tool," *Food Service Marketing* (April), pp. 39–40.

RAUNICK, D. A., and A. G. FISHER (1972). *Journal of Purchasing* (February), pp. 63–80.

SHIH, W. (1979). "General Decision Model for Cost-volume-profit Analysis Under Uncertainty," *Accounting Review* 54 (October), pp. 687–706.

TERESKO, J. (1978). "Make or Buy? New Issues Force the Decision," *Industry Week* (September 4), pp. 34–37.

THAL, L. S. (1982). "Sensitivity Analysis—A Way to Make Feasibility Analysis Work," *Appraisal Journal* (January), pp. 57–62.

WALKER, G., and D. WEBER (1987). "Supplier Competition, Uncertainty and Make-or-Buy Decisions," *Academy of Management Journal* 30 (September), pp. 589–596.

WESTON, F. C., JR. (1981). "The Multiple Product Make or Buy Decision," *Journal of Purchasing and Materials Management* (Winter), pp. 17–22.

16

Justifying
Strategic Investments:
The Case of Flexible
Manufacturing Technology

RAJ AGGARWAL*

ABSTRACT

Justifying strategic investments, such as investment in new manufacturing technology, is usually very difficult since the most important benefits are often difficult to quantify and convert to incremental cash flows. While traditional capital budgeting procedures that rely on such return measures provide much needed discipline to the process of allocating capital, they do not normally capture the strategic benefits of higher quality, faster responses to a wider range of customer needs, and the options for future growth made available by flexible manufacturing technology. Adding to these limitations is the difficulty of using traditional cost accounting systems to generate the information necessary for justifying strategic new manufacturing investments. This article reviews these problems, develops and recommends procedures useful for assessing strategic investments, and illustrates them with the case of investments in flexible manufacturing technology.

*I thank the Edward J. and Louise E. Mellen Foundation for research support, and David Schirm and the participants in the May 1990 Cleveland Advanced Manufacturing Program Seminar on Justifying and Financing New Technology in Manufacturing for useful comments.

I. INTRODUCTION

Capital budgeting procedures, as traditionally. practiced, have been widely criticized as having a number of limitations. It has been contended that the widespread adoption of discounted cash flow techniques has resulted in "myopic" policies with an excessive focus on the short run and a resulting loss in global competitiveness.[1] In addition, traditional capital budgeting procedures are often considered unsuitable for assessing strategic investments where the projected cash flow impacts of the benefits may be difficult to estimate.[2] For example, while traditional capital budgeting procedures that rely on incremental cash flows as return measures provide much needed discipline to the process of allocating capital, they do not normally capture the strategic benefits of higher quality, faster responses to a wider range of customer needs, and the options for future growth made available by flexible manufacturing technology. This chapter proposes the use of a modified version of the adjusted net present value (NPV) technique to value strategic investments. While the case of justifying strategic investments in flexible manufacturing technology is used as an example in the rest of the chapter, the proposed procedures are applicable to other strategic investments.

Spurred on by global competition, microprocessor-based advances in automation and technology, and the successful experiences of other firms, many manufacturing firms are planning large amounts of capital investments in flexible manufacturing equipment. Investments in new flexible manufacturing technology at Allen-Bradley, Baldor, and Deere have been widely credited with helping these firms survive global competition and enhancing their competitive positions. However, many other companies have not been as successful. While Cummins Engine managed to achieve major reductions in unit manufacturing costs by using flexible new capital equipment, its competitive position did not improve because prices for its products fell even faster. General Motors added over $50 billion in new capital equipment in the first 7 years of the 1980s, and their Saturn flexible manufacturing project leapfrogged them over their Japanese competitors by reducing their unit costs. Unfortunately, GM suffered a significant drop in market share and changed from the lowest to the highest cost U.S. automobile manufacturer during the same time period.[3]

These are only a few examples of the challenges facing manufacturing firms evaluating investments in flexible new manufacturing technology since the optimal amount of investment in such equipment or the optimum degree of flexibility is far from clear. Consequently, some firms have overinvested in such equipment, resulting in a heavier than necessary financial burden, while other firms have been overcautious, with a resulting loss of their competitive position and market share.

Justifying new manufacturing technology is difficult in most cases since the most important benefits are often strategic and difficult to quantify. Traditional capital budgeting procedures that rely on return measures based on direct cost savings and well-identified incremental future cash flows are not normally implemented to capture the strategic benefits of higher quality, faster responses to a wider range of customer needs, and the options for future growth made possible by flexible manufacturing technology.[4] Adding to these limitations is the difficulty of using traditional cost accounting systems to generate the cash flow information necessary for justifying new manufacturing investments. This article reviews these problems and recommends the use of adjusted net present value calculations based on strategic analysis as a procedure for assessing investments in flexible new manufacturing systems.

The rest of the chapter is organized into four sections that discuss the nature of traditional capital budgeting procedures, the need for investments in flexible manufacturing technology, the intangible and strategic aspects of the benefits from investments in flexible manufacturing technology, and the recommended model for assessing strategic investments as applied to the case of justifying investments in new flexible manufacturing technology.

II. TRADITIONAL CAPITAL BUDGETING PROCEDURES

The allocation of capital in a firm is an important topic. Many contend that the focus on discounted cash flow techniques for evaluating new capital investments is inappropriate because it leads to a loss of international competitiveness. Others have contended that such criticisms are incorrect and that capital budgeting techniques are not inappropriate but are often misapplied.[5] In any event, the evaluation of new investments is an important part of the process whereby firms create value and thus can have significant implications for the competitive position of a firm or a country.

Traditional capital budgeting procedures depend on the ability to convert *all* costs and benefits to incremental cash flows. These cash flow estimates must include consideration of all project interdependencies with other operations and the values of any and all options for future growth that are generated. Naturally, there are many difficulties in estimating the project costs and benefits, especially when they depend on competitor reactions, and in estimating the risks involved over long time horizons. Capital budgeting analysis also requires an estimate of the appropriate investment horizon, the terminal value, and the discount rate. Thus traditional capital budgeting can have many limitations, especially when it is applied to strategic investments.

First, even for well-defined, tangible, and fairly certain benefits, there are a number of sources of estimation and measurement error. For fairly stable environments, capital budgeting procedures are being improved with better statistical forecasting tools that reduce estimation errors. An additional source of measurement and estimation errors can be cost accounting systems that often involve approximations in overhead allocation. Further, because of the unique nature of each application, new capital equipment may not work exactly as estimated, with resulting unexpected variations in labor, material, inventory, or other costs.[6]

Second, all positive net present value projects depend explicitly or implicitly on some natural or artificially created market imperfections. It is often difficult to forecast the stability of market imperfections over time, especially since they are likely to depend on competitor reactions. There may be a number of discontinuities in the effect of competitor actions, particularly for strategic capital investments subject to positive feedbacks, where an initial competitive advantage can lead to additional advantages. Such discontinuities make it difficult to estimate future benefits from an investment.[7]

Third, traditional capital budgeting procedures have generally ignored the valuation of options created by an investment. Such options are valuable whether or not they are exercised and should be included in the benefits of such an investment. The valuation of real options associated with an investment is often difficult, and it depends on estimates of the uncertainties being reduced by the real options. A set of options commonly given inadequate attention in traditional capital budgeting procedures involve the continuing management of an investment after the initial accept/reject decision. As an example, management has the option to delay the investment. Another option available to management in each time period is the option to continue or to temporarily or permanently shut down the project. In addition, management generally also has options to make changes in operating procedures to enhance the value of the project as new information becomes available.[8]

Fourth, as the burgeoning research on risk assessment indicates, there is considerable imprecision and systematic bias in the estimation and valuation of risky alternatives. For example, probability estimates are subject to bias because of phenomenon such as anchoring, framing, and regret. Fifth, in addition to uncertainties in the estimation of future benefits and costs, uncertainties in inflation and interest rates, capital market imperfections, and changing tax rates also make the estimation of an appropriate discount rate difficult and subject to error, especially when its is difficult to distinguish between systematic and total risk, when there are capital market imperfections, and when there are unexpected variations in inflation and interest rates.[9]

Sixth, agency costs and information asymmetry can also influence the efficiency of the capital budgeting process, particularly as practiced in large multidivisional companies. For example, agency costs resulting from differences in goals, objectives, and utility functions among owners, managers at different levels, creditors, and other stakeholders introduce inefficiencies in each stage of the capital budgeting process, and the selection and management of new investments may not be economically optimum. The capital investment process can be segmented into three phases: identifying the set of investment alternatives, selecting the right investment, and implementing and managing the investment. The capital budgeting process has to work well in each of these phases for investments to be value-enhancing. Mistakes and inefficiencies in any one of these phases can offset even outstanding skills and efficiency in the other phases. These problems can arise not only because of differences in utility functions and attitudes toward risk among these various agents but also because of the search and information costs made necessary by information asymmetries among the various parts of a company.[10]

Thus it has been contended that traditional capital budgeting procedures are useful mostly for deciding between comparable tactical alternatives where the intangible and long-term costs and benefits are similar and where there are low levels of uncertainty and risk. Such procedures are, therefore, often considered best for decisions made during the mature part of the product life cycle and where strategic competitor behavior and uncertainty are not critical.[11] However, as discussed in the next section, flexible manufacturing seems more important early in the product life cycle or in other situations where there is great emphasis on product customization and where traditional capital budgeting procedures may be particularly unsuitable.

III. THE NEED FOR FLEXIBLE MANUFACTURING TECHNOLOGY

It is clear that manufacturing firms are now in an era of global competition being spurred on by continuing advances in communications and transportation, the rise of the newly industrializing countries of Asia and Latin America, and the emergence of Western Europe and Eastern Europe as new centers of manufacturing competition. Markets for an ever-larger number of products are becoming global and, in addition to the adoption of more competitive manufacturing strategies, many firms are responding with increased cross-border trade, licensing agreements, joint ventures and strategic partnerships, and direct foreign investment.[12]

This new era of global manufacturing competition is also characterized by a sharper focus on product differentiation, reliable quality, just-in-time delivery, and ever shorter design-to-delivery times and product life cycles. Given the strengths and weaknesses of the U.S. free enterprise system, many U.S. firms are focusing on high value-added manufacturing that involves rapid product innovations and manufacturing flexibility. While companies like Hewlett Packard, 3M, and Rubbermaid are well known for having adopted specific goals regarding the proportion of their sales that must be in new products, most businesses now recognize the need to be more competitive and to work with shorter product life cycles. Increasingly larger numbers of world-class businesses are now proactive and no longer wait for products to become obsolete. In order to survive, U.S. firms not only must lower labor and material costs, delivery times, and inventory levels, but must also improve quality, reduce economic batch sizes, learn concurrent engineering, and work with ever shorter design, engineering, production, and overall product life cycles. Thus, many firms are beginning to realize the importance of the phrase, "Automate, migrate, or evaporate."[13]

However, a number of U.S. manufacturing firms still rely on functioning but obsolete manufacturing processes and equipment. The necessary improvements in organizational and manufacturing capabilities in such firms will require major new investments in new technology and capital goods. Such firms must make distinctions between enhancing economies of scale by expanding dedicated production lines and enhancing economies of scope by investing in often higher-cost flexible manufacturing systems.[14] Unfortunately, as indicated earlier, the optimum degree of cost-effective flexibility is often unclear. For example, flexible manufacturing has been highly successful at many firms such as Baldor, which now designs, produces, and delivers new motors in as little as 6 weeks. However, other firms have had less success. For example, a new flexible tractor plant in Waterloo, Iowa, cost Deere $1.5 billion, and while it works very well, it is considered to be much more flexible than Deere's needs. In addition to its troubles with the Saturn project, GM is also having productivity troubles with its highly automated large-car plant in Hamtrack, Michigan. Thus, it seems that while some companies seem to have done well in assessing investments in flexible manufacturing, others have done very poorly. As Dana's CEO Mitchell said, "We're not alone in having spent a tremendous amount of money on fancy equipment where it didn't work for us."[15] The next two sections review some of the reasons why it is difficult to assess the optimum amount of investment in flexible manufacturing.

IV. THE NATURE OF FLEXIBLE MANUFACTURING
TECHNOLOGY

As the earlier discussion indicates, there are a number of reasons why it
is difficult to assess the optimal amount of investment in flexible manufacturing technology. First, new flexible manufacturing technology encompasses a wide range of capabilities and must be distinguished from
dedicated automated mass production lines. The degree of manufacturing flexibility can vary from stand-alone robots and numerically controlled machine tools to groups of machines such as in cells and in group
technology, to linked islands of automated machines, and finally to flexible manufacturing systems and computer-integrated manufacturing.
Figure 16.1 illustrates these different levels of manufacturing flexibility
and the trade-offs between flexibility in handling wide ranges of outputs
and the ability to achieve economies of scale with systems dedicated to
volume production. Generally, each step of the increase in manufactur-

Figure 16.1

Productivity versus flexibility in manufacturing systems.

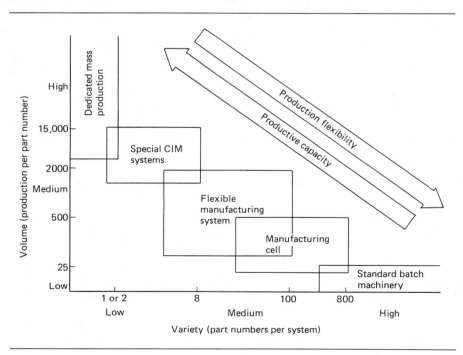

Source: Based on Canada and Sullivan (1989, p. 48).

ing flexibility involves a higher level of investment and decreasing reliance on tangible benefits.[16]

Second, flexible manufacturing systems differ with regard to the degree to which they can be integrated with and can benefit the rest of the business, for example, design and engineering as in the case of Baldor which now has a design-to-delivery cycle for a new motor of as low as 6 months, and marketing and distribution as in the case of The Limited and other retailers who now have manufacturing and distribution systems tied directly to sales on a daily basis.[17] As these examples illustrate, the benefits of a flexible manufacturing system depend on the degree to which flexible production capabilities are part of overall corporate strategy.

Third, many of the benefits of flexible manufacturing technology are intangible and hard to measure but nevertheless real. The tangible benefits include lower inventory levels and lower labor, material, and space costs. Intangible benefits include higher quality and better customer service, faster response times, and enhanced economies of scope rather than economies of scale. The strategic benefits include a greater capability for longer-term strategic partnerships and the development of new revenue sources, better retention of current customers, and an enhanced ability to adjust to competitive changes. These new capabilities can also decrease a firm's risk of bankruptcy and its cost of capital by providing more stable and possibly higher profit margins. Table 16.1 illustrates the differences among tangible, intangible, and strategic benefits of investments in flexible manufacturing technology.

However, the strategic benefits of flexible manufacturing also depend on technological advances and competitor reactions to the use of new technology. Unfortunately, it is difficult to forecast competitor reactions and technological advances. Recent research has contended that

TABLE 16.1   Tangible, Intangible, and Strategic Benefits of Flexible Manufacturing

Tangible Benefits	Intangible Benefits	Strategic Options
Labor savings	Increased product uniformity	Shorter and better product life cycles
Material savings	Increased quality	Lower cost of capital
Reduced inventory	Shorter delivery times	Increased ability to enter new markets, adjust to competition, adopt new technology, survive economic lows, form strategic partnerships
Reduced space needs	Reduced expediting	
Reduced defects and scrap, inspection, rework, warranty, and service costs	Increased safety	
	Better customer service	
	Increased goodwill	
	Increased revenues and market share	

Source: Based on Noori (1989, p. 205) and others.

competitive advantage is often characterized by temporal instability influenced by positive feedback because competitive advantage can be
self-reinforcing. For example, higher levels of resources made available
as a result of an initial competitive advantage can lead to new competitive advantages that are further enhanced by the learning curve advantages of implementing new technology earlier than others. Thus an early
lead in flexible manufacturing may be critical, and there may be significant disadvantages of not investing early in new flexible manufacturing
technology. For example, a common rule of thumb in the electronics
business is that "the first two manufacturers that get a new generation
product to market lock up as much as 80% of the business."[18]

Fourth, firms that rely heavily and exclusively on traditional methods of evaluating capital investments may be at a serious disadvantage
not only because most cost savings, benefits and new revenues from new
flexible manufacturing technology are not easily estimated but also because existing cost accounting and other measurement systems are usually unsuitable for the new manufacturing environment. For example,
traditional cost accounting systems depend heavily on labor hours to
allocate overhead. While overhead is particularly high with flexible
manufacturing technology, labor is generally only 8 to 12% of average
production costs and may be only half that in some industries such as
electronics. As a consequence, overhead costs are often misallocated in
modern manufacturing.[19]

Thus a firm trying to assess the benefits of new flexible manufacturing technology faces large amounts of uncertainty and measurement error in estimating the costs and benefits of such equipment. It has to
develop the ability to estimate both soft and hard or measurable costs
and benefits and to assess its strategic dependence on future events in
the industry and the reactions of its competitors. Unfortunately, traditional capital budgeting methods are often unsuitable for valuing many
of these soft and uncertain benefits. Consequently, justification methods
that depend on a leap of faith or intuition are often used even though
such methods are not disciplined, replicable, or optimizable.[20] The next
section makes some recommendations for developing appropriate procedures for augmenting traditional analysis of investment proposals to assess investments in flexible manufacturing technology.

V. ASSESSING STRATEGIC INVESTMENTS IN MANUFACTURING TECHNOLOGY

Traditional capital budgeting procedures need to be modified and augmented in a number of ways in assessing strategic investments, such as
in new flexible manufacturing technology. It must be recognized that

flexible manufacturing technology investments are part of corporate strategy and should be assessed in a strategic framework. While it is important for a firm to distinguish between strategic analysis of manufacturing needs and capital budgeting analysis for tactical alternatives, it should be noted that success in implementing new technology is often enhanced when it is possible and appropriate to implement such technology in the form of small incremental changes. Most importantly, assessing investments in flexible manufacturing often requires a fundamental change of focus and corporate culture from "How can we be more productive?" to "How can we be more competitive?"

Strategic analysis for assessing investments in flexible manufacturing technology should include an analysis of industry and competitive strengths, weaknesses, opportunities, and threats (SWOT). Proposed flexible manufacturing investments should be evaluated with regard to their ability to enhance the competitive position of the firm given the results of the SWOT analysis; the marketing, production, and financial strengths and weaknesses of the firm and its competitors; and the possible nature and sources of new competition, for example, foreign, domestic, horizontal, or vertical. Proposed new investments should also be assessed with regard to their effects on possible strategic alliances and mergers, given the nature of the entry and exit barriers in the industry and an assessment of current and future competitor technical, financial, and marketing abilities. In some cases, it may not be enough to compare a company with other firms in the industry, and in such cases strategic analysis should include an analysis of the future viability of the industry. Most importantly, flexible manufacturing investments should be assessed against conditions of declining competitiveness and loss of market share and not against the usual capital budgeting assumption (often implicit) of no response by competitors.

A firm that plans to develop a competitive strategy based on flexible manufacturing capabilities needs to develop systems to assess intangible and strategic benefits and options related to increased levels of quality, customer service, and technical capacity that result from the new manufacturing capabilities. The value of flexible manufacturing depends on the nature of the business, for example, on the complexity in the mix of production lot sizes, the range of products, and the degree of strategic advantage achieved by production flexibility, faster delivery times, reliably higher quality, and faster conformity to customer demands.

Many of the benefits of flexible manufacturing systems also depend on the extent to which they are integrated with the rest of the business to provide economies of scope. The system used to value investments in flexible manufacturing technology must be able to assess the relative importance and trade-offs between scope economies and scale economies. Such systems should also be able to estimate the increased revenues, reduced risk levels, decreased costs, and benefits of being able to manage greater product diversity, as well as volume, customer, and supplier instability resulting from the new flexible manufacturing system. According to option theory in finance, the value of real options for future growth generated by flexible manufacturing systems increases with increases in uncertainty regarding the future.[21]

Based on this analysis of manufacturing systems, flexible manufacturing systems are particularly good in managing an unstable, competitive, technological environment. However, because production costs for flexible manufacturing systems are not as low as for dedicated mass production systems, economic justification of the former depends on the importance of product differentiation and a lack of heavy price competition. Figure 16.2 summarizes this discussion and illustrates the optimality of various manufacturing systems in dealing with instability in the competitive, technological environment versus the competitive nature of the product market as indicated by the importance of price competition.

While Figure 16.2 provides broad guidelines for the economic justification and selection of manufacturing systems, it seems that a more disciplined and accurate system for justifying investments in flexible manufacturing technology should include both capital budgeting procedures and strategic analysis. The uncertain benefits of such investments must be assessed, perhaps using tools such as scenario analysis and multicriteria decision models.[22] The assessment of these benefits should

Figure 16.2

Economic optimality of manufacturing systems.

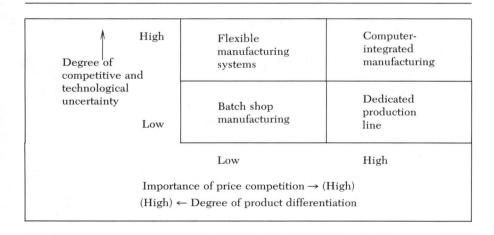

then form the input for the capital budgeting process augmented to account for the strategic and soft benefits of investments in flexible manufacturing systems. It is shown below that the traditional formulation of net present value can be modified to reflect the differing degrees of riskiness inherent in the different types of cash flows associated with strategic investments such as in flexible manufacturing technology.

A form of net present value formulation that may be used in such cases is adjusted net present value (ANPV) analysis. ANPV analysis is based on the value additivity principle and encourages a decision maker to account explicitly for the various special characteristics of the proposed investment including variations in riskiness and changes in capital structure associated with a new investment. As an example, the form of ANPV suitable for justifying investments in flexible manufacturing technology can be expressed as

$$\text{ANPV} = -I + \sum \frac{\text{TS}_i}{(1 + k_d)^i} + \sum \frac{\text{TCF}_i}{(1 + k_t)^i} + \sum \frac{\text{ITCF}_i}{(1 + k_n)^i}$$

$$+ \sum \frac{\text{CFRE}_i}{(1 + k_r)^i} + \sum \frac{\text{OPTS}_i}{(1 + k_0)^i} + \sum \frac{\text{DCFWOI}_i}{(1 + k_w)^i} + \frac{\text{TV}}{(1 + k_t)^N}$$

where ANPV = adjusted net present value

I = initial investment

TS = tax shields from project-related debt

i = subscript indicating time period i

k_d = discount rate applicable for debt shields

TCF = net tangible cash flows, for example, savings in labor, material, inventory costs, space costs, and other tangible and identifiable savings

k_t = discount rate reflecting the riskiness of the tangible cash flows[23]

ITCF = net intangible cash flows from better quality and delivery times and other soft benefits

k_n = discount rate reflecting the riskiness of intangible cash flows

CFRE = net cash flows from revenue enhancements which may depend on competitor and industry reaction

k_r = discount rate reflecting the riskiness of cash flows from revenue enhancements

OPTS = values of options for future growth created by the new investment. These values depend on the degree of underlying uncertainty in the variable being optioned, the time period for which this option is available, and the cost advantage of exercising the option[24]

k_0 = discount rate reflecting the riskiness of the value of options for future growth

DCFWOI = decline in current levels of cash flow in the absence of the new investment

k_w = discount rate reflecting the riskiness of cash flow estimates regarding the decline

TV = terminal value of the investment

N = number of time periods in the investment horizon

In case of significant variations in the riskiness of the cash flows within any one of the above categories, it may be useful to segregate such cash flows and discount each subcategory at its own appropriate discount rate. In addition to these ANPV calculations and the strategic analysis outlined above, investments in flexible manufacturing technology also can be compared to investments in other traditional manufacturing systems using exit NPV (ENPV) analysis. ENPV analysis may be especially useful in assessing the risks of loss resulting from changing or unstable economic and technological environments.[25] It should be noted that continuing investments in flexible manufacturing technology may change the nature of a firm's fixed assets and thus may have important implications for the capital structure of the firm. For example, because of the flexibility-related decline in firm riskiness and the embedded growth options in such assets, their collateral value is likely to be lower than their economic value, leading possibly to a lower-than-optimal debt ratio. Such changes in asset structure may also have important implications for managerial compensation policies favoring a heavier reliance on incentive-based compensation. These and other related implications of the increasing flexibility of the asset structure should be considered in evaluating investments in flexible manufacturing technology.[26]

In order to implement this strategic and an adjusted NPV approach to the assessment of new manufacturing investments, it is useful for a firm to conduct an audit of its organizational structure and capabilities to ensure that it can undertake such a strategic analysis. Implementing the strategic ANPV approach involves not only integration of the capital budgeting and the strategic planning processes but also procedures for ensuring the involvement of top management and a need to educate and provide incentives for production personnel at all levels to encourage proposals for appropriate new investments in flexible manufacturing. While this chapter has focused on use of the adjusted net present value rule for the valuation of investments in flexible manufacturing technology, the procedures outlined here can be modified to assess other strategic investments. As indicated in prior research, there are many situations where finance and strategy seem to clash with regard to their recommendations for the allocation of capital, especially in large multidivisional firms.[27]

VI. CONCLUSIONS

Justifying strategic investments, such as investment in new manufacturing technology, is usually very difficult since the most important benefits are often difficult to quantify and convert to incremental cash flows. While traditional capital budgeting procedures that rely on such return measures provide much needed discipline to the process of allocating capital, they do not normally capture the strategic benefits of higher quality, faster responses to a wider range of customer needs, and options for future growth made available by flexible manufacturing technology. Adding to these limitations is the difficulty of using traditional cost accounting systems to generate the information necessary for justifying strategic new manufacturing investments. This article has reviewed these problems, developed and recommended procedures useful for assessing strategic investments, and illustrated them with the case of investments in flexible manufacturing technology.

This chapter shows why and how traditional capital budgeting procedures can be supplemented by strategic analysis using an adjusted net present value framework for guiding the calculations. While the case of justifying strategic investments in flexible manufacturing technology is used as an example in the chapter, the proposed procedures are applicable to other strategic investments as well.

NOTES

1. See, for example, Hayes and Garvin (1982) and Hodder (1986).
2. For a review of the issues related to the problems of evaluating strategic alternatives in a traditional capital budgeting framework, see, for example, Myers (1987).
3. These examples are documented in Gene Bylinsky, "A Breakthrough in Automating the Assembly Line," *Fortune*, May 26, 1986, pp. 64–66; James Cook, "Back to Simplicity," *Forbes*, August 25, 1986, pp. 32–33; Alan Farnham, "Baldor's Success: Made in the U.S.," *Fortune*, July 17, 1989, pp. 101–106; Nick Garnett, "The Long Hard Road to Automation," *Financial Times*, October 21, 1988; Ronald Henkoff, "The Engine That Couldn't," *Fortune*, December 18, 1989, p. 124; Robert E. Huber, "Deere's Run for Manufacturing Excellence," *Production*, June 1989, pp. 36–40; Doron P. Levin, "In a High-Tech Drive, GM Falls Below Rivals in Auto Profit Margins," *Wall Street Journal*, July 22, 1986, pp. 1, 14; and Richard Rescigno, "Race to the Future: Can Billions and Mr. Smith Make GM a Winner?" *Barron's*, June 30, 1986, pp. 6–7, 30–31.

4. See, for example, Mensah and Miranti (1989), Fine and Freund (1990), and Milgrom and Roberts (1990).

5. For details of these contentions, see, for example, Hayes and Garvin (1982), Hodder (1986), Landau (1988), and Myers (1987).

6. See, for example, Johnson and Kaplan (1987) and Kaplan (1984).

7. Competitive effects including destabilizing positive feedbacks of an initial competitive advantage associated with new investments have been modeled by, for example, Arthur (1990), Bailey and Friedlaender (1982), Dixit (1989), Mills (1988), and Roberts (1987).

8. The literature exploring the role of real options in valuing new investment proposals is expanding rapidly and includes Aggarwal and Soenen (1989), Baldwin (1982), Brennan and Schwartz (1985), Carlsson (1989), Kester (1984), Majd and Pyndick (1987), Mason and Merton (1985), McDonald and Siegle (1985, 1986), Sick (1989), Siegle et al. (1987), Stulz (1982), and Trigeorgis and Mason (1987).

9. See, for example, Arrow (1982), Machina (1987, 1989), and MacCrimmon and Wehrung (1986).

10. Agency and information asymmetry issues in capital budgeting have been explored in many books and papers including Aggarwal (1978), Heckerman (1975), Jensen and Meckling (1976), and Myers and Majluf (1980).

11. See, for example, Aggarwal and Soenen (1989), Falkner and Benhajla (1990), Michael and Millen (1985), Neises and Bennett (1989), and Sullivan and Reeve (1988).

12. See, for example, Jaikumar (1986), Aggarwal (1987), Landau (1988), and Noori (1990).

13. "CE Roundtable: World Class Manufacturing," *Chief Executive,* November–December 1987, pp. 46–59.

14. For a discussion of the economics of scope see, for example, Bailey and Friedlaender (1982) and Goldhar and Jelinek (1983).

15. "CE Roundtable: World Class Manufacturing" *Chief Executive,* November–December 1987, p. 55.

16. For details of variations in flexible manufacturing systems see, for example, Canada and Sullivan (1989), Meredith and Hill (1987), Noori (1990), and the references cited in Singhal et al. (1987).

17. See Woody Hochswender, "How Fashion Spreads Around the World at the Speed of Light," *New York Times,* May 13, 1990, p. E5.

18. See, for example, Kulatilaka (1985), Burstein and Talbi (1985), Gaimon (1986), Roberts (1987), Arthur (1990), and "A Smarter Way to Manufacture," *Business Week,* April 30, 1990, pp. 110–117.

19. See Howell and Soucy (1987), Hunt et al. (1985), Johnson and Kaplan (1987), Kaplan (1984, 1986), Krause and Keller (1988), Noori and Radford (1990), Skinner (1986), and "How the New Math of Productivity Adds Up," *Business Week,* June 6, 1988, pp. 103–112.

20. See, for example, Bennett et al. (1988), Currie (1989), Dean (1988), Meredith (1986), and Meredith and Suresh (1986).

21. The use of option pricing theory to value capital investments is gaining popularity. See, for example, Mason and Merton (1985), Siegle, Smith, and Paddock (1987), Stulz (1982), and Trigeorgis and Mason (1987).

22. See, for example, Falkner and Benhajla (1990), Fine and Freund (1986), Graham and Huber (1988), Neises and Bennett (1989), and Sullivan and Reeve (1988).

23. This should be the discount rate for an all-equity firm with these cash flows.

24. References that discuss the use of option pricing theory to value capital investments were cited in an earlier note. See, for example, Mason and Merton (1985), Siegle, Smith, and Paddock (1987), Stulz (1982), and Trigeorgis and Mason (1987).

25. For details of the ENPV procedure, see Aggarwal and Soenen (1989).

26. While development of the details of these corporate finance implications of flexibility in a firm's asset structure are beyond the scope of this article, they would be a suitable topic for further research. For additional details on the interaction of the investment and financing decisions, see as a start, for example, Cooper and Franks (1983), Myers (1977), and Myers (1987).

27. See, for example, Barwise et al. (1989), Hayes and Garvin (1982), and Myers (1987).

REFERENCES

AGGARWAL, RAJ (1980). "Corporate Use of Sophisticated Capital Budgeting Procedures: A Strategic Perspective," *Interfaces* 10 (No. 2, April), pp. 31–34.

AGGARWAL, RAJ (1987). "Strategic Challenge of the Evolving World Economy," *Business Horizons* 30, (No. 4, July–August), pp. 38–44.

AGGARWAL, RAJ, and LUC A. SOENEN (1989). "Project Value as a Measure of Flexibility and Risk Exposure," *Engineering Economist* 35 (No. 1, Fall), pp. 39–54.

ARROW, KENNETH J. (1982). "Risk Perception in Psychology and Economics," *Economic Inquiry* 20 (No. 1, January), pp. 1–9.

ARTHUR, W. BRIAN (1990). "Positive Feedbacks in the Economy," *Scientific American* 261 (No. 2., February), pp. 92–99.

BAILEY, E. E., and A. F. FRIEDLAENDER (1982). "Market Structure and Multiproduct Industries" *Journal of Economic Literature* 20 (No. 2, June), pp. 1024–1048.

BALDWIN, CARLISS Y. (1982). "Optimal Sequential Investment When Capital Is Not Readily Reversible," *Journal of Finance* 37 (No. 3, June), pp. 763–782.

BARWISE, PATRICK, PAUL R. MARSH, and ROBIN WENSLEY (1989). "Must Finance and Strategy Clash?" *Harvard Business Review* 67 (No. 5, September–October), pp. 85–90.

BENNETT, EARL D., and JAMES A. HENDRICKS (1987). "Justifying the Acquisition of Automated Equipment," *Management Accounting* 69 (No. 7, July), pp. 39–46.

BENNETT, EARL D., SARAH A. REED, and DON ROBERTSON (1988). "A Survey: How Do You Justify an Investment in Technology?"*Financial Executive* 4 (No. 5, September–October), pp. 44–48.

BRENNEN, MICHAEL J, and EDUARDO S. SCHWARTZ (1985). "Evaluating Natural Resource Investments," *Journal of Business* 58 (No. 1, April), pp. 135–157.

BURSTEIN, M. C., and M. TALBI (1985). "Economic Evaluation for the Introduction of Flexible Manufacturing Technology Under Rivalry," in K. Stecke and R. Suri (eds)., *Flexible Management Systems: Operations Research Models and Applications* (Basel: J. C. Baltzer), pp. 81–112.

CANADA, JOHN R., and WILLIAM G. SULLIVAN (1989). *Economic and Multi-Attribute Evaluation of Advanced Manufacturing Systems* (Englewood Cliffs, N.J.: Prentice Hall).

CARLSSON, BO (1989). "Flexibility and the Theory of the Firm," *International Journal of Industrial Organization* 7 (No. 2, June), pp. 179–203.

COOPER, IAN, and JULIAN R. FRANKS (1983). "The Interaction of Financing and Investment Decisions When the Firm Has Unused Tax Credits," *Journal of Finance* 38, (No. 2, May), pp. 571–583.

CURRIE, W. L. (1989). "The Art of Justifying New Technology to Top Management," *Omega: International Journal of Management Science* 17 (No. 5, September), pp. 409–418.

DEAN, JAMES W., JR. (1988). *Deciding to Innovate: How Firms Justify Advanced Technology* (Cambridge, Mass.: Ballinger).

DIXIT, AVINASH (1989). "Entry and Exit Decisions Under Uncertainty" *Journal of Political Economy* 97 (No. 3, May), pp. 620–638.

FALKNER, CHARLES H., and SAIDA BENHAJLA (1990). "Multi-Attribute Decision Models in the Justification of CIM Systems," *Engineering Economist* 35 (No. 2, Winter), pp. 91–114.

FINE, CHARLES H., and ROBERT M. FREUND (1986). "Economic Analysis of Product-Flexible Manufacturing Systems Investments Decisions," in K. Stecke and R. Suri (eds.), *Proceedings of the Second ORSA/TIMS Conference of Flexible Manufacturing Systems: Operations Research Models and Applications* (Amsterdam: Elsevier), pp. 55–68.

FINE, CHARLES, H., and ROBERT M. FREUND (1990). "Optimal Investment in Product-Flexible Manufacturing Capacity," *Management Science* 36 (No. 4, April), pp. 449–466.

GAIMON, CHERYL (1986). "The Stragetic Decision to Acquire Flexible Technology," in K. Stecke and R. Suri (eds). *Proceedings of the Second ORSA/TIMS Conference of Flexible Manufacturing Systems: Operations Research Models and Applications* (Amsterdam: Elsevier), pp. 69–81.

GOLDHAR, JOEL D. (1983). "Plan for Economies of Scope," *Harvard Business Review* 61 (No. 3, May–June), pp. 141–148.

GRAHAM, PEARSON, and ROBERT F. HUBER (1988). "Guidelines for Better Investment Decisions." *Production* (March), pp. 42–71.

HAYES, ROBERT H., and DAVID A. GARVIN (1982). "Managing as If Tomorrow Mattered" *Harvard Business Review* (No. 3, May–June), pp. 71–79.

HECKERMAN, DONALD G. (1975). "Motivating Managers To Make Investment Decisions," *Journal of Financial Economics* 2 (No. 2, June), pp. 273–292.

HODDER, JAMES E. (1986). "Evaluation of Manufacturing Investments: A Comparison of U.S. and Japanese Practices," *Financial Management* 15 (No. 1, Spring), pp. 17–24.

HOWELL, ROBERT A., and STEPHEN R. SOUCY (1987). "New Manufacturing Environment: Major Trends for Management Accountants," *Management Accounting* 69 (No. 7, July), pp. 21–27.

HUNT, RICK, LINDA GARRETT, and MIKE C. MERZ (1985). "Direct Labor Cost Not Always Relevant at H-P," *Management Accounting* 67 (No. 2, February), pp. 58–62.

HUTCHINSON, GEORGE K., and JOHN R. HOLLAND (1982). "The Economic Value of Flexible Automation," *Journal of Manufacturing Systems* 1 (No. 2), pp. 215–228.

JAIKUMAR, RAMCHANDRAN (1986). "Postindustrial Manufacturing," *Harvard Business Review* 64, (No. 6, November–December), pp. 69–76.

JENSEN, MICHAEL C., and WILLIAM H. MECKLING (1976). "Theory of the Firm: Managerial Behavior, Agency Costs, and Ownership Structure," *Journal of Financial Economics* 3 (No. 3, October), pp. 305–360.

JOHNSON, H. THOMAS, and ROBERT S. KAPLAN (1987). *Relevance Lost: The Rise and Fall of Management Accounting* (Boston: Harvard Business School Press).

KAPLAN, ROBERT S. (1984). "Yesterday's Accounting Undermines Production," *Harvard Business Review* 62 (No. 4, July–August), pp. 95–101.

KAPLAN, ROBERT S. (1986). "Must CIM be Justified by Faith Alone?" *Harvard Business Review* 64 (No. 2, March–April), pp. 87–95.

KESTER, W. CARL (1984). "Today's Options for Tomorrow's Growth," *Harvard Business Review* 62 (No. 2, March–April), pp. 67–75.

KRAUSE, PAUL, and DONALD E. KELLER (1988). "Bringing World-Class Manufacturing and Accounting to a Small Company," *Management Accounting* 70 (No. 11, November), pp. 28–32.

KULATILAKA, N (1985). "Capital Budgeting and Optimal Timing of Investments in Flexible Manufacturing Systems," in K. Stecke, and R. Suri (eds.), *Flexible Managment Systems: Operations Research Models and Applications* (Basel: J. C. Baltzer), pp. 35–57.

LANDAU, RALPH (1988). "U.S. Economic Growth," *Scientific American* 258 (No. 6, June), pp. 44–52.

MAC CRIMMON, KENNETH R., and DONALD A. WEHRUNG (1986). *Taking Risks* (New York: Free Press).

MACHINA, MARK J. (1987). "Choice Under Uncertainty: Problems Solved and Unsolved," *Economic Perspectives* 1 (No. 1, Summer), pp. 121–154.

MACHINA, MARK J. (1989). "Dynamic Consistency and Non-Expected Utility Models of Choice Under Uncertainty," *Journal of Economic Literature* 27 (No. 4, December), pp. 1622–1688.

MAJD, SAMAN, and ROBERT S. PYNDICK (1987). "Time to Build, Option Value, and Investment Decisions," *Journal of Financial Economics* 18 (No. 1, March), pp. 7–27.

MASON, SCOTT P., and ROBERT C. MERTON (1985). "The Role of Contingent Claims Analysis in Finance," in Edward Altman and Marti Subrahmanian (eds.), *Recent Advances in Corporate Finance* (Homewood, Ill.: Richard D. Irwin), pp. 149–158.

MCDONALD, ROBERT L., and DANIEL R. SIEGLE (1985). "Investments and the Value of the Firm When There Is an Option to Shut Down," *International Economic Review* 26 (No. 2, June), pp. 331–349.

MCDONALD, ROBERT L., and DANIEL R. SIEGLE (1986). "The Value of Waiting to Invest," *Quarterly Journal of Economics* 101 (No. 4, November), pp. 707–727.

MENSAH, YAW M., and PAUL J. MIRANTI, JR. (1989). "Capital Expenditure Analysis and Automated Manufacturing Systems: A Review and Synthesis," *Journal of Accounting Literature* 8, pp. 181–207.

MEREDITH, JACK R. ED. (1986). *Justifying New Manufacturing Technology* (Norcross, Ga.: Institute of Industrial Engineers).

MEREDITH, JACK R., and MARIANNE M. HILL (1987). "Justifying New Manufacturing Systems: A Managerial Approach," *Sloan Management Review* 28 (No. 4, Summer), pp. 49–61.

MEREDITH, JACK R., and NALLAN C. SURESH (1986). "Justification Techniques for Advanced Manufacturing Technologies," in Jack R. Meredith (ed.), *Justifying New Manufacturing Technology* (Norcross, Ga.: Institute of Industrial Engineers), pp. 82–97.

MICHAEL, G. J., and R. A. MILLEN (1985). "Economic Justification of Modern Computer-Based Factory Automation Equipment: A Status Report," in K. Stecke and R. Suri (eds.), *Flexible Management Systems: Operations Research Models and Applications* (Basel: J. C. Baltzer), pp. 25–34.

MILGROM, PAUL, and JOHN ROBERTS (1990). "The Economics of Modern Manufacturing: Technology, Strategy, and Organization," *American Economic Review* 80 (No. 3, June), pp. 511–528.

MILLS, DAVID E. (1988). Pre-Emptive Investment Timing," *Rand Journal of Economics* 19 (No. 1, Spring), pp. 114–122.

MYERS, STEWART C. (1977). "Determinants of Corporate Borrowing," *Journal of Financial Economics* 5 (No. 2), pp. 147–175.

MYERS, STEWART C. (1987). "Finance Theory and Financial Strategy," *Midland Corporate Finance Journal* 5 (No. 1, Spring), pp. 6–13.

MYERS, STEWART C., and N. MAJLUF (1984). "Corporate Financing and Investment Decisions When Firms Have Information Investors Do Not Have," *Journal of Financial Economics* 13 (No. 2, June), pp. 187–211.

NEISES, STEVEN J., and ROBERT E. BENNETT (1989). "AutoMan—Decision Support Software," *Management Accounting* 71 (No. 11, November), pp. 58–60.

NOORI, HAMID (1990). *Managing the Dynamics of New Technology: Issues in Manufacturing Management* (Englewood Cliffs, N.J.: Prentice Hall).

Noori, Hamid, and Russell W. Radford, eds. (1990). *Readings and Cases in the Management of New Technology: An Operations Perspective* (Englewood Cliffs, N.J.: Prentice Hall).

Roberts, John (1987). "Battles for Market Share: Incomplete Information, Aggressive Strategic Planning and Competitive Dynamics," in Truman F. Bewley (ed.), *Advances in Economic Theory* (New York: Cambridge University Press), pp. 157–195.

Sick, Gordon (1989). *Capital Budgeting With Real Options*, Monograph Series in Finance and Economics, no. 1989-3, (New York: New York University), pp. 1–78.

Siegle, Daniel R., James L. Smith, and James L. Paddock (1987). "Valuing Offshore Oil Properties With Options Pricing Models," *Midland Corporate Finance Journal* 5 (No. 1, Spring), pp. 22–30.

Singhal, Kalyan, Charles H. Fine, Jack R. Meredith, and Rajan Suri (1987). "Research and Models for Automated Manufacturing," *Interfaces* 17 (No. 6, November–December), pp. 5–14.

Skinner, Wickham (1986). "The Productivity Paradox," *Harvard Business Review* 64 (No. 4, July–August), pp. 55–59.

Stulz, Rene (1982). "Options on the Minimum or Maximum of Two Risky Assets," *Journal of Financial Economics* 10 (No. 2, July), pp. 161–185.

Sullivan, William G, and James M. Reeve (1988). "Xventure: Expert Systems to the Rescue," *Management Accounting* 70 (No. 10, October), pp. 51–58.

Trigeorgis, Lenos, and Scott P. Mason (1987). "Valuing Managerial Flexibility," *Midland Corporate Finance Journal* 5 (No. 1, Spring), pp. 14–21.

Raj Aggarwal
The Edward J. and Louise E. Mellen Chair in Finance
John Carroll University Cleveland

Professor Aggarwal's teaching and research interests include finance and business strategy and their global dimensions. In addition to John Carroll, he has taught at Harvard University, University of Hawaii, University of Michigan, University of South Carolina, University of Toledo, and the International University of Japan. He has a Bachelor of Technology degree in mechanical engineering, an MBA (operations management), and a DBA (corporate finance and international business), and has done postdoctoral work in international trade and economics. He attended the Indian Institute of Technology, Kent State University, and the University of Chicago. His experience includes work in academic administration, as a production engineer, as a financial analyst, and as a member of senior management. He has been a consultant to management and boards of directors at Asahi Life Insurance (Japan), BP America, Dana Corporation, Marine Midland Bank, Owens-Illinois, Perfect Circle Victor (India), and others. He currently serves as a board member at Manco and at Advanced Clinical Diagnostics.

Dr. Aggarwal's publications include the books *Financial Policies for the Multinational Company, International Dimensions of Financial Management, International Business, Management Science, Discounting in Financial Accounting and Reporting,* and *Advances in International Planning and Forecasting,* and over fifty scholarly papers in the *Journal of Banking and Finance, Journal of Financial Research, Journal of International Money and Finance, Journal of Portfolio Management, Financial Review, Financial Management, Journal of Business Finance and Accounting, Engineering Economist, Decision Sciences, Business Horizons, Journal of International Accounting, Columbia Journal of World Business,* and *Journal of International Business Studies.* His research has been reprinted and cited in journals and books and has received awards such as "best contribution of the year." He is or has been a member of the editorial boards *Financial Review, Journal of Financial Practice and Education, Journal of International Business Studies, Quarterly Review of Economics and Business, Journal of Cash Management,* and *Global Finance Journal.*

Professor Aggarwal has held a number of leadership positions including Vice-President and Program Chairman of the Academy of International Business and of the Eastern Finance Association. He has presented keynote speeches at annual meetings of the National Association of Accountants, the Association of Japanese Business Studies, and the Midwest Academy of International Business. He has received research grants from the National Science Foundation, the Cleveland Foundation, and the Financial Executives Research Foundation. In 1984 he was Senior Fulbright Research Scholar in South-East Asia. He is listed in *Who's Who in America* and *Who's Who in Finance and Industry.*